BROKEN
PROMISES

BROKEN PROMISES

How Americans Fail Their Children

With a New Postscript

W. NORTON GRUBB

MARVIN LAZERSON

The University of Chicago Press
Chicago & London

The University of Chicago Press, Chicago 60637
The University of Chicago Press, Ltd., London

97 96 95 94 93 92 91 90 89 88   5 4 3 2 1

Library of Congress Cataloging in Publication Data

Grubb, W. Norton.
  Broken promises.

  Reprint. Originally published: New York : Basic Books,
c1982. With new pref. and postscript.
  Bibliography: p.
  Includes index.
  1. Family policy—United States. 2. Children—
Government policy—United States. 3. Child welfare—
United States. I. Lazerson, Marvin. II. Title.
HQ536.G78   1988   306.8'5'0973   88-1165
ISBN 0-226-31004-3 (pbk.)

CONTENTS

PART TWO
CHILDREN'S INSTITUTIONS

Contents

PART THREE

BEYOND CHILDREN'S INSTITUTIONS

PREFACE

WE BEGAN this book as members of the Childhood and Government Project at the University of California at Berkeley. Our greatest debt is to Charles Benson, who encouraged us to extend our early writings on children and the state beyond the life of the Project. Our thanks go also to the Ford Foundation and the Carnegie Corporation, who funded both the Project and our subsequent writings. Of the many individuals who have helped us, particularly in the writing of the Postscript, we would like to thank Julia Brody, David K. Cohen, Maria Garza-Lubeck, Harold Howe II, Martin Kessler of Basic Books, and Steven Schlossman.

In *Broken Promises*, completed in the spring of 1981, we argue that Americans have failed to fulfill their public responsibilities to children. Americans have not neglected children; indeed, in the realm of private and personal commitments we can claim to be a child-centered nation. But in the public sphere we are much less so, and our failed obligations to poor children are especially disheartening.

Writing in the late 1970s and early 1980s, our views were powerfully influenced by the optimism of the Great Society legislation, but also by the evident contradiction of those policies and the slow deterioration of children's programs during the 1970s. We were concerned that the plight of children could not be significantly improved unless public policies were rethought and expanded. But whatever the original limitations of these programs, subsequent events have damaged them even more. One purpose of the paperback edition is to describe what has happened most recently (in the Postscript beginning on page 309), and to show how these developments confirm our earlier analysis.

Writing about children in the early 1980s provoked little public interest. The Reagan administration had cast a pall over most social policy. Its insistent rhetoric about fraud, waste, and abuse in government led many citizens to believe that public programs could do no good. With deep cuts in federal spending, children's advocates were on the defensive. Calls to reconstruct social programs in order to fulfill our historic promises to children were pointless at a time when the Reagan administration seemed intent on demolishing public commitment to those in need.

The pendulum has now begun to swing back. Children are once again the focus of concern. Increasing poverty among children has alarmed many people, and the damage wrought during the last decade has become more widely recognized. As the nation revs itself up for the 1988 elections and a new administration, it seems appropriate to reissue *Broken Promises.* In the current atmosphere our central message—the importance of public programs for children, and the necessity of detecting and transcending program limitations—is more likely to be recognized.

Because of the events of the 1980s, some details of *Broken Promises* are now outdated, some numbers are old, and some reform proposals are no longer hot. But we are convinced that our analysis remains valid. The Postscript shows how the developments of the 1980s illustrate the analytic points of our book. We think it important to recognize that the harm done to children during the past decade, including the spending cuts of the Reagan administration, was not an aberration; it was instead the logical consequence of innate limitations and internal contradictions in the programs we have inherited.

The Postscript also includes an agenda for reform, designed to clarify the implications of our analysis. Of course, we would be gratified if children's advocates or other social reformers adopted our agenda, but that is not our primary goal. Our aim instead is to provide a deeper understanding of how programs for children have developed, why they have remained so limited, and what barriers need to be overcome to fulfill our historic promises. Without this understanding, we fear that our country will continue to lurch between periods of reform like the 1960s and those of contraction and self-protection like the 1970s and 1980s, with little permanent improvement in the conditions of childhood. Americans owe their children more than that.

We dedicate this edition again to *our* children: to Hilary Maia Grubb, now 13; Alexander Jason Grubb, age 7; and Jared Michael Lazerson, age 18. They continue to amaze and educate us, to create great stress and to give us great joy. They convince us that life without children is in many ways impoverished, and that children—all children—deserve our fervent support.

W. NORTON GRUBB

November 1987   MARVIN LAZERSON

BROKEN
PROMISES

Introduction

DURING the past decade, alarm over the "breakdown of the family" has reached hysterical levels. Public discussion of the family has become a ritual. High divorce rates, low birth rates, and high levels of maternal employment are cited as indicators of family breakdown, a breakdown that is linked to a glut of social pathologies: child abuse, juvenile delinquency, teen-age pregnancy, illiteracy, and a diminished work ethic. Both moderate and conservative commentators blame women for neglecting motherhood by remaining childless or "dumping" their children in day care centers. Others, especially feminists, identify traditional concepts of motherhood and nuclear family as oppressive to both women and children. Perhaps the most heartfelt jeremiad is the lament that two-earner families, higher divorce rates, and a greater tendency to remain unmarried mark the decline of the family as a refuge of affection, leaving America a nation of disconnected, self-centered individuals in an aggressive and brutalizing society.[1]

The "crisis of the family" has proved to be a catchall for every social problem and every ideological position. Arguments about the decline of the family have something for everyone, from the politicians and academics who claim they can do something about the family's deterioration to the professionals and parents fighting over whom to blame. Opportunism, alarmism, muddled thinking, and worn-out myths abound. Forecasting the "death of the family" has become a popular pastime, despite the persistence of families and the development of another school stressing the "strength and resilience" of family life.[2] Professionals have used the image of the family in decline to hint at new arrangements replacing the family, arrangements both vague and ominous in suggesting the need for

3

supervision. As the chair of the Joint Commission on the Mental Health of Children stated, "There is serious thinking among some of the future-oriented child development research people that maybe we can't trust the family alone to prepare young children for this new kind of world which is emerging."[3] The Moral Majority and the right-wing "profamily" movement have extolled the mythical family of the past, with women happy at home, masculine breadwinners, and obedient children, as a way to attack feminism. Politicians like Jimmy Carter have espoused the family's cause in an effort to seem concerned and caring, but they do so without any real commitment to disentangling the difficult political issues raised by the sense of family "crisis."

Yet discussions about the family do express real fears and angers. Families have changed substantially in the postwar period: increases in the number of women working and in the number of single-parent families have been substantial, divorce rates have continued to increase, doubts about how best to rear children have been exacerbated by the uncertainties of schooling and the economy and by the contradictory messages of professionals. Feminists and those living in communes have challenged conventional family norms, so that the image of "the family" itself is shifting and unstable. Institutions outside the family—both public institutions like the schools and nominally private institutions like television—now play a greater role in childrearing than ever before. Events have moved quickly in the postwar period, creating new anxieties and real confusion over how to respond. The dilemmas of men and women searching to construct family lives amidst the winds of feminism and anti-feminism and the bewilderment of parents facing economic uncertainties and mounting criticism of public institutions are real enough; and the poverty of many children, especially those in female-headed and minority families, is more than sufficient to justify public concern.

Although much has changed in American families, the current *angst* over the family is hardly novel. Concern for the family has been a perennial phenomenon stretching back to the colonial era, and the same issues have emerged again and again: the effects of poverty and racial discrimination on childrearing, debates about changing sex roles, and the difficulties parents have guiding their children through the welter of institutions outside the family. During certain periods of rapid change—especially the decades before the Civil War, the progressive era around 1900, and the Great Depression of the 1930s—anxiety has become especially acute, generating institutional reforms and ideological revisions with lasting implications for families and children. Evidently the family has withstood social dislocations repeatedly, though it has changed in the process. The false sense that the family "crisis" of the 1970s and 1980s is unprecedented and that changes in family life must portend the decline of the family has itself contributed to the anxiety.

In every period of crisis, the feeling that families are in trouble has invariably focused most intensely on the fear that *children* are being harmed by family dissolution. As Lyndon Johnson remarked in his speech at Howard University on black families:

> The family is the cornerstone of society. More than any other force it shapes the attitudes, the hopes, the ambitions, and the values of the child. When the family collapses, it is the children that are usually damaged.[4]

Now, as in previous periods, changes like increasing poverty rates, rising divorce rates, and increasing maternal employment rates have been assessed for their effects on children. In fact, present debates about the family often make it seem that only children matter. Maternal employment and divorce have come to be public issues because of the children involved, not because of their effects on adults. Poverty has been a special concern because of its effects in stunting a child's normal development, while the poverty of parents has been all but irrelevant. Many commentators with no discernible interest in families have taken up the cause of children—critics of television, those concerned about nutrition and environmental hazards, proponents of children's legal rights, and adults in the vanguard of "kid's lib." Whatever else it might be, the crisis of the family has been most forcefully expressed as a crisis in childrearing.

Public discussions of childrearing problems have inevitably turned to public resolutions because individual approaches to complex issues like poverty and social cohesion are patently inadequate. In every period of "family crisis," concern for children has led to an expansion of public responsibilities. The nineteenth-century movements establishing public schools to socialize children appropriately, the early twentieth-century efforts at "child saving" through child labor legislation and rudimentary welfare programs, the social programs of the New Deal and Johnson's War on Poverty have institutionalized a set of public obligations to children: to spare innocent children the ravages of poverty, to provide for those children whose parents are unable or unwilling to nurture them, to provide every child a decent opportunity for adult success. In these efforts we have provided public support for children where we are unwilling to reform conditions for adults, and children's institutions have been made responsible for creating a just and equitable society from one riddled with inequities. Yet our implicit promises to children have been only partially fulfilled. Childhood poverty remains first on the list of family problems, and equality of opportunity remains as distant now as it did in the mid-nineteenth century. The same problems besetting children and families keep reemerging because the reforms to treat them have always been contradictory and incomplete. The recurring cycles of crisis and reform are evidence of our broken promises.

Our task is to analyze the possibilities and limits of public responsibility for children and families, to understand the relationship between the American state and children. That relationship has been paradoxical. On one hand, the boundaries between the private and the public—between the private family and the public world of government and the economy—have shifted constantly, especially with the expansion of the state, so that the distinction between the public and private has become blurred. Yet our rhetoric and public policies continue to refer to the family as a private and personal sphere insulated from the world outside, even as the state's activities have become more elaborate. Ideologically, the family remains the "basic unit of society," even though our economic and social policies make clear that the family is not the primary unit of production nor even the only institution socializing children. In part, we continue to insist on the family's privacy because we have nothing to replace it as a refuge of affection and intimacy. But this insistence has generated the central dilemma: if the state must assume some responsibilities for children, how can it discharge those responsibilities when childrearing is still considered a private responsibility? The dominant solution ever since the early nineteenth century has been to allow the state to intervene into childrearing only when families are considered to have failed. This constraint—the doctrine of *parens patriae*—has itself limited and distorted public programs for children, in ways we describe throughout this book.

Our promises to children have also been broken by our collective failure to overcome the inequalities that affect their lives. Poverty—especially the poverty of racial minorities and recent immigrants—has always been recognized as central to the sense of families in crisis. That recognition has in turn, generated reforms to reduce unemployment, to minimize the effects of poverty through welfare programs, and to eradicate poverty by providing educational opportunities so that the next generation would not repeat the conditions of their parents. Yet efforts to cope with inequalities have always been resisted. Some have been hostile to spending public money for "other people's children"; others have been hostile to poor children themselves, fearing that they constitute a threat to social peace. Both conservatives and liberals, who have been divided over how to respond to poverty, have ignored the origins of income and racial inequalities in the class divisions of a capitalist economy and have tended to ignore as well the other consequences of class for children—the stresses that work produces within the family, the different values that children of different class backgrounds receive from their parents. Structural inequalities have therefore generated both the imperative for the state to intervene and the political resistance that keeps the state's efforts on behalf of poor children relatively feeble.

Because of the limits on what the state can do for children, the effects of expanding public responsibility have usually been ambiguous and contradictory. Welfare programs have provided resources to poor families, but they do so in ways that are demeaning and that restrict the choices poor mothers can make. The public schools have provided opportunities that some parents cannot provide for their own children, but they have also incorporated class and racial biases. Professionals in public institutions have enhanced the well-being of families and children at the same time that they have diluted parental control and contributed to the feeling that families are becoming powerless. The failures have permitted conservatives to assert that state policies are always ineffective and that public responsibility should be minimized. The successes have prompted the belief of modern liberals that further state expansion can solve social problems.[5] Both views are incomplete: the conservative response emphasizes the ineffectiveness of the state without recognizing the valid reasons for its expansion, while the liberal insistence on the state's power to resolve social problems fails to acknowledge the limits of the American state. Both fail to consider explicitly how the state has responded to changes in family life, though both sides recognize that the family has changed. Neither side considers very deeply the economic basis of family life, though both understand that families are often at the mercy of economic forces.

To avoid the limitations of the current debate, we must understand the simultaneous evolution of family life, state policies, and the economic system underlying both of them. The task is not easy. The accumulated myths, the unexamined assumptions, and the enormous passions generated over the appropriate role of the state in personal life all hamper coherent analysis. Even the hardest statistics are open to conflicting interpretations. Some mourn high divorce rates as signs of the "death of the family," while others stress that high remarriage rates signal the robustness of marriage. The harm to children caused by divorce is countered by emphasizing the harm of bad marriages. Disentangling the changing roles of families with respect to other institutions is complicated by contradictory myths. One myth invokes a golden age of the past when loving parents sacrificed all for their children, children obeyed their parents, families provided an emotional haven, and extended families and stable communities provided supports for parents and children. A contrary myth, oblivious to the first, asserts that family life and childrearing have continuously improved, rising out of the cruelty and insensitivity of the feudal ages to an enlightened and liberated present.[6] Differing views of what "the family" means, unstated but powerful, have generated ideological conflicts without the protagonists being sure what they are fighting about.

To avoid conflicting myths in our discussion, we consistently turn to historical perspectives. While historical analysis can never indicate what the resolution of current problems will be, it can distinguish the persistent issues from those that are more ephemeral. In addition, since many current attitudes toward children and families and most public institutions that affect them originated in the nineteenth century, an appreciation of their origins helps us understand why we believe and act as we do. It can also help us counter both the simple alarmism that so often afflicts discussion of families, children, and government policies and the naive expectation that reforms can be easily accomplished.

As another antidote to conventional wisdom and muddled thinking, we emphasize in Part 1 the most basic principles underlying the state's relationship to children and families, principles that have become embodied in public institutions treating children. In Part 2, we analyze four children's institutions to see the particular form these assumptions take: public schooling; institutions for youth, especially training and juvenile justice programs; Aid to Families with Dependent Children, the basic welfare program; and early childhood programs, specifically child care and parent education. However, children's institutions do not exhaust the influence of the state on children. The burgeoning interest in "family policy" in the 1970s has turned attention to other state programs that affect children through their effects on families. An examination of what family policy might be (in chapter 9) raises questions about the state's influence over the most fundamental factors—unemployment and macroeconomic conditions, sex roles and sex discrimination, various forms of racial discrimination, and the origins and consequences of class. Since ideological and institutional constraints that restrict the state's influences on children and families are historically rooted, they are difficult to change; since they are internally consistent, they are interrelated and difficult to alter in a piecemeal fashion. While the sturdiness of these principles may seem discouraging to reformers, it is necessary to understand them in order to see why past reforms have been so incomplete and what assumptions and practices need to be changed to go beyond the limited reforms of the past.

Although the problems of families and children now seem especially urgent, heightened attention to the family has waxed and waned in the past; the historical record implies that the recent sense of family crisis is

8

also likely to be transitory. The family as a special political issue may disappear, because of reforms that appear to resolve some of the problems, because of the ascendance of politically more powerful issues, or simply because the "crisis" has been overblown and the "death of the family" proves an unreliable forecast. Signs of waning interest in the family crisis appeared as early as 1978, as former President Carter extolled the strengths of the American family just two years after he declared it to be "in trouble,"[7] and as those preparing for the 1980 White House Conference on Families discovered the "resilience" of American families.

But we should not be misled by the shifting winds of political attention. The underlying issues that have generated a sense of crisis are not so quickly resolved, nor are they ephemeral. Concern for childrearing, horror over the inequalities of income, race, and (in veiled form) class, anxiety over the changing roles of men and women, and debates over what the state ought and ought not to do have been among the most enduring issues Americans have faced. These issues are larger than the recurring sense of family crisis. They have persisted well after each immediate crisis has run its course, after journalists, politicians, social reformers, and academics have moved on to other topics. The underlying problems—the boundary between the private and the public, the relative values of individual and collective responsibility, the appropriateness of market mechanisms versus political decisions, the nature of democracy—are grand and recurring questions. Every generation must struggle with their resolution, as the conditions of family life and childrearing shift, as the economy and the state develop, and as new versions of old problems emerge.

In particular, our generation must struggle with the nature of the state. Since the state has become omnipresent—in the "private" life of families as well as in the economy—the role of the state for good or evil cannot be ignored. Despite the misleading rhetoric of conservatives led by Ronald Reagan, the state will not wither away; even for conservatives, an activist state has become necessary to address the various social and economic problems that cannot be resolved by individuals. The significant issue remains—who will control the state and for what purpose? The challenge is to replace the principles that now govern public institutions with more progressive ones. While such changes may seem bewildering, we suggest in the concluding chapter that Americans can draw upon widely accepted ideals to reconstruct the state. The reforms necessary to implement these principles will still be threatening, contentious, and protracted. But without these changes we will be doomed to repeat the cycles of crisis and reform, and we will be unable to fulfill the promises to children which have been among the most generous impulses of American life.

1

Family Crises and
Public Responsibility

THE BELIEF that families are in trouble has been persistent in American history. Colonial Americans expressed the "greatest trouble and grief about the rising generation" and brooded about "the great neglect in many parents and masters in training up their children in learning and labour." They sought to stabilize families through statutes enforcing parental responsibility and through the scrutiny of public officials over family life.[1] In the early nineteenth century, alarm over family stability generated a profusion of guides to childrearing, often combined with calls for philanthropic efforts and public measures to "shore up" family life. Social reformers expressed similar concerns during the rest of the nineteenth century and into the twentieth century: they blamed parents for youthful misbehavior and criticized mothers in particular for failing to take the obligations of motherhood seriously. It often seems that each generation has discovered in the "decline of the family" the source of its troubles and the rationale for a variety of public policies.

While the sense of family disruption has been constant, the conditions underlying periods of anxiety have shifted. The family itself has changed, and ideological conventions about the family have been modified, especially in times of rapid economic and social developments. As factory production replaced family-based farming and craft work in the early nineteenth century, the ideology of the separation of the private family from the public world of production developed. The emergence of a "cult of true womanhood" complemented the vision of "separate spheres" for men and women, and changing concepts of children led to an emphasis on socialization in the home and in schools rather than in the community and at work. At the turn of the century, labor force developments increased the proportion of women in the labor force and increased the years of schooling for children, in both cases modifying relationships within families and generating new concerns for family life. Similar trends in the post–World War II period have generated more recent anxieties. The conditions of family life have changed drastically, but the very process of change has recreated old fears about the family's functioning.

The relationship of extra-familial institutions to families has also changed. The growing number of public institutions designed to supplement families during the nineteenth century—schools, juvenile houses of refuge, and asylums for physically and mentally handicapped children—increased the institutional contacts of families at the very moment when the ideology of the "private" family was developing. The expansion of state institutions during the progressive era continued to enlarge public responsibility for children, and new governmental roles in regulating economic and social conditions extended public responsibilities into the "private" economy as well. During the 1930s, these developments were all extended in response to the depression, and then again in the post–World War II period. By the 1960s and 1970s, when the family seemed once again "in trouble," childrearing had changed radically from a hundred years before, when the public influences on children were considerably less pervasive. In the nineteenth century, parents and public officials debated the state's right to enforce child labor laws and compulsory school attendance. Today, whatever the merits of that enforcement, few Americans doubt the state's right to act. Public responsibility has become institutionalized through schools and other children's institutions, in welfare programs, and in macroeconomic and regulatory policies.

The historical record suggests a complex pattern. On the one hand, discussions of the family have been dominated by rhetorical flourishes about the decline of the family and about the family as a private institution. On the other hand, economic and social changes have altered relationships within families and between families and other institutions. A marked continuity in discussions of family life has thus masked dramatic changes in the circumstances of families and in the state's relationship to families. Americans desperately maintain the ideology of the private family and private responsibility for childrearing, long after the prerequisites for truly independent families have disappeared and public responsibility has expanded. They bemoan changes in sex roles, even though women have been increasing their labor force participation for over a century and several feminist movements have developed alternative conceptions of women's roles. In constantly reasserting that the family is the "basic unit of society" Americans have ignored evidence that some institutions—corporations, for example—profoundly shape family life and that parents share their socializing influences with a host of extrafamilial influences. The irony is that each assertion of family crisis has been accompanied simultaneously by a call to strengthen the private family and by an effort to develop alternatives to families, particularly through public institutions to socialize children and do for them what their parents are failing to do. Nicholas Hobbs's seemingly innocuous statement of the family crisis in the mid-1970s summarizes the attitudes and options that have been restated by a thousand commentators from the 1830s to the present:

> The family in America is in deep trouble. It may or may not prove to be adequate to its childrearing responsibilities. If it is to survive as the basic structural unit of society, the family must be strengthened or replaced by some new structural unit fully adequate to its childrearing responsibilities. The survival of our society depends on it.[2]

Americans have historically tried to fulfill both of the alternatives which Hobbs describes. They have consistently articulated the sanctity of the private family and reaffirmed private responsibility for childrearing in order to "strengthen the family"; at the same time they have adopted policies and supported institutions that claim public responsibility, "replace" the family, and assert that families cannot be private. The emergence of this duality can be illuminated by examining two earlier periods of major historical change—the mid-nineteenth century and the beginning of this century—when the sense of family crisis reached fevered levels and new forms of public responsibility for children emerged.

Dual Conceptions of Responsibility

The first half of the nineteenth century was a period of substantial economic transformations. Revolutions in transportation and communication opened vast new areas of the continent to settlement; agriculture became overwhelmingly commercial, displacing farming for self-sufficiency; banking and commerce expanded and became specialized. Above all, the transformations of entrepreneurial capitalism changed the organization of work and of families themselves. Entrepreneurial firms emerged, emphasizing mass production for markets rather than limited production for local households and replacing household-based craft production with factory-based production carried out by wage laborers. The capital requirements of large-scale production and industrialization forced entrepreneurs to go beyond the resources of the family-based firm in favor of joint stock companies independent of families ties.[3]

Developments in the shoe industry illustrate the replacement of family-based production. Before the nineteenth century, shoemaking was carried on by artisans in their own households, usually at the request of individual customers. Even as custom production gave way to production for markets, shoemaking remained within the household: journeyman and apprentice, wife and children lived and worked within a household directed by the master shoemaker, who was simultaneously husband, father, teacher, overseer of a small work team, and small-scale capitalist. In the early nineteenth century, growing pressure to expand production and increase profits led to specialization and the location of some phases of production in centralized workshops outside the household. From that stage, it was a small step in the 1840s and 1850s to the establishment of shoe factories where all production took place. Most shoemakers themselves became wage laborers rather than small-scale capitalists, and families lost their role in production. The separation of families from production took place in a similar way in other sectors which had previously been craft enterprises, like textiles, and through the creation of new industries, like large-scale locomotive production. The transformation of the household economy occurred at different rates in different places; it was more an urban than a rural phenomenon, and in no part of the country were households entirely eliminated as producers. Nonetheless, almost everywhere the ties that had linked families to production became tenuous.[4]

The consequences of these changes were enormous. The amount of self-employment was reduced, and the differences between skilled artisans and unskilled laborers were eroded. These changes generated a larger class of urban wage laborers. The process of creating new class divisions also exacerbated inequalities in wealth and income. In 1860, 5 percent of all families held 55 percent of the reported wealth, and half of all American families had no wealth at all. In urban areas the economic disparities were worst of all. Immigration from Europe added racial and ethnic divisions to the divisions of class and income. Migration from rural to urban areas increased as small-scale farming diminished. Poverty, the divisions of class and ethnicity, urbanization and urban crowding, mobility and instability, the development of inhuman industrial processes—whatever capitalism promised in terms of greater production, its costs in terms of social problems were enormous.[5]

To some extent, social commentators in the ante-bellum period under-stood that economic and social changes were transforming families. They complained that urban conditions made it difficult for families, especially poor families, to live decent lives. They acknowledged that changes in sex roles were the consequence of the shifting organization of production and that class, racial, and income divisions were producing social conflict. Yet they tended to blame families themselves for the social turmoil.[6] Fathers, "eager in the pursuit of business," toiled "early and late" and neglected their paternal responsibilities.[7] Mothers showed "a conspicuous lack of maternal instinct"[8] and were charged with being too distracted by fashion and entertainment to care for their children. Those bemoaning the crime, vagrancy, and general disorder of the cities were quick to cite the family backgrounds of criminals as responsible and to blame the "almost univer-sal prostration of family government and the almost entire absence of parental restraint."[9] Responsibility for the decay of society was clear: "the State is stabbed at the hearth-side and here liberty and honor are first sold. It is injured by family neglect."[10]

The tendency to blame families was in part a holdover from the colo-nial period, when the family was regarded as a "little commonwealth" responsible for preparing citizens for the larger commonwealth. But the social context had changed: the separation of production from the family in the nineteenth century meant that families were now seen as separate from the outside world. Rather than stressing the colonial vision of fam-ilies as replicating the structure and values of the larger society, nine-teenth-century Americans began to view the family as a retreat from the harsh realities outside, a "haven in a heartless world."[11] The family func-tioned best when it constituted a bulwark against the crass materialism and the disorganizing effects of production and politics; as *Godey's La-dies Magazine* urged its readers, in words echoed from countless pulpits and journals, "Look to the *sanctuary* of the home; there sympathy, honor, virtue are assembled; . . . there disinterested love is ready to sacrifice ev-erything at the altar of affection."[12] In order to realize the image of the home as a sanctuary, a literature flourished on the architecture and orga-nization of homes. Houses were to be protected from the outside; they needed fireplaces to provide the physical analogue of the emotional "warmth" that would pervade the happy home. Reflecting the ideology of the family as a private sphere, the architecture of private homes and public buildings became increasingly distinct; patterns of mixed use, where a building would incorporate both workshops and family living quarters, were gradually abandoned.[13]

In reconstructing the home as a sanctuary for the proper raising of children and the reconstitution of men ravaged by the world of work, the

15

domestic ideology gave a special role to women: "To render *home* happy is women's peculiar province; home is her world."[14] In contrast to the seventeenth century, when fathers were considered important child-rearers, by the early nineteenth century it was overwhelmingly assumed that mothers would be the primary caretakers.[15] If today we interpret the domestic ideology as imprisoning women within the home, domestic writers of the nineteenth century assured women that in creating the family home and rearing the next generation women liberated their real capacities and gained moral authority. As Lydia Sigourney, one of the country's most popular writers, told her readers in 1838: "If in becoming mothers you have reached the climax of your happiness, you have also taken a higher place on the scale of being . . . you have gained an increase in power."[16] Maternal responsibility and sacrifice would determine the success of the family enterprise, which would shape society itself through its influence on future generations. "When our land is filled with virtuous and patriotic mothers," wrote the author of the widely read *The Mother at Home,* "then it will be filled with virtuous and patriotic men."[17]

Domesticity was an ideal that applied to all families, but social commentators discovered special problems when they turned to poor and immigrant families. For the first time, Americans began to discuss poverty as a group phenomenon rather than one caused by the moral failings of individuals. As was true for many domestic writers, those bemoaning the disorderly conduct of urban youth began by condemning urban life as antithetical to proper childrearing and ended by condemning families themselves for ethnic and cultural deviations that led to poor childrearing, poverty, and disorder. The existence of poverty among urban immigrants in the 1840s and 1850s generated new ideas about a "culture of poverty" which explained social problems; entire immigrant groups were condemned for their failures. The secretary of the New York Association for Improving the Condition of the Poor described the Irish in 1856 as

> content to live in filth and disorder. . . . Instead of putting their children to school, or to some useful trade, they are driven out to beg, pick up fuel, sweep the street crossings, pedal petty wares, etc., that they may themselves live lazily on the means thus secured.[18]

The deterioration of family life ascribed to blacks was still worse. Even as perceptive an observer as de Tocqueville missed the extent to which black slaves managed to maintain family alliances through complex extended families. He concluded that the wretched state of black families was due to the "profound and natural antipathy between the institution of marriage and that of slavery."[19] More often, whites simply blamed racial inferiority for the failures of black parents in their childrearing obligations. The ideology of domesticity outlined the proper way to rear children and the duties of parents, but it presented ideals that lower-class parents and slaves could not possibly fulfill. Domesticity therefore allowed commentators to concentrate on the failings of parents, ignoring the real sources of poverty and racism.

While generations of domestic writers attempted to reconstruct families through ideological exhortations, other reformers lamenting the disruption of family life—especially those concerned with the urban poor—proposed alternative institutions to fill the vacuum caused by the decline of family, church, and community. The extent of institution building at mid-century was astounding. Specialized institutions—initially philanthropic but increasingly state-funded—opened to deal with education, crime, poverty, disease, mental illness and mental subnormality, deafness and blindness. Their founders claimed that these institutions would act as moral and disciplinary forces, creating social order, shielding children and adults "from the temptations of a sinful world," and aiding them "in forming virtuous habits, that they may finally go forth, *clothed as in invincible armour.*"[20] In one sense, the new institutions followed precedents from the colonial period, when children were sent to other families for discipline, moral training, and occupational preparation if their parents were lax in discipline or too poor to provide for them adequately. The new institutions thus extended the assumption that children should be removed if their parents failed them, and reformers were explicit that the new institutions would stand *in loco parentis*. This assumption is clear in a description of the duties of Boston school masters in 1836: "As the master stands in place of the parents, he should perform the duty of a parent; and examine closely the characters, morals, and habits of each pupil."[21] Yet the creation of new institutions in place of parents represented a profound shift in social policy away from the care of dependent and deviant children within households toward care in public institutions independent of families. The shift in social responsibilities paralleled the shift in production; families were in every way becoming more private.

Urban public schools and houses of refuge for wayward children were the archetypes of the new institutions. In cities, public schools were advocated for those poor and minority children whose families appeared to be in most disarray, and "visitors" were sent to "persuade the indifferent and careless to send their children to school."[22] For such parents, unable to raise their children correctly, "the teacher becomes their agent, supplying their place and doing their duty."[23] The superiority of public schools to home life was clear to early educators, as in this statement from 1851:

No one at all familiar with the deficient household arrangements and deranged machinery of domestic life of the extreme poor and ignorant, to say nothing of the intemperate—of the examples of rude manners, impure and profane language, and all the vicious habits of low-bred idleness, which abound in certain sections of all populous districts—can doubt that it is better for children to be removed as early and as long as possible from such scenes and such examples and placed in an infant or primary school, under the care and instruction of a kind, affectionate, and skillful female teacher.[24]

To be sure, reinforcing moral and religious codes had always been the school's obligation, an extension of communal and familial responsibilities; the moral mission to educate the child "to a regard for the laws of justice, integrity, truth, and reverence, so that he shall grow up mindful of the rights of others, a good neighbour, a good citizen, and an honest man" extended beyond the lower-class to middle-class children as well.[25] But in the cities, where economic and social tensions were high, the public school received its most forceful support as a way of replacing families in disarray, a relatively novel public response to problems that were now beyond private solution.

Houses of refuge and reform schools, the precursors of the juvenile justice system, were even more clearly designed to replace defective families. The fashion of blaming youthful crime on bad family influences led the founders of these new institutions to propose that they provide parent-like supervision while keeping children—usually poor and immigrant children—as far from their own parents as possible. As one prominent spokesman urged in 1832, "Have not they the most emphatic claim to the charity of public instruction who have the misfortune to be drawn into the vortex of crime, by the force of inevitable suffering, by the urgency of guilty parents, by the excitement of wicked associates?"[26] Such institutions were necessarily residential facilities, to minimize contact with evil influences; and they were often in the country, inaccessible to parents and closer to the supposedly wholesome influences of rural life. The schools themselves were designed to replicate the model family; the first reform school for girls, established in 1856 in Lancaster, Massachusetts, claimed that each matron would serve as mother, provided each girl with her own room, forbade the use of corporal punishment, and stressed love and homemaking skills as the cure for waywardness.[27] The control of youthful crime—the central social problem to many nineteenth-century reformers—required an institution that replaced the family as completely as possible.

With the development of new public institutions, Americans had established by mid-century a dual and potentially contradictory conception of responsibility for children. One strand emphasized the private family, including the responsibility of parents for children, the primary role of mothers, and the separation of the child-centered family from the harsh world outside. The second stressed the responsibility of the state where families failed to meet their responsibilities, a role discharged through children's institutions like the common schools and the juvenile reform schools. The two conceptions of responsibility developed almost simultaneously: public institutions expanded at the same time that the doctrine of private responsibility was clearly articulated.

In practice, the state's role remained limited. In contrast to the colonial period, when families had only limited privacy rights against the community, the nineteenth-century assumption was that the state should not normally intervene in family life but should be called in only after the response of private institutions—including churches and philanthropic institutions—to family failure was found inadequate. An age that stressed individualism and voluntarism was unwilling to allow extensive intervention into families.[28] In fact, many of the children in state institutions were placed there by parents unable to control disobedient youth or faced with the difficulties of rearing a handicapped child. Most important, the conflict between the conception of private responsibility and the emerging institutions of public responsibility was minimized because the children in need of the state's protection were so often poor, immigrant, and black, from families unable to live up to middle-class domestic ideals. Yet the willingness to define some children as needing the intervention of the state portended a very different world from the one implied by the ideal of private responsibility.

Families and the State in the Progressive Era

In the magnitude of their transformations, the decades around 1900 were similar to those of the mid-nineteenth century. By World War I the United States had become the world's dominant economy, sufficiently expansive to attract eighteen million immigrants between 1890 and 1920. The growth of large corporations had changed the economic structure of the country: the economy of the ante-bellum period, in which relatively small entrepreneurs produced single products for local or regional markets, gave way to an economy increasingly dominated by large, multiproduct corporations in which ownership and management were separated and which produced for national and international markets. Independent entrepreneurs and self-employment became marginal, workplaces were increasingly large and impersonal, and the further introduction of new machinery and new work processes (like the assembly line and the reforms of scientific management) continued to reduce craft work and skilled work. The growth of large corporations did not eliminate small businesses; many small farms continued, and small firms grew up in trade and retailing. But the large corporations became dominant, and they shaped both the economy and the role of the government.[29]

The shifts in the scale of business often made the economy seem uncontrollable; urban growth and large-scale immigration further exacerbated the turmoil and the sense of disorder. The expectation that private initiative with benign state sponsorship would create economic prosperity was dashed by the depressions of the 1870s and 1980s. The labor violence that mounted near the end of the century indicated how contentious society had become. The influx of unskilled labor and the further conversion of craftsmen into relatively unskilled workers meant that the distribution of income became more unequal, making poverty more extreme.[30] The progressive reformer, Robert Hunter, wrote in 1904 that even in prosperous times "No less than ten million persons in the United States are underfed, underclothed, and poorly housed."[31] The new industrial system reshaped hiring patterns and diminished the importance of family ties in employment, and workers were increasingly confronted by sustained efforts to inculcate patterns of industrial discipline—punctuality, adherence to order, efficiency—which further enhanced the role of nonfamilial institutions like the schools in preparing youth for employment.[32]

The expanding industrial economy increased the amount of work available to women. Between 1890 and 1910 the proportion of women in the paid labor force increased from 16 percent to 25.5 percent. The variety of occupations open to women also increased: by 1910, 9.1 percent of working women were in retail jobs, compared to less than 1 percent forty years earlier; women constituted 36 percent of the rapidly expanding clerical work force, compared to less than 3 percent in 1879. Declining fertility rates among native-born white women reduced some of the constraints of childbearing. The growth of public schooling, health and social services, and college opportunities opened the way for some women to enter the professions. To be sure, in every occupation women were at the bottom, in the lowest paid positions with the slightest chances for advancement. Female employment continued to be dominated by young single women, with most women leaving employment when they married. Sharp class and racial differences also existed, with the participation rates of immigrant women 50 percent higher than those of native-born white women, and the participation of black women much higher than for white women.[33] Maternal employment, therefore, continued to be relatively limited, but the available options had expanded significantly, compared to those available in the nineteenth century. Marguerite Dixon, a conservative vocational guidance counselor, summarized the ambivalent acceptance of employment for women. She wrote that women should remember that their highest vocation was the home, but at the same time they ought to know what the labor market was like. They should know "local conditions with respect to working hours, character of work, wages, possible advancement, dangers to health, moral conditions, advantages over other occupations open to girls. . . . Girls should at least go into factory work with their eyes open."[34]

As in the ante-bellum period, much of the anxiety about changing social and economic conditions focused on the family. Reformers and journalists rediscovered poverty and decried the threat that inadequate income, urban crowding, and chaotic housing conditions presented to family life. As one educator stated the problem in 1917:

> Conditions of modern life have created a large class of society whose social or industrial circumstances are such that children cannot be well educated from or in the home. In many cases the social duties of the mother and the business cares of the father leave no time for that home life and parental care so necessary to the regular and natural development of child life. In many other cases the surroundings of the home are such that parents feel constrained to send the child away for his education. Crowded apartment houses, lack of play room, want of neighbourhood life, street companionship of uncertain or evil character, the overcrowding of the public schools—these and other reasons are literally forcing thousands of our city population to seek boarding schools for their children.[35]

Though some reformers recognized that social and economic conditions of lower-class families made an ideal family life nearly impossible, others blamed changing conditions within families for urban decay, rising crime, and the sense of disorder. Immigration from Europe increased the variety of "un-American" family patterns and customs, and immigrant parents were in turn chastized for failing to rear their children adequately; as the social historian Arthur Calhoun wrote in 1919, "Children of immigrants lose respect for parents and the home becomes practically non-existent."[36] Even more than before, ethnic group culture—"cultures of poverty"— were held responsible; as Josephine Baker, a public health physician for the New York City Department of Health, described the problem of infant deaths:

[Hell's Kitchen's] residents were largely Irish, incredibly shiftless, altogether charming in their abject helplessness, wholly lacking in any ambition and dirty to an unbelievable degree. . . .The babies' mothers could not afford doctors and seemed too lackadaisical to carry their babies to the nearby clinics and too indifferent to carry out the instructions you might give them. I do not mean that they were callous when their babies died [from dysentery]. Then they cried like mothers, for a change. They were just horribly fatalistic about it while it was going on. Babies always died in the summer and there was no point in trying to do anything about it.[37]

Immigrants and the poor were not the only groups blamed for failing as parents. The declining fertility rate and the increasing divorce rate among native-born whites furthered the sense that the family was in disarray. Middle-class native-born white women were accused of committing "race suicide" by having fewer babies then did immigrant women. The divorce rate jumped from 1.5 to 7.7 divorces for every 1,000 marriages between 1879 and 1920. In searching for the causes of divorce, many commentators blamed women in particular; a group of women panelists discussing the topic "Are Women to Blame?" concluded that the unrealistic and romantic expectations of women about married life, their impatience, inconsiderateness, and tendency to usurp traditional male functions were indeed to blame.[38] Others were more concrete in pointing to maternal employment as the cause for "abandonment" of the home. The author of "The Transitional Woman," published in 1880 before the large influx of women into employment had really begun, complained that

Women do not care for their home as they did; it is no longer the focus of all their endeavours; nor is the mother the involuntary nucleus of the adult children. . . . Professional women have found that however dear the home is, they can exist without it.[39]

To be sure, the attack on women was challenged: feminists and liberals contended that divorce was a necessary evil and that the family was less a place of nurture than a source of oppression for women, a legitimized form of prostitution. The sharp disagreement about the causes of family "decline" itself indicates how troubling the issues of the family were.

Social commentators of the progressive era repeated the contradictory reactions established in the nineteenth century: they reasserted the primacy of the family's responsibilities *and* the importance of public responsibility, especially the necessity of new and more expansive children's institutions. The ideal of domesticity took on new life, with a novel emphasis on "scientific" home management and childrearing. Courses in home economics and domestic science proliferated; a flood of pamphlets, articles, and books provided instruction outside the schools. Mothers' clubs and organizations like the National Congress of Mothers (the forerunner of the PTA) were established to emphasize the importance of the family and to provide parent education. The "house beautiful" movement and the growing popularity of magazines like *Good Housekeeping* extended the earlier emphasis on the household as necessary to healthy family life, with a new emphasis on science and efficiency. Much of the literature on housekeeping before the Civil War took the form of a dialogue, with an older woman passing on her knowledge and experience to a younger woman; after 1890, the literature was couched in the language of science, of facts and figures, of economics and efficiency, with experts doing the talking. Mary Pattison's *Principles of Domestic Engineering* (1915) epitomized the trend; the book was introduced by Frederick Winslow Taylor whose *The Principles of Scientific Management* it emulated.[40]

Above all, supporters of the family reaffirmed motherhood as the highest role of women. The author of *A Study of Child Nature from the Kindergarten Standpoint*, a book which went through fifty editions, wrote that motherhood "demands of woman her highest endeavor. It demands of her that she become a physician, an artist, a teacher, a poet, a philosopher, a priest."[41] Even feminists like Charlotte Perkins Gilman, who urged women to enter employment, subscribed to the centrality of motherhood for women: "Because women's first place is at home is no reason why her last and only place should be there."[42] To help women perfect their "highest endeavor," various experts began to educate mothers in the science of childrearing, which included child psychology, pedagogical techniques, nutrition, and moral instruction; the published advice of childrearing experts, special courses offered by women's organizations, and the teachings of charity workers providing instruction to the poor were all manifestations of the new, "scientific" attention to domestic roles.

The affirmation of the family and of maternal influences spilled over into public policy as well. Moral conservatives formed groups like the League for the Protection of the Family to fight the tide of divorce and to press for more stringent divorce laws.[43] The clearest expression of the need to "shore up the family" came in the 1909 Conference on the Care of Dependent Children, the forerunner of the decennial White House Conference on Children. The conference summarized the conventional wisdom that children were "natural resources" requiring parental protection to become healthy, productive adults and defended the institution of the family in ringing terms:

> Home life is the highest and finest product of civilization. It is the great molding force of mind and of character. Children should not be deprived of it except for urgent and compelling reasons.[44]

The conference repeated the prevalent view that reformatories, orphanages, and other extrafamilial institutions for deviant and dependent children could not replicate families and that the state should seek reforms to support children within their families rather than institutionalizing children.

The attempts to develop a public policy in support of the family's private responsibilities produced a variety of reforms during the progressive era. Mothers' pensions—the forerunner of the current Aid to Families with Dependent Children—provided state funds to eliminate the necessity for maternal employment, in theory allowing poor mothers to give full attention to childrearing. The practice of parole in the juvenile justice system allowed delinquent children to be supervised in their families rather than remain in institutions, respecting the sentiment of the 1909 conference that even the worst families were better than the best institutions. Similarly, the establishment of day care for the poor was designed to keep families intact by enabling women who had to work to keep custody of their children.[45]

Even more prominent than reforms to "shore up" the family and reassert the primacy of parental responsibilities was the second strand of reform: the extension of public responsibility for children through public institutions. The public schools expanded, especially at the high school level, systematizing their practices and further sharpening the distinction between school and family. In a period of transition and uncertainty, the schools were promoted to resolve various social problems by replacing family influences with more appropriate teachings: to Americanize immigrants and socialize rural migrants, to teach respect for property and government, to mute the antagonism between capital and labor. A new emphasis on the entry of youth into the labor force emerged, a response to complaints that the work ethic had deteriorated and demands that schools had to prepare students more directly for vocations;[46] the vocational emphasis of schooling confirmed the century-long decline in the ability of families to prepare their children for occupational roles. Developments within the schools—like tracking and ability grouping—that continued the separation of middle-class and lower-class children were justified by the different childrearing abilities of their parents.

The compulsory attendance movement affirmed the trend toward increased public responsibility even more strikingly. While mid-nineteenth century reformers had expressed concern about children out of school, they hoped that persuasion and the advantages of school attendance would convince parents to send their children to school. At the end of the century, however, those hopes seemed unfounded. The issue was, as it had always been, the need to police lower-class families who would otherwise be derelict in their duties. The secretary of the Connecticut State Board of Education wrote in 1872 that "we have imported parents [immigrants] so imbruted as to compel their young children to work for their grog and even to beg and steal in the streets when they should be in school." Compulsory attendance legislation and its active enforcement confirmed the dominance of state responsibility over parental prerogatives, as the Supreme Court of Illinois declared in a 1901 ruling upholding the state's compulsory attendance statute:

> The natural rights of a parent to the custody and control of his infant child are subordinate to the power of the State. . . . One of the most important natural duties of the parent is his obligation to educate his child, and this duty he owes not to the child only, but to the commonwealth. If he neglects to perform it, or willfully refuses to do so, he may be coerced by law to execute such civil obligation. The welfare of the child and the best interests of society require that the state shall exert its sovereign authority to secure to the child the opportunity to acquire an education.[47]

Outside the schools, new institutions developed to discharge public responsibilities. The juvenile court and the institution of probation—designed for "the retention of natural conditions, in the home, if it is at all fit," rather than institutional treatment of delinquents—allowed state supervision over a larger number of families found derelict in their child-rearing. As a juvenile court judge described the advantage of the new practices:

> With the great right arm and force of the law, the probation officer can go into the home and demand to know the cause of the dependency or the delinquency of a child. . . . He becomes practically a member of the family and teaches them lessons of cleanliness and decency, of truth and integrity.[48]

The establishment of the U.S. Children's Bureau, in the wake of the 1909 conference, meant an ongoing (if small) federal presence to monitor the condition of children and advise on their upbringing.[49] The well-being of the child—"child saving"—became the justification for a host of other measures, from child labor legislation to health centers, playgrounds, and better housing in immigrant and working-class districts. But the irony is that even those practices designed to support home life, the "highest and finest product of civilization," had the contradictory result of expanding the state's role. The mothers' pensions, small as they were, still meant that the support of poor children had become in some part a public responsibility rather than the responsibility of parents or of private philanthropy.

Probation may have reduced the rates of institutionalized wayward youth, but the practice allowed public supervision of delinquent behavior to expand. Child care facilities may have diminished institutional placement of poor children, but they also shifted significant childrearing responsibilities out of families and away from mothers.

The reforms of the progressive era thus consistently expanded the institutions of public responsibility which had emerged in the nineteenth century. Grace Abbott, the second chief of the federal Children's Bureau, articulated this dramatic reordering of the relations among the state, children, and families:

> The state has recognized certain obligations to all of its children. For example, it has expended large sums for free schools and playgrounds to aid parents in their common-law duty to educate their children. This has been done in part because collective provision is the best way to meet a universal need. But in its public-school program the state also recognized it had a responsibility for the training and protection of children, which would be met only by providing the necessary facilities for such training and ensuring the use of those facilities by prohibiting the employment of children and requiring their attendance at schools.... For those children who are wholly dependent on the state, who are especially handicapped by reason of birth or physical or mental defect, who are becoming delinquent or are delinquent, the state has a special responsibility.[50]

Despite the further development of domestic ideals and the restatement of maternal responsibilities, most reformers of the progressive era stressed the state's parental role—its "obligations to all of its children"—rather than the limited state responsibility that had prevailed in the nineteenth century.

The expansion of public responsibility was as evident in economic policy as in social policy. The scale and abuses of corporate power, the disruptive impact of competition, and the development of a national economy all thrust the federal government into more active economic policies: the Sherman Antitrust Act and the Clayton Act provided some power against monopolistic practices; the Federal Reserve Act of 1913 extended governmental regulation of the monetary system; and a variety of regulatory efforts—in the Pure Food and Drug Act and legislation covering hours, wages, and working conditions, for example—extended federal powers into the "private" economy.[51] The potential role of the state in social and economic policy was not fully realized until the 1930s, but compared to what had occurred before the Civil War, the policies of the progressive era were more coherent, involved federal and state governments to a far greater extent, and were more widespread in their effects.

At the same time, the shift toward public responsibility should not obscure the continuing ideology of private responsibility, both in familial and economic matters. If the progressive state took on the responsibilities of parents—indeed, if reformers sometimes assumed that the state could be a better parent than many parents—it also incorporated a distorted view of parenting. As Grace Abbott criticized the limits of public benevolence:

> In its provision for the children in need of special care the state has ... undertaken to provide for their care only when the evidence of need made such action inevitable. Reluctant to undertake a clear duty, it is not surprising that legislators have sought to provide not "what the best and wisest parent wants for his own child" but the cheapest possible care, and that law-makers have been slow to recognize that this not only violated sound humanitarian tenets but was in the long run a very costly economy.[52]

Even as the state intervened in families and expanded the scope of children's institutions like the schools and the juvenile court, the model family remained "private," relatively untouched by public institutions (except perhaps the public schools) and responsible for rearing its own children (perhaps with the help of childrearing experts). Since financial support of children was ideally a private responsibility, the funding of public institutions remained inadequate; public schools, juvenile facilities, and day nurseries were often grim places, and mothers' pensions were stingy and their recipients stigmatized. Finally, though the state's prerogatives over parents in theory applied to all parents, in practice public responsibility for children took class-biased and racially motivated forms, with the surveillance powers of the juvenile court and the reforming impulses of the schools aimed at lower-class families whose childrearing "failures" threatened to produce class revolt in later generations. The real legacy of the progressive era, then, was the reaffirmation of the two competing conceptions of responsibility for children which had been tentatively formulated in the nineteenth century. The uneasy coexistence of public responsibility with an ideology of private responsibility provided the setting for the subsequent expressions of family "crisis."

The Great Depression of the 1930s was in one sense a special case. In contrast to earlier periods of family crisis, when the transformations in society and families were unclear, the nature of the crisis was obvious: with official unemployment rates as high as one-quarter of the labor force, and reduced wages for those lucky enough to have jobs, the daily struggle for survival was intense. Beyond that obvious fact, the strain within the family worsened when the man of the house became unemployed for extended periods. When the wife entered the job market to compensate for the decline in family income, this often shifted the division of labor and the balance of power within the family. The usual indicators of strain appeared: rates of separation increased, marriages were postponed, and the birth rate plummeted. Although many families suffered, those children most harmed were in lower-class families or families under stress before the depression hit.[53]

The sheer enormity of the depression severely challenged the liberal principle of self-reliance, both for individuals no longer able to count on private resources and for the federal government forced into massive programs to stave off widespread rioting. The Federal Emergency Relief Act to provide welfare to "all needy unemployed persons and/or their dependents," the Works Progress Administration to provide public works to heads of households, and finally the Social Security Act of 1935 all expanded the scope of federal intervention.[54] Some policies tried to address the problems within families more specifically: parent education classes were established to guide parents in a difficult period, and home economics classes taught women how to stretch tight budgets. But the magnitude of the depression was too great for such efforts to have much effect. Building upon the governmental activities of the progressive era, the New Deal established public responsibilities that went considerably beyond those of the nineteenth and early twentieth centuries. In doing so, it laid the foundation for basic "family policies," aiding families by supporting their economic conditions and using welfare programs and macroeconomic policies to reduce the inequalities and wrenching economic cycles of a capitalist economy.

However, even as the conception of what government might do changed, the principles of private responsibility and the notion that families were to blame for the conditions of their lives continued. Even as massive federal programs were enacted, public opinion and the expectations of politicians like Roosevelt continued to view federal activity as a temporary expedient in a time of crisis, expecting the governmental role to "wither away" after the crisis was over. Yet the government's role did not wither away, even though its welfare activities diminished temporarily during the boom times of World War II. Instead, the growth of relief programs and experimentation with direct control over the economy extended public activities further into what had been private domains. In many ways the new policies of the depression extended the changes begun in the progressive era, expanding the state's role while maintaining the ideology of the private family and the private economy.

The Legacy of Family Crises

The substantial changes of the ante-bellum period and the progressive era, as well as the more obvious dislocations of the depression, generated feelings of families in crisis. The crises were real, not because the family was disappearing or deteriorating but because deep social changes were altering all aspects of American society, and the appropriate responses were unclear. Previous periods of family stress have been times of fundamental transformations in capitalism. They have also coincided with deteriorating economic conditions caused by increases in relative poverty or high unemployment, exacerbated by pockets of hard-core poverty among immigrants and blacks. Immigration, internal migration, and urbanization have compounded the sense of dislocation. Periods of family crisis have also been times when families themselves have been in the midst of fundamental changes, particularly in the roles of women and secondarily in the roles of children.

To be sure, every period of change has also suffered from mild hysteria; alarmism about the imminent "death" of the family has been common in every period. Changes have often been misconstrued as originating in families, apparently confirming that the essential problems have been the deterioration of families rather than other social changes. The responses to family crises have also been contradictory, fueling the sense of uncertainty and turmoil: in every period (including the present) reformers have wavered between "strengthening" the family and "replacing" the family. They have usually attempted a little of each, combining ideological exhortations in support of the family with institutional changes that expanded state responsibilities. The historical record thus reveals an extraordinary phenomenon. Every period of major social change has seen an expansion of public responsibility for the plight of families and children, blurring the distinction between public and private. Yet Americans have continued to insist that families are private, and that public policies should "shore up" the private family as the "basic unit of society."

The conception of the family as the "basic unit" has confused the relationship of private to public responsibility. Despite the vast transformations in the role of the family, Americans have consistently been treated to a rhetoric of the family as the "cradle of civil society," the agency responsible for all behavior. In words that almost repeat those of the 1909 Conference on the Care of Dependent Children and countless other pronouncements, the Family Protection Act of 1979 declared that "a stable and healthy American family is at the foundation of a strong American society."[55] Most often this phrase has referred to the family of the domestic ideal—the father at work, the mother at home rearing children and nurturing her husband—despite the extensive changes in sex roles over the past century.

Yet in many important ways the family has not been the basic unit of society for at least a century. Corporations are now the basic units of economic life, not families. Individuals participate in political life through parties, interest groups, and coalitions, not primarily as individuals or family members. Nor are families basic in the sense of providing all the socializing experiences of their children, since these have been supplemented by schools, child care facilities, the health system, television and other media, and the influence of professionals. Few supporters of the family have argued for eliminating all other socializing institutions, and fewer still have argued for a return to the self-sufficient producing family of the seventeenth and eighteenth centuries (although there are some communes which attempt just that). It is, therefore, difficult to know what it might mean to reestablish the family as the "basic unit of society." Still, the rhetoric continues, its primary effect being to focus responsibility for lapses in social discipline on the family rather than on the social and economic conditions that have themselves unsettled family life.

Blaming families for social problems has also muddied public debates by generating a confusing discussion about the state's role in "strengthening the family." To some extent, this is simply a rhetorical device, since no one is in favor of "weakening the family" and since anyone who is "for the family" must also be good-hearted, caring, and concerned. But this apparently innocent phrase has masked a debate about what families should be. To conservatives, strengthening the family has meant reverting to nineteenth-century domestic ideals by restoring paternal authority, restricting options for women, keeping children dependent and under firm adult supervision, and reducing state programs. Modern liberals, on the other hand, have embraced a conception of the family (less well codified than the domestic ideal) with more egalitarian relationships between husband and wife and between parents and children. Since family relationships can be undermined by a lack of economic resources or restricted opportunities for women, liberals have pressed for expanded state action to correct these problems. For each group, "strengthening the family" implies widely different positions on social programs. Welfare programs "undermine the family" for conservatives, but "strengthen the family" for liberals; for conservatives, child care programs "undermine" the family because they help revise sex roles, but to liberals they "shore up" the family by providing financial and emotional resources. Some reforms have strengthened the position of children against parents, or wives against husbands; whether these "strengthen" or "weaken" the family depends on ideological positions about the appropriate power of men over women and of parents over children. The goal of "strengthening the family," attractive as it sounds, is therefore unspecific and useless as a guide for policy.

In part, the tendency to hold onto slogans about the family reflects nostalgia for a world we have lost, a lament for the demise of families which were presumably more cohesive, more stable, and more powerful in their control over social conditions. Mid-nineteenth–century reformers mourned the passing of an earlier family, in which the patriarch directed the family's production. Social critics in the progressive era longed for the discipline and moral standards of the Victorian family. The romanticization of the past has much the same flavor today: laments over the decline of the extended family, the passing of the family as a "haven in a heartless world," and the disappearance of women happy with home-bound roles indicate a longing for the Victorian family of our nineteenth-century ideals. These nostalgic visions falsify the past by insisting that the family was, just a few years earlier, a "haven"; they ignore the dark side of family life in earlier periods, especially the drudgery and isolation of rural life, the distant and often harsh relationships within families, and the oppression of women in the patriarchal family.[56]

Efforts to establish a golden age of the family, as mistaken as they are, have still served an important purpose: they have been used to argue that the family is responsible for social problems. Perhaps no legacy has been more prominent; even as Americans have acknowledged that social and economic changes were changing the family, they have insisted that the family was itself to blame for its own plight and for the social turmoil around it. As we have seen, the tendency to make the family a scapegoat is one of the striking phenomena of the ante-bellum period and the progressive era. It has been equally apparent during the last two decades, particularly in debates over black and Hispanic families and the roles of women.

From E. Franklin Frazier's *The Negro Family in the United States* (1939) through Gunnar Myrdal's *An American Dilemma* (1944) to Daniel Patrick Moynihan's *The Negro Family* (1965), the litany surrounding black families has been the same: the problems of poverty, limited educational achievement, and low occupational status that blacks have faced since emancipation are attributable to unstable, weak families—fatherless, matriarchal families with illegitimate children and high rates of divorce and separation. In Moynihan's words, "It was by destroying the Negro family that white America broke the will of the Negro people," leaving a "tangle of pathology."[57] A similar though less visible discussion of Mexican-American families has taken place, portraying them in terms of deviations from American familial and cultural norms and describing the pathological consequences for children. The values often associated with Chicanos—*machismo,* orientation to the present, unwillingness to strive for future success (as through schooling), passivity, resistance to change— have been portrayed as the residues of Mexican peasant culture and then blamed for the failures of Chicano children.[58]

Like commentators on family life in the ante-bellum and progressive periods, those who have focused on the problems of minority families have often acknowledged that forces external to the family are responsible for the conditions of family life; Moynihan, for example, called for a national plan of action to counter unemployment and low educational achievement. But the constant reiteration of inadequacy, of parental failure and neglect, and of marital instability has easily led to the view that minority families and minority culture are to blame, trapping children in a "culture of poverty" from which they are powerless to escape. Discussions that emphasize the details of family life have neglected the effects of racial discrimination and class divisions and have made it difficult to shift the discussion away from the family to economic and social problems. As one black described his reaction to the Moynihan report:

> [Most Negroes] want what is *due* them, rather than pity and sympathy. They think that if you have to make people look *bad* or broken up before you can get the country to give them what they should have by right, then that's the same old racism and segregation at work. . . . all our worst points were brought up, and so again the country has the image of the poor, shiftless Negro—or nigger. . . . We know Negroes have suffered, and we know how a lot of our children have to grow up. We just don't believe our family trouble should be emphasized; particularly when everyone has family problems, and the divorce rate among whites is almost thirty-three percent. We want the *causes* of our troubles licked, not the symptoms paraded up and down—which always happens to us anyway.[59]

Ascribing the blame to black and Hispanic families has been based on several historical fallacies. Recent studies in the history of black families now make clear how resilient those families have been; even under slavery, the vast majority of American blacks have always lived in nuclear, two-parent families. Even though a higher proportion of black children than white children have lived in female-headed households, this can be attributed primarily to the poverty caused by racial discrimination rather than to a cultural allegiance to matriarchy, as has often been asserted.[60]

The characterization of Chicano families as dominated by an anachronistic *machismo* has also been proved false.[61] Rather than being completely "pathological," black and Hispanic families have been effective in establishing extended kin networks to provide emotional and financial support, allowing them to survive under extreme conditions of poverty and discrimination.[62]

Yet the tendency to dwell on the details of family life rather than on external economic conditions and racial discrimination has been a trap even for the defenders of minority families. In response to the denigration of minority families, the "revisionist" portrayal has stressed the strength and resilience of black and Hispanic families, emphasizing how many minority families are intact and rediscovering the power of kin networks.[63] Although this view has forced a reexamination of old myths, it also runs the risk of romanticizing minority families and minimizing the cruel effects of poverty and discrimination. As one black psychiatrist reacted:

> We hear a lot of discussion by black scholars . . . praising the strength of black families. Nonsense! You can't talk about strength and then talk about oppression![64]

From either the "pathology" or the "resilience" perspective, then, the discussion of minority families has too often tended to ignore the causes of problems and to foster the attitude of "benign neglect" which suggests that nothing need be done to improve the lives of minority families and children.

A second prominent form of blaming the family for social problems has been the tendency to indict women and mothers for the "deterioration" of family life and thus the deterioration of society. In the ante-bellum and progressive periods and again today, evidence of more women working, rising divorce rates, and declining birth rates have been used to show that women have been disrupting civil society. Working mothers have been accused of ignoring their children's "birthright" to full-time mothering, and single mothers have been castigated for denying children the care and influence of fathers. In the words of a prominent child psychiatrist, Selma Fraiberg, "Our survival as a human community may depend as much upon our nurture of love in infancy and childhood as upon the protection of our society from external threats," and that love requires full-time mothering. Continuing a theme elaborated since the early nineteenth century, Fraiberg argues that women who work are likely to leave their children neglected, left to "learn that the world outside of the house is an indifferent world, or even a hostile world," and that adults "are interchangeable, that love is capricious, that human attachment is a peril-ous investment."[65] The U.S. Women's Bureau made the point even more precisely when it officially announced in 1964 that it was not the bureau's policy "to encourage married women and mothers of young children to seek employment outside the home. Home and children are considered married women's most important responsibilities."[66] Those women at-tempting to alter that assumption have been subjected to harsh criticism, as well as political efforts to constrain their choices. The outpouring of anti-feminist sentiment during the 1980 White House Conference on Families and the recent assertion of anti-abortion, anti–day care, and anti–Equal Rights Amendment activities are only the most current ver-sions of the persistent tendency to claim that family life would be resur-rected, and thus a moral society reestablished, if only women would as-sume traditional sex roles.[67]

The attempts to blame women for the dilemmas experienced both within and outside families are clearly rooted in nineteenth-century do-mestic ideology. Since these ideals gave central responsibility for family life and childrearing to mothers, any deficiencies in families—and by ex-tension the wide array of social problems which might be traced to defi-cient childrearing—could be blamed simply and precisely on mothers. During the twentieth century the tendency to blame mothers has been reinforced by psychoanalytic and child development research, providing a "scientific" base that has seemed impregnable to alternative interpreta-tions. Psychoanalytic theory, often drawing upon research on highly de-prived children, has stressed the importance of a single strong bond be-tween mother and child for all subsequent development. Child development researchers reinforced the same argument; their *observa-tions* of children in a period when only mothers cared for children led them to normative *prescriptions* that mothers were the most effective parents, with warnings of dire consequences for children if mothers went to work.[68] In the post–World War II period, no individual more effective-ly communicated this message to the public than Benjamin Spock:

> You can think of it this way: useful, well-adjusted citizens are the most valuable possessions a country has, and good mother care during the earliest childhood is the surest way to produce them. It doesn't make sense to let mothers go to work making dresses in a factory or tapping typewriters in an office, and have them pay other people to do a poorer job of bringing up their own children.[69]

Although Spock subsequently changed his opinions, a new generation of childrearing experts has been eager to reinforce the notion that there is nothing women can do that is as valuable as mothering.[70] Despite deter-mined efforts to alter its ideological power, the nineteenth-century ideal has survived, and it remains the essential underpinning for conservative efforts to reinstate traditional sex roles.

Like the debate over black families, the persistent tendency to blame women for family crises has distorted actual changes and hampered a clear understanding of public responsibility. The assertion of "educated motherhood" during the progressive era ignored increasing employment for women, just as the reassertions of domesticity during the 1950s ignored massive maternal employment during World War II and the steadily increasing rates of female employment from 1946 on. Particularly as new evidence has accumulated, the conventional wisdoms about the sanctity of mother-child relations have become obsolete. The findings that maternal employment does not by itself harm children, that children can benefit from multiple attachments, that active fathers create richer possibilities for the child's development and do not weaken the maternal bond all contradict what has previously passed for scientific evidence. Contrary to assertions that women can only be fulfilled when they are wives and mothers, the evidence indicates that working women are usually better off than their nonworking peers—more self-assured, less prone to depression and anxiety over the future, more powerful in decision making within their families—as well as having higher incomes.[71] As revised sex roles have generated evidence about the effects of maternal employment, dire warnings about the effects of changing families on children have been revealed as overblown myths.

Above all, the consistent restatement that mothers alone bear responsibility for raising the next generation has constrained the development of public policies which would accommodate maternal employment. As we will see in analyzing the welfare system, child care, and parent education, public programs have often forced mothers into the dilemma of choosing between staying at home with low incomes or working under conditions of terrible stress to increase their earnings. The expansion of child care facilities has foundered on reluctance to accept the legitimacy of maternal employment. The inability to develop employment policies which would facilitate combining employment and childrearing—maternity and paternity leaves, part-time work, and flexible working hours, for example—has placed greater strains on mothers and fathers than are necessary. The attempts to blame women for the family crisis, to limit public support for maternal employment, and to return to conventional sex roles have had no power to retard the movement of women out of the home and into the labor force, which has been under way for over a century, but they have made it more difficult to understand the implications of these changes for private lives and public practices.

In a society that glorifies individuals, the tendency to emphasize the failures of parents and mothers in particular, rather than the economic and social conditions that shape family life, is consistent with prevailing norms. The exclusion of references to the economic underpinnings of family life and the effects of class and racial discrimination leaves only discussion of intrafamily relationships. As Urie Bronfenbrenner, a prominent developmental psychologist, complained, in describing a television program on the family which systematically eliminated every reference to external conditions, the result is to portray family life as:

> a series of soap operas, with comments from the sidelines by the experts—a panel of psychologists, psychiatrists, and family specialists—on the characters in each story; the strengths and weaknesses that accounted for their personal failures, or, less frequently, their personal successes against overwhelming odds . . . and not a word about the circumstances under which the families lived, the conditions that needed to be changed, the actions that had to be taken at the national or local level. "That's the way it is," said the media message. "It's up to these people themselves to come to terms with their problems; some do, some don't."[72]

Yet in addition to the continued assertion of the privacy of the family and the tendency to blame families and mothers, every period of family "crisis" has had another side: the expression of public responsibility for the plight of families and children. Generations of "child savers" have sought to improve the lives of children. In addition to their concern for children themselves, social reformers have also feared that the "failure" of families would lead to other problems—badly reared children, poor workers and low productivity, the decay of cohesive values and the resulting social chaos—and they have advocated the development of public institutions to "shore up" the family as a defense against these threats. The promises of educators and juvenile corrections officials to restore social harmony, the efforts of those promoting mothers' pensions and the other reforms of the progressive era, the justification for the welfare programs and the regulatory efforts of the 1930s all have rested on the assumption that public action should be used to correct social problems.

These assertions of concern and public responsibility have, since the early nineteenth century, invariably faced a dilemma: how to implement public responsibility when the family and childrearing have been considered private, and when the economy is also private. In contrast to the colonial period, when church fathers and town officials could literally walk into a family home to supervise parental behavior, the privacy rights of the nineteenth-century and twentieth-century family have forbidden such intrusion. Colonial communities also had direct ways to alleviate poverty, by requiring families to take the poor into their households or by apprenticing poor children to craftsmen, but the development of the private economy in the nineteenth century made such direct correction of poverty impossible. Every family crisis has therefore generated an imperative to act on behalf of children, and yet the privacy rights of both family and business have constrained the most forthright public action.

Since the early nineteenth century the dominant solution to this dilemma has been the establishment of children's institutions. These institutions have stood *in loco parentis,* doing for children what their parents could not do. Many children's institutions have been based on the assumption of family failure and embodied the hope that public institutions could compensate for that deficiency. They have promised to socialize children when their parents no longer could, to prepare them for adult occupations when fathers could no longer pass on occupations to their sons, to affirm national norms when class, racial, and ethnic heterogeneity threatened the nation. They have promised to alleviate the worst aspects of poverty and to inculcate the values necessary to maintain social integrity—respect for property and authority, acceptance of individual initiative, and a particular form of the work ethic. Children's institutions have promised to improve the lives of children while still respecting the privacy rights of families; they have been promoted to enhance equality of opportunity where it has been impossible to intervene into the private economy and reduce inequality itself. The result has been to make children's institutions carry the weight of improving the lives of children and creating a just and equitable society. In Richard deLone's apt phrase, children have been the "bearers of the American Dream": our ideals for a fair and moral society have rested on the hope that children's institutions can provide every child with an equal chance of adult success.[73]

Although anxiety during periods of family crisis has been widespread, the sense of alarm about family life has always been most intense for lower-class families, and the public responses through children's institutions have therefore embodied class biases. Ever since the early nineteenth century, alarms about family life have usually expressed fears that lower-class children have not been socialized in appropriate ways—to obey laws, to obey their superiors, and to accept the ethic of self-improvement through individual effort—rather than concern about the ravages of poverty on children. Ante-bellum worries about an emerging "culture of poverty," apprehension during the progressive era about labor unrest, James Bryant Conant's fear of "social dynamite" in the ghettos of the late 1950s, the Moynihan report's prediction of a new crisis in race relations, and the alarm over juvenile crime during the 1970s all exemplify the image that has dominated discussions of poverty, of lower-class socialization gone wrong and lower-class families failing in their basic duty as bulwarks against social disorder.[74]

As a consequence of that image, children's institutions have been premised on class-biased conceptions of family deficiency, and they have embodied a class-differentiated conception of their goals. The schools have defined the disabilities of lower-class and middle-class parents in different ways and have consistently established mechanisms of class and racial segregation to treat children differently according to the "evident or probable destinies" inferred from their class backgrounds. The juvenile justice programs and the welfare system have consistently emphasized the need to watch over lower-class families and prevent their excesses. Again and again, as we will see in subsequent chapters, the fear of lower-class children has converted the promise to "save the child" into the goal of protecting the community from their disruptive potential. This conversion has itself undermined the humanitarian impulses of public institutions, while masking disciplinary impulses in the confusing rhetoric of concern for the best interests of children and for the family as the "basic unit of society."

Apart from the inheritance of confusing rhetoric and myth, the legacies of previous periods of family crisis include both the ambiguous relationship of the state to children and a set of institutional responses to the dilemma of discharging public responsibility. But these responses have proved to be incomplete, either inadequate to the tasks they were meant to address or hopelessly contradictory in their effects. The incomplete resolution of social problems in earlier periods of reform has created the conditions for subsequent periods of "crisis," as in the postwar period when familiar issues—of poverty and welfare programs for poor children, of discrimination and equal educational opportunity for minority children, of changing sex roles and the need to "shore up the family," of rapid social changes and the "decline of the family"—generated yet another stage of family crisis. This has in turn set off another round of grappling with the issues of public responsibility: whether we should respond to family "crises" by increasing the scope of public activities or by retreating to private responsibilities; whether we can design public programs that do not infringe on the privacy rights of families (including lower-class families); whether we should strengthen the family by increasing welfare programs or decreasing them, by expanding child care or eliminating it.

The conventional debates between modern conservatives and liberals have largely involved just these issues. But these debates have been incomplete, partly because neither side has examined the nature of the state itself. In attempting to return responsibility to private hands, conservatives have consistently acted as if state involvement has been unwarranted. Yet the state has historically been pressed to act precisely because the consequences of not acting—recurring depressions, for example, or poverty widespread enough to cause social disorder—have been unacceptable. Conservatives thus ignore why the state has expanded and fail to assess which of its policies are critical—even to the continued functioning of capitalism itself. Modern liberals have similarly ignored the nature of the state, an ironic conclusion because they have been the most insistent about its expansion. At the same time that liberals criticize the inadequacy of existing welfare programs—the insufficiency and stigma of Aid to Families with Dependent Children, the ineffectiveness of education programs, the contradictory effects of social services—they continue to call for the reform and the expansion of such programs, hoping that this time around the earlier problems will be eliminated by careful attention to administration and planning. In the succession of the New Deal, the Fair Deal, the New Frontier, and the Great Society, there has been little attention to the systematic failures of liberal agendas or to the conflicts embedded within the state itself which constrain efforts on behalf of children.

The debates between conservatives and liberals have also been incomplete because of their neglect of class divisions. This neglect has allowed conservatives to call for "shoring up the family" by reducing public programs for children, a policy that would let the full consequences of class-based inequality fall on children. The assertion that such reductions would strengthen the family assumes at best that families by themselves can be equally strong in financial and psychological resources, equally self-reliant, and equally able to guide their children through school and into the occupational structure; at worst, the conservative position glories in the inequalities produced by class divisions. Liberals have been more sensitive to how the divisions of income and race affect children, but in their appeals for public resources they have concentrated on the worst consequences of class—the extremes of poverty, of ill-treatment in schools and in the juvenile justice system, of poor health and living conditions—without coming to terms either with the origins or with the full consequences of class differences.

The historical record suggests how difficult it has been to confront the child's relation to the state. Much of the debate over families and children has always been empty, confusing, and even harmful. When pronouncements about the family are not self-seeking or demagogic, they nevertheless tend to rely on the old myths articulated in the nineteenth century which only obscure the changes of the past two centuries. The myth of the family as the "basic unit of society" has led us to ignore the social and economic basis of family life and to blame the family for its problems. Tying women's identities to mothering has meant that each change in sex roles presents itself as a catastrophe for children. The myth of the classless society has blurred the effects of class on families and clouded the class bias that suffuses every children's institution. Failing to analyze the limitations inherent in public responsibility for children, particularly in a class-divided society, has guaranteed the repetition of family crises: even as major changes have been made in state institutions and in the conception of public responsibility, reforms have been incomplete and their partial benefits always under attack. To overcome these cycles of crisis and reform we must turn to a fuller understanding of the child and the state as a first step in reshaping this relationship.

PART ONE

THE CHILD AND
THE STATE

2

The Corruption of Public
Responsibility for Children

SINCE the early nineteenth century, a dual solution has emerged
to the dilemma of fulfilling public responsibilites for children. One strand
has been to justify public action when parents have failed in their childrearing responsibilities. Such justification has often drawn upon the English legal doctrine of *parens patriae,* which gives the state ultimate
parental powers; this doctrine evolved in the nineteenth century into a
conception of limited public responsibility, superseding private responsibility only under the conditions of familial disorganization and pathology.[1] The second strand has been to sidestep the economic and social basis
of family life by creating children's institutions, that in theory compensate
for parental deficiencies without intruding into private families and without intervening into the private economy to change the material conditions of family life. Even as public responsibility expanded, the assumption remained that both families and the economy would remain private.
The state would do only what parents could not do, and it would do so "in
the best interests of the child," as parents would. As John Dewey expressed the hopes of child savers in every era:

> What the best and wisest parent wants for his own child, that must the commu-
> nity want for all of its children. Any other ideal for our schools is narrow and
> unlovely; acted upon, it destroys our democracy.[2]

In practice, Dewey's ideal has rarely been achieved. The promise of
benevolence toward children has invariably fallen short, not—as today's

43

conservatives would have it—because the state is necessarily intrusive and destructive of family life, but because the assumptions under which the state has acted have themselves been limiting. The reconciliation of public responsibility and private responsibility has remained imperfect, and so battles between conservatives and liberals over the appropriate scope of state action, followed by the expedient policy changes, have seriously impaired children's institutions. Still more damaging to children, the assumption that state intervention should be premised on the failure of more "natural" private institutions like families and firms has given public policy a peculiar cast. Public action is a second-best resort, aiding those who are often considered second-class citizens. *Parens patriae* has labeled public intervention as an abnormal activity, a label that serves to limit the scope of public responsibility and keep public funds low. The presumption of parental failure has similarly labeled the children in public institutions as potential failures, adding a form of stigma which has often undermined benevolent intentions.

The potential of children's institutions has also been constrained by the special scrutiny required of public funds, which subjects children's institutions to cost-benefit criteria that are not central to the decisions parents make for their own children. Public investments in children must "pay off" in terms of future benefits, primarily future benefits to the state. If early childhood programs and nutrition programs, for example, do not increase cognitive abilities, and therefore adult success, beyond the shadow of a doubt, they are likely to be considered worthless investments, even if they benefit children in other ways. Americans lack any sense of "public love" for children, which would parallel parental love;[3] therefore public institutions are more concerned with children as instruments to achieve other social goals efficiently—high growth rates, lower welfare costs, social peace—than with children's well-being.

Parents themselves further undermine the intentions of children's institutions: in a world of parental responsibility for children, parents are driven to use public institutions exclusively to advance their own children. All parents use public institutions for private gain, but some parents—those with high incomes, professional status, and white skins—are better able to shape institutions to their own ends. As a result, children's institutions designed to compensate for structural inequalities often end up replicating these inequalities.

In a society so dominated by ideals of private responsibility and by structural inequalities, where public institutions have so consistently been subordinated to private goals, the very principle of public responsibility for children proves to be questionable. Contrary to Dewey's ideal, in which the distinction between public and private provision for children vanishes, the difference has remained substantial. The universal promises to act on behalf of children—to nurture "our most precious natural resources," to provide for "unlucky children," to protect the "truly needy" from the ravages of poverty, to provide equal opportunity—have been undermined by various forms of private responsibility. Relying on children's institutions and on *parens patriae* has not been a satisfactory way to reconcile public responsibility with private interests, since public programs on behalf of children so often prove to work against them.

Private Responsibility and *Parens Patriae*

Since the mid-nineteenth century, most Americans have assumed that parents are responsible for their children's upbringing. In contrast, colonial communities (like some communitarian groups today) were more inclined to think of children as the responsibility of the whole community. Churches, schools, and other community institutions were active participants in rearing children, and town fathers and other public officials could enter homes to observe and correct family life. They could warn parents, publicly or privately, about too much or too little punishment, about inattention to religious instruction, unclean homes, and ill-kept children. In extreme cases town fathers would place children in other families who would exercise parental responsibilities more diligently; in Massachusetts, for example, the 1735 assembly ordered children found in "gross ignorance" placed in other families that would not neglect their instruction. Children were frequently sent by their own parents to live and work in other families, another indication that childrearing was not solely the responsibility of parents.[4] The overlap between public and private responsibility diminished considerably during the eighteenth and nineteenth centuries, as the emergence of family privacy rights made public surveillance of childrearing patterns more difficult and as growing class and ethnic heterogeneity made the "sharing" of childrearing responsibilities almost inconceivable. By the mid-nineteenth century, the decline of public responsibility and the enlargement of private responsibility became rationalized by a domestic ideology that declared the family independent of other institutions and parents superior to all other influences on children. Ever since, childrearing has been presumed the responsibility of the "private" family.

However, private responsibility for children has never been total. The corollary of vesting childrearing responsibility with parents has been that the community or state might intervene under the doctrine of *parens patriae* when parents fail to rear their children correctly. This intervention into family life was considered normal and essential for the maintenance of social order in colonial America. With the flowering of distinctions between "public" and "private" spheres, however, the state's right to intrude into the private family was severely circumscribed, and intervention required more forceful rationale than had previously been the case. If the state was to be as separate as possible from the family, then state intervention ought to be abnormal, justified only when evidence of family disorganization was overwhelming. The presumption of private responsibility therefore came to place effective restrictions on the state: rather than affirming broad public responsibility for the welfare of children, *parens patriae* has taken on the negative cast of intervention only in exceptional cases of parental failure.

A related assumption about the state's intervention also emerged in the nineteenth century; when the state intervened on behalf of the child, it did so in the *child's* best interests. While the state might have to be the adversary of particular parents, the state and child could never be in any serious conflict—not in proceedings to remove the child from parents, not in the juvenile courts, not in compulsory school attendance laws—since the state's goal was to enhance the child's welfare. In modern terms, there existed no reason to protect the child's rights against the state.[5] The ideology of beneficent state intervention was frequently articulated during the nineteenth century, in the course of developing new institutions; as the Massachusetts minister Edward Everett Hale expressed this ideal:

> . . . wherever there are parents, incompetent to make their homes fit training places for their children, the State should be glad, should be eager to undertake their care. Nay more, its own means for training those children, must not be merely such as will suffice for the waifs and strays whom no one else shall care for. They must be so thorough, and so successful, that parents shall not themselves regret the care which is given to their children; and that, as often as possible, selfish and incompetent parents, too poor to educate their children well, may be willing to give them up to care which is so much better. The arrangements should be so wide, that the State should never refuse the care of children who may be offered to it by those who have them in charge.[6]

Most explicitly developed in the courts as the right of the state to take a child away from derelict and potentially harmful parents, the doctrine of *parens patriae* was reformulated to fit other institutions developing in nineteenth-century and twentieth-century America. The expansion of urban public schools was predicated in part on the need for a public institution to stand *in loco parentis* for the children of lower-class and immigrant parents. The early juvenile justice system was similarly aimed at children thought to be beyond the control of their parents, and in need of the discipline and instruction that more capable parents would provide. During the progressive era, mothers' pensions extended the same principles of public support in cases of failure, and these principles have continued to dominate the expansion of income supports and social services to children throughout this century.

During the 1960s, the programs of the Great Society and the War on Poverty enormously enlarged state programs for children and continued to base them on *parens patriae*. The concern for children underlying these programs was unmistakable, but so was the assumption of parental failure. In the twentieth century the failure of parents whose children need public help has not necessarily been considered individual failure, as nineteenth-century reformers often assumed, but instead failure rooted in a "culture of poverty," an environment that made it impossible for children or parents to escape the cycle of poverty. The new children's institutions developed during the 1960s were to replace the culture of poverty with a healthier environment, replacing the deficiencies of parents and community in the most literal sense. Sargent Shriver, former director of the Office of Economic Opportunity, described the motivation for the War on Poverty programs in terms not very different from those of the nineteenth century:

> During my stay in Chicago, I recall driving through depressed communities in the city and seeing groups of youngsters standing on street corners. One can do the same today. It's a national tragedy. . . . As an educator I asked myself, "Couldn't we start boarding high schools rather than just day high schools, take these kids out of that environment, and put them into a controlled environment, where we could teach proper work habits, perserverance on a job, what a job is, etc." When they attend day school, they go right back into an environment that often is anti-work and anti-job. Nobody in the community has a job. For many of these kids, nobody in their family has had a job for *three* generations! . . .
>
> For this reason, it seemed to make sense that for older children growing up in poverty we needed to develop a strategy that competed with the social environments from which these children were coming. We were trying to "break the cycle of poverty." . . . When I became director of OEO, I thought, "Here's my chance. We'll start Job Corps centers and we'll take them out of that environment of poverty and put them into a place for two years, and we'll really break the cycle." People said at the time, "Why don't you just send them there for six months, teach them the skills?" But that's not enough. They say in the army and navy that it takes four years at West Point or the Naval Academy to

make an army or navy officer. And they're starting with the best kids in the country![7]

To varying degrees, all the compensatory programs of the Great Society—Head Start, Follow Through, Title I, Job Corps—and the philosophy of the War on Poverty in general recapitulated these assumptions, with their peculiar combination of humanitarian zeal and condemnation of the poor. Rather than diminishing with the expansion of children's institutions, the doctrine of *parens patriae* has flourished. Indeed, there seems to have been little alternative, given the dominant ideologies of parenting: providing public services to children without the demonstration of parental failure would contradict the presumption of private responsibility for children.

The inability to imagine an alternative rationale for public institutions is so pervasive that all the major ideological positions on the appropriate role of government reflect the logic of *parens patriae*, with slight modifications. The conservative position, distrustful of any programs that smack of egalitarian sentiments, has emphasized giving public aid only to the "truly needy"; as Martin Anderson, a principal adviser to Ronald Reagan, expressed one principle of welfare:

> Practical welfare reform . . . requires that we affirm our commitment to the philosophical approach of giving aid only to those who cannot help themselves, while abandoning any thoughts of radical welfare reform plans that will guarantee incomes. The American people want welfare reform that ensures adequate help to those who need it, eliminates fraud, minimizes cost to the taxpayers, and requires people to support themselves if they can do so.[8]

Although who is "truly needy" is usually left unclear, in practice the conservative insistence on reducing government services amounts to a simple reaffirmation of private responsibility, with the view that "need" should be as severe as possible to justify state action and public remedy as limited as possible. A widely supported moderate view, articulated by Gilbert Steiner in *The Children's Cause*, argues that public policies should be directed only at "unlucky children" whose parents cannot provide for them:

> The children's policy most feasible—and most desireable—is one targeted on poor children, handicapped children, and children without permanent homes: unlucky children whose parents cannot provide them a start equal to that provided most children. . . . Ultimately, a far more complex, universal program may be warranted. It may develop that private families really are not equipped to meet most children's needs. . . . Unless and until that case is made more persuasively than it has been, however, a children's policy will be successful

enough if it concentrates on ways to compensate demonstrably unlucky children whose bodies and minds are sick or whose families are unstable or in poverty.[9]

Even modern liberals, who have been most insistent on extending public responsibility, have regularly resorted to the language of familial disorder and collapse to justify expanded programs. Often, they have applied such descriptions to the majority of families, where once the specter of family crisis applied primarily to lower-class families. The quintessential liberal position, argued by the psychologist Kenneth Keniston and the Carnegie Council on Children, has justified income redistribution, full employment, and expanded services to children in just these terms: "Recognizing that family self-sufficiency is a false myth, we also need to acknowledge that all today's families need help in raising children."[10] Despite its commitment to public programs, the liberal position nonetheless reinforces the belief that governmental programs for children can be justified only when parents are inadequate and "need help." Thus conservatives, moderates, and liberals continue to battle over the magnitude of the state and the boundary between the private world of the family and the public world of government, but not over the basic rationale of the state's relationship to children.

The logic of *parens patriae* has therefore had considerable power in shaping the state's approach to children since the nineteenth century, and in defining the scope of ideological debate over the state's appropriate role. On the whole, however, this justification for public responsibility has not been beneficial to children, since the logic of *parens patriae* is inherently limiting. Most obviously, if the state can intervene only in situations that are construed as abnormal or pathological, then by definition governmental programs can be extended only to the minority of families who are considered the poorest, the most disorganized, and the least effective in socializing their children. In contrast to the positive construction of the colonial era, in which *parens patriae* affirmed widespread responsibility for all children, the negative interpretation of the nineteenth and twentieth centuries has worked to limit public programs and to subordinate public efforts to private responsibilities. Keniston's interpretation of *parens patriae*, that all families "need help," seems to assert that most families are pathological and disorganized, but (with the possible exception of public schooling) this expansive interpretation has never been acceptable. The result has been to reinforce the tendency toward "private wealth and public squalor," with public programs short of funds, limited in the number of children they can serve, and by design inferior to the alternatives that parents finance privately. Thus welfare grants have always been kept substantially below the wages available to unskilled workers, public health care has been inferior to that privately available, public social services like day care are worse than those that middle-income families can buy, and public education is less effective than private schooling. Complaints about "unmet needs" and inadequate funding have become routine among those who run children's programs, not simply because they are partisan but also because the restriction of programs to the "truly needy" leaves many children—especially the children of the "near poor" or the "working poor," for example, or the children whose school performance is mediocre but not abysmal—without appropriate help. Even as it has generated public programs for children, *parens patriae* has assured that they would be restricted in scope and short of funds, contradicting the image of state benevolence.

Defining public responsibility in terms of *parens patriae* has also led to a pernicious labeling. If the state can intervene only in cases of inadequacy, then children who receive special government support must be in some way deficient. When children are considered deficient, that label can become a self-fulfilling prophecy as others come to view them as deficient and perhaps incapable of improvement, and as children themselves come to see themselves as failures. Compensatory education programs—by definition designed to compensate for "educational deprivation"—often suffer from "pygmalion effects": children told that they are failures needing special help come to act like failures, behaving badly and becoming inattentive. Just as often, other teachers perceive children from compensatory programs and special education as "slow learners," unlikely to do well and unworthy of serious attention. Juvenile justice programs brand youths caught within them as troublemakers, undisciplined and untrustworthy if not actually criminal, and so hamper their future employment.[11] The labeling of children in publicly subsidized child care as deficient—neglected, ignored, or even abused—has generated the "pathology" model, underfunded, custodial, and dominated by the conception of child care as "substitute mothering" inferior to maternal care.[12] When the labeling is pervaded by class and racial bias, the effects are all the more vicious. *Parens patriae* assumes a benevolent state, but the assumption that the state serves deficient and neglected children—potentially deviant, perhaps unreachable—makes that benevolence hard to achieve.

The stigma attached to children in public programs extends even more forcefully to their parents, who are by definition inadequate and therefore to blame for their children's plight. The result has been, in various subtle ways, to undermine programs for children. In the schools, the tendency of teachers to identify children with their parents, and specifically with their class and racial backgrounds, becomes a way of linking the deficiencies of children to the deficiencies of parents. The teacher who claims that "if there is a relationship between the parent and child *at home*, then we can teach them in school"[13] is implicitly claiming that teachers cannot help those children with neglectful or absent parents— precisely those whom the schools ought to help most in the logic of *parens patriae*. The tendency, visible since the nineteenth century, to link criminal behavior to family histories has often implied that troublesome youth cannot be rehabilitated because the influences of their parents have been so negative and so powerful. In Aid to Families with Dependent Children, the basic income support program designed for *children*, the antipathy to "welfare queens," deserting fathers, and welfare "bums"—the *parents* who are considered undeserving—has consistently emerged as hostility to funding welfare programs that would support those parents, but this hostility has unavoidably hurt poor children. Because the ability of the state to stand *in loco parentis* and to break the link between parent and child has necessarily been incomplete, children in public programs have always suffered for the deficiencies attributed to their parents.

As subsequent chapters will demonstrate in greater detail, justifying public responsibility for children by the failures of their parents has therefore been contradictory. Each time children are found in need, humanitarian and benevolent activists propose government programs to overcome the deficiencies of family life. Yet we invest reluctantly in those programs, clinging to a desperate wish that parents would adequately fulfill their private responsibilities and resenting their children for requiring public attention and for making demands on our private incomes. The result is that public programs are the "cheapest possible care," as Grace Abbott complained. We end up with a corrupted notion of public responsibility in which the benevolent assumptions of *parens patriae* are subordinated to private responsibility.

Instrumental Conceptions of Children

The distortion of public responsibility inherent in the doctrine of *parens patriae* has been reinforced by the differences between our private and public conceptions of children. Our private, family-based conceptions reveal an "irrational commitment" to our own children, and parents are willing to sacrifice to make them happier in the present as well as in the future—even as they weigh the economic costs of their decisions. In the public realm our commitments are considerably more restrained. We are unwilling to make "irrational commitments," since we are more concerned about how much programs for children—other people's children—will cost us. In contrast to the deep love we feel and express in private, we lack any sense of "public love" for children, and we are unwilling to make public commitments to them except when we believe the commitments will pay off. As a result, cost-benefit criteria have dictated the kinds of activities the state might support, while *parens patriae* has stipulated which children might receive state benefits.

The tendency to assess public responsibility by the calculus of economic costs and benefits and the return on investment is pervasive. Even those with the broadest sense of that responsibility tend to express personal suffering in economic terms and to justify government programs according to the money that will be saved in the long run. As Hubert Humphrey expressed the consequences of unemployment:

> The 1.4 percent rise in unemployment during 1970 has cost our society nearly $7 billion in lost income due to illness, mortality, and in added State prison and mental hospital outlays. To this must be added public outlays of some $2.8 billion annually over the 1970–1975 period for jobless and welfare payments associated with the sustained 1.4 percent rise in unemployment. Additional outlays not included here are the costs of care in Federal institutions. Even excluding these latter outlays, the cost of the sustained 1.4 percent rise in unemployment during 1970 is at least $21 billion. . . . These dollars represent resources lost or diverted from productive use. They represent wealth never to be realized, lost forever to our economy and society. They, in part, measure the human tragedy of unemployment. But most significantly, their loss could have been avoided.[14]

In this discussion the "human tragedy" of unemployment is an afterthought, the economic consequences—the wealth "lost forever," the unnecessary public outlays—the central concern.

While this logic is ubiquitous, children are particularly susceptible to its application precisely because they are in the process of growing up. The 1930 White House Conference on Child Wealth and Protection provides a splendid example of economic logic—and our ambivalence towards it—in a passage justifying classes for partially blind children:

> It would seem almost unnecessary to have to justify, in these United States, the cost of the education of any child who is educable. Humanitarianism alone would seem a sufficient justification. Yet it must be remembered that the state is responsible to the taxpayers for the use of public moneys and that in conse-

quence the state tends to look upon all education as an investment that will pay justifiable dividends.

The object in educating partially seeing children is the same as in the education of any group—to prevent illiteracy and so to develop the innate powers of the individual that he will not become a liability to the state but an asset of the greatest possible value. . . . To give a partially seeing child an even chance with the normally seeing to become an asset to the state, it is necessary to provide for him the opportunity to overcome his handicap. . . . it is obvious that such facilities cost more than those provided for the normally seeing. If by providing them the state is enabled to change potential liabilities into actual assets, no further justification is necessary.[15]

Despite its obligatory mention, "humanitarianism" proves an insubstantial motive. Instead, the solvency of the state is the goal that justifies the effort to transform a potential "liability" into an asset, an independent taxpayer. Economic arguments have shaped the vocabulary in which we conventionally refer to children in the public realm: they are "our most precious natural resource," a resource which needs to be "developed" in order to yield the most productive adults. As a recent report on children's health care summarized its recommendations: "What we offer is a prospectus for a sound investment in America's future, in economic as well as social terms. Healthy children represent a major economic asset."[16]

Embedded in this conception of the state's responsibility for children is an instrumental view: children are valued not for the individuals they are, but as instruments in achieving other goals—economic growth, the reduction of welfare costs, stable and fluid labor markets, a high level of profits, social peace. The prime object of concern becomes the public budget, and the highest goal becomes achieving a high rate of return on current public expenditures and economizing on future expenditures. The questions about costs and benefits and the intense worry over the state treasury are not invalid concerns, but they have tended to narrow the conception of public responsibility by making what is measurable—expenditures, adult earnings, IQ scores, crime rates—the basis for justifying programs for children and by shifting all attention to future outcomes. The child's present well-being, the well-being of those around the child (like parents), and moral concerns are relegated to secondary considerations, if they are considered at all. What the sociologist Sara Lawrence Lightfoot has written about the schools is equally true of child care, social services for handicapped or disturbed children, correctional institutions for juveniles, and vocational training programs:

Part of the focus away from the child as a whole person . . . reflects the broad social and economic functions of the schools in our society. Schools are considered transitory, preparatory institutions where the child's *future* status becomes the overriding concern of his adult sponsors. The preoccupation with anticipated potential rather than with the present realities of the child's life, therefore, is symbolic of a more general tendency not to view children as functionally whole until they become members of the economic structure.[17]

Contrary to the assumptions embedded in *parents patriae* that the state acts "in the best interests of the child," the instrumental conception of the state's role makes the welfare of the child relevant only insofar as it will benefit the state.

Although economic logic has suffused discussion of children's institutions since the nineteenth century, it has become even more pervasive in the post–World War II period. The development of cost-benefit analysis and associated planning mechanisms like Planning-Programming-Budgeting Systems and zero-based budgeting has extended utilitarian logic to all public programs and makes the application of cost-benefit conceptions automatic. The development of computers and statistical methodology and the use of social science research in policy issues have changed the nature of evaluation. These developments have meant that the casual assertion of benefits or the easy use of anecdotal evidence which has often justified public programs can no longer stand the test of "scientific" validity and that more rigorous and better quantified examinations are necessary. Formal evaluation methods have become the clearest expression of instrumental thinking because they judge the worth of a program in terms of specific, measurable goals for the child, like test scores, adult earnings and unemployment rates, rates of welfare dependence and crime.

The development and application of instrumental conceptions of children has been most obvious in education. When mid-nineteenth–century educational reformers like Horace Mann affirmed that education increased productivity, they referred to its role in inculcating personal values and the elements of character—discipline, sobriety, thrift, hard work—believed essential to adult success. After 1900 that emphasis on personal traits was partly replaced by the assertion that schooling taught skills directly applicable to jobs and prepared students for labor markets, and increased schooling levels came to be justified by their "money value."[18] The development of human capital theory in the 1960s completed the identification of education with income returns, and codified the basic principle for evaluation: investment in children, and in educational programs specifically, ought to be undertaken only when the return in the form of increased earnings is at least as high as the return to private investment. The power of this viewpoint is illustrated by the recent concern with "over-educated Americans," youths who have graduated from college but for whom the return on their educational investment is lower than the return on private investment. Given instrumental justifications for public programs, it follows that schooling levels need to be reduced.[19]

During the 1960s, the development of formal methods evaluating the effectiveness of schools reinforced instrumental conceptions of educational programs. The Coleman Report of 1966 provided early statistical evidence about the influence of school resources on one measurable outcome—student performance on achievement tests. While the analysis was intended to buttress the conventional wisdom that more spending would improve learning, particularly for poor and minority children, the results failed to substantiate this claim. As other studies confirmed the findings of the Coleman report—or failed to overturn them convincingly—enthusiasm cooled for spending more public money on the schooling of low-income and minority children and for redistributing resources to low-spending schools. The doubts that spread during the 1970s about the efficacy of schooling for vocational ends and cognitive development undermined the fundamental rationale for public expenditures on education.[20] It has become impossible to justify public spending on schools that are challenging, enjoyable places for children; only the demonstration of future benefits—in cognitive skills, in reduced delinquency and crime, above all in earnings differentials—is regarded as a legitimate argument.[21]

Specific educational programs have similarly been evaluated in terms of future returns, especially compensatory programs for the "educationally deprived." Head Start, originally justified by the long-term cognitive benefits (and assumed economic benefits) it would bring to poor children, was dealt a serious blow by a 1969 evaluation claiming that its cognitive effects were uncertain and short-lived. Parental enthusiasm for the program generated enough political support to keep Head Start alive. But rather than relying on noninstrumental justifications or community support, advocates looked for instrumental evidence, undertaking a frantic effort (ultimately successful) to find evidence of cognitive gains.[22] The necessity for instrumental justifications has been evident in other compensatory programs, like Follow Through and Home Start, and the successful demonstration by the Perry Preschool Project of a 9.5 percent rate of return for one year of compensatory preschool education attracted national attention.[23] Countless noneducational programs also illustrate the demand to justify public programs for children in terms of future benefits, especially economic benefits. Nutritional programs for children, like the Women, Infants, and Children (WIC) program for pregnant mothers and infants, have been justified in terms of future outcomes rather than on moral and humanitarian grounds: malnourished children are unacceptable because they may suffer brain damage and then become future dependents of the state, not because of the immorality of malnutrition in a land of plenty. Innovative juvenile delinquency programs are funded if they can reduce rates of recidivism or increase employment; the humanitarian arguments that youth should be treated more gently than adults, in de-institutionalized settings, have a long history behind them but little evidence of transforming programs. To the extent that public subsidies for abortions have any support left, the politically most powerful arguments have been the instrumental view that publicly funded abortions will reduce future welfare costs. Even the purest forms of publicly subsidized enjoyment for children—parks, recreational facilities, and sports programs—have been justified in terms of their developmental results: advocates of such programs have historically argued that organized recreation teaches children the cooperation and social skills necessary for future success.

In many ways the tendency to view children as vehicles of investment seems completely natural, especially in a capitalist economy where we use utilitarian calculations in every aspect of our lives, where investment is the engine of economic progress and the return on investment is sacred. The emphasis on the future effects of present costs seems particularly appropriate for children, since they are obviously in the process of growing up, and concern over what kinds of adults they will become is legitimate. However, confining public justifications for children's programs to instrumental views is not inevitable, nor is it always beneficial to children. Most obviously, it has limited children's policies by insisting that programs be justified as economically efficient. Any expenditure whose contribution to a child's development is uncertain, or which merely contributes to the well-being or enjoyment of children as children, cannot be justified as a public expense but must remain a private expenditure. Pleasant schools, well-staffed day care centers, adequate nutritional programs, and programs for handicapped children which may not show a return have always had to fight for their existence. Similarly, the efforts to improve the quality of public facilities have been difficult, partly because the effects of quality are nearly impossible to substantiate. Limiting public responsibility in this way has reinforced the tendency towards "private wealth and public squalor." Some parents—those who have enough income—spend lavishly on their children, generating the notion that we are a child-centered society. But public spending for children is often meager and always surrounded by contention, and it embodies the peculiar conception that children are not valuable as persons in their own right but only for the adults they will grow up to be.

Another pernicious consequence of applying instrumental criteria has been the distortion of what children's institutions do, by limiting the goals of public programs to those consistent with cost-benefit criteria. Within education, for example, the power of instrumentalist views has collapsed the goals of schooling into the vocational purpose of earning a living, and that purpose now dominates the thinking of students, administrators, and legislators. Older ideals of a liberal education which offered a variety of benefits—fostering curiosity, creativity, critical thinking, intellectual and political independence, and preparation for avocations—still exist, but they have been effectively undermined by vocational objectives. In the area of child care, the search for economic returns has emphasized the welfare savings that result from maternal employment—a rationale for public support of child care that has come to be known as the "welfare model." In the process, the varied possibilities of child care have been ignored in most public programs, including the ways child care promises to aid in the redefinition of sex roles, to reduce the boundaries among families by fostering new "communities" or "extended families," to provide a wider variety of adult figures, and to provide a richer environment for young children.

Instrumental conceptions of children and cost-benefit calculations by themselves distort public programs, but these distortions have become more powerful with the formalization of evaluation. The requirement that outcomes be specified in readily measureable terms has shaped the goals of many public programs. As a result, educators have become obsessed with test scores, despite the fact that educational consequences are complex and goals typically differ among teachers, parents, and students. Those public preschool programs like Head Start which do not follow the "welfare model" have to concentrate on preparation for school because later school results have come to be the measure of success, with a tendency to deemphasize the social and emotional aspects of development which used to dominate early childhood education.[24] Evaluation methods may also be responsible for the perceptions that many children's programs have failed to reach their objectives. Conventionally, evaluators assume a simple causal mechanism in which a specific program is responsible for change. Since a variety of social institutions influence a child's development, changing a single influence is likely to have only a marginal effect. The finding of relatively small effects may therefore indicate that changing one out of a variety of influences is insufficient, rather than proving that a program is ineffective.[25] Formal evaluation methods are not necessarily neutral, therefore, since they lead us to ignore the variety of outcomes and social influences at work in complex social institutions.

The development of formal evaluation methods also shifts the burden of proof for justifying public actions, in ways that reinforce the limited conception of public responsibility embedded in *parens patriae*. If the social commitment to public responsibility for children (or any other group) is strong—or if political power behind a program is substantial—then state actions of uncertain effectiveness but possible benefits are acceptable. In the absence of a strong commitment or political power, the programs that appear uncertain in their effects, as measured by conventional evaluations, will not be funded; only programs that are unambiguiously beneficial have a chance to survive. Particularly during conservative periods like the 1970s and 1980s, children's advocates bear the burden of demonstrating that their programs pay off. The sense of children's programs being constantly under attack by hard-nosed evaluators reflects the corrosive effects of research and evaluation on the simple faiths that have always motivated reformers and child advocates—faith in the value of keeping children well-fed and healthy, faith in the value of education, faith in the value of public programs which embody some concern for the child as a person, faith in the assertion of moral responsibilities. In a world where public decisions are made on the basis of economic criteria and formal evaluations, there can be no simple faiths, only demonstrable results.[26]

The twisting of moral and humanitarian arguments for children into economic calculations has seriously limited programs that have difficulty justifying themselves in instrumental terms. It has made it almost impossible to provide food and housing to poor children on moral grounds, to provide schools where children enjoy themselves rather than being psychologically assaulted, to provide supportive facilities for those judged delinquent, or to provide facilities for handicapped children which further develop their capacities. Public programs to feed children exist not because of a moral commitment to children, but because in the long run it is more expensive not to feed them. Childhood poverty has a special horror not because the plight of poor children moves us, but because the developmental consequences of poverty are economically inefficient. As long as programs must be justified by future returns on investment—ultimately, in terms of reduced burdens on the public purse—then programs that might be justified on moral grounds or in "softer" terms, in making life richer and more supportive for children and their parents, remain unfunded. Implicitly, instrumental perspectives deny the contention that we value children. In the public realm, we do not value children very highly; we care only for adults who have grown up "right," and we focus all programs on that future.

The contrast between public and private conceptions of children is remarkable. Of course, parents hold instrumental views of their children: they may use their children as a source of adult status and meaning, as a justification for their sacrifices, or as a way of competing with other parents.[27] They often live through their children vicariously. But a critical difference remains between public and private views of children: parents also value their children as children, not simply for the adults they will become. Most parents enjoy their children, find their companionship rewarding, love them and are loved in return, find them funny as well as enraging. Even while they are preparing their children for adulthood, parents enjoy their childish qualities. The decisions they make for their children—spending decisions, schooling decisions, decisions on where to live—must sometimes consider calculations of future benefits versus present costs; since incomes are usually limited, the question of whether a particular expense is "worth it" will invariably arise. But parental decisions are not confined to close calculations of benefits and costs. Parents also consider the child's present enjoyment and base their decisions on a much looser sense of the conditions under which a child would be better off. Indeed, the ideal of sacrifice suggests that parents should spend any amount to improve their children's lives and chances for future success. Parental decisions thus reflect altruistic motives that do not always ask whether a particular expenditure is "worth it" in terms of the child's future success.

In the public realm, altruism is not entirely absent. *Parens patriae* assumes benevolent motives; reformers in every period, from the child savers of the progressive era to the planners of Great Society programs, have invoked altruistic motives, partly in an effort to move the citizenry beyond conventional utilitarian calculations. Public altruism remains the foundation of our ideals for children, as in Dewey's maxim that "what the best and wisest parent wants for his child, that must the community want for all of its children." But this conception is invariably corrupted by the distinctions we make between private conceptions of children and our treatment of children in the public realm—distinctions that Dewey was trying to eliminate. The dominant social attitude toward children in the aggregate—children who are not our own, other people's children, children unknown to us—is fear of the havoc they can cause and distrust of their influence on our own children. We assume that enjoyment of children (and expenditures for them) ought to be a private experience within the family, and our ideological commitments to the private family limit the ability of parents to view their children as part of a larger group of children, or to feel affection for other children like the affection they feel for their own. In the world of private families created during the nineteenth century, the possibilities for a community of concern focused on children have rarely been achieved.

The instrumental conception of children adds new problems to the expression of public responsibilities. In place of the concern for the child's welfare expressed in *parens patriae*, it substitutes a concern for the public treasury, economic growth, or other future goals that may be irrelevant to the child's well-being. In place of the benevolence that is nominally the basis for the state's concern for children, it expresses an indifference to children as individuals. The lack of any "public love" for children makes it difficult to persuade taxpayers to approve funds for programs that cannot be justified in instrumental terms and distorts the content of existing programs. Even when we acknowledge some social obligations to children, instrumental conceptions limit and corrupt what we do for them.

The Private Use of Public Institutions

The limits of *parens patriae* and instrumental conceptions of children are the two most striking constraints on the fulfillment of our benevolent concern for the young. But public responsibility has also been corrupted by a lingering adherence to the ideology of parental determinism, the notion that parents alone determine the futures of their children. We continue to assert that parents raise their children privately and are wholly responsible for their successes and failures, despite the ubiquity of social institutions and public decisions in the lives of children. Public schooling extends through high school for almost all children, and the expansion of higher education has extended public schooling beyond the high school for about one-third of youth. Income support programs, health programs, and nutrition programs affect the basic necessities available to poor children; many public subsidies flow disproportionately to middle-income and upper-income families, including subsidies for home ownership and health insurance through the income tax system and subsidies for higher education. The importance of monetary and fiscal policies for the economic conditions of family life implies that all families are affected by state policies, not merely poor families or those "deviant" families unable to carry out childrearing responsibilities. The enormous amount of childrearing literature indicates that even the earliest actions of parents are shaped by influences outside families, and the influences of television and other public media are ubiquitous. Above all, much of what looks like the effect of parents turns out to be the effect of class, as the next chapter will demonstrate. The range and power of extrafamilial institutions has become too vast to contend that public policies are limited to the abnormal, the pathological, and the irresponsible, or to claim that the family is still private.

Yet these simple points are almost neglected in the pieties of parental determinism. Drawing its inspiration from a nostalgia for preindustrial families engaged in farming and skilled crafts, when parents had a direct hand in the success of their children by training them and passing on property, parental determinism first took its modern form in the mid-nineteenth century as an extension of the domestic ideology, placing special responsibilities on mothers. Initially, parental determinism was a defensive attempt to assert the primacy of parents at a time when increasing numbers of parents could not pass property on to their children, when fewer parents were training their children directly in adult skills, and when schools were beginning to shape access to adult occupations.

In the twentieth century, parental determinism has been reinforced by various psychological concepts, which have led some professionals to assert the dominance of parents even as public institutions have gained greater influence over children. Concepts loosely based on Freudian thought present an image of the vulnerable child, easily damaged by traumatic events and emotional stress, and psychoanalytic theory has emphasized the importance of the earliest interactions with parents for the psychological health of the adult. Behaviorists have viewed the child as essentially malleable, completely responsive to parental influences. John Watson, the founder of behaviorism, once declared:

> Give me a dozen healthy infants, well-formed, and my own specified world to bring them up in, and I'll guarantee to take any one at random and train him to be any type of specialist I might—doctor, lawyer, merchant, and yes, even beggar man and thief![28]

The Freudian and the behaviorist perspectives, different as they are, both emphasize the centrality of parents in the child's development, and this perspective dominates the research on child development. Despite recent challenges by theorists like Piaget who stress that the child is an active and independent participant in his or her development, and those like Jerome Kagan who question the rigid model in which infant experiences determine adult behavior, the notion of parental determinism continues to dominate most discussions of childrearing and provides the rationale for the enormous volume of childrearing advice in this country.[29]

As a way of understanding the relationship between children and parents, parental determinism has been confusing both to families and to public policy. It fosters both the awesome fear and the incredible enthusiasm with which parents confront childrearing. It leads parents to take credit for their children's successes and find justification for their own lives in the sacrifices they make on behalf of their children:

> If you can't improve yourself, you improve your posterity. Otherwise, life isn't worth nothing. You might as well go back to the cave and stay there. I'm sure the first cave man who went over the hill to see what was on the other side—I don't think he went there wholly out of curiousity. He went there because he wanted to get his son out of the cave. Just the same way I want to send my son to college.[30]

At the same time, "living through one's children" places enormous burdens on parents. Parental determinism also has its darker side: it implies that if children fail, parents have failed. The burden this imposes can generate an intense ambivalence:

> To me the prospect of rearing a child is also a very frightening one. All along the way loom pitfalls and the possibility of errors. What if, in spite of our best efforts, our child turned out to have severe emotional problems, to be a drug addict or a criminal? . . . I worry that just loving your children and doing your best may not be enough to prevent such a tragedy. So even though nowadays I frequently long to hold and cuddle a baby of my own whenever I see someone else's, my fears soon come to the surface to confuse me and make me hesitate.[31]

Living by the dictates of parental determinism, especially as established by experts, is therefore a nerve-wracking business. As one mother in the 1920s expressed the dilemma of responding to the advice of childrearing professionals: "I try to do just what you say, but I am a nervous wreck trying to be calm."[32]

If the ideology of parent determinism has brought undue stress to childrearing, its consequences for understanding what parents actually do have been disastrous. In the simplest terms, it denies that parental roles are constrained and supplemented by other institutions, both public and private.[33] In the public realm, a lingering belief in parental determinism distorts the rationale for state responsibilities. If parents determine the success of their children, then remedial institutions may be sufficient to counter parental failure. If, on the other hand, a variety of social, economic, and parental influences shape a child's development, then the implications for public action are more complex, and public influence over these social and economic institutions—including those of the "private"

economy—may be warranted. By drawing attention away from these possibilities and back to parents, the notion of parental determinism embedded in *parens patriae* has generated a limited conception of public
responsibility.

Given the many institutions that influence children, it is more accurate
to describe parents not as determiners but as *managers* of their children's
lives.[34] Parents have the responsibility for guiding their children through
the maze of institutions which shape their futures, and they can modify,
actively or passively, the influences on their children. For the most part
they do not affect the institutions themselves, but they can—within the
limits of income, race, and class—choose among alternatives: which community to live in, which school and which classes their children attend,
which television programs their children watch, which doctor to visit. The
conception of parents as managers explicitly acknowledges the importance of children's institutions and the proliferation of extrafamilial influences. The managerial conception still recognizes the importance of parents in shaping their children's development, and the role that children
play in their own development, but it also accepts the reality of state
power.

Considering parents as managers does not imply that they are powerless. Many parents successfully manipulate the institutions confronting
their children. They change teachers and school assignments, prevent
their children from being assigned to low tracks, criticize teacher behavior, or voice disapproval of textbooks. They can undercut or reinforce the
message of television by their own reactions and attitudes toward television; they can (with some difficulty) restrict the amount of viewing. Yet
the extent to which *some* parents effect such changes does not imply that
all parents have such power. On the contrary, the power of parents as
managers varies with income, with class, with race, and with their previous education, experiences, and sophistication in dealing with bureaucratic institutions. The importance of income is clear: parents with higher
incomes can afford to send their children to private schools; they have a
greater choice of medical care and of childcare facilities; they can more
readily buy legal services; they can provide expensive alternatives to television like toys, lessons, and summer camp; and they can avoid welfare
institutions altogether. Given the class and racial biases of most extrafamilial institutions, the value of managerial or professional class standing and
a white skin is evident. Privileged parents can manipulate schools, doctors,
police, and officers of the court while others are more likely to be treated
with contempt. Parents with higher levels of education have a special
advantage, particularly in dealing with those institutions like schools and

63

hospitals that depend for their power on professional status. Viewing parents as managers is more realistic than the myth of parental determinism, then, but the problems of inequalities among parents remain.

Even where structural inequalities weigh lightly, the role of parents as managers generates new problems. In acting on behalf of their children, parents face a variety of institutions. Yet parents *as individuals* have little power to influence institutions. They may be able to choose the schools their children attend, but changing the school system itself—by pressuring teachers and administrators, instituting lawsuits, and lobbying for legislative changes—is a much more difficult tactic. They can control the specific programs their children watch, but influencing the general content of television requires concerted, collective, and political action (as a number of children's television groups have demonstrated). Individual parents may find satisfactory doctors, but they are limited in their collective influence on the health system not only by the political power of the medical establishment but also by the trappings of professionalism, the aura of competence, and the mystique of expertise. Even the most powerful parents at times feel powerless in the face of institutions that are national in scope, that depend for their legitimacy on expertise, and that have attained the size and power that corporations and governments in this country enjoy. At best, parents become guides for their children through institutions that they cannot readily control.

Thus parents as managers are usually driven to individual or "private" solutions to the problems their children face. The tendency to resort to private solutions is deeply rooted in the individualistic ethic and in the doctrine of private responsibility for children. Private solutions therefore seem natural and appropriate: parents promote the welfare of their own children, and they avoid the costs of acting collectively for the benefit of others' children. The result is a situation in which parents seek purely private solutions to social problems common to many parents, like the problems of inadequate schools, unsafe streets, unavailable and inappropriate medical care, and exploitive television programming.

The tendency to focus on the success of one's own children in turn generates another dilemma. While parents' goals remain private—limited to their own children—the means that they use on behalf of their children are public; the institutions through which parents guide their children are generally open to all children, and many are governmental institutions subject to political pressures. The private use of public institutions is to some extent illegitimate, since public institutions are supposed to serve all children, not merely one's own. In practice, many of the issues about access to and control of the public institutions of childrearing are conflicts among parents battling for their own children. Even the limited conceptions of public good based on *parens patriae* and simple equity—desegregated schools, equitable school financing, programs for handicapped children, or the elimination of sexual bias, for example—become mired in contention because they threaten the interests of other parents seeking privileges for their own children. As long as parents view public institutions in private and individualistic terms, we can expect such conflicts to be continuous and bitter.[35]

We can also expect the conflicts to be unequal: some parents are more successful than others in using public institutions for their own children. Inevitably, inequalities of class and race among parents generate inequalities in the treatment of their children in public institutions, rather than the equality of opportunity these institutions often claim to provide. As Marion Wright Edelman of the Children's Defense Fund argues:

> If I [as a middle-class parent] don't like the teacher or the schools, I can yell until I'm satisfied with a change, or I can take my children elsewhere. In many ways middle-class parents don't exercise much control over their children's school. But we generally have more political clout and more choice about the kind of education and treatment our children will get. Poor parents have less of a choice in both areas.[36]

The commitment to universality, equality of opportunity, and a common citizenship fostered through the schools commonly founders because of the inability of different groups of parents to force educational changes in their own children's best interests. Middle-class parents are also better able to persuade the police not to detain their unruly adolescents. The political power of the middle class has generated a system of taxes and transfers that is favorable for middle-class children and families. For example, tax expenditures for home owners and for the health care of middle-income families are greater than direct spending for public housing and Medicaid; middle-income children benefit disproportionately from the tax credit for child care even as direct expenditures for child care of low-income children are declining rapidly. At the same time that middle-income and upper-income children benefit from various other tax expenditures, it proves politically impossible to expand and reform welfare programs for the poorest children.[37] Examples are ubiquitous. As long as institutions are evaluated for the individual gains they can confer, even the limited conception of public responsibility requiring special obligations to some children is difficult to implement.

We are left with a feeble conception of public responsibility for children, inaccurate in its assumptions, weakened by the various forms that the ideology of private responsibility takes, and undermined by the tendency to evaluate public institutions in terms of individual gains. Even periods of expanding public responsibility for children—like the progressive era and the 1960s—contain the seeds of failure and retrenchment because children's insitutions are underfunded, distorted in their purposes, and inevitably inadequate to the tasks set for them. Even programs that are undeniably necessary and beneficial to children—Aid to Families with Dependent Children and the public school system, for example— prove to have various detrimental consequences. The result has been to substitute a "narrow and unlovely" set of principles for the visions of reformers and to turn Dewey's ideal on its head: too often, what the community provides for its children is what the best and wisest parent must shun for his or her own child.

3

Public Responsibility in

a Class Society

AMERICAN IDEALS for children rely on an image of a society without class divisions. Even though children do not begin life as equals, there is still a pervasive belief that every child ought to have an equal chance of success, limited only by innate ability and motivation but not by family background. Indeed, the American dream of mobility has been most frequently expressed in terms of children—not as the ideal that every adult can advance as far as he or she is capable, but as the ideal that all children face equal opportunities and that parents can rise through their children if success has been denied them. These egalitarian ideals are precisely reflected in the aspirations that parents have for their children. Parents across all classes, races, and income groups share much the same hope: they want their children to become well educated, to have good jobs, to earn enough to live comfortably, to enjoy stable, happy family lives, to have some measure of control over their own lives, not to live at the mercy of others.[1]

Children have been the "bearers of the American Dream," and children's institutions have usually borne the responsibility for fulfilling this version of the American dream. Most obviously, reformers in every period have identified poverty as ruinous to family life and childrearing and have proposed mechanisms of redistribution—from private charity to mother's pensions, Aid to Families with Dependent Children, and the present complex of income support programs—to reduce poverty as a barrier to later success. Since the early nineteenth century educators have offered equality of opportunity through schooling, as in Horace Mann's famous declaration that universal education could be the "great equalizer," the "balance wheel of the social machinery." Even earlier, in 1834, Pennsylvania legislators justified common schools in egalitarian terms:

> Common schools, universally established, will multiply the chances of success, perhaps of brilliant success, among those who may forever continue ignorant. It is the duty of the State to promote and foster such establishments. That done, the career of each youth will depend upon himself. The State will have given the first impulse; good conduct and suitable application must do the rest. Among the indigent, "some flashing of a mounting genius" may be found; and among both the rich and poor, in the course of nature, many no doubt will sink into mediocrity, or beneath it. Yet let them start with equal advantages leaving no discrimination then or thereafter, but such as nature and study shall produce.[2]

To be sure, some interpretations of equal opportunity have been inegalitarian: the provision of "separate but equal" schools for black pupils has historically made a mockery of equal opportunity; the development of vocational education after 1900 prompted the view that equal opportunity means giving every student an education appropriate to his "evident or probable destiny," even when that destiny was based on class and race.[3] Nonetheless, even the most perverse statement of equal opportunity has still affirmed some duty of the state to help children overcome the circumstances into which they are born, and the rhetoric of equal opportunity has helped blacks, immigrants, and lower-class children to gain access to public institutions. By providing equality of opportunity in a country where there has been little support for equality itself, children's institutions could reconcile the American dream and egalitarian visions with the reality of a class society.

But this vision of the state's responsibilities has consistently been thwarted by other consequences of inequalities. From its very inception, *parens patriae* incorporated a peculiar blindness to inequalities, particularly in its conception of the private family and private responsibility for children. Although the inequalities of income, race, and class shape every aspect of childrearing, public discussions of parental deficiencies have invariably focused on the effects of inequalities rather than on their origins—on the dirtiness and foul manners of poor children, for example, rather than on the economic conditions that have made the lives of their parents so desperate and degraded. Not even the most sympathetic observers have been immune from responding to structural conditions in personal terms: the reactions of Josephine Baker in Hell's Kitchen and Sargent Shriver in Chicago are laments about poverty, but they also express revulsion about the way the poor live their lives. The view that poverty is due to the personal characteristics of the poor, or to a "culture" in which they are trapped, has proliferated. The dominant interpretation of *parens patriae* has tended to blame childrearing deficiencies on parents themselves, thereby ignoring the origins of the problems in income inequalities, in poverty, in racial discrimination, and in class differences. Children's institutions have therefore been forced to cope with the effects of structural inequalities without being able to remedy the inequalities themselves. Schools have provided remedial education and welfare programs have partially compensated for low income, but without changing the underlying inequalities of resources among families.

Compensating for structural inequalities and providing equality of opportunity in an inegalitarian society has proved to be politically impossible. Quite apart from the limitations on public responsibility inherent in *parens patriae*, class and racial biases have shaped attitudes toward children which have in turn constrained public programs. The division of children into a parent's own children, who are the focus of intense affection and high hopes, versus other people's children, who are potential threats to one's own, has been intensified by class and racial divisions. The most immediate result has been to compromise the benevolence of *parens patriae* with the public miserliness of citizens who don't care to support other people's children. In the process, the rhetorical claims that children are "our most precious natural resources" have been overshadowed by pessimistic views that children—especially other people's children supported by public programs—are social liabilities rather then social assets, and are unworthy of public support.

Beyond the constraints of public miserliness, our ambivalence toward children has often taken the form of hostility toward other people's children, especially toward lower-class children who seem most threatening. This perception has generated various efforts to control lower-class children, to limit their influences on other children, and to socialize them in the interests of social peace. Even among the best-intentioned reformers, the assertion of benevolence has been compromised by the assumption that the neediest children come from these classes most threatening to society.[4] The various forms of segregation in public institutions, the use of the schools, juvenile institutions, and work-related programs to inculcate appropriate values, and the development of schools and training programs that serve principally as warehouses rather than as developmental institutions have reflected the coexistence of controlling impulses, in the interests of the community, with child-saving impulses, in the best interest of the children. Sometimes, the goal of social peace has overridden the concern for the welfare of lower-class children; consistently, the coexistence of two competing goals—social peace and the enhancement of individual opportunity—has distorted the content of children's institutions and limited their ability to overcome inequalities.

Structural Inequalities and Family Life

Few issues have been more confusing and discomforting to Americans than inequality. The Declaration of Independence claimed that "all men are created equal" and de Tocqueville in the 1830s asserted that the United States had come closer to "an almost complete equality of condition" than any other nation,[5] but the inferiority of nonwhites and the nonparticipation of women was built into the Constitution, and Americans have throughout their history regarded immigrant groups as inferior. Despite celebrating the United States as a classless nation "in which some people [are] more middle-class than others,"[6] Americans have allowed differences of income and class to persist, and some have rejoiced in these differences as evidence of merit and opportunity at work. Child savers have consistently decried the evils of childhood poverty, but parental determinism and *parens patriae* have emphasized the failures of parents rather than inequalities of the economic system.

The tendency to mask inequalities with ideologies of equal opportunity, merit, and classlessness has made it easier to ignore the most salient aspect of an economic system based on wage labor: an income distribution in which the richest fifth of the families receive *eight times* as much income as the poorest fifth, a proportion that has remained highly stable in the postwar period.[7] Inequality of income has meant that by any standard poverty is widespread: in 1978, 15.7 percent of children were considered to be in poverty by federal standards, and according to other standards of poverty between 15.5 percent and 24.5 percent of children were poor in 1974.[8] In 1977, the Carnegie Council on Children expressed the problem more starkly still: "We estimate that a *quarter to a third* of all American children are born into families with financial stress so great that their children will suffer basic deprivations."[9] As large as they are, these figures still hide the dynamic aspect of poverty: families move in and out of poverty at an astonishing rate. Using individual rather than family data and a conservative definition of poverty, one survey found that between 8 and 11 percent of individuals were poor during any one year between

1967 and 1972, but 21 percent were poor for *at least* one year between 1967 and 1972.[10] For those at the lower end of the income spectrum, economic security can never be assumed:

> The worries are always there—whether it's about the kids, or our families, or how we're getting along, even about money. He makes most of it, but it's never enough. And I have to worry about how to pay the bills.[11]

The precariousness of family life is partly caused by low-paying jobs. Jobs at the bottom of the hierarchy pay so little that a parent cannot earn enough to keep his or her family out of poverty, even with full-time work. At the 1978 minimum wage of $2.65 per hour, a full-time worker earned only $5,300 in income, just at the official poverty threshold of $5,201 for a family of three and below the $6,662 threshold for a family of four.[12] The problems of the "working poor" have been compounded by unemployment, which (like poverty) has been a constant feature of capitalism, particularly in the recessions that have regularly plagued market-based economies. While the postwar cycles in unemployment rates have been serious, the larger problem has been the continuing upward trend of unemployment, from an average of 4.5 percent in the 1950s and 4.8 percent in the 1960s to more than 6 percent in the 1970s; older conceptions of "full employment"—3 percent unemployed in the 1950s and 4 percent in the 1960s—now seem unattainable.[13] Even these figures are underestimates, since they fail to consider workers who are involuntarily employed half-time, "discouraged workers" who have stopped searching for work because the search appears futile, and those who are employed at jobs below the level at which they have been trained. Adding the various measures of underemployment to the official unemployment rates increases them up to 40 percent.[14] Like poverty, unemployment has a dynamic aspect: during 1974, when the overall unemployment rate was 7 percent, 17.8 percent of all individuals in the labor force were out of work for some period.[15] The fear of unemployment so often mentioned in studies of working-class life reflects this grim reality: as one working-class woman recalled her childhood, "It seemed like every three months my father was on strike or laid off."[16]

The most obvious consequence of unemployment is the loss of earnings: unemployment quintuples the probability that a family will be poor.[17] But there are more subtle effects on family relationships. In a country where market worth is a measure of personal worth, an unemployed individual has few other comparable sources of status, esteem, or meaning. Periods of unemployment intensify feelings of insecurity and loss of self-respect, and can generate irritability and frustration as well as violence. Taken together, these economic and psychological losses create strains on families with disastrous consequences for children and adults. Poverty and unemployment seem to be related to a host of severe familial problems: separation and divorce, alcoholism, mortality, and child abuse.[18] In her study of working-class families, Lillian Rubin found that 40 percent of the adults she interviewed grew up with at least one alcoholic parent, almost as many were children of divorce or desertion, and 10 percent spent part of their childhood in institutions or foster homes. Poor youths are more likely to marry early, have children early, and divorce or separate than are more affluent youths.[19] As Joseph Califano summarized the views of several hundred responses to Jimmy Carter's 1976 campaign task force on families, "The central conclusion is that the most severe threat to family life stems from unemployment and lack of adequate income."[20]

The effects of racial discrimination exacerbate the problems of poverty and unemployment. For full-time workers, media earnings for black men tend to be slightly higher than media earnings for Hispanics, but both groups earn only two-thirds of what white men earn. Surprisingly, black and white women working full time have almost the same earnings on average, with Hispanics earning about 85 percent of what Anglo women earn.[21] For blacks, discrimination in labor markets appears to be the overwhelming factor, accounting for one-half to three-quarters of the earning differences between blacks and whites; for Hispanics, discrimination in education is a more formidable barrier to labor market opportunities than it is for blacks.[22] For both blacks and Hispanics, the forms that labor market discrimination can take are varied and sometimes subtle; one form is the tendency for blacks and Hispanics to be limited to occupations of low pay and low class stature,[23] and another is the relatively high unemployment that minorities suffer, typically twice as high for blacks as for whites, and about 50 percent higher for Hispanic men than for white men.[24] The consequences for minority incomes are staggering; mean family income in 1978 was $14,657 for Hispanics, $13,409 for blacks, and $20,860 for whites. The differences in terms of poverty are even more grotesque: in 1978, 20.4 percent of Hispanic families and 27.5 percent of black families were officially considered to be in poverty, while the rate of poverty was only 6.9 percent for whites. For children, the differentials in poverty rates become truly alarming: 11 percent of white children were poor, compared to 27.2 percent of Hispanic children and 41.2 percent of black children.[25] One black psychiatrist has described the consequences in the clearest possible terms: "Black people do not have families—we have survival units. That is all we are allowed to have."[26]

Income inequalities, unemployment, and discrimination in labor markets are often hidden by the various ideologies surrounding family life, but they are still familiar terms to most Americans; despite limitations, various policies do exist to attack these structural inequalities. In contrast, the origins of inequalities in the hierarchy of occupations and the nature of work—the causes and consequences of class differences—have been almost completely absent from public discussions. The concept of class has itself been complicated by the elaboration of the American occupational structure over time. In the colonial period, when there were few unskilled laborers and the differences among independent farmers and craftsmen were small, the American class structure was relatively simple; the vast majority of men were self-employed, small-scale capitalists. The expansion of wage labor, the division of workers into skilled and unskilled laborers, and the increasing differences in the size of firms in the nineteenth century complicated the class structure, creating differences among capitalists and wage laborers, large and small-scale capitalists, skilled and unskilled workers. The constant process of restructuring jobs by dividing skilled from unskilled work has continued to expand the range of class differences, and the tremendous increase in professional and managerial occupations has blurred the division between owner and hired worker. As a consequence of increasing complexity, older conceptions of class have lost their applicability; the simple division between capitalist and worker of Smith, Ricardo, and Marx is no longer sufficient, and the more recent distinction between white-collar and blue-collar work has almost lost its usefulness as working conditions and pay between the two groups now frequently overlap.

Since the concept of class is difficult to use in its totality, for simplicity we will often refer to two or three class groupings: a middle class, characterized by a high degree of autonomy in work and clear career progressions, who are typically highly paid, well-educated managers and independent professionals; and a working class with comparatively little autonomy in work, in turn divided into two segments. One is composed of individuals with relatively stable but highly supervised employment, often in unionized sectors, typified by operatives, clerical and retail workers with limited prospects for advancement. At the bottom is a lower class with unstable and intermittent employment, where employment (when it is available) is low-skilled, casual, and unlikely to lead to more stable prospects.[27]

Most obviously, class differences influence income, since positions higher in the occupational hierarchy pay more; class is also associated with social status and esteem. Class differences and unemployment are related: lower-class jobs tend to be less stable, with more layoffs and quits. Since racial discrimination often takes the form of "crowding" minorities into unstable, poorly paid, and subordinate jobs, race and class status are also linked. But the effects of class extend beyond its influence on the basic structural inequalities of income, unemployment, and racial discrimination. Lower-class individuals tend to have poorer physical working conditions, partly because they have little control over any aspects of their jobs. The nonphysical conditions of work tend also to be worse than for individuals of higher class standing, with greater stress and fewer sources of satisfaction. Values and attitudes tend to vary with class position, as those values important to particular jobs come to dominate lives outside of work. Class divisions shape political alliances and attitudes toward other groups in society, including other groups of children. These varied consequences of class are worth distinguishing, for in different ways they have profound effects on family life.

At the most obvious level, one's place in the class structure shapes the daily experiences of family members. Although a wide variety of occupational settings can be harmful to physical and mental health, jobs at the bottom of the class hierarchy—with inferior status, with little autonomy, isolated from other workers, characterized by low skill levels and dull, repetitive, and physically hazardous work—have been most strongly linked to low levels of job satisfaction, and then to low self-esteem, anxiety, tension, and psychosomatic illness.[28] The conclusion that relationships within the family are affected is not surprising: when the conditions of work are stressful and draining, satisfying relationships at home are difficult to achieve.[29] Interviews with working class adults confirm the influence of work in thousands of ways. A thirty-seven-year-old male laborer in a steel mill told Studs Terkel, "I'm a dying breed. A laborer. Strictly muscle work," and then added, "When I come home, know what I do for the first twenty minutes? Fake it. I put on a smile."[30] Children quickly feel the impact. An eleven-year-old daughter of a hospital attendant has no trouble telling when her dad has had a bad day "just by looking at him":

> When he's has a bad day at work or something like that he comes in stormy— something like that. . . . I tell my mother sometimes, and she tells him that the kids don't like the way he's acting. Sometimes he says he can't help the way he acts because if he's had a hard day, and he doesn't want people bugging him, and my mother says, "Well, you don't have to blame them—the kids—just because it happened at work."[31]

These are situations all parents and children encounter—the spill-over of working conditions into family life. But "bad days" are not random occurrences; they are more likely to occur in working-class and lower-class jobs than in middle-class jobs. The higher the occupational category, the more likely relationships at home will be companionate, emotionally rewarding, defined by sharing of conflict, and with less antagonism between spouses; parents who come home from more supportive middle-class occupations have more energy for emotional involvement with their children.[32] To be sure, middle-class life cannot be completely insulated from the pressures of work: the effects of pressure among high-level managers—alcoholism, divorce, and emotional neglect—imply that the image of the family as a refuge from work is false for even the most privileged individuals.[33] But the available evidence does indicate that inequalities in working conditions tend to be replicated within families: those with satisfying jobs tend to have more satisfying family lives as well.[34]

The conditions of class also profoundly influence the messages parents give to their children about success. Like middle-class parents, working-class parents want their children to do better than they did. In the mid-1920s, a pipe fitter's wife who had gone to work as a cleaning woman justified working for the luxury goods it brought (an electric washing machine, electric iron, and vacuum sweeper), for her enhanced sense of freedom, and because "the two boys want to go to college, and I want them to."[35] The working-class women Lillian Rubin interviewed in the mid-1970s were unanimous in hoping that their daughters would "be independent and not have to rush into marriage"; "I don't want the girls to have the regrets I've had."[36] One father told Studs Terkel, "This is gonna sound square, but my kid is my imprint. He's my freedom."[37] Their aspirations are succinctly stated: "I just want them to be happy, that's all. I want them to have everything they want, all the things we couldn't have."[38]

Yet right from the beginning the aspirations of parents are compromised by the reality of class. Those in subordinate class position are invariably uncertain about how to assure their children's success. They soon discover the barriers—the difficulty of gaining equal treatment in the public schools, the long and risky battles of adolescence, the economic costs of higher education, the difficult transitions into college and into jobs with some chance of advancement—which they are, relative to middle-class parents, powerless to affect. The clash between aspirations and expectations becomes poignant: when asked if they hope their children will go to college, most working-class parents respond, "If they want to." The response protects them against the real possibility that aspirations for their children cannot be achieved and mask the growing feelings that they can do little to help their children toward these aspirations.[39] As sociologist Hylan Lewis described a group of lower-class black mothers:

As children grow older there seems to be a cut-off point at which parents express impotence and bafflement. Although there are anxieties, the fate of these growing children is written off as out of parents' hands. There recurs in the records a mixture of hope and resignation: "I do hope they don't get in trouble. I tried to raise them right." "The Lord will have to look out for them." "I'm glad mine are little. I kinda hate to see them grow up. At least I can do something for them now." [40]

At the same time that class affects the balance between aspirations and expectations, conditions of employment shape the values parents pass on to their children. Middle-class parents are more likely to value independence, self-direction, self-control, and dependability—the characteristics necessary for their work—and emphasize these to their children. Working-class parents tend to stress obedience and conformity, the characteristics that determine success (or at least survival) in their own spheres of work.[41] As a result, children of different class backgrounds are prepared for institutions outside the family in different ways. For example, Robert Hess and Virginia Shipman, two developmental psychologists, typified the teachings of a middle-class mother as stressing the participation of the child with the teacher as well as obedience:

> First of all I would remind [my child] that she was going to school to learn, her teacher would take my place, and she would be expected to follow instructions. Also that her time was to be spent mostly in the classroom with other children and that any questions or any problems she might have she should consult with her teacher for assistance.[42]

The lower-class mother, in contrast, tends to stress obedience only, sometimes in harsh ways:

> Mind the teacher and so do what she tells you to do. The first thing you have to do is be on time. Be nice and do not fight. If you are tardy or if you stay away from school your marks will go down. The teacher needs your full cooperation. She will have so many children she won't be able to pamper any youngsters.[43]

Class also conditions the attitudes the parents impart toward mobility and achievement.[44] Seeing that educational achievement has meant rather little to their own lives and to their work, working-class parents often subtly degrade the value of schooling even as they express the hope that education will be a mechanism of advancement. As an appliance repairman recounted the values of his childhood:

> There was no demand on any of us for any goal. You see, my father wasn't an educated man. He was taken out of school when he was nine, and him not having an education, it kept him from seeing a lot of hopes for his kids. . . . Oh,

> I guess he didn't want us to be just ordinary laborers like he was, but it wasn't ever talked about. Like, going to college was never discussed. It never occurred to me to think about it. That was something other kids—rich kids—did. All I know was that I'd have to work, and I didn't think much about what kind of work I'd be doing. There didn't seem much point in thinking about it, I guess.[45]

This man's reminiscence illustrates another pitfall for working-class children—the inability to plan, itself rooted in the realities of working-class life. Buffeted about by unemployment and other economic forces beyond their control, with the future capricious and uncontrollable, planning seems pointless; with limited possibilities for advancement in most working-class jobs, there is no reason to prepare for future job advancement and little reward for planning, as there is for middle-class professionals and managers. Working-class parents have few ways to pass on a sense of the future to their children, and economic requirements reinforce the inability of their children to chart a future for themselves:

> I didn't think much about [planning]. I just kind of took things as they came. I figured I know I'd work; I worked most of my life. I started working at real jobs when I was fourteen. I worked in an upholstery place then. I used to carry those big bolts of material and keep the workers supplied with whatever they needed, and I kept the place clean. There wasn't much point in dreaming. I guess you could say in my family we didn't—maybe I should say couldn't—plan our lives; things just happened.[46]

For the working-class parents, then the high aspirations of the American dream give way to more "realistic" expectations and to working-class conceptions of what "real jobs" are; and the values and attitudes necessary to realize the promise of that dream are unavailable to working-class children. In these patterns, lower-class parents and working-class parents are themselves the agents of making the American dream unattainable, invisibly discouraging educational attainment when schooling remains almost the only mechanism of advancement, communicating to their children their own sense of powerlessness and of unconquerable constraints which are rooted in their own work and lives. In these patterns, we can see the evidence that can be interpreted as parental determinism: the actions of parents shape the futures of their children. But the origins of these patterns lie not with the parents themselves but with the class structure in which they live; the "failures" are not those of individual parents, as *parens patriae* would have it, but are instead the limitations of a class society.

The portrait that emerges from considering class is one of family life as exceedingly vulnerable to the characteristics of jobs, contradicting the image of the "private" family. The irony is that the ideal of the family as a

77

private refuge—as a locus of emotional support and as a childrearing environment—tends to work best where it is least necessary. When jobs provide autonomy, control, and some sense of meaning and purpose, then parents can more readily bring to their families not only the adequate income typically associated with such jobs, but also the emotional and psychological resources necessary for strong family relationships and the values and attitudes most useful to their children. But when the jobs themselves are most devastating, when they provide little challenge, little esteem, few personal relationships aside from the hostile attentions of supervisors, then—just when an alternative source of meaning and support is most needed—the family bears the brunt of the frustration generated by work, and family relationships become aggressive and unrewarding. Rather than a sphere of affection and nurturance, the family comes to focus the strains of work and extend them to all family members; rather than a springboard for adult success, many parents come to limit the future possibilities for their children. In such cases the effects of production have succeeded in standing the modern conception of family on its head: instead of a sphere in which economic relationships are excluded, it becomes one in which their effects dominate.

Other People's Children

Structural inequalities affect family relationships and shape opportunities for children, but their consequences for the larger society are still more complex and pervasive. The failures of public responsibility reflect in part a sharp differentiation between one's own children and other people's children, especially those in the public world of government institutions.[47] Other people's children, those who are different from one's own, are to be mistrusted. They may be shiftless or dangerous influences on one's own children; they may be potential competitors to one's own children in schools or in entry into limited occupations; they may impose social costs that detract from one's own children's opportunities. The differentiation among children becomes most powerful in an unequal society. Class and racial biases harden the negative perception of other people's children, and income differences, with the implication that public responsibility requires a redistribution from rich to poor, reinforce the fear that other people's children are costly liabilities. Above all, in a society of sharp inequalities the sense of children as a group meriting special concern becomes difficult to sustain. The unwillingness to assume the financial burdens of other people's children undermines the promises of children's programs and often reduces them to institutions merely containing those children who seem threatening or socially costly.

The tendency to differentiate sharply between one's own children and other people's children has been reinforced by the development of the private family and the evolution of childrearing as a private responsibility. In colonial America children were viewed as both public and parental responsibilities. That participation—what we would now consider the intrusion—of town and church fathers in childrearing was constant, with community officials chastising lax parents and even entering households to survey family life. Children often left the parental household by age seven or eight to work in another household, a signal that children were members of a wider community of families and not of a single family. Parental love reflected the social conception of children: while parents expressed affection for their children, parental love was a kind of "rational" love, moderated by the knowledge of high death rates among children, the fear that evil tendencies could easily flourish in children, and the sense of responsibility toward the community. The relationship between parent and child was not predominantly an emotional and personal one. The Virginia planter, William Byrd, made the point succinctly when he noted in his diary, after having dinner with his young daughter, that he had "dined by [him]self," his companion "nobody but the child." In modern terminology, the notion of the parent-child bond was lacking from the ideology and much of the practice of childhood.[48]

With the advent of the "private" family in the nineteenth century, children came to be less public members of the community and more members of their own families. The decline of communal oversight meant that parental responsibilities were defined as the duties of individual parents to their own children, not to children in general; no longer were children placed in other families, nor were poor children apprenticed as a way of providing them vocational training within another family. The social roles of children also changed: the decline of child labor (particularly in middle-class families who established the norms of childrearing) meant that children were perceived less as economic assets and more as children as we now think of them, without economic and social duties and with predominantly emotional ties to their parents. As enshrined in domestic ideals, the emotional relationship between parents and children and the notion of childrearing as a private prerogative came to dominate the ideology of childrearing.[49]

Conceptions of childrearing as a private responsibility have shaped the dichotomy between one's own children and other people's children. Because of the emotional nature of parental love, parents identify with their own children, delight in their development, and project their own hopes onto them. The ethic of "living through one's children," the view that "if you can't improve yourself, you improve your posterity," have suffused the ideology of parenting. Other people's children, in contrast, can be only a threat: they threaten to corrupt one's own children and, in a competitive society, to succeed at the expense of one's own. The battles over busing have brought out the fears of "other people's children" in the starkest forms. As one white mother declared:

> I know what it's like to live in a tough neighborhood where the kids take turns beating you up every time you walk around a corner. I fought desperately to better myself and to get out of that neighborhood. Then all of a sudden they were talking about busing my children back there to the same school where I went. If they think they can do that to me they're crazy.[50]

As always, racial and class dimensions heighten such feelings: the fear parents have that their children will mix with the wrong crowd and their hostility to their children's peers often reflect the feelings that lower-class shiftlessness and pleasure-seeking may corrupt one's own children. Both residential and school segregation have exemplified the effort to subject one's own children to only the best influences—that is, to children of one's own class and race.

If private responsibility for children has had a consistent meaning, in a society where children's institutions have been expanding, it has meant that parents should bear the financial responsibility for their own children, but not for other people's children. The theme of sacrifice for children, so much a part of the child-centered American family, has been an ethic of sacrifice for one's *own* children. The ethic has sometimes seemed fragile: if too many other parents do not sufficiently sacrifice for their own children, but instead resort to public resources, the concept of sacrifice itself can be thrown into doubt. The ethic of sacrifice, then, entails the corollary that other parents should sacrifice as well, rather than having their responsibilities relieved through public funds. As one father, threatened by those who have "gotten away with it," expressed his anger:

> You don't work, you don't live, right? . . . I *work* for *my* money. My job is to work for my family. [Those on welfare] don't wanna work, they live for nothing but kicks, nothing but good booze and good sex. . . . I go out, I work sometimes nine, ten days in a row, I got five children. That's what burns me, when someone else—like this woman on the street here that collects welfare.[51]

The intensity of sacrifice for one's own children and the fear that other parents may not be sacrificing to the same extent generate a deep hostility toward those public programs that confer on other people's children a favoritism not granted one's own. The hostility emerges in countless ways: in the resistance of parents to paying for educational programs their children do not use, in taxpayer revolts against Aid to Families with Dependent Children and food stamps programs, in attacks on recreational programs and other public services used heavily by children whose parents cannot afford to provide private alternatives. Ultimately, this hostility adds to the pressures from others—from adults without children, from adults beyond their childrearing years—who also object to bearing the costs of other people's children.

Of course, public miserliness toward other people's children has never been monolithic. One obvious division between modern conservatives and liberals involves willingness to spend on social programs for children. Conservatives, wedded to the old image of the private family, have resisted public support for what they consider private responsibilities; especially recently, they have urged that the government confine its spending to the few they presume to be "truly needy." However, conservatives are not particularly careful with public money: they delight in defense spending, even when defense budgets are demonstrably wasteful; budget cuts proposed by Ronald Reagan attacked Medicaid but not health care subsidies through the tax system, which benefit upper-income families; public housing funds were cut, but not mortgage subsidies through the income tax, which benefit middle-income home owners; federal subsidies to lower-income college students were reduced, while Reagan pledged to pass a tax credit for private education, which would be of more benefit to upper-income families; the Aid to Families with Dependent Children program, child nutrition programs, and social services for the poor were severely cut, while Social Security, Medicare, and Unemployment Insurance—programs that benefit those with more stable employment records, sometimes referred to as "middle-class welfare"—have been left with only marginal changes.[52] Thus conservatives have been hostile not to public spending itself, but to public spending that benefits the poor. Modern liberals, on the other hand, have more consistently opposed public subsidies to middle-income and upper-income families and supported redistributional program benefitting low-income families and children. The conflict over the composition of government spending, then, has partly reflected differing views of spending for other people's children.

Economic and social conditions have also affected public willingness to spend for children. During the 1950s, after two decades of depression and war, the desire for children and home life took on euphoric overtones. Economic growth appeared strong and certain, assuring a positive future for children. The birth rate was high; parents were supposed to enjoy their children, as Spock and other childrearing experts reminded them.[53] Despite some concerns about permissiveness and delinquent youth, children were considered assets, both to their families and society. The growth of the suburbs, encouraged by tax credits for home ownership and publicly funded highways, provided the physical setting for this child-centered world; because of the baby boom, funding for public education grew enormously with scarcely a note of protest, and public higher education began to displace private colleges. To be sure, the child-centeredness of the 1950s was a middle-class celebration of the private family; there was little recognition of lower-class children, and the basic welfare programs for poor children remained constant even as other public funding began to rise.

Positive attitudes toward children spilled over into the 1960s. High growth rates and the apparent elimination of business cycles made the first half of the decade a time of economic optimism. The discovery in the Sputnik crisis of 1957 that American children were lagging behind their Russian peers stimulated greater investment in schooling. The "human capital" school in the early 1960s continued to justify schooling and other training programs by their future returns. With the rediscovery of early childhood, positive returns on public investment also justified the Head Start programs for poor children, and then compensatory education programs funded through the Elementary and Secondary Education Act of 1965. As Lyndon Johnson remarked when he signed this act, "Better build schoolrooms for 'the boys' than cells and gibbets for 'the man.'"[54] The real growth in federal spending came through the major income support programs of the Great Society—Medicaid, food stamps, the school lunch and breakfast programs, and the expansion of Aid to Families with Dependent Children. These programs reflected optimism about investing in children and an insistence that poor children be provided greater access to the prerequisites for normal development—food, income, education, and health care.

In the late 1960s and the 1970s, the social and economic conditions that had generated positive views of children during the 1950s and the early 1960s changed. The economic optimism of the early 1960s dissipated as growth rates began to fall, as the reappearance of business cycles (in 1969–70 and 1973–75) made it clear that uninterrupted growth was still unattainable, and as stagflation—the simultaneous existence of high unemployment and high inflation—presented new and apparently insoluble economic problems. The certainty that investment in children would pay off began to pale. Two initial sources of doubt were the Coleman Report of 1966, which found that increased educational resources did not necessarily lead to higher achievement test scores, and the Westinghouse study of 1969, which reported that Head Start did not improve the cognitive abilities of small children. The criticism that schooling serves merely as a credential without substantial content grew throughout the decade, and falling returns to college education generated the image of the "overeducated American" with more schooling than was economically valuable.[55]

In part, changing attitudes may have been caused by the increasing costs of raising children. Because prices for food, housing, medical care, and education rose faster than the general rate of inflation, the cost of a "higher budget" for an urban family of four with two children—a standard of living that prospective parents would prefer for their children—rose 82 percent between the spring of 1967 and the autumn of 1976, while the Consumer Price Index increased by 70.5 percent.[56] The tendency for mothers to work had increased another cost of children; the potential earnings that women must forgo in order to bear and rear children—the opportunity costs—went up. Even if mothers returned to work when their children were young, the "interruption effect" of reduced and interrupted experience still decreased their subsequent earnings.[57] Quite apart from the rising costs of children to their own families, the public costs of children—the burden of other people's children—had risen substantially during the 1960s. Between 1964 and 1976, as total federal outlays increased by 233 percent, federal spending on education—almost all of it for compensatory education and other programs for special populations—increased by 671 percent; income support programs increased by 1,587 percent, health spending by 1,080 percent, child care expeditures by 1,470 percent, and employment-related programs for teen-agers by 1,371 percent.[58] In some areas—compensatory education, housing, child care, health, and employment, for example—the creation of programs as part of the War on Poverty had created new federal roles. Even if children were "America's richest resources," as Lyndon Johnson claimed,[59] the very expansion of public programs meant that poor children were social liabilities in the most immediate sense of costs. As doubts about the Great Society programs and children's institutions spread, even the vision that programs might convert potential liabilities into "social assets" came under serious attack.[60]

In the public realm, negative attitudes toward other people's children have strengthened resistance to public programs. During the 1970s and the early 1980s, a fiscal backlash against expenditures for children developed at all levels. At the local level, the rising costs of schooling led to "taxpayer revolts," sometimes in the refusal to levy additional taxes to keep schools open, and more often in spending limits for education.[61] Many towns passed zoning ordinances and building codes restricting housing for families with children, to avoid child-related expenses (particularly schooling) borne by local governments. At the state level, attacks on public spending were led by referenda to limit state and local spending. In California, after the success of Proposition 13 which reduced property taxation drastically, a sample of voters listed welfare, day care, and parks and recreation programs—all of them essentially programs for children, especially poor children—as their first three priorities for spending reductions; these public opinion polls apparently influenced the state legislature to reduce welfare spending and protect the traditional public services, fire and police protection.[62] One cogent explanation for the power of tax limitation movements blames the shifting composition of state and local spending during the 1960s: between 1956 and 1973 social welfare spending increased from 17.4 percent to 22.3 percent of state and local spending, while the traditional and universal services (fire, police, and sanitation) fell from 32.1 percent to 21.6 percent and local education fell from 30.4 percent to 26.9 percent.[63] Although the tax limitation movement has several other strands, resistance to redistributive programs and to funding other people's children appears to have been a central motivation.

At the federal level, a similar reaction to redistributive programs for children took place during the 1970s. The idea of a governmental "overload," of too many functions for too many groups, became popular among neoconservatives. One prominent cause of "overload" has been what Samuel Huntington, a prominant neoconservative, called the "welfare shift" during the 1960s, when the proportion of the total direct government spending for education, health, and income transfers rose while the proportion for defense dropped.[64] Since the beneficiaries of the "welfare shift" were—with the possible exception of college students—largely poor and lower-class, attacks on direct government spending unavoidably reflect a dislike of redistribution and of the poor themselves. The hostility toward recipients of Aid to Families with Dependent Children—the most threatening of other people's children—has been especially severe; benefit levels declined in real terms during the 1970s, and children became the age group with the highest rates of poverty and the slowest progress out of poverty.[65] Other federal expenditures on children at the end of the 1970s also declined in real terms, with nutrition programs, social services, and child health care programs especially vulnerable; efforts by Ronald Reagan to cut social programs have accelerated the trend, reducing federal programs for poor children while maintaining subsidies (including tax subsidies) benefiting middle-class children.[66]

The resistance to supporting other people's children adds to the fiscal limits on children's institution inherent in *parens patriae*. Children's programs that might reduce the effects of structural inequalities have then been distorted: public miserliness has undermined expensive compensatory education programs, promoted cheaper training programs over more expensive employment programs for adolescents, replaced truly rehabilitative (but costly) programs in the juvenile justice system with institutions of incarceration, generated "custodial" rather than "developmental" child care, and limited the scope of welfare payments and other transfer programs. The cycles in redistributive programs indicate that our special promises to children—to mitigate the effects of poverty, to provide some greater equality of opportunity through the state—are no more binding than any of the other ideologies that Americans have erected to cover their discomfort with structural inequalities. The saccharine myth of America as child-centered society, whose children are its most precious natural resources, has in practice been falsified by our hostility to other people's children and our unwillingness to support them.

Ambivalence Toward Children in a Class Society

The weak public commitment Americans feel toward other people's children is, in the first instance, rooted in the nineteenth-century conception of the private family with responsibility for its own children only. A different set of attitudes has compounded these divisions: Americans are ambivalent toward all children, and ambivalence has sharpened the distinction between one's own children and other people's children. Structural inequalities have affected the balance between positive and negative views of children in a class-divided society: the latent hostility toward children has often become a hostility toward lower-class and minority children—those who are most threatening, most costly, and least like middle-class children. In turn, hostility has undermined public responsibility for such children and has reinforced the efforts to control them.

Despite the long standing view of themselves as "child-centered," Americans have always been ambivalent about children. During the seventeenth and early eighteenth centuries, the dominant view of children as damned by original sin required authoritarian childrearing to break their wills and assure obedience. In the words of a prominent Puritan minister:

> Surely there is in all children . . . a stubborness, and stoutness of mind arising from natural pride, which must, in the first place be broken and beaten down;

that so the foundation of their education being laid in humility and tractable-ness, other virtues may, in their time, be built upon.[67]

During the eighteenth and nineteenth centuries, a notion of childhood innocence, of children as young plants that had to be nourished and pro-tected but not overindulged, became dominant. The stress on the fragility of childhood and the essentially positive view of childhood innocence greatly expanded the range of conceptions about childrearing. Many com-mentators were explicit about the warring elements in the child's nature; the Congregational minister Horace Bushnell, a strong advocate of milder childrearing techniques, asserted:

> The good in [the child] goes into combat with the evil, and holds a qualified sovereignty. And why may not this internal conflict of goodness cover the whole life from its dawn, as well as any part of it? . . . Never is it too early for good to be communicated. Infancy and childhood are the ages most pliant to good.[68]

The assumption that children were both innocent and potentially evil suffused many of the debates about children in the nineteenth century. Controversies over childrearing practices debated the extent of discipline necessary. Public schooling moved toward factory-like settings and work-oriented pedagogies, even while reformers like Friedrich Froebel defined children's "work" as play and developed softer, less constrained teaching methods. To some extent, the ambivalence toward children reflected a dichotomy between familial and extrafamilial experiences. At home, par-ents (more particularly, mothers) could be soft and permissive. Outside the home, especially in school, moral training and discipline had to be firm. The concern that innocent children could be easily contaminated by idleness and unproductivity contributed to a distrust of children and the fear that, despite all efforts within the home and outside, they would grow up lacking discipline, industriousness, and diligence.[69]

In the twentieth century, the legacy of an explicitly positive yet essen-tially ambivalent conception of childhood has continued. Freudian theo-ries, for example, resurrected the view of the child as antisocial and domi-nated by a mass of uncontrolled impulses that had to be firmly redirected in order to achieve a healthy adult. But even more often, Freud was inter-preted as calling for greater freedom for children if their personalities were not to be repressed. It was important, one Freudian pedagogue of the mid-1920s wrote, "to create a child's world and then for the most part to stand aside and watch the children grow in it under conditions of real freedom."[70] The two sides of the child were frequently expressed in debates over controlling the "natural" impulses of children versus fostering their independence, debates over restrictiveness and permissiveness, work and play, which continue to shape child advice literature and teaching methods.

Ambivalent feelings toward children are also a daily aspect of being a parent. The experience of children as both good and bad is familiar to every parent; extremes of emotion, from elation at a child's development and independence to overwhelming anger at disobedience and defiance, are inevitable. Such emotions start from birth:

> In my arms, I held my baby. After he drank from me, sometimes he would sleep. I stayed still for hours, then, staring at this face, comparing his to mine, finding a turn of his mouth which reminded me of my sister's, discovering in the shape of his torso the suggestion of his father's body. . . . At other times, during and after feedings he would cry and scream. I would walk him through the house, weeping with him for my incompetence, apologizing for my anxious and jittery soul, which was clearly the wrong style for good mothers. Sometimes I hated him for rejecting me so completely; "Shut up! I'll kill myself if you don't shut up!" I'd yell. Then I would try to shove my nipple into his mouth and he would push it away, his face distorted with pain.[71]

The disparate feelings continue as children age. On the one hand, American parents—particularly middle-class parents—raise their children to become independent; on the other, they want their children to be well behaved. Children continue to be both tremendous drains of energy and resources and tremendous sources of pleasure.

As they grow up, their successes may be gratifying to their parents, but here too parental goals for their children deepen their ambivalence. "Living through one's children" both promises and threatens. Children who surpass their parents may give them joy and meaning, but their success may also represent a repudiation of parental values and status; generations of immigrants have been particularly vulnerable to this bitter-sweet combination of reward and rejection. As one working-class father reacted:

> I always let [my sons] fear me. "Because you got an education under you, you gonna push me around," I says, "I'll throw you out of this house bodily. I don't need you." I make them understand who is the boss and they respect me. 'Cause I let them get away with it, they'd start, you know . . . working on me.[72]

If the success of a child is double-edged, a child's failure mocks the ability of parents to provide and invalidates their sacrifices. Failure thus generates parental anger alongside parental love. As one son, whose father had spent his whole life "trying to get enough money so my boys'd get what I didn't have," expressed the resulting conflict: "I look at my father and I want to cry ... but he's getting almost to hate me because I don't want to be a lawyer or doctor or someone respectable."[73] Identifying with the success of one's children is thus a risky prospect, inviting disappointment as well as elation no matter what the outcome.

Social and economic conditions can modify the ambivalence we feel toward children. In the 1950s, for example, growth stimulated highly positive views of children, though these coexisted with some concerns for juvenile delinquents and gangs. Ambivalence toward children became more polarized during the 1960s: reactions to young people, particularly college protestors and hippies, varied between strong hostility and positive assertions that the young were the most progressive force for change.[74] However, the anger directed at demonstrators and hippies, who were largely middle-class youth, never resulted in any real programs; instead positive feelings toward children seemed to predominate, in expanding education, in the new concern for the young child, in experiments with free schools and softer pedagogies, and in the efforts to de-institutionalize the juvenile justice system.

In contrast, the bleak economic conditions of the 1970s fostered more obviously hostile feelings. High unemployment rates, low growth rates, and economic malaise made it more difficult to be optimistic about the future, creating insecurity for adults and for children. With the inability of the labor market in the 1970s to absorb all college graduates, not even college seemed a reasonable assurance of success. The problems of steering one's own children through the bewildering array of extrafamilial institutions and activities—neighborhoods, television, and schools—and avoiding the pitfalls of bad peers, drugs, and sex sometimes appeared overwhelming to parents and prospective parents. As a result, the concepts of sacrifice and of "living through one's children," so fundamental to American childrearing attitudes, were challenged. Even while participating in the future through one's own children continued to be a social norm, few parents believed that their children would grant them any measure of immortality.[75] By the end of the decade, the feeling that "living through one's children" was precarious and uncertain had emerged from the comments of parents themselves:

> Other people argue that [our legacy] need not be our children, especially since there is no guarantee that our children will choose to represent us and stand for our goals and interests. . . . In fact, if we count on our children to represent us, we are likely to be disappointed. By asking that of them we are type-casting them, putting pressure on them to perform according to our needs and expectations. It's a set-up for disappointment.[76]

During the 1970s, bearing children ceased to be an automatic part of adulthood. The rise of voluntary childlessness (though statistically small) and organizations like the National Organization for Non-Parents signaled a willingness to consider the burdens children impose and an acknowledgment that children may not be worth the necessary sacrifice. We no longer have to consider children adorable. In fact, popular movies and literature in the 1970s (*Rosemary's Baby*, *The Exorcist*, and *The Omen*, for example) often portrayed children as demons visiting death and destruction on the adults around them.[77] In a period of rising costs and poor future prospects, our negative feelings toward children have become magnified.

Ambivalence toward children—both children in general and one's own children—is thus deeply embedded in modern conceptions of childhood and parent-child relationships. Potentially, this ambivalence could weaken the separation between one's own children and other people's children: one's own may be badly behaved, expensive little wretches; other people's children may be social assets, our "most precious natural resources." The hope that we can reduce the distinction between our own and other people's children is often expressed as the dream of a universal childhood; in the poetry of Carl Sandburg:

> There is only one child in the world,
> And that child's name is All Children.

In practice, however, ambivalence has intensified the separation. Rather than admit our negative feelings toward our own children, we tend to deny them; as Kenneth Keniston has noted, we displace our anxieties and fears onto other people's children.[78] In a society of intense identification with one's own children, the process of displacement is one way to maintain positive views of one's own. As expressed in doggerel:

> When my child hits your child he has not yet adjusted;
> But when your child hits my child he simply can't be trusted.[79]

We thus compound the already existing tendencies to ascribe the bad behavior and poor discipline of our own children to other children. The fear that our own children can get into various kinds of trouble—poor grades, juvenile delinquency, dropping out of school, teen-age pregnancy—becomes transformed into suspicion of the effects of peers, who are by definition other people's children. Parents consistently report their own children to be well-disciplined and just as consistently blame the sorry state of the schools on the lax discipline of other parents.[80]

Our own children may be wonderful to us—sources of great joy, justifications for our sacrifice, and guarantees of immortality—but other people's children are threatening as well as costly: they threaten to corrupt one's own children, and they may threaten social peace. As a result, another public goal has always coexisted with benevolent intentions toward children, albeit a goal less overtly argued and rhetorically less popular: if a child might grow up undisciplined and a threat to community peace, then the state might intervene to protect the community.

However legitimate the concern for social order, it has historically been distorted by class and racial biases. The fear of social disintegration in this country has almost always been a fear of lower-class disorder or working-class rebellion. Even in relatively homogeneous colonial America, with its much broader conception of public responsibility for childrearing, poor children were singled out for community and church intervention, to socialize them properly and to prevent unruly behavior. The fragmentation of urban communities and the increased stratification of the population by income, class, race, and ethnicity in the nineteenth century increased the fear posed by "others." The urban chaos of the nineteenth century, the violent strikes at the end of the century, the marches and rioting of the unemployed during the Great Depression, the "social dynamite" of ghetto youth in the 1950s, the race riots of the 1960s, and the swelling of juvenile crime in the 1970s have consistently threatened the middle class and caused it to act in its own protection. The fear that the inability of lower-class families to socialize their children would lead to social disorder has been a potent stimulus for state intervention, from the provision of schooling *in loco parentis* to the expansion of police powers to incarcerate disruptive juveniles.

The fear of social disorder has been so consistently class-related that identical behavior among middle-class youth and lower-class youth elicits very different responses. A sociologist, William Chambliss, has detailed the experiences of the "Saints," a gang of upper-middle-class boys, and the "Roughnecks," a gang of lower-class boys in the same town:

> The Saints were constantly occupied with truancy, drinking, wild driving, petty theft, and vandalism. Yet not one was officially arrested for any misdeed during the two years I observed them. . . . The Roughnecks were constantly in trouble with the police and community even though their rate of delinquency was about equal with that of the Saints.[81]

Indeed, the good reputation of the Saints seemed impervious to any evidence of their exploits, while the reputation of the Roughnecks was always much worse than their actual behavior. Judge David Bazelon has commented on the same tendency in the courts to intervene more harshly with lower-class children:

> When a child from a well-to-do family needs special attention, he and his parents are less dependent upon court facilities. His parents are likely to seek help privately . . . [and the] courts are willing to accept assurances from families that the child will receive private care and attention, even when quite serious offenses are involved. . . .
>
> When a well-to-do child offends, particularly in a vicious or violent way, we tend immediately to think of mental illness. After all, a nice child would not do such a thing unless he "wasn't right." When a ghetto child commits the same act, however, we may assume that such behavior is merely normal in view of his upbringing.[82]

The threat of other people's children has prompted those fearful of lower-class behavior to use children's institutions for purposes very different from the benevolent assertions of public intervention in the child's interests. Although the primary justifications for children's institutions have usually been phrased in terms of *parens patriae,* some reformers have explicitly recognized the dual nature of public goals. As the first superintendent of Chicago's public schools described the central purpose of education:

> Though common school is a civil, rather than charitable institution, it must be admitted that a primary object is, to bring under a wholesome influence, the classes of children [whose parents do not regard the education of their children with sufficient interest to induce proper individual action]. Whether we regard this subject in reference to *their* interest, or that of the whole people forming the state, it is of too much importance to be passed over lightly, or justify, for a moment, the conclusion that any portion of the rising generation, on whom must devolve the government of the country, can be abandoned to accident or certain ruin.[83]

The existence of two different and potentially incompatible goals governing the state's relation to children, a reflection of our basic ambivalence, has had several consequences. Most obviously, modern conservatives and liberals have divided over the most appropriate goal of the state. Conservatives have been more concerned about community peace and conserving social institutions by mechanisms which keep the class structure intact; they have, for example, been champions of stricter punishment for juvenile offenders, foes of most forms of compensatory education efforts (particularly busing), and opponents of efforts to redistribute income through welfare programs and social services. As Daniel Patrick Moynihan, shifting toward a more conservative position in the wake of the 1967 ghetto riots, argued to liberals, "They must see more clearly that their *essential* interest is in the stability of the social order."[84] Modern liberals have tended to emphasize the welfare of the child and to de-emphasize issues of control; they have promoted de-institutionalization, de-criminalization, and other "softer" treatment of youth in trouble, fought for compensatory efforts and redistribution in all forms which might help children, and generally minimized the danger to social stability which looms so large to conservatives.

Similarly, the periods of time with a liberal or conservative cast to them have differed on the main goals of government programs. The periods of liberal reform, like the progressive era and the 1960s, were notable for programs to promote the well-being of poor children. Conservative periods like the 1970s and 1980s, when more hostile feelings toward children and youth have surfaced, have also been dominated by obvious efforts to reassert controls over young people and subject them to new forms of discipline, especially the discipline of work. Career education, work experience programs, options to leave high school early to enter the work force, and a general emphasis on discipline and testing in the schools have proliferated.[85] A variety of youth employment and training programs were developed under the Comprehensive Employment and Training Act of 1973 and then the Youth Employment Demonstration Projects Act of 1977, but the largest number of positions for youth involved summer work programs to keep them off the streets and out of trouble. The increasing threat of juvenile crime has been met with pressure to treat juveniles as adults and to impose longer sentences in secure prisons. In these responses and in the general failures of the schools, the promises of education, training, and rehabilitation—the benevolent ideals of *parens patriae*—seem to have been forgotten.

A more complex consequence of the dual goals of the state is that every children's institution embodies both goals. The schools provide opportunities for adult success—indeed, they are almost the only avenue to success for lower-class children—but from their inception they have also been concerned with controlling behavior, providing the moral "character" and the values that some parents were thought not to provide their own children. The special promise of the juvenile justice system has been the hope of rehabilitating wayward youth, providing for them the guidance unavailable from parents or educators, but juvenile justice has obviously been pulled by the need to keep the community safe from dangerous youth. Manpower programs and other training programs have offered some hopes of improved access to stable jobs, but like the schools they have also been concerned with minimizing unruly behavior. Welfare programs like Aid to Families with Dependent Children and social services have provided financial resources to poor children and their parents, but the public concern that the poor should try to work their way off welfare has resulted in a variety of regulations governing the behavior of welfare recipients. The result is that almost every public program for children—particularly those for lower-class children—has some beneficial consequences but some negative results as well, which are destructive of the program's original intent.

The predominance in children's institutions of "help that can hurt," as Richard deLone has described this phenomenon, has complex origins.[86] The ethic of private responsibility for childrearing has always been invoked to disclaim public responsibilities and to limit the scope of public programs for other people's children. Public stinginess has itself hurt poor children, since they are the children most in need of public support. But the injuries go further: in a class society, the hostility toward children—never far from the surface—tends to manifest itself in particularly potent ways for other people's children, the lower-class and minority children who are so threatening. Fears of other people's children then compromise whatever public commitment to children exists by elevating social peace to a goal equal to that of supporting children suffering from structural inequalities. The result is to place benevolence toward children in contention with controlling impulses, and to further limit the promise of *parens patriae* that the state will always act in the best interests of the child.

The Dominance of Control over Benevolence

In the public realm, the tension created by ambivalence toward children has been eased by the hope that we can enhance each child's welfare while simulaneously guaranteeing social peace. A variety of programs have promised to combine the child-centered benevolence of *parens patriae* with a concern for the community: education programs that enhance a child's future earnings and simultaneously decrease the chance of his becoming a criminal or a welfare dependent; preventive nutrition and health programs that improve a child's health and decrease the likelihood of brain damage and chronic illness; public employment programs that simultaneously provide income and work experience, offer training for better jobs, and keep youth out of trouble. Lyndon Johnson's remark—"Better to build schoolrooms for the 'boys' then cells and gibbets for 'the man'"—Sargent Shriver's ideals for Job Corps, and the vocabulary of investment in children typify our hopes that the interests of children in personal advancement and the community's interest in social order are congruent rather than incompatible. These hopes have asserted the most noble promise of *parens patriae:* that public institutions can improve a child's life and simultaneously convert a "potential liability" into a "social asset."

In practice, however, the dual goals of the state have seldom been compatible because programs that are truly rehabilitative, compensatory, or preventitive have rarely been achieved. On the simplest level, controlling of hostile impulses have often come to dominate benevolent intentions: our reluctance to provide for other people's children prevents us from doing much for children and youth, and our fears of other people's children lead us to be primarily concerned with control. Most citizens want to make sure that, whatever the fate of other children, their own children are not harmed and their own lives are not disturbed. The unwillingness of most communities to accept community-based programs for juvenile delinquents is the clearest example, where no group is willing to risk higher crime rates in their neighborhood for the sake of programs which in the long run might benefit adolescents. The hostility of middle-class suburbanites to low-income housing has shown a similar unwillingness to accept the potential problems associated with lower-class and minority families; suburban location may be beneficial for children, according to the conventional wisdom of the postwar period, but middle-class parents have been unwilling to extend its benefits to lower-class children. The furor over school integration and busing and the phenomenon of "white flight" have similarly reflected the unwillingness of white parents to risk any potential (or even imagined) injuries to their children simply to improve the education of black or Hispanic children. As one white mother objected to the idea of sending her child to a poor black school, "I'm not willing to experiment with my children. They have only one chance to get educated."[87] Sometimes all children suffer these insults: the growth of "adult communities" where children are not allowed signals the unwillingness of some adults to suffer any disruptions of children. More often, however, lower-class and minority children are the targets. In all these cases, class and racial biases magnify the potential injuries from other people's children and generate a resistance to public programs which no amount of rhetoric about rehabilitation—or converting social liabilities into social assets—can overcome.

The public stinginess generated by the unwillingness to support other people's children also contributes to the decline of programs which promote the interests of children, rather than those of the community. Particularly as cost-benefit calculations—distorted by considering only those outcomes that can be measured—have become the dominant form of evaluation, we consistently see an unwillingness to bear the high costs of decent programs and an impulse to substitute cheaper palliatives that undermine the intent of the original programs. Reducing welfare costs through administrative changes that make it harder for welfare recipients, efforts to cut the costs of day care programs and promote "custodial" care, and the constant efforts to reduce funding for nutritional programs—even those like the WIC program that have shown real benefits in reducing nutritional deficiencies and later health problems[88]—all represent this sort of economizing. The preponderance of short-term summer employment programs, which are of little value as training but are useful in keeping troublesome youths off the streets, similarly indicates an unwillingness to fund more thorough and more expensive programs that might provide some long-term advantages rather than short-term control. No matter what their justification, programs to provide for poor children and to equalize opportunity are often weakened by our reluctance to support other people's children.

Finally, the restriction that public programs alleviate the effects of structural inequalities without dealing directly with inequalities themselves complicates the development of truly compensatory programs. This restriction often leads to meaningless or insufficient programs in place of obviously necessary ones: social services in place of income support, counseling and training programs instead of efforts to increase employment levels. Public programs usually address the symptoms of inequalities rather than inequalities themselves, so that the basic problems can never be resolved. For example, the state has provided remedial health care rather than eliminating the poverty and miserable community conditions that lead to poor health, developed compensatory education rather than improving the class-related experiences that lead children to do poorly in school, and institutionalized a juvenile court system that concentrates on bad behavior rather than on the conditions which lead to crime among lower-class youth. These programs fail to correct the underlying causes of health differentials, educational deprivation, and alienation, so that the same problems present themselves generation after generation.

Sometimes the restriction that children's institutions leave structural inequalities untouched generates insuperable challenges. The problems of overcoming the differences among children which emerge in their first five or six years—differences of health, of values, of cognitive stimulation, of experiences—through compensatory programs of relatively short duration seem impossible on the face of it; the idea of overcoming in training programs of several months the disabilities of teen-agers which ten years of schooling have not corrected is ridiculous. Under the best of circumstances, devising programs that can enhance the welfare of poor children is difficult, but when constrained by children's institutions which deal only with the symptoms of inequalities rather than their origins that task becomes close to impossible.

Because rehabilitive intentions prove so difficult to implement or are incompatible with controlling impulses, programs for children often fail to fulfill the promises underlying them. Training programs and vocational education fail to prepare youth for occupations, even though they keep youth out of trouble. Compensatory education programs have not equalized the educational attainments of all children, although they offer some evidence that the schools are trying to provide equal opportunity to all children. Welfare programs have done relatively little to reduce poverty rates among children, even though they do provide some material benefits to poor children. The health and nutrition programs begun since the 1960s have failed to eliminate the tremendous disparities (especially the racial disparities) in health indicators. The failures often produce so much frustration that many have abandoned support for public programs and have advocated purely controlling efforts. The response of neoconservatives to the apparent failure of children's institutions has been to eliminate public programs as hopelessly ineffective and to reassert private responsibility, while making sure that children in the remaining programs cease to be "troublesome" and that their costs are kept as low as possible. The abandonment of the Great Society programs—the abandonment of the very idea that public programs can overcome social problems like poor schooling, poverty, bad health, and unemployment—has been the most prominent retreat from public responsibilities, increasingly widespread as taxpayer revolts and a general mood of conservatism has swept the country. In the process, the chance that the state might intervene on behalf of poor children—never a strong possibility to start with—has been further undermined.

As long as enhancing the child's welfare is incompatible with controlling impulses, the state is in an inescapable dilemma. The structural inequalities of a capitalist society create barriers to stable family life and to decent childrearing conditions for poor, lower-class, and minority children. These inequities in turn generate the pressure for the state to alleviate poverty and to provide some semblance of equal opportunity. But structural inequalities simultaneously generate the public attitudes and political pressures that prevent the state from discharging these responsibilities. Public responsibility for children is thereby reduced to remedial programs that usually prove insufficient and children's institutions that are consistently unable to redress the problems they were created to solve.

4

Public Power and Children

AKEN to its extreme, the ethic of private responsibility and *laissez faire* creates innumerable problems. Capitalism has generated inequalities of class and income and has exacerbated racial discrimination, which families acting alone have been unable to control. The dislocations of urbanization, of immigration, and of social change in its many forms have created still other social problems that have often overwhelmed individuals. The cycles of capitalist expansion and contraction, the abuses of "vicious combinations" and monopolistic corporations, and the pollution and other dangerous conditions created by unregulated firms are other evils that have affected both families and businesses. Acting collectively, Americans have always rejected the full consequence of laissez-faire capitalism. They have repeatedly replaced economic decisions with political decisions, attempted to reduce the inequalities generated by capitalism, and established public regulation where private markets have failed.

Families and children have always been central to these democratic and egalitarian initiatives.[1] Democratic politics has improved the lives of many children, yet the promise of democratic politics has invariably fallen short of its professed aims. Intervention on behalf of children has remained haphazard and inadequate; despite the good intentions of child savers, too many children are still poor, undernourished, ill-housed, and barely educated. Children's institutions remain ambiguous in their effects, helping children in some ways and limiting them in others. While campaigns of child saving can generate enormous public support for humane principles and even a consensus on the need to revise existing programs, implementing those principles has been nearly impossible. Nearly fifty years ago, Grace Abbott of the Federal Children's Bureau proclaimed her commitment to children in a fantasy which has remained an inspiration for all children's advocates but which also expresses the pathetic weakness of the children's cause:[2]

> Sometimes when I get home at night in Washington I feel as though I had been in a great traffic jam. The jam is moving toward the Hill where Congress sits in judgment on all the administrative agencies of the Government. In that traffic jam there are all kinds of vehicles moving up toward the Capitol. . . . There are all kinds of conveyances that the Army can put into the street—tanks, gun carriers, trucks. . . . There are the hayricks and the binders and the ploughs and all the other things that the Department of Agriculture manages to put into the streets . . . the handsome limousines in which the Department of Commerce rides . . . the barouches in which the Department of State rides in such dignity. It seems so to me as I stand on the sidewalk watching it become more congested and more difficult, and then because the responsibility is mine and I must, I take a very firm hold on the handles of the baby carriage and I wheel it into the traffic.[3]

Evidently, the simple dedication of reformers has never been enough; advocates for children have usually been pushed aside by more powerful interest groups, either the tanks (now the missiles) representing military spending, the limousines of the business classes, and even the hayricks of the common farmer, better organized and more serious than babies seem to be. The discrepancy between the potential power of child saving movements and the reality of their outcomes sharpens the dilemma we have continuously posed: why has public responsibility for children been so difficult to implement, even within a democratic state?

Children suffer an obvious liability within democratic politics: they cannot vote, and many of them cannot even speak on their own behalf. Instead others speak for children in public. In fact, despite a wistful view that children's issues should be above politics and that family issues should remain private, there is no dearth of interest groups and professionals speaking for children. Yet the representation of children by organized groups and by professionals generates special dilemmas, which explain why democratic mechanisms have been relatively ineffective.

Although representation by interest groups allows children to have some public voice, it has generally compromised the children's cause. To be politically powerful in America requires organizing on self-interested and narrow grounds. Disinterested and humanitarian groups can only rarely generate sufficient political power to pass legislation or to remain cohesive enough to assure that reforms are implemented. Thus the most powerful advocates for children, like the National Education Association and the American Federation of Teachers, are strong precisely because they build upon teachers' self-interests, but they then represent children well only when children's interests and teachers' interests happen to coincide. Other disinterested advocates for children are generally weaker, since they lack the basis in self-interest which generates the most cohesive, unified interest groups; purely humanitarian advocates, like the "hunger lobby" or the "children's television lobby," either fail or find their success so fitful as to be of marginal influence. Organizing interest groups to represent children is, paradoxically, often destructive to the children's cause, since children's groups are often fragmented and in competition with one another. Most devastating of all, in a political process dominated by self-interested groups, it has become impossible to develop a coherent conception of the "best interests of children" or to implement programs based on principles rather than power. Our willingness to allow interest groups to dominate politics has thereby impeded the cause of children.

Both in politics and within children's institutions, professionals have become the most powerful group who defines the interests of children and who speaks for children. Yet the results of professional power have been ambiguous. While professionals often possess expertise and experience that are helpful, they also act out of self-interest and the desire to solidify their status, distancing themselves from parents in the name of professional autonomy. Those efforts have been only partially successful, however, because parents have resisted "professionalized childrearing" and because the location of childrearing professionals in public institutions subjects them to public control. The consequence has been to limit the potential of childrearing professionals: their power is often contested, and they remain semiprofessionals rather than fully autonomous professionals like doctors and lawyers; their claims to expertise and benevolence are clouded by self-interest; and conflicts between parents and professionals are unavoidable. As a result, the promise that professionals would use their power "in the best interests of children" has been compromised.

Democratic politics therefore turns out to be less promising for children than it should be. The hope that democratic mechanisms and reform movements can help children escape the limitations of nineteenth-century liberalism turns out to be naive. Instead, the political representation of children proves to be distorted by the same self-seeking behavior, the elements of *parens patriae,* and the compromise of moral principle that child advocates have always sought to avoid. When we understand who speaks on behalf of children in public, then the present structure of American democracy itself becomes questionable—not because democracy itself is no longer admirable, but because we have created a distorted notion of democratic politics and citizenship. A strong and humane sense of public responsibility cannot be fully developed and implemented as long as the only political question is who can organize effectively enough to get what they want; the interests of children cannot be fully represented as long as professionals remain the dominant groups speaking on behalf of children. To the extent that democracy has become corrupted and unrepresentative of all its citizens, public responsibility for children will continue to be contradictory and confused, and children will continue to suffer.

Interest Groups and Children's Interests

The conventional explanation for the weakness of the children's cause is that children cannot vote. The power of this explanation has been strengthened in the postwar period when the other major group of dependent Americans—the aged—have increased their political power through greater numbers and more effective organizing. The relative political power of the young and the old has been starkly illustrated by the spending cuts proposed by Ronald Reagan and enacted in 1981: while the major federal programs benefiting the elderly—Medicare and Social Security—remained relatively intact, the major programs for children—Aid to Families with Dependent Children, food stamps, child nutrition programs, social services, housing programs, employment and training programs, and education—bore the brunt of efforts to reduce social spending. In the political choices among competing priorities, most politicians have been more afraid of retributions from elderly voters than of the wrath of children.

While there is considerable truth to the view that children are powerless because they cannot vote, a more sophisticated explanation is necessary. The solution to the inability of children to vote—like the inability of the mentally retarded or the insane—has always been to organize groups that act *on behalf of* children, representing the interests of children to the state. Parents are the most obvious representatives of children, of course, but as we have seen they usually represent their own children, not children in general. Sometimes their self-interest coincides with that of a class of children—when parents organize to oppose education cuts, for example, or when parents of handicapped children press for special services—but by and large the divisions among parents and the ethic of childrearing as a private responsibility have prevented them from speaking publicly for children. However, there is no lack of other groups representing children: they include organizations of professionals who serve children, like the American Federation of Teachers and the National Association of Social Workers; academic groups whose interests include children and child development, like the American Psychological Association; child advocacy groups, like the Children's Defense Fund; groups organized to advocate a particular program, like the Day Care Council of America; coalitions of children's groups like the Coalition for Children and Youth. Most of the national interest groups have state or local branches, and advocacy groups at the local level have proliferated with the expansion of children's programs. Many other groups support children's issues where they coincide with their primary interest: the National Organization of Women and other women's groups have supported child care, and labor organizations have been advocates for welfare programs.

The problem in the political representation of children is not the absence of groups speaking on their behalf, but their relative powerlessness. Some obvious characteristics contribute to their weakness. Many of them are dominated by women, and the issues of childrearing have been intimately connected to the roles and rights of women; as a result, the political underrepresentation of women has limited the responsiveness of politicians to children's issues. The vision of men far removed from childrearing responsibilities debating children's issues among themselves has often seemed ridiculous to child advocates; the emergence of a few politicians identified as spokesmen on children's issues—Walter Mondale until 1976, Alan Cranston since then—is evidence of how rare such a concern has been, compared to the numbers who press to be on the Senate Foreign Relations Committee or the House Ways and Means Committee. Poor and minority groups similarly lack power within the state in proportion to their numbers; as in the case of women, their exclusion is critical because many of the most burning public issues involve poor and minority children. Many of the groups advocating on behalf of children are academic and professional groups, which are often ambivalent about acting politically and would prefer that children's issues be "above politics."

But deeper reasons for the weakness of the children's cause lie in the nature of American democracy, and specifically in the limits of representation by interest groups. Over the past two centuries, democratic practices in America have changed dramatically. The purest image of democracy Americans share—the New England town meeting, with the direct participation of individuals—has gone the way of the self-sufficient families and the homogenous communities of the colonial period, replaced by more collective forms of political representation. Even political parties, the nineteenth-century solution to the problem of organizing political expression, have given way in the twentieth century to more specialized interest groups, self-interested and often unreconcilable. During the entire twentieth century, the expansion of state activity has been paralleled by an expansion of interest groups, pressuring voters, shaping legislation, influencing regulatory and administrative decisions, and thereby reducing the influence of formal democratic mechanisms in which individual voters debate issues and cast ballots. While individuals still vote—though in declining proportions—they are powerful only to the extent they are organized into interest groups, both because such groups influence voting (particularly in an era of costly media campaigns) and because they influence the administrative aspects of government which are only indirectly affected by voting.[4]

In a democracy dominated by interest groups, factions are powerful in proportion to the number of voters they can mobilize, not the number of individuals they represent, and they are powerful in proportion to their economic power. Unions can influence their workers to vote in particular ways: corporations can buy political influence or threaten to use their considerable economic power in retribution against their enemies. In contrast, the claim to represent a large but voiceless group like children carries no real weight. The most powerful interest groups speaking for children—teachers' groups like the American Federation of Teachers and the National Education Association—act like unions asserting the voting power of their members, not like representatives of children; advocacy groups which claim to represent large numbers of children—like the Children's Defense Fund and various children's rights groups—have relatively less power because they represent neither votes nor the money to buy votes. In the final analysis, interest groups can only organize those who vote; they cannot represent those, like children, who have no vote.

Naming the most powerful interest groups acting on behalf of children suggests another reason why children have not fared well in the democratic state: the self-interest of groups acting on behalf of children—particularly groups of professionals—and the interests of children do not always coincide. Higher pay and greater status for professionals working with children may improve children's lives, by regularizing the conditions of teaching or child care and by creating careers to which individuals can devote themselves, for example; and organized teachers have supported compensatory education and bilingual education because these programs would increase employment. But in other cases, self-interest and the quest for pay and status have little to do with the welfare of children or the effectiveness of teaching. The successful effort of the National Education Association to establish a separate Department of Education during the

Carter administration provides a good example of political power expended without a clear regard for children; there was never any substantial evidence that a new federal department would enhance the education of children, even though it was expected to increase the power of teachers' groups. Teachers' groups have successfully opposed vouchers and community control as being against their own interests, even if such initatives might improve education;[5] they have also opposed the Child Development Associate credential, designed to certify child care workers through proficiency tests rather than formal education, since the Child Development Associate challenges the usual methods of licensing professionals.[6] The drive for professional standing—in the efforts to require more credentials, in the efforts to monopolize public institutions, and in the attempts by teacher unions to control publically subsidized child care[7]—are still other examples of how self-interest in the political process may not benefit children. Yet within a political system dominated by self-interested groups, there is no escaping the danger that the groups representing children may not be disinterested advocates for them.

The potential difference between professional self-interest and the welfare of children reflects a special irony: the groups that represent children are often politically weak, but those that are least self-interested are especially weak. The forces in the formation and cohesion of interest groups are responsible, for they make interest group politics based on humanitarian and moral grounds extremely difficult. Interest groups are powerful to the extent they can mobilize identification among members in support of political positions. Invariably, the strongest interest groups—corporate lobbies and unions—are based on the simplest forms of economic self-interest, and because simple self-interest is involved such groups can usually generate the money to finance organization and lobbying. In the realm of children's issues, the ability to organize on the basis of self-interest occurs most commonly among professional groups who have a direct stake in government programs, and among parents of handicapped and retarded children who desperately need expensive services that can only be collectively provided. Although parent groups supporting services for the handicapped and retarded have been relatively powerful, their interests are necessarily narrow and include only children like their own. Professional groups—especially teachers' unions like the American Federation of Teachers—and other self-interested service providers have thus become the most powerful political advocates on a range of children's issues, despite the fact that these groups are not exclusively interested in the welfare of children. As Gilbert Steiner—a political scientist at the Brookings Institution and ever the political realist—has concluded:

103

No lesson seems more important than that of involving groups with a self-interest in the children's cause. School food service personnel have been important to school feeding; project directors have been important to maternal and child health projects. And any prospects for child development legislation depend on the comparable anxiety of public school teachers to protect their job opportunities by reaching for younger clients to keep the pool full.[8]

In contrast, those groups that do not have a self-interested stake in children's issues rarely possess the sustained discipline and commitment to political activism necessary for effective interest group politics because they can appeal only to humanitarian principles and the moral outrage of their members, or (depending on their abilities) to public opinion. The "hunger lobby" organized to expand food and nutrition programs is an example of a purely humanitarian group which has lobbied actively and gained the attention of the media, but which has never been as influential in passing legislation as the self-interested agriculture lobby.[9] Even those on the extreme right specializing in moral outrage, convening in single-issue groups to oppose abortions, homosexuals, and the decline of the family as they see it, have seen their power within the Reagan administration diminish in deference to moderate conservatives with ties to corporate America rather than to religious and ideological groups. Ironically, then, those groups that are economically self-interested are the most powerful, and the most disinterested groups—which might best represent the interests of children—are relatively weak.

Of course, there are some disinterested children's groups with consistent access to political decision making, just as there are occasions when humanitarian appeals have political influence. But their power seems serendipitous. The Children's Defense Fund is one such organization, largely built on the personal power of its director, Marion Wright Edelman. The ability of charismatic individuals—almost all women—to gain political access on children's issues has a long history, from Julia Lathrop of the early Children's Bureau to the influence of Mary Dublin Keyserling on child care issues during the 1960s.[10] Quite apart from the fact that such individuals may abuse their power, their influence has been limited precisely because they do not represent large and powerful organizations, as business and union leaders do. Other children's organizations have gained a voice because of their longevity and exclusive interest in narrowly defined issues, as in the case of the Child Welfare League and its lobbyist William Pierce; but again this power is idiosyncratic, linked to a specific set of traditional child welfare issues and the visibility of one organization and one person. Other than individual power, the only way to achieve political influence has been through identification with a particular children's institution—like the role in public education that Albert Shanker of the American Federation of Teachers has played—but this source of power again means that institutional and professional self-interest may come to dominate.

Interest group action on behalf of children is further complicated by the problem of deciding which issues to address and which to ignore. While there are many interest groups with a broad range of political activity—the AFL-CIO and the Chamber of Commerce, for example—generally the influence of an interest group diminishes as its agenda strays from a relatively single-minded goal. The conception of an interest group as one with limited purposes is fundamental to the pluralist model,[11] and interest groups are becoming increasingly limited as single-issue groups have burgeoned in recent years. Among children's advocates, different groups concentrate on child care, nutrition programs, health programs, traditional child welfare issues, mental health programs, and education. In fact, the strategy of limiting an organization's goals to a few issues has sometimes worked well, as in the success of the Child Welfare League of America in the area of foster care, adoption, and child abuse; but the very source of its success—its ability to provide services to specialized adoption and foster care agencies—has also prevented the league from extending its concern to all children.[12] The efforts to develop groups representing children with a broader scope have been generally unsuccessful, and the demise in 1980 of the Coalition for Children and Youth—an umbrella organization attempting to provide some coordination among children's advocates—testifies to the difficulty of combining narrow interest groups.

Another example of the tendency to define issues narrowly has been the attempt to develop family impact statements, modeled on environmental impact statements. The idea behind family impact statements—and the search for a family policy in general—has been to examine the range of government action and inaction and provide some coherence to the existing chaos. However, because of "limited time and resources" the initial efforts to catalogue federal policies influencing families examined only those federal programs "whose primary goal is the provision of financial assistance, in-kind subsidies, or services to individuals or families (such as social security benefits, subsidized school lunches, or health services, respectively)"—that is, traditional income support programs, with tax policy, macroeconomic policies, regulatory agencies, court decisions, and employment-related issues specifically omitted.[13] But in the realm of children, narrowing the focus of concern is self-defeating. The conventional approach of addressing specific programs—for example, child care, foster care, or health screening—may be politically necessary, but it forces children's groups to neglect the most important influences on children, like poverty, macroeconomic policy, or the effects of job conditions on family life. The issue of scope therefore presents an inescapable dilemma for any group representing children: if the group narrows its scope to a few issues with immediate possibilities of political passage, it may contribute to the chaos of policy making on behalf of children and run the risk of irrelevance; if it expands its scope and addresses some of the central issues affecting children, its success rate is likely to be low, and it may be criticized for moving out of "children's issues" and into areas where it has no business.[14]

The fragmentation into groups concerned with narrow issues has in turn generated the intense internecine warfare that so frequently afflicts children's lobbies. These battles have sometimes been portrayed as merely petty;[15] though they are at times mean-spirited, they are more appropriately seen as rooted in the logic—the illogic—of representing children by interest groups. The conflicts over "turf" among different professional groups seeking monopolies over children's programs are unavoidable where groups are so fragmented, where self-interest is the primary basis for the formation and internal coherence of interest groups, and where there is so little public funding for children's programs. The debates between educators and social workers over child care, for example, reveal substantive differences, but they also display simple self-interest in seeking control over a new and potentially large social service. Faced with declining enrollments and budget cuts, educators have argued that child care ought to be part of the public school system on the grounds that they are the only professionals trained to teach children and that location in the public schools is the only way to make child care universally available. Social workers have expressed concern about the efficacy of schools and about the loss of family-centered resources if child care funding is channeled through the public schools. In both cases, however, the issue of professional control and self-interest has dominated the public rationales. The resistance to new forms of licensing professionals reveals a similar process; battles over control are debated in terms of the child's best interests, without those interests ever being assesed. To be sure, the inability of children's groups to present a united political front sometimes reflects different conceptions of children and what they need, and the resulting debate is basically healthy and consistent with democratic principles. But in a political system dominated by interest groups, debate is supposed to occur among competing interests, and the failure to achieve a consensus on "the best interests of children"—whether for self-interested or disinterested reasons—becomes a political liability. The withdrawal by Senator Alan

Cranston from the Child Care Act of 1979, partly because of the unwillingness of child care advocates to unite behind the bill, provides one example of the consequences for children.

While the nature of interest groups has been detrimental to the children's cause, a different aspect of American democracy has been even more devastating: the drift towards a purely self-interested and adversarial form of democracy. While we now take this form of democracy for granted, it has been—like the shift toward interest groups—a development of the last two centuries. Colonialists in the seventeenth and eighteenth centuries often expressed a strong sense of the common good. In their governing practices, they took for granted that responsibility to the community's common welfare was every citizen's obligation, and the community good tended to override private interests in a variety of areas: monopoly pricing was regulated, the need to care for the indigent meant that wealthier members of the community were required to support poor children in their own homes, and even the residential location of community members was the subject of community decision since compact communities were essential for protection from Indians and for moral surveillance.[16] The architects of the American revolution condemned the "factionalism" and self-serving interests of the British government as sure sign of its internal corruption and moral decay.[17] Different political theories have reinforced conceptions of disinterested politics; theorists like Montesquieu and Rousseau emphasized the search for the common good and for the elements of civic responsibility,[18] and others like John Stuart Mill envisioned a "developmental democracy," one that fostered the development of citizens through the "advancement of community . . . in intellect, in virtue, and in practical activity and efficiency."[19] These conceptions of democracy asserted above all that democracy was a moral system, a view that received its fullest expression in Rousseau's belief that only by acting in the common good could individuals become moral beings.[20] The ideals of developmental democracy have continued to live on: the 1962 Port Huron Statement of Students for a Democratic Society advocated democratic participation to reduce apathy and improve the quality of citizens' lives, and the Community Action Program and "maximum feasible participation" of the War on Poverty supported similar goals. However, these ideals—even those less than twenty years old—now sound either archaic or millenarian because contemporary politics have changed so drastically.

Even by the end of the seventeenth century, the vision of a moral democracy of disinterested citizens, pressing toward the common good, began to vanish. The molders of the Constitution continued to believe in the "public good" and "true interest of [the] country," but by then they recognized that the "causes of faction"—self-interest and economic divisions—could not be eliminated. As James Madison described it, the task for the Constitution was therefore the "regulation of the various and interfering interests."[21] According to de Tocqueville, Americans were unique in converting individual self-interest into "self-interest rightly understood," as he described the American way of establishing a common good and the dominance of public responsibility over the private interest.[22] However, de Tocqueville was not especially optimistic that Americans would hold to their unique conception of self-interest. He recognized, without fully elaborating it, that slavery and an emergent aristocracy of commerce and manufacturing threatened to eliminate the common good in favor of an unequal division according to selfish interests. By now, the fears of Madison and de Tocqueville have been confirmed. Democracy in America has become an adversarial relation in a relatively narrow sense: each individual and each group has its own interests, and each seeks a greater share of political power and the material benefits which can flow from the state.[23] In place of earlier theories of "developmental democracy," we now have more "realistic" theories that deny the possibility of the public interest or the common good. As David Truman, author of the most influential analysis of interest groups, dismissed the idea of a common good, "We do not have to account for a totally inclusive interest, because one does not exist."[24] Instead of the search for the common good, the dominant political theories now view democracy as a mechanism to establish equilibrium between demand and supply, with different groups demanding their own goals from the state and politicians supplying those groups with the greatest political power.

In an adversarial democracy, politics depends upon the self-interest of the most powerful groups. No other conception of politics can emerge; it is impossible to act on the basis of consistent principles, no matter what the consensus on those principles is, unless they coincide with the self-interest of the most powerful groups. This is the reason why the lack of the vote and the weakness of representation by interest groups are so devastating to children: in a principled democracy, one that strives to define the common good and to implement that definition, the direct representation of children's interests would be unnecessary because the interests of all would be equally considered. But in an adversarial democracy there is no substitute for the vote and no substitute for organization into powerful groups. The efforts of child savers and reformers to define the "best interests of children," to promote moral and humanitarian justifications for children's programs, and to identify the community's interest in protecting small children from hunger, poverty, danger, and vice have largely been submerged in the press of purely self-interested politics.

The principle that "no child shall starve," for example, would be supported by all but the most mean-spirited Americans and could therefore generate coherent policies to enhance child nutrition. In 1969, for example, 68 percent of Americans favored (and only 25 percent opposed) free food stamps for families with income under $20 per week, ten years before free food stamps for the poorest families were provided.[25] In practice, groups acting in their own self-interest have prevented the consistent implementation of the principle:[26] fiscal conservatives and employers have opposed the expansion of welfare programs and food stamps; farmers have pressured for the highest prices possible, sometimes in the form of reduced output; the food industry has resisted any regulation of the nutritional content and toxicity of the food it processes. Even the Women, Infants, and Children (WIC) program of nutritional supplements to infants and to pregnant and lactating women, a program that seems as impossible to oppose as motherhood itself, has been consistently undermined by Republican and Democratic administrations and by an unenthusiastic Department of Agriculture, who have responded to fiscal conservatives and agricultural groups with more political clout than the merely humanitarian cause of malnourished children can muster. The 1975 federal budget, for example, called for a $600 million cut in food stamps and a $53 million cut in maternal and child health, including the elimination of the Women, Infants, and Children program; the 1976 budget attempted reductions in Medicaid and school lunch expenditures, cuts of $12 million for child and maternal health, and a 23 percent reduction in child nutrition, all during a period of 6 percent inflation. Children fared no better under Jimmy Carter. In response to the mood of budget cutting, Carter proposed trimming the 1980 budget for the child care food program, the school lunch and breakfast program, the special milk program, and WIC appropriations—under the ridiculous logic that WIC is inflationary—in a period of 18 percent inflation.[27] Children have fared least well under Ronald Reagan: while promising to provide "safety nets" for the "truly needy," he proposed in 1981—a year of about 12 percent inflation—to cut food stamps by 15 percent, other child nutrition programs by 35 percent, and the Women, Infants, and Children program by 30 percent.[28]

Other principles that by themselves generate widespread support have similarly been thwarted by the realities of politics. The "right" to decent health care, also widely supported in principle, has in practice been compromised by fiscal conservatives and doctors preserving their own self-interest. Another principle that many Americans support—that children (if not adults) should not suffer the ravages of poverty—has similarly been weakened, as we will see in chapter 7. In some cases, widely held principles have been embodied in legislation: "high" employment in the 1947 Employment Act, "decent housing for all" in the 1949 Fair Housing Act, and "full employment" in the 1978 Humphrey-Hawkins Act are prominent examples, all with potentially important consequences for children. But we conventionally understand these not as principles to be consistently implemented but as rhetorical devices to attract political support, inevitably undermined by those powerful interest groups who are not well served by low unemployment and decent housing.

Adversarial and self-interested politics also tends to generate chaos in place of coherent programs which can consistently implement a specific goal. Since every group tries to pass legislation tailored to its own interests, legislated programs are uncoordinated and unrelated. The examples of programs operating at cross-purposes are ubiquitous: welfare programs and income tax codes contain incentives against marriage; housing subsidies are unrelated to other income support programs; the various efforts to prepare youth for work in the schools, in manpower programs, and in the juvenile justice system are uncoordinated; social services are poorly planned, with the result that many children "slip through the cracks" or fail to have urgent needs addressed because diagnosis and cure take place in separate agencies; the efforts of health screening programs to identify health problems and those of Medicaid to provide health care are unrelated; different forms of child care subsidies are provided through Head Start, Title XX, the income tax code, and the welfare system, all uncoordinated, with different eligibility criteria and standards.[29] Mechanisms to coordinate and consolidate services to children and youth are part of every reform agenda, particularly attempts to enact state-level offices for children and youth[30] and to establish "family impact statements" to examine the coherence of programs. The recent calls to generate a coherent "family policy" also emphasize the potential benefits from articulating and implementing more consistently what the state ought to do for families and children. Such attempts have often been prompted by the belief that the lack of coherence is inadvertent or thoughtless, an "unintended consequence." But coordination efforts reveal the extent to which interest groups are responsible for the chaos: modifying programs and reorganizing agencies invariably founder on the objections of interest groups. The chaos and inconsistency that mark children's programs—the lack of a real "children's policy" or a "comprehensive family policy"—are not accidental; they are the result of a state which responds to interest group pressures, one which is unable to proceed according to clearly specified principles.

The best evidence of the failure of conventional politics for children has been the dismal record of White House Conferences on Children. Meeting every decade since 1909, the conferences have regularly convened a variety of advocates and professionals to establish agendas for children, with participation becoming increasingly broad in the conferences of 1960, 1970, and the 1980 White House Conference on Families. At every conference, the same shining principles have emerged: the elimination of discrimination, equality of educational opportunity, the elimination of poverty, the need for parental love and strong families.[31] Even the 1980 White House Conference on Families, nearly torn apart by the efforts of the conservative "profamily" forces to dominate the conference, still managed to produce recommendations consistent with those of past conferences, including more help for the handicapped, "family-oriented personnel policies" like flexible and part-time work, support for full employment, the elimination of employment discrimination, adequate welfare assistance, and more public funding for day care.[32] Yet—with the possible exception of the first conference, which played an important role in promoting mothers' pensions—the effort to reach a consensus on public priorities for children has never had any real effect on government policies. As one lobbyist forecast in 1969, with complete accuracy:

> We are going to have a White House Conference in 1970 on [children and] youth. We have had one every ten years. I can write the resolutions for them now, because they will be the same ones as passed in 1909. . . . You can roll eggs on the White House lawn and it will have the same effect on legislation.[33]

In part, the failures of the White House Conferences are due to the indifference or powerlessness of their sponsors: Richard Nixon in 1970 had already established his social policy agenda and was not to be swayed, and Jimmy Carter was in no political position to make any but the most pitiful efforts to implement the recommendations of the 1980 White House Conference on Families. For the 1981 White House Conference on Children, President Reagan has replaced a national conference with state conferences, a sure way to guarantee public anonymity. Aside from being unable to overcome the indifference of particular presidents, the conferences have never fulfilled their goal of establishing the agenda for the coming decade. The division of children's advocates into splintered interest groups is partly responsible: although all can agree on basic principles, few are willing to abandon their own special concerns to press for a cause different from their own, and so the child care lobby, the mental health lobby, the child welfare lobby, the education lobby, and the hunger lobby all go their own ways.[34] Since unified political pressure from the community of child advocates proves impossible to sustain, the recommendations of decennial conferences are left as collections of well-meant principles that have no power whatsoever to motivate legislation. The visible results are therefore symbolic, like the response of Carter to the 1980 conference in proposing an end to the "marriage tax" and in creating an Office for Families. The conferences become celebrations of children and family life without any consequences, testimony to the failure of self-interested and adversarial democracy for children.

Unfortunately, the limits of interest group politics on behalf of children have not yet led people to reconsider the nature of interest group democracy. Instead, efforts to enfranchise children continue to generate still more interest groups working on their behalf, with mediocre success. Efforts to organize parents on behalf of their children, for example, have been effective only around single issues like busing or sex education. Organizing parents as a general purpose advocacy group would mean rejecting the ideal of the private family and private responsibility for childrearing. Such organizing is also impossible as long as parents use public institutions on behalf of their own children and view other people's children as hostile competitors. Without a collective sense of the value of children—"public love"—and without the notion that public institutions ought to serve collective rather than individual ends, parent groups inevitably deteriorate into class or racial self-interest organizations. Groups representing minority children, like the Black Child Development Association, groups organized on behalf of low-spending school districts and groups supporting high-spending districts, groups promoting busing and those opposed to it, all tend to replicate the existing inequalities among families and to reinforce the practice of self-interested and fragmented politics in which some children consistently lose. In a society so dominated by private responsibility for childrearing, without any collective concern for children, it has proved impossible to develop long-lived, general advocacy groups. In a system of politics which degrades humanitarian and altruistic motives, disinterested children's groups will continue to be relatively powerless.

The recognition that children's interests have been consistently underrepresented led in the 1960s and 1970s to still another approach, in which the state itself was to foster the development of children's interest groups.[35] The creation of state offices for children, intended to be advocates as well as administrative agencies, and federal mandates requiring citizen participation in government programs like Head Start and Title I compensatory education are examples of the public promotion of interest groups. The problem remains how to use state power to create groups that can represent children's interests more powerfully against other, better established groups. The record of state offices for children does not warrant much optimism since most of them have remained relatively powerless or have become part of the government bureaucracy without a substantial constituency to back their efforts; the creation of a state office without a corresponding interest group has been pointless. While parent participation requirements have in some cases fostered active political groups—notably in Head Start—in other cases mandated citizen groups have merely been legitimizers for professionals and may even have drained political energy better spent elsewhere.[36] Even success can be a failure: one of the most successful interest groups fostered by parent participation requirements—the Mississippi Child Development Group, which extended its efforts to other kinds of organizing among poor blacks—incurred the wrath of Senator James Eastland of Mississippi and almost caused the demise of Head Start.[37]

Establishing more complete representation of children remains an intractable problem, then, within our current structure of interest group politics. Since self-interested and adversarial politics also thwarts the development of principled goals and their systematic implementation, it will remain impossible to represent the interests of disenfranchised children by appealing to moral and humanitarian principles. The concept of the "best interests of the child" will remain elusive since it is impossible to begin the serious political discussion that would allow such a concept to emerge, and such an exercise will remain pointless because any consensus would still have to battle with self-interest. Indeed, as long as the outcome of interest groups opposing one another is the only conception of democracy, the very idea of "the public interest" or "the welfare of children" as public goals is absurd, as "realists" like David Truman have often told us. To improve the representation of children's interests, it will be necessary to reconsider our political arrangements, to think of democracy as a set of institutions every bit as variable as economic institutions and other public programs and correspondingly in need of self-conscious reform.[38] The likelihood of developing new structures of democracy quickly is less important than the goal: if we are to have a state capable of principled politics, then we will have to remake the political process of the democratic state. Until we do that, we will have to remain content with a state whose political processes invariably leave all children underrepresented and compromise our public commitments to children through the battles of self-interest.

113

Professional Power and Its Consequences

Among those who speak publicly for children, professionals tend to have the greatest stature and influence. Professional groups with obvious self-interest have been able to form cohesive, unified interest groups, in contrast to other groups that tend to be held together with the weaker glue of altruism. In part, the power of professionals comes from their importance within the public institutions of childrearing. Professionals have considerable power over the lives of children on a daily basis, in addition to their political power, and they often define the best interests of children. To understand the public voices speaking on behalf of children, we must therefore analyze the ambiguities of professional power.

The development of children's institutions in the nineteenth and twentieth centuries simultaneously fostered the major and minor professional groups treating children: first teachers, then juvenile court workers and probation officers, social workers, and child development experts. In the assertion of public responsibilities for children, the relationship between the state and professionals was symbiotic: each reflected the presumed benevolence of the other, each relied on the other for legitimacy. The professional claims of expertise and competence were a necessary corollary of *parens patriae:* those supporting public institutions for children have relied on professional claims of benevolence and service "in the best interests of the child" to guarantee that state intervention would improve the welfare of children rather than harming them. As one juvenile court judge asserted in explaining the effectiveness of the court, the professional "becomes practically a member of the family and teaches them lessons of cleanliness and decency, of truth and integrity."[39] Particularly since the progressive era, with its characteristic emphasis on scientific rationality, the professional reliance on expertise has promised that the decisions of parent-surrogates would be correct, even incontrovertible. The lofty claims of professionals have always worked to mute possible conflicts: those parents fighting teachers or juvenile court workers on behalf of their own children have found it difficult to argue with professionals, who are more educated and have claims to special competence. In every way professionalism has been consistent with the premises of children's institutions: professionals have promised a special concern for children, superiority to parents, and an ability to reduce social conflicts.

In turn, the expansion of children's institutions has provided greater power to professionals, as they have gained control over children's institutions and pressed claims to special power and status for their own benefit.

Professionals have also justified their own existence in terms of *parens patriae,* claiming that parental limitations require expert intervention if children are to thrive. Professionals have thus become the leading advocates of expanded state responsibility, stressing both the state's duty on behalf of children and the inadequacy of parents as arguments for the greater use of professionals. Professionalism and *parens patriae* have become intertwined: expansion of the state has meant expanded authority for professionals as more competent than parents, while professionalism has in turn justified intervention into "failed" families in the "best interest of the child."

While professional power has been justified by its claims of benevolence and expertise, these promises have not always materialized, and professionalism itself has been much disputed. During the 1960s liberal and radical critics challenged the class and racial biases of professionals and complained that professionals were selfishly frustrating reform of the institutions they dominated; groups interested in greater parent participation in the schools attacked the tendency of professionals to treat parents as second-class citizens and to limit their participation.[40] Some critics like Christopher Lasch and Jacques Donzelot have interpreted professionals as agents of social control only, "policing the family" and usurping its functions.[41] These attacks have been joined in the 1970s and 1980s by criticism from right-wing critics complaining that professionals—especially teachers—have undermined parental prerogatives over their children. The groundswell of conservative reaction against the Child and Family Services Act of 1975 contained a strong protest against "rearing children by the government,"[42] and Senator Paul Laxalt's Family Protection Act of 1979—also a right-wing document—contained various guarantees of parental rights over educators. To be sure, professionals are not a homogeneous group, and public perception of different professionals varies: conservatives have been most critical of "human service professionals" and teachers, and more respectful of doctors; liberals have distrusted teachers and social workers, and have sometimes argued that doctors—the model professionals—and the medical establishment are inequitable, inefficient, and callous. Teachers and social workers have borne a disproportionate amount of abuse, while public health nurses and librarians have rarely been seen as villains. Still, the trend of the last two decades has been an increasing distrust of professionals, bringing simultaneously a healthy suspicion of professional claims and an overwrought tendency to blame professionals for every ill of modern life.

The challenges to professionals reflect, first and foremost, an uncertainty over what professionals can or should do in children's lives. One basic reason for this uncertainty involves the heart of professional status: the claims to expertise and competence. In contrast to medicine and law, the "high professions," childrearing has always been the province of "amateurs." Indeed, the superiority of amateur parenting itself has a well-developed ideology embedded in domestic ideals and the principle of private responsibility. Since the mid-nineteenth century, the notion of expertise as essential for childrearing has clashed with the assumption that parents—especially mothers—are instinctively capable of rearing their children. Domestic ideals have asserted the superiority of "natural" mothers in caring for children because of the power of the mother-child bond. The very notion of "professional childrearing" is therefore a contradiction in terms:[43] the suspicion that parents know best how to rear children always constitutes a challenge to the claims of professionals, even in situations where parents turn to professionals for help. As one teacher perceived the feelings of parents:

> . . . mostly mothers feel that their areas of competence are very much similar to those of the teacher. In fact, they feel they know their child better than anyone else and that the teacher doesn't possess any special field of authority and expertise. Especially now when mothering is *learned* through books, when educated mothers are reading books about child care, child development, "good" parenting. . . .[44]

Simultaneously, professionals have suggested that parenting is too critical to remain a natural process. A vast literature giving parents expert advice has transformed childrearing into a highly self-conscious and socially manipulated process, reducing the emphasis on the "natural" competence of parents. Every conceivable aspect of childrearing has been the subject of expert dicta—permissiveness, restrictiveness, discipline, toilet training, affection and attention, sleeping, feeding, masturbation—under the dual presumption that there is a best way of raising children and that parents without expert help may be inadequate to that task. In fact, professionals have claimed that parents could too easily and completely undermine even the best professional advice. As one prominent childrearing guide has stated:

> If a family does its job well, the professional can then provide effective training. If not, there may be little the professional can do to save the child from mediocrity. . . . From all I have learned about the education and development of young children, I have come to the conclusion that most American families get their children through the first six to eight months of life reasonably well in terms of education and development; but I believe that no more than ten percent at most manage to get their children through the eight- to thirty-six month

age period as well educated as they could and should be. . . . Given the importance of the parental role in early childhood development, it is ironic that so few parents are prepared for parenthood.[45]

As ways of claiming superiority over parents, professionals have invoked the experimental results of child development research, generated a "science of teaching," and developed supposedly scientific instruments like IQ measures and achievement tests. Professionals have tried to depoliticize knowledge, making it seem rational, precise, and neutral with respect to class, race, and sex. Often, these efforts have generated new anxieties in parents, as one teacher remarked:

> The discrepancies between the realities of their daily lives and the "experts'" words of advice and warning make them feel great ambivalence about their competence as mothers. The more they know about the potential psychoemotional and intellectual dangers of childrearing, the more inadequate and fearful they feel about their mothering and their child's healthy development.[46]

Thus professionals have both affirmed the importance of parenting, especially in stressing the mother-child bond and the dangers of any form of maternal deprivation,[47] and have undermined the place of parents—often unwittingly—by the supposition that they possess knowledge and skills superior to those of parents.

Yet the validity of professional expertise has always been ambiguous at best. The criticism of the 1960s and 1970s clarified the class and racial biases of professionals and the middle-class standards of child development theory. The sexual bias of Freudian theory and conventional writing on the maternal bond have been challenged by feminists, and the imprecision and biases of tests have been debated. The disagreements among childrearing experts and the shifts in thinking over time have contributed to the feeling that much "knowledge" about children is not scientific and enduring but is instead the codification of childrearing practices—usually those of white, middle-class, educated parents—that themselves vary over time and among families. The shifts in what is considered "appropriate" childrearing and the challenges to professionals reveal that parents and professionals can have different and conflicting bases to their claims over children, with professionals standing on claims of expertise and parents asserting their natural rights over their children. As long as the expertise of professionals remains uncertain and can be countered by parental perceptions of what is best for their child, professionals and parents will conflict and will remain unsure of their status. As one teacher described her dilemma:

You have to be very careful what you say about parents, and you have to be very careful what you say to parents. And also you have to be very careful sometimes what you say to children, because they go back to the parents and say something that might be offensive.... [especially with black parents] I have to chose my words very carefully and I have to make sure that I'm not degrading the child in any way or patronizing the mother.... I don't know whether this is always true, but it seems that quite a number of the black parents tend to take this antagonistic attitude towards the school.[48]

Childrearing professionals have consistently responded to the ambiguity of their expertise by denigrating parental abilities, reasserting their superiority and the "scientific" basis of their knowledge. The teacher who proclaimed her superiority to the "immoral" parents of poor children; the settlement house worker who asserted that "slum babies" were better off with her than at home; the parent educator who affirms that she could be a better mother than those she teaches; the pediatrician who condemns parents for not listening to him, all are examples of professionals who are arrogant and disdainful of parents. In the extreme case of handicapped children, John Gliedman and William Roth have argued that professionals treat parents themselves like patients, as a way to exert professional dominance and dampen parental challenges.[49] In the ensuing battles with parents, professionals can then rely on their expertise to confirm their superiority. As one early childhood educator justified her request for more in-service discussion of child development theory, "It's not that these discussions really help me with my teaching—but they're really useful for dealing with parents ... they make me 'authoritative.' When they challenge me on something I'll just throw [Eric] Erikson at them."[50]

In the continuing struggle to convince parents of professional superiority, class and racial biases have played their inevitable role. In part, personal prejudices are a factor, since most professionals are middle-income, middle-class, and white, and they carry the norms and biases of their class and race with them. But there are more subtle origins as well. The superiority that professionals claim over all parents is more easily asserted over poor, lower-class, minority parents, who are usually considered to be "failures" under the assumptions of *parens patriae*. The differences in education levels reinforce the status differences between middle-class professionals and their lower-class clients, making it more difficult for them to challenge professional expertise and reinforcing the feelings among professionals that they know better than do lower-class parents what is best for their children.

Bigotry, demeaning attitudes toward parents, and cynical approaches to knowledge are not ubiquitious, of course. Countless professionals are dedicated, sensitive, and humanitarian individuals who provide valuable services to parents and children. However, the complaints of both left-wing and right-wing critics reflect the feelings that the professionals have all too often trampled the prerogatives of parents and demeaned their real abilities. The problem is that the tendency to demean parents is inherent in the dominant conception of professions: we demand that professionals be superior to their clients by virtue of their special knowledge or experience, and we provide in the doctrine of *parens patriae* further support for their assertion of superiority. Indeed, if professionals cannot be considered superior, then we have difficulty justifying their intervention into the lives of children. We place on professionals the responsibility to convince parents and the public that they know considerably more about children then anyone else, and then resent the fact that they assert their superiority in ways which are unconvincing, prejudiced, or demeaning.

The ambiguous nature of childrearing professionals is also a product of the settings within which most of them work. Public institutions like schools, welfare agencies, family courts, and child care centers must "save" and rehabilitate the child but must also control the child so that he or she does not disrupt social stability and conventional norms. Professionals have tried to minimize the conflicts by asserting that professional interests, institutional stability, and the child's best interest are congruent, which is sometimes true. For example, teachers have called for smaller classes and higher salaries in the best interests of their pupils, and welfare workers have pressed for more funds to increase grants and improve services to their clients. Professionals also tend to stress the rehabilitative aspects of their work because they are more consistent with the professional ethic of service to the child. As one juvenile corrections worker described her role:

> I don't see this position as corrections as much [as a] social work role. . . . I accept the fact that my decision [is important] in whether [or not] a girl comes to this locked setting which she sees as a punishment. I can accept that it is a form of protection and for the girl. But I see [the correctional institution] as being very treatment-oriented and not just a closed placement.[51]

No matter how professionals wish to see themselves, the institutional pressures on them are enormous and often conflict with the ethic of service. Professionals are simultaneously our child savers and our police; they are social advocates for children, fighting to address the greatest social problems—illiteracy, poverty, poor health, the lack of employment opportunities, even neglect and abuse—but they are given insubstantial resources and told to economize. Teachers must regularly make decisions about which children to send to underfunded enrichment programs, case-workers must alleviate the poverty of welfare families while keeping public costs low by minimizing overpayments and error rates, and policy makers must weigh the merits of serving more children through lower-cost social services versus serving fewer children with better services. In addition to the fiscal pressures, professionals are caught in the contradictory goals of public institutions. Those working in the juvenile justice system call for more flexible rehabilitation programs while they are being pressured to exert tighter controls over youth; social workers press for more programs and funds for their clients while their daily activities are concerned with minimizing state outlays; teachers espouse individualized instruction and developing the child to the limit of his or her capacities while racial, sexual, and class-based stereotyping and stratification in schools subvert these goals. Frustration levels and "burn-out" rates are high, testimony to the insuperable dilemmas of these "street-level bureaucrats." As one social worker described the constraints:

> You know, the basic frustration of the caseworker is that you can only help your client's material needs. What they really ought to have is help in getting rehabilitated, in taking a big step along the way toward becoming better citizens. But you have sixty cases to take care of and a mountain of paperwork. The department sets up no program of effective rehabilitation. And it seems to have an attitude like a vindictive parent. It's tough to do the kind of job you'd like to do.[52]

While the contradictions in what childrearing professionals do have often been ascribed to selfishness or a lack of commitment, those contradictions are more appropriately seen as institutional; as long as childrearing professionals serve in underfunded public institutions that control children as well as serve them, the professional ethic of benevolent service will always be compromised.

The conflicting purposes of children's institutions are also responsible for the curious fact that professionals have been attacked by both the right and the left. Conservatives, hostile to the very existence of welfare programs, have attacked "human service professionals" for characteristics that liberals find admirable; as one right-wing attack on the liberal "human services orthodoxy" complained about its lack of concern for the public purse and moral standards:

> The central tenets of the human service orthodoxy are flexibility and responsiveness. According to the orthodox approach, we must accord people the freedom to define their own needs and the conditions under which assistance can be provided. We must not impose any restrictive ideas of morality upon recipi-

ents, and we should not set eligibility requirements which might deprive people in need.[53]

In contrast, liberals have charged social workers with doing too little for their clients, for serving as police, for being inflexible, unresponsive, and bearers of conventional ideas about family and work which are repressive because the poor have so few choices. Conservatives have attacked teachers for their liberal ideas about integration, sex education, and compensatory education, while liberals have charged them with perpetuating class and racial biases in the schools. At one time or another everyone has criticized professionals for interfering in family life, while different kinds of professionals have been entrusted, *faute de mieux,* with alleviating problems involving the most intimate phenomena—child abuse and neglect, wife abuse, divorce—which have been consistently in the public eye. As long as we freight our public institutions with conflicting goals, those who work within these institutions will remain subjected to conflicting pressures and contradictory criticisms.

The institutional location of childrearing professionals creates still another dilemma: In contrast to doctors and lawyers, who (until quite recently) have usually been independent entrepreneurs, most professionals involved with children are identified with *public* institutions: teachers with the public schools, social workers with welfare programs, correctional and probation officers with the juvenile justice system. Their status— their very existence—has been bound up with the financial health and public acceptance of their institutions. Unlike professionals operating in private markets, "public professionals" cannot seek to establish market power as a way of gaining greater stature and control, because they do not operate in conventional markets.[54] Instead, they have sought to expand children's institutions as the most appropriate means of obtaining power, status, job security, and higher incomes. To achieve these gains, childrearing professionals must secure public support, mobilizing their clients to agitate for expanding funding or to fight against budget cuts. The mobilization of clients is risky business, however, because it means that professionals are dependent on their clients rather than their clients being dependent on them. As a price for such support, clients may demand a say in how the institution is run and how the services are provided. As sociologist Carole Joffe puts it, parents who become "overly involved" may "pose a threat to the political order of the school. If parents could in fact run the school by themselves, there would be no need for teachers."[55]

Childrearing professionals have also tried to control the internal workings of their institutions as part of their professional prerogatives, but here too their location in public institutions has limited their efforts. The archetypical professions, doctors and lawyers, have been able to control almost every aspect of medical and legal institutions, and other professions have emulated them. In Carole Joffe's words, "the profession, ideally, is mandated to define the public interest in matters relating to its particular speciality. In this sense professionals not only perform services but also dictate policy."[56] Thus teachers have tried to define education, and social workers to specify the appropriate treatment of the poor. More specifically, by establishing the rules and methods by which their institutions operate and by controlling the procedures which declare a child (or family) a success or a failure, childrearing professionals have enhanced their own control and reaffirmed their superiority over parents and clients. But in contrast to doctors and lawyers, who tend to dominate private institutions insulated from democratic participation, teachers, social workers, policemen and probation officers, and early childhood educators work in public institutions subject to some measure of democratic control.[57] Even where parents have no pretentions to participate directly in children's institutions, the legitimacy of public participation has limited the power of professionals. Challenges to school teachers in the community control movement provide one clear example of this; community challenges to juvenile court proceedings and negotiations between parents and professionals over the content of day care provide others.[58] Legislative discussions to foster competitors to public institutions, as in debates over funding for private education, and public decisions about professional credentials indicate other ways the autonomy of childrearing professionals is circumscribed. The many possibilities for public control have prevented professionals in children's institutions from enjoying the power typical of doctors and lawyers: they have remained semi-professionals, with limited autonomy, status, and income, rather than full professionals.[59]

The dilemmas of public professionals have meant that parents are both partners and antagonists.[60] Parents and professionals are partners in a variety of ways. They share responsibilities for children; since they are likely to be more effective when they agree than when they conflict, it is in everyone's interests—especially the child's—for there to be agreement. Professionals need parents and clients for political support, to pressure for expanded funding, and to legitimize their special roles. But parents and professionals are antagonists, too. The claims of expertise and ability justifying the special role of professionals have depended on the assertion of superiority over parents. This by itself has tended to distance parents from children's institutions, as have the efforts of some professionals to limit outside involvement in the institutions they run. The efforts of teachers to limit the influence of parents, the impregnability of welfare offices to recipients trying to discover the rules for themselves, the resistance of the juvenile justice system to community participation, and the resistance to cooperation with parents when parent participation is required in child care and educational programs are all examples of the use of professional status to distance parents. The frequent experience of professionals as antagonists, rooted in the basic conception of professionalism, means that conflict between parents and professionals is always latent.

Under certain conditions, the elements of partnership vanish and conflict between parents and professionals becomes open and bitter. Although the prerogatives of professionals in childrearing institutions can usually be challenged, some parents and clients are not in a strong position to do so. Those parents who have few alternatives to public institutions—who have, for example, little choice but to turn to welfare or little chance to change their location for better schools—are at a disadvantage compared to middle-class parents who have greater power of "exit" from public institutions they loathe; the lower-class and minority parents who are uneducated and unsophisticated about bureaucratic institutions and must suffer the disdain of professionals are at a disadvantage compared to the middle-class parents who can more readily negotiate with professionals. When parents are both trapped in public institutions and do not accept professionals as especially knowledgeable or as beneficial to their children, the potential for open and continuing conflict is real. Community control of schools, community resistance to police and juvenile court activities, the organization of welfare recipients to open welfare institutions to greater public scrutiny, and the battles over busing, textbooks, and sex education have all followed the same pattern: parents with few alternatives for their children have denied the claims of institutional benevolence and professional expertise, and the challenges to public institutions have been direct and rancorous.

Because of the dilemmas of public professionals and their potential conflicts with parents and clients, it has been impossible to answer clearly the question of when professionals speak in the interests of children. When parents and professionals conflict, the choice between them is a devil's dilemma. Sometimes the conflicts of professionals with parents reflect the legitimate role of professionals in weaning children away from their parents into the larger social world, exposing children to a wider range of values and experiences than their parents know; this role may generate resistance from parents who resent the options schools and other extrafamilial influences provide and are ambivalent about their children growing up.[61] Sometimes the conflicts represent the justifiable exercise of expertise: *in extremis*, the cases of pediatricians gaining custody of children from Jehovah's Witnesses and Christian Scientists who do not believe in certain medical procedures illustrate cases where professionals do speak in the child's interest. But just as often the expert claims of professionals are themselves ambiguous, or mask more self-serving efforts to gain power over parents, or reflect the biases against the poor embedded in *parens patriae*. As long as professionals argue from a basis of expertise which is suspect and not always disinterested, and parents rest their claims on their more intimate concern for their child and the presumption of parental responsibility, they will conflict in a variety of areas where the claims of each side are impossible to evaluate.

The conflict with public institutions and the professionals in them has generated a hostility toward professionals which has sometimes declared that professionals can do no good for children and that the solution is to eliminate professionalism.[62] A more appropriate view is that professionals have always had distinctly ambiguous consequences for children because of the nature of professionalism itself. The attractiveness of expertise is undeniable. Many parents benefit from educative, supportive, and thera- peutic services, and the proliferation of childrearing advice literature and various self-help groups suggests that professionals can often be helpful in assuaging the anxieties of parents. Quite apart from the fact that few parents have the time to teach their children, teaching requires some skills that—while not the monopoly of trained teachers—are enhanced by training and experience. While the scientific basis of child development research is unclear, it at least provides a closeness of observation and a breadth of experience which individual parents cannot hope to match. At the same time, the attempt to establish professional superiority has often worked to distance parents from the rearing of their own children, to generate conflict even where that is not in the best interests of children.

Given a genuine ambivalence toward professionals, the appropriate re- sponse to the abuses is not to abolish all expertise but to redefine the nature of professionalism. In the wake of the sharp criticism of profession- alism in the 1960s, a few small groups have experimented with different concepts of professionalism, and in other cases clients have pushed profes- sionals toward new power relations. The efforts to develop "new profes- sionals" generally recognize that expertise is not absolute or scientific but is value-laden and contingent, that knowledge can be shared with parents rather than hoarded and mystified, and that professionals need not dis- tance themselves from clients. The development of the Child Develop- ment Associate is the most formal example of the attempts to develop a new style of professional with a different kind of credential. In place of formal schooling, the Child Development Associate credential requires experience, and it evaluates competence through an on-the-job review process which includes parents rather than relying on grades. The Child Development Associate acknowledges that traditional professional preparation is particularly inappropriate for child care, where a close relation with parents is necessary, and that a credentialing process that includes parents is more consistent with the goal of parent participation than is counting course credits.[63] Different groups of teachers and social workers, often considered radical fringes, have tried to open up the schools to parents and welfare offices to recipients and to make their institutions more democratic and participatory. Even in medicine and law, efforts to incorporate a sense of identification with clients have begun. Within the legal profession, the development of a public interest bar with public funding through the Legal Services Corporation has encouraged the identification of lawyers with their clients on political and moral grounds, in contrast to the conventional bar in which legal services are purchased. The concept of community medicine, with responsibility to a community in addition to professional norms, has generated different kinds of training programs.[64] In various ways citizen pressure has begun to modify some professions. The requirements of citizen participation in federal programs, as in Head Start and compensatory education, are efforts to alter the power relations of public institutions so that professionals must change the ways they behave with parents and other citizens. Greater patient control has transformed birthing practices, which under pressure from the women's movement have become more natural processes in which mothers and fathers have greater participation and decision-making power; the development of medical review boards is still another recognition that professional power must be modified by granting power to clients.[65]

New forms of professionalism are barely visible, particularly at a time when increasing educational levels have forced the licensing of more occupations. Nevertheless, they do indicate that the conventional model of professionals is not inevitable: it is possible to have special knowledge and training without at the same time using that special status to exclude parents and clients. For children's institutions, such an approach is the only way to reap the benefits of expertise without risking the specter of "rearing children by the government" or exacerabating conflicts between parents and professionals.

To understand the possibilities and difficulties of redefining professionalism, we must remember that the basic dilemmas of professionals express the larger contradictions of the state's relation to children. Childrearing experts have come to personify the state's relation to the child, with all its possibilities for good as well as evil, for benevolence as well as control, for providing greater equality as well as replicating inequality. They are given public responsibility for children in a society that still defines child-rearing as a private responsibility. They intervene under the claim that parents have failed but are limited in their ability to overcome the problems children suffer. While they express humanitarian concern for children, they must justify their actions in instrumental and cost-efficient terms and must assure that the controlling goals of children's institutions are met. Professionals are responsible for overcoming structural inequalities in the pursuit of equality of opportunity, but they have the power to do little more than replicate existing inequalities. Within children's institutions they are often pulled apart by the private use of public institutions: parents demand that professionals do right by their own children, even at the expense of other people's children. As the personification of these contradictions, professionals have been easy and obvious targets of abuse, as well as the focus of whatever optimism we can muster about public responsibility for children. They are consistently condemned for being inadequate and still urged to do better.[66]

The problems of professionals, then, are the general problems of the state's relationship to children. It will not be possible to resolve these problems simply by eliminating professionals or by making marginal improvements in professional training. The central issue remains the same as it has been for all children's institutions: to carry out our public responsibilities toward children and to fulfill the promises of benevolence and service which professionals have always offered, we will have to revise our fondest myths about children and our most deeply-rooted institutions. Until we do so, the political representation of children's interests will remain incomplete and contradictory, subject to the familiar limitations of *parens patriae*, corrupted by self-interest and the compromise of moral principle, and undermined by the structural inequalities that generate so many problems for children in the first place.

PART TWO

CHILDREN'S INSTITUTIONS

5

Public Responsibilities

and Private Gains:

The Conflicts within Schooling

AMERICANS hold great expectations for public education, yet they are continually disappointed with their schools. They support public schools more enthusiastically than any other children's institution, yet many have rejected them for private alternatives. Public schools are open to all children without the assumptions of failure and deviance so typical of other children's institutions; indeed, the historic commitment to universality has been the most distinctive characteristic of American education. Yet this universality is deceiving: many children have been denied access to education, and the class, racial, and sexual divisions within the educational system have mocked the ideal of equal educational opportunity. At its best public education incorporates familial, local, and national values, but the differences among these values have often been the source of conflict. Originally defined as agents of the common good and designed to enhance social responsibility, the public schools have more and more come to be evaluated in individual terms, by how well they enhance personal gain.[1]

Of the different tensions within American public schooling, the conflict between universality and the reality of class stratification has been especially powerful. Even as Horace Mann argued for universal public schooling as the "balance wheel of democracy," what aspired to be a homogeneous institution was divided by class and race. At best, nonwhites were segregated; more often they were denied any schooling at all. For lower-class children, schools stood *in loco parentis* and were prepared to provide the personal traits necessary for stable work performance and social peace. For middle-class children, public schools extended rather than ne-gated parental influences and were often mechanisms of individual advancement. From the very beginning, then, mechanisms of class and racial segregation undermined the common school ideal. As schooling became more vocationally oriented in the early twentieth century, the conflict between the promise of universality and the reality of class stratification intensified. The schools promised equality of opportunity at the same time that they prepared students for an inegalitarian society, in part by differentiating students in vocational tracks and ability groupings. The tensions could be minimized as long as people believed that educational achievement reflected the merit of individual children. But evidence that school attainment depended upon a child's economic background, race, and sex helped undermine the assumption that schools evaluated students on merit and in turn generated challenges to the ways schools are organized and to the school's legitimacy in reproducing social stratification.

Conflicts over schooling have also reflected the differences between the public purposes and the private goals of schooling. The public responsibilities are vast: developing human capacities, creating a common set of values, preparing a literate and critical citizenry, providing equality of opportunity, moving children and youth from their families into the larger social world, and serving as the prime avenue to occupation, income, and status. In their managerial roles, however, parents have assumed that public schooling should be used for private ends: to ensure their own ethnic or religious values, to reaffirm childrearing as a familial rather than a social responsibility, and above all to ensure the success of their own children. The clash of public purposes and private goals has meant that public responsibilities are always likely to be diluted. The values of a liberal education have been undermined by vocational goals and universal literacy ignored because it threatens a class society. Equality of opportunity has fallen before the pressure of parents seeking advancement for their own children. At the same time that we look to the schools for collective solutions to social and economic problems, individual parents work to make sure the schools serve primarily their own children.

The mixture of public and private goals has meant that the public schools have always had peculiar and ambiguous relationships to families. Few parents can afford to ignore public education, for in the schools the most deeply held values are supported or challenged, and a child's vocation and adult success are likely to be determined. Most parents have thus been forced to embrace public schooling even when they are ambivalent about its treatment of their own and other people's children. Often, the stress has been too great, and conflict has erupted—in controversies over religion and science, segregation and desegregation, IQ testing and vocational education.[2] The conflicting expectations that schools should both replace parents and act as their agents have placed parents in an ambivalent relationship to public education, as both partners and antagonists. Teachers are supposed to work with parents and yet, especially where parents are considered inadequate, educators have assumed their superiority to parents.

Despite their claims to universality, then, the public schools embody the contradictions common to other children's institutions. In fact, the power of the schools comes from this special combination: the norms of universal access and public responsibility ensure their importance to all children and all citizens, while biased treatment and the power of private goals assure that the schools perpetuate the divisions of class, race, and sex, and control some children rather than educate them. This combination has made conflict endemic to American education. The severity of protest has reached new heights in the last two decades. As the occupational dimensions of schooling became more pronounced, as economic growth diminished, and as the struggle for places in the educational hierarchy intensified, the contradictory purposes of schools could no longer be muted. The resulting conflicts—between minorities and whites, middle class and working class, city dwellers and suburbanites, Catholics and non-Catholics, students and teachers, men and women—shifted the emphasis of educational reform. By the late seventies, the historic expectations that schools could overcome inequality and provide opportunity for all were countered by claims that too many Americans were "overeducated." Efforts to equalize educational opportunity—through integration, compensatory programs, equalized financing, and special admissions—are being contested or dismantled, replaced by expanded subsidies to middle-class students and a retreat from public schooling itself.

In the reactions of the 1970s and early 1980s, American education has been caught in its most fundamental contradiction. It aspires to use public resources to enhance egalitarian goals, but those in privileged positions are unwilling to allow public responsibility to threaten their own—often insecure—positions. While Americans want to use the schools for private gains of their own children, they resist the gains of other people's children, fearing they will come at the expense of their own. As long as parents use public institutions for private ends, the public responsibilities of

131

the schools will remain embattled and compromised, and the promise of public education will remain distorted by the demands of individualistic ends.

Vocational Goals and the Dual Roles of Public Schooling

The tensions between the public responsibilities and the private uses of schooling were less readily apparent in colonial America, when schooling was unsystematic and limited for almost all children. Schools reinforced basic literacy and religious values taught in families, and some schools taught occupational skills, but formal schooling was decidedly secondary to more informal ways of learning. The growth of entrepreneurial capitalism in the nineteenth century, which generated class heterogeneity at the same time that immigration made cities ethnically heterogeneous, increased the importance of schooling. Americans turned to public education to build a Protestant-republican country, to contain the social disruptions of entrepreneurial capitalism, and to prepare youth for occupational success. Private ends were never absent, but in the dramatic expansion of public education in the mid-nineteenth century, public purposes overwhelmingly predominated.[3] The Boston School Committee described the social purposes of the schools succinctly in 1847: "Our schools are our hope—we look to them, and their effects upon the intelligence of our citizens, as the Ark of Safety to our Institutions."[4]

Even as schools were conceived as the central institution to socialize children in a new and shifting world, conceptions of socialization took on class distinctions. Educating poor children became synonymous with overcoming the childrearing deficiencies of poor families—"nurseries of indolence, debauchery, and intemperance."[5] Since so many lower-class children were immigrants, the antidote to lower-class disorder was to "draw in the children of alien parentage with others, and assimilate them to the native born." As one prominent educator remarked in 1857, in arguing for the further expansion of public education:

[The censuses] show an adulteration of our population annually to an appalling extent, and yet we are boasting of our schools as if they were more than sufficient to remedy every evil that impends. . . . if you would save your institutions, teach these [immigrant] children.[6]

Nowhere was the assumption that poor parents failed to socialize their children more apparent than in the debates about teaching the work ethic. All children needed to learn how to work, but some needed it more than others, particularly immigrants who came from precapitalistic, preindustrial rural areas where patterns of work differed from those required by wage labor. Immigrant adults would learn the new rhythms—governed by the clock rather than the sun, demanding punctuality, regularity, docility, deferred gratification, and subservience to work routines—directly at the workplace. But for their children, the school would be the central agency of transmission.[7] By the late nineteenth century the internal procedures of urban public schools mimicked the workplace in their adherence to routine, insistence on punctuality, hierarchies of authority, and rote learning, providing by example and long exposure the necessary work-related values.

Middle-class children too had to learn the ethic of work. Late nineteenth-century educational reformers complained about permissive middle-class childrearing patterns. The ideal family sustained by particularistic and affectionate relationships was a liability in a world of universalistic norms, impersonal authority, interpersonal competition, and ruthless entrepreneurial activity. But for middle-class children the emphasis was less on the school as a replacement for family life than as its extension or a mild corrective of some of its deficiencies. The enhanced role of schooling in middle-class life was due in part to the transformations in the occupational structure, especially the growth of professions and careers tied to educational certification and the decline of inheritance in passing on occupations. Middle-class families able to forgo their children's earnings allowed them to stay in school longer; the advantages that middle-class children once received directly through inheritance or joining the family firm continued indirectly through more schooling and access to middle-class occupations. Schooling for the middle class became a mediator that eased the transition between the private family divorced from production and the public world of vocational achievement.[8]

By the end of the nineteenth century, schooling had come to stand *in loco parentis* for all children, to remedy the different deficiencies of both poor and middle-class parents. In differentiating students by class and race while claiming universality and promising to mold one country out of a heterogeneous population, nineteenth-century public education established the duality that has been elaborated ever since: the schools replicated class and racial differences while their advantages—the promise of upward mobility—were theoretically available to all; they served individual ends (especially for middle-class children) while trumpeting the social goals of common values and social peace. The balancing act did not always work, as challenges from blacks wanting access to public schools and from Catholics wanting to establish their own schools indicated. In addition, as schools became more vocationally oriented, they began to degrade older conceptions of liberal education on which they were founded. The goals of schooling which Thomas Jefferson had promoted—to provide every citizen of the republic with critical facilities, "to diffuse knowledge more generally through the mass of the people"—were potentially disruptive in a class society. In the increasingly class-differentiated society of the nineteenth century, private gain and social control became more important than universal literacy. Lower-class children needed moral training, not extensive knowledge, and education valued for its own sake became a luxury for an elite few.[9] While all should go to school, all children would not be equally educated.

The enhancement of the vocational roles of education around the turn of the century intensified the conflicts between public goals and private ends. Formal schooling, which had previously prepared individuals for only a few occupations like teaching and bookkeeping, became necessary for more and more positions. The decline of child labor and the availability of a large unskilled immigrant and nonwhite work force pushed adolescents out of the labor market. The growth of occupations for which formal schooling was useful—clerical and managerial positions, and the various professional occupations—increased the occupational relevance of schooling and, in all likelihood, its economic returns as well. Corporate hiring procedures were routinized, with informal and personal criteria replaced by formal criteria such as schooling. The vocational direction of the schools transformed their very nature. As the president of the Muncie, Indiana, school board affirmed in the mid-1920s, "For a long time all the boys were trained to be President. Then for a while we trained them all to be professional men. Now we are training boys to get jobs."[10]

The growth of the high school after 1900 meant that working-class immigrant and black youth had more access to schooling, but increased access did not lead to positions of higher earnings and status. The influx of the "children of the plain people" into the high school was a source of considerable anxiety to educators. Within schools, elaborate mechanisms of segregation developed—differentiated curricula, internal tracking and ability grouping, elite high schools with admissions requirements, and the development of testing to place segregation on a more "scientific" footing—to assure that children of different classes and races would not mix and that their education would differ according to their "evident or probable destinies."[11] The rationale for differentiation was outlined by two educators early in the century:

> It is obvious that the educational needs of children in a district where the streets are well paved and clean, where the homes are spacious and surrounded

by lawns and trees, where the language of the child's play-fellows is pure, and where life in general is permeated with the spirit and ideals of America—it is obvious that the educational needs of such a child are radically different from those of the child who lives in a foreign and tenement section. . . . [12]

Just at the point when schools were becoming the most important mechanism for access to jobs and social position, and when attendance in high schools was expanding, the simultaneous development of internal differentiation meant that schools continued to operate in favor of middle-class, native-born, and white male children to the detriment of others.

However, the role of schools in stratification was always accompanied by the expectation of equal opportunity. Because of its economic value, schooling was promoted as a way of resolving the problems of poverty: by giving immigrant and black children the capacity to earn adequate incomes, schooling would integrate those groups that had historically been at the bottom of society. The concept of educational opportunity which emerged in defense of this role was singularly inegalitarian. Boston's superintendent of schools declared just before World War I that the schools "have offered equal opportunity for all to receive *one* kind of education, but what will make them democratic is to provide opportunity for all to receive such education as will fit them *equally* well for their particular life work." [13] A democratic educational system was one geared to the "evident or probable destinies" of youth, with working-class children tracked into vocational programs and middle-class children in academic programs. The articulation of equal opportunity as an ideology, weak as it was, nonetheless reflected egalitarian pressures on the schools. The ideal of equal access prompted conflicts over stratification within schools during the progressive era, like the struggles of blacks to gain access to public education and the efforts of working-class parents to resist a second-class vocational education for their children.[14] As schooling has become more important in certifying for occupational placement since World War II, equality of educational opportunity has generated a variety of educational reforms and increasingly intense political battles.

The growing vocational importance of schooling in the twentieth century has meant that those discriminated against cannot simply dismiss the schools as irrelevant to their own needs. As the most obvious mechanism of social mobility, schools have become almost the only hope for children whose parents have no wealth or position. Black and working-class parents have often realized that their children were treated shabbily, but they have simultaneously embraced public education as the best hope for their children's success. The result has been a new intensity to conflicts over access to schooling.

Simultaneously, vocationalism further narrowed the value of education.

135

Beginning with the rhetoric of "learning to earn" in the progressive era and culminating in the human capital theory of the 1960s, the justification of schooling in terms of increased earnings has eliminated the other values once associated with education. The moral values that dominated nineteenth-century schooling have progressively fallen away, except when applied to the "immoral" behavior of black and immigrant children— other people's children. Even for middle-class students, literacy and critical capacities have become useful only to the extent they lead to economic returns. Other purposes have persisted, as the recurring battles over sex education, religious teaching, and "values clarification" illustrate, but economic efficiency has come to dominate all other functions of the schools.

By World War II the critical roles of public schooling had been well established. A vocational purpose dominated. In their nonvocational functions the schools continued to be viewed as a replacement of the family, particularly in the Americanization of immigrants and the socialization of rural blacks. The schools balanced—indelicately, to be sure—two contrary roles: while schools by and large perpetuated differences based on class and race from one generation to the next, they also provided upward mobility for a few, based on an ideology of universal access and equal opportunity. In both of these roles schools pursued various social goals— the goals of greater equality, of cultural homogeneity, of social stability— while parents increasingly concentrated on the "private" use of the schools to promote the success of their own children. For very different reasons, then, both parents and social reformers who saw schooling as a solution to social problems pressed for continued expansion. Although prior to the 1940s the tensions inherent in these roles were effectively limited to local conflicts of short duration, the basis for more prolonged and nation-wide battles had been established.

The dilemmas of public schooling continued in the dramatic expansion of higher education after World War II. Part of the pressure for expansion was economic: the relatively small numbers born during the Great Depression meant that new college graduates were relatively few, while sectors with high demands for educated labor—including the defense sector and education itself—expanded rapidly. The resulting shortage of college graduates caused the earnings advantage of college to increase precipitously. In 1954 the earnings advantage of a college graduate over the average worker was 10 percent; by 1958, it had almost doubled to 19 percent, and it further increased to 25 percent by 1966.[15] With high returns, the incentive to attend college led to the expansion of state systems of higher education and to increasing federal funds for both public and private colleges. During the period of expansion, the different purposes of education meshed nicely: well-paid, high status jobs for college graduates were readily available, and the social purposes of higher education had been convincingly reaffirmed, particularly in stimulating growth and in assuming Cold War responsibilities after Sputnik. The expectations were neatly summarized by social commentator Peter Drucker in 1958:

> Today . . . we cannot get enough educated people. . . . In the past the question has always been: How many educated people can a society afford? Today it is increasingly: How many people who are not highly educated can a society afford?[16]

Yet expansion created a number of problems, particularly in changing the purpose of higher education. For much the same reasons that high schools had expanded earlier, students were attracted to college by the promise of higher earnings and higher status, and colleges became increasingly vocational.[17] In the area of greatest growth—the two-year colleges—higher education was largely an extension of high school vocational courses. Ironically, however, vocational goals also fostered the irrationality of demands for higher education. As college attendance became more common, the educational requirements for jobs became inflated,[18] generating the phenomenon of "credentialing" and making college attendance increasingly necessary as a defensive measure. Although the earnings advantage to college attendance had fallen by 1974 to the relatively low levels of the early 1950s, rates of college attendance nonetheless remained high: in the fall of 1972, 52 percent of those between the ages of eighteen and twenty-one were enrolled in higher education, compared to 26 percent in the fall of 1953.[19] With high enrollments and lower rates of return, charges of "over-education" mounted; Drucker's optimism of two decades earlier vanished, as he and others became proponents of reducing our expectations. The phenomenon of expanding enrollments has exposed a central dilemma: while school attendance for private ends—greater earnings and status—is individually rational, the use of public institutions for private ends has generated the socially irrational phenomena of educational inflation and spiraling credentials.

Expansion created a second problem: like the earlier growth of the high school, the greatest increase in post-1960 attendance was among working-class and minority youth, an increase that threatened the historic role of higher education in perpetuating class and racial differences. Again, the conflict inherent in the rush for places was muted by combining "equality of opportunity" with the creation of alternative institutions and programs for "appropriate" students. The principal mechanism of stratification was the expansion of the community college, which—because of its lower entrance requirements and because of barriers of distance and money—tended to attract students of lower incomes and lower class standing and more minority students than four-year institutions, and to prepare them for working-class rather than middle-class jobs.[20] Other mechanisms of stratification have included the differentiation of state colleges from state universities, the development of specific campuses of a state university system with special prestige and status, and the distinctions of prestige and "quality" among all institutions of higher education. As had been true with the high school, the differentiation of higher education proceeded under the rationale of providing educational opportunity according to merit. The mechanisms of segregation at the college level—tests, grouping by ability, counseling—were familiar from practices in the high school, developed and legitimized decades earlier. The process of "cooling out"— adjusting student aspirations to the reality of class and racial bias—had become so smooth that it had become a well-accepted aspect of public schooling.[21] Once again the concept of equal educational opportunity was compromised: while promising to be a route to social mobility for all, in reality education continued to distinguish students by their class and racial backgrounds.

At the same time that the stratification of higher education maintained privileged access, the vocational importance of higher education caused reformers to press for expansion of programs of equal opportunity at the college level. There was little alternative: the close connection between college attendance and occupations of higher class status has meant that equal access to college is fundamental to equal opportunity through the schools. The effort to improve access to college has been the basis of federal subsidies to low-income students, special admissions programs, the passage and (sometime) enforcement of Title VI of the Civil Rights Act prohibiting racial and sexual discrimination in federally subsidized higher education, and the experiment in "open enrollment" at the City University of New York.

During the 1950s and early 1960s, growth muted the contradiction inherent in the equalizing and stratifying roles of higher education, allowing colleges to accept increased proportions of lower-income and minority youths while still providing places for middle-class youth. Only since the mid-1960s, in a period of stagnant growth, declining advantage of college attendance, and taxpayer revolts, has access to favored positions in colleges and universities become relatively scarce. The result was predictable: intensified battles over additional subsidies to middle-income (rather than low-income) students, over special admissions programs for minorities, and over open enrollment indicate how desperate the battle for access to college has become.

The growing vocational importance of higher education in the postwar period has distorted the content of education in ways that have exacerbated these conflicts. The nonvocational purposes that lie outside economic considerations—the goals of liberal education, including literacy, critical citizenship, a sense of participation in a community and of social responsibility—have been diminished. Schooling has been stripped to its economic essentials, evaluated almost entirely in terms of its rate of return to individuals, the basis for private gains. In the process the conflict between using education for private ends, in which middle-class parents have greater political clout, and using education for the social goals of equalization and integration has become exposed.

Conflicts over Educational Opportunity

While schools have always conferred advantage on privileged children, the ideology of public schooling as a universal and egalitarian institution has served as the basis for widespread gains among disadvantaged groups. Minorities have asserted the ideology of universality to gain access to schooling and to limit the most discriminatory features of the school system. Working-class parents have used it to resist class-segregated schools and programs. Racial integration, compensatory education, and attacks on spending inequalities in the postwar period were stimulated and legitimized by the ideology of equal opportunity. Yet the attainment of egalitarian ideals has never been successful, despite numerous gains. The political power of those fearful their children will lose if other people's children gain and the belief that schools should serve private ends have made each step toward more egalitarian goals conflict-ridden and partial at best.

Political pressure to fulfill the promise of equal access to public schooling increased considerably after World War II, especially in attacks on racially segregated schools, in the development of compensatory education programs, and in efforts to equalize school resources. In one of the fullest statements of the egalitarian ethic, the Supreme Court argued in *Brown* v. *Board of Education* that it was "doubtful that any child may reasonably be expected to succeed in life if he is denied the opportunity of an education," and concluded that segregation "solely on the basis of race . . . deprives the children of the minority group of equal education opportunities." Integration through desegregation and busing was extended to other minorities, with Hispanics also pressing for bilingual education to overcome language barriers.[22]

By the mid-1960s, integration efforts were reinforced by a barrage of compensatory education programs, most legislated in the Elementary and Secondary Education Act of 1965. Head Start represented an effort to give "educationally disadvantaged" young children the chance to begin schooling on a more equal footing with their privileged peers. Follow Through, a compensatory program for children in the early elementary grades, was instituted to try to retain the cognitive gains of Head Start. At the other end of the educational spectrum, various programs of special admissions and scholarships were established to provide easier access to higher education for those historically excluded due to outright discrimination, for economic reasons, or because their secondary schooling was deficient. Despite the variety of these programs, they often shared a common premise: the deficiencies of their families caused nonwhite and lower-class children to lag behind white middle-class children in their preparation, and these children required special remedies to bring them up to their white peers. The War on Poverty, Johnson declared, "can be won *only* if those who are poverty's prisoners can break the chains of ignorance."[23] The chains might be broken by public programs, but their initial forging was the responsibility of parents. In these programs, *parens patriae* was reborn, with the same mixture of concern and revulsion which marked most earlier efforts to help children in need.

Still a third mechanism for enhancing opportunity through schooling was the effort to equalize the financing of elementary and secondary education. Although attempts to decrease gross inequalities in spending levels had been undertaken at the turn of the century, the slow pace of equalization through integration and compensatory education led civil rights activists to challenge these inequalities in financing. Lawsuits proliferated, especially after the California case of *Serrano* v. *Priest* generated a favorable decision in 1971, with a ruling that articulated the ideology of equal opportunity and invoked Horace Mann for support:

> We have determined that [the California] funding scheme invidiously discriminates against the poor because it makes the quality of a child's education a function of the wealth of his parents and neighbors. Recognizing as we must that the right to an education in our public schools is a fundamental interest which cannot be conditioned on wealth, . . . we have concluded, therefore, that such a system cannot withstand constitutional challenge and must fall before the equal protection clause. . . . By our holding today we further the cherished idea of American education that in a democratic society free public schools shall make available to all children equally the abundant gifts of learning. This was the credo of Horace Mann, which has been the heritage and inspiration of this country. "I believe," he wrote, "in the existence of a great, immortal immutable principle of natural law, or natural ethics—a principle antecedent to all human institutions, and incapable of being abrogated by any ordinance of

man . . . which proves the *absolute right* to an education of every human being that comes into the world, and which, of course, proves the correlative duty of every government to see that the means of that education are provided for all."[24]

The resulting legal and political pressure to equalize school revenues caused another surge of legislative reforms, leading to increases in state funds relative to local taxes and to changes in the distribution of state monies in order to equalize school resources.[25]

Despite frustration and resistance at every turn, the various equalization efforts have had some effect. Schools in the South are now much more integrated than they were in 1954, though there has been no progress whatsoever in the North. The gap between white and black educational attainments has narrowed, though the gap for Hispanics remains just as wide as it ever was. There has been some equalization in total spending levels, though the changes have not done much to benefit poor children or equalize instructional expenditures.[26] Yet progress has been slow in each of these areas, the political battles have been intense and bitter, with equalization resisted by parents protecting their "private" prerogatives in the public schools and their rights to manipulate the schools on behalf of their own children. Almost invariably, court challenges have been necessary to compel the state to enforce its own constitutional and legislative principles: the long, drawn-out court battles over desegregation in the wake of the *Brown* decision, the thirty court cases filed in twenty-six states challenging school financing provisions, and the endless skirmishes between the Department of Justice and institutions of higher education over minority admissions indicate how slow and reluctant compliance has been. More recently, the courts have begun to overturn earlier decisions, signaling the most obvious retreat from the principles of equal access. *Bakke* v. *Board of Regents of the University of California*, in which a white male successfully challenged a special minority admissions program, and *Crawford* v. *Los Angeles Board of Education* overturning the need for busing to correct school segregation caused by segregated housing, are two examples. Like all other principles in the American state, the ideal of equalization through the schools has been difficult to implement under the pressures of interest group politics and the defense of one group's position over another's.

Desegregation, compensatory education, and school finance reforms illustrate the war between the ideal of equalizing opportunity and the presumption that the state should not provide undue advantage to "other people's children." The tragedy is that the deterioration of urban public schooling has exacerbated conflict. Actions in defense of integrated

141

schools have been attacked for seeming to undermine the quality of schooling. In the desegregation battles, court-ordered busing has met with serious resistance from whites, arguing in one form or another that integration threatens the quality of their own children's education. The struggle over integration has been argued in terms of the effect of integration on the school achievement of black and white children, an instrumental view of integration having nothing to do with moral issues.[27] Not surprisingly, racial animosity has emerged in its most naked form, but the insecurities whites feel in their social and economic condition and their fear that "other people's children" threaten their own also play important roles. As a result, one of the most powerful responses to desegregation has been "white flight" from urban public schools to predominantly white suburbs and private schools. White parents can thereby recapture the image of schools as extensions of families, consistent with local values and working in the private interest of each family, symbolized by the rhetoric of the "community school." The irony is apparent: at precisely the point when schools might become truly communitarian, many whites have decided that they would have none of it. As long as the private outcomes of schooling appear to pit some children's advancement against others', the public goals of greater equality remain subordinate.

After an initial round of success, the efforts to reduce inequalities in school spending also generated resistance. Wealthy school districts banded together to protect their own interests and to file lawsuits of their own contending that equalization would eliminate "lighthouse districts," those beacons of excellence that stood as models for other school systems, and that state grants to equalize funding would dilute local control. In several states, legislatures rescinded parts of reform legislation, and in other states progress toward court-ordered reform has been slow and recalcitrant; in the extreme case of New Jersey, the state supreme court took on the operation of the schools to force the legislature to comply. One critical blow to equalization efforts has come from evidence that redistributing school resources might not lead to different cognitive outcomes because the causal relationship between spending and educational outcomes is so uncertain. Although the instrumental argument against fiscal equalization should apply symmetrically to spending for all children, it has been used only to attack increased resources for poor districts, not to attack high public spending levels in wealthy areas. As in the busing controversies, the sanctity of local control over school policies and resources and a distrust of higher-level governments have been invoked in defense of spending differences, despite evidence that such arguments are essentially self-serving.[28] Again, we can see that the use of schools for private gain—in the prerogatives of high-income parents to segregate themselves in wealthy suburbs for the advantage of their own children—has been deeply ingrained.

Compensatory education programs have also been attacked, though usually by academics and policy makers citing their ineffectiveness rather than by parents who felt their children were unfairly treated or left out.[29] Special admissions programs in higher education have come under even more vigorous, often hysterical attack—not surprisingly, for no other educational reform is more directly related to future success. Moreover, special admissions programs have been especially vulnerable because they appear to contradict the principle of admission according to merit. Indeed, in special admission programs the dual roles of schooling are most strikingly illustrated: the schools can be used to equalize access to valued occupations, according to egalitarian and political criteria, or they can perpetuate the inequalities into which children were born, legitimized by an ideology of merit and an apparatus to administer that ideology (including biased tests). Where the two roles have come squarely into conflict in special admission programs, as in the minority admissions program at issue in the *Bakke* case, the result has been the most bitter conflict.[30]

The attacks on the various equalization programs have been facilitated by the dominance of instrumental conceptions in public policy toward children. In almost every case, proponents argue that a reform will cause specific educational outcomes, usually increases in cognitive test scores. High scores are assumed to lead to adult success, a concern which should not be dismissed. But the exclusive focus on long-term cognitive effects, essentially as proxy for access to occupations later on, illustrates the use of schools in a purely instrumental fashion, ignoring the broader range of criteria which might govern public programs and which usually govern the schooling of privileged children. A purely utilitarian conception of integration ignores the moral and symbolic aspects of integration and suggests that integration be abandoned if it does not increase test scores. The focus on cognitive effects in Head Start ignores the efforts to develop an institutional model quite different from the public schools, in which parents, community, and school are integrated, in which a child-centered institution can become a social advocate for children and families.[31] The constant justification of equalization formulas in terms of cognitive outcomes similarly ignores broader conceptions of the effects of spending, including the symbolic aspects. In the press to find cognitive effects, the possibility that schools might be pleasant and stimulating places for children—including poor children—has been almost uniformly forgotten.

Given the extent to which public schooling is now defined by private gains and the inequality of power to affect educational policy, the reversal of equalization efforts appears to be inevitable. While all parents struggle on behalf of their own children, middle-income and white parents are better able to press their interests (both in schools and in the political arena) than are lower-income and minority parents. Middle-income and white parents can more readily "exit" from a school they dislike, moving to a new neighborhood or placing their children in private school, as the white flight from desegregation efforts illustrates. Indeed, middle-class parents have even demanded public funds in the form of tax credits to facilitate their flight to private schools.

Providing equal opportunity through the schools has been one of the most consistent and one of the most benevolent hopes of child savers in every period of reform, including the postwar period. Educational opportunity has taken on special importance as prospects for equality itself have seemed impossible to some Americans and undesirable to many, and schools have therefore been the central expression of the public responsibility to achieve a just society. Yet providing equal educational opportunity in an inegalitarian society has proved impossible. Limited progress in some areas has invariably been followed by backlash and retrenchment, reassertions of private goals, and inegalitarian outcomes. Try as we might to make public schools the avenue of our deepest democratic commitments, we invariably fall short. The result has been to undermine public responsibility in the institution which is the most critical for all children.

Schools and Parents: Partners and Antagonists

More than any other institution, schools share childrearing with parents.[32] Although relations between parents and schools are usually experienced in personal terms, in fact conflict and cooperation are structured by the institutions themselves, by the differences in their goals, the ways they operate, and their relations to children. Because of their importance, the schools illustrate better than any other children's institution the dilemmas and conflicts—some inevitable and others fortuitous, some legitimate and others illegitimate—typical of the state's relation to children.

In preparing children for adult life, schools try to meet the aspirations parents have for their children. But schools also exist to prepare children to leave their families. For rural and ghetto children, schools can open a world their families barely know; for the children of non-English–speaking parents, they have been places where the language of success is taught; for middle-class and working-class children alike, they offer the possibility of going beyond parental status. The vocational potential of schooling has placed parents in an especially ambiguous relationship to the public schools. To the extent that schools further the success of their children, parents must support schools and teachers. At the same time parents may resist the ways in which teachers treat their children and exercise professional prerogatives over parents. The norms and goals of each differ: schools are designed to move children from the affection-based, personal, cooperative, and protected family to a world that operates by more universalistic norms, requires independence, and provides little protection for those who are unable to cope on their own.[33] The process of weaning the young child away from the home may itself produce ambivalence in parents. As one teacher described the situation:

> Mothers seem to be in subtle competition with teachers. There is always an underlying fear that teachers will do a better job than they have done with their child. They are also somewhat ambivalent about relinquishing control. . . . So a great deal of their self-esteem and self-worth hangs on their child's successful transition from home to school and on his achievement and advancement through school. The teacher is a threatening figure because her evaluation of the child can enhance or negate the *mother's* self-image.[34]

Conflicts may also emerge over public education's role in teaching relatively homogeneous values in a heterogeneous country. These kinds of conflicts have been most intense where schools confront strongly held ideological, communal, or regional differences. The most extreme examples have come in the cases of communities like the Amish, who have fought to escape the public schools in the belief that the schools would undermine Amish values, and that once exposed to the world outside the Amish community their children would be more likely to leave the community. Expressed as an issue of parental prerogatives against the state, this conflict has for the moment been decided in favor of parents in the case of *Wisconsin* v. *Yoder*.[35] Conflicts over religious values have surfaced between Catholics and non-Catholics, Jews and Gentiles, and in the revival of fundamentalist religious objections to the teaching of evolution. The perennial conflicts over sex education and over book censorship can be interpreted as clashes between "liberal," more tolerant schools and more conservative communities that resist the schools' values.[36] The ceaseless battles over maintaining small rural schools versus consolidating them in the interests of efficiency and uniformity have demonstrated the conflict between parents who wish to maintain local schools as reflections of their

145

own ways of life versus educators who have assumed that consolidation is in the best interests of children. As one West Virginian mother described the issues:

> We had a fine little school here. It was small, and the teachers knew how to get on with our kids. We had no trouble sending them off; everyone loved school. They "consolidated.". . . It was called "progress." Well, we were all for that! But what happened? What did we get? We ended up with our kids being lost in that building; and hearing how "ignorant" they are. It's no good, when you have your kids coming home and telling you that the teacher is all the time looking down her nose at people like us.[37]

Unsettling as these conflicts over moral values and social norms have been, they are inevitable in a heterogeneous society. As long as the division of labor between parents and schools is ill-defined, we can expect parents to assert their prerogatives and schools to assert the necessity and superiority of national norms. These are also legitimate conflicts: as long as schools and parents share responsibility for socializing children, they should each be able to make claims on behalf of certain values. But if some conflicts between parents and schools are necessary if the child is ever to grow up—and some are inevitable given the overlapping influence of parents and teachers—others are more obviously illegitimate because they grow out of patterns of discrimination.

The line between legitimate and illegitimate conflict is not easily drawn. Often, conflicts based on class, race, and sexual discrimination have been portrayed as conflicts among regions or among different educational ideologies, portrayals that tend to legitimize opposition to egalitarian measures. Efforts to integrate Southern schools, for example, were initially depicted as an imposition of northern values on the South. Racial battles on the North have typically been formulated as battles over the "neighborhood schools" and the self-determination of communities. Efforts to eliminate sexual biases have been resisted as the imposition of federal controls on communities with different values, and efforts to equalize expenditures have been attacked as undermining local control. In these efforts, specific inequalities have been reinterpreted as the results of parental preferences and community control, which are then considered legitimate. This interpretation has been extremely difficult to counter, in part because local control and pluralism are so deeply ingrained in American education.

The difficulty in identifying biased and illegitimate treatment of children within schools has been reinforced by the subtle ways schools reproduce class, racial, and sexual patterns. Often, mechanisms of stratification are hidden from parents, since they occur within classrooms, beyond the parents' view.[38] Sometimes they are beyond the control of either parents or teachers, as are the complex of forces which generate school systems of high and low quality. Yet the unfair treatment of children in the schools is still sufficiently clear to cause conflict when some parents perceive that their children are getting less than other children, particularly white, middle-class children.

In these conflicts, we can often see the doctrine of *parens patriae* at work: with some children considered inferior in their preparation for school—explicitly so in the case of compensatory programs, implicitly in the case of racial and class labeling—teachers begin to treat some children as incapable, a process that extends blame to parents and makes the parent-teacher relationship potentially explosive. Sara Lawrence Lightfoot has clarified the process whereby teachers blame parents for their children's failures by contrasting two kinds of teachers. One teacher takes the child as an individual, divorced from his or her family. The other identifies the child's family background and infers from that background the child's characteristics:

> Although [she] seeks to establish a comfortable distance from the families of the children in her class, in her interactions with the children she carries around images of their families in her head. Even as she relates to a child, she is seeing him as the shadow of his parents. As a matter of fact, [she] finds it very difficult to describe the individual nature of the child without reference to the sociological dimensions of family structure, social class, race, and ethnicity. . . . Ironically, [she] yearns for a classroom setting that is free from the "negative" impact of families and community, but her view of children is shaped by the very forces that she seeks to avoid.[39]

In such a situation, relations between parents and teachers can at best achieve a stalemate and are more likely to be antagonistic: the children are doing poorly in school partly because of the teachers' labeling, the parents blame the teachers for the poor performance of their children, and the teachers in turn blame the parents. Most of the time the resulting conflicts between parents and children remain submerged; occasionally, as in the struggles in the late 1960s over community control in New York, these conflicts attain the level of collective and political action. Whatever their level, the conflicts are worrisome not only because they testify to patterns of bias and exclusion within the schools, but also because such conflict undermines the educational potential of the schools for lower-class and minority pupils since children learn better when parents and teachers work as "partners" rather than "antagonists."[40] The poor performance of some children results in part from a self-fulfilling prophecy:

the conflict between parents and teachers, born of the assumption that lower-class and minority pupils will do poorly, helps ensure that this will be so.

The latent conflicts between teachers and parents of lower-class and minority pupils are pervasive precisely because they are reflections at the classroom level of institutional biases that can be traced back to the nineteenth century. Recent changes have exacerbated these conflicts, especially the nationalization of educational issues and the increased vocational importance of schooling. Supreme Court decisions, federal programs, standardized testing and curricula, and coverage by the national media have forced parents and teachers to contend with issues that are rarely initiated locally—racial integration, sex discrimination, financing patterns, standardized testing, special admissions, and bilingual education, to cite the most obvious. The vocationalization of the schools has sharpened the battles: conflicts over access to the schools, over integration and special admissions, for example, have become more intense as the stakes have increased.

At the same time, the schools have become more immune from parental intervention, as the bureaucratization of the schools has centralized and standardized educational practice, introduced layers of administrators and specialists, and converted political issues into administrative problems. The professionalization of teaching and the increased militancy and political power of teacher organizations have shifted the balance of power between teachers and parents, particularly lower-class and minority parents, in favor of teachers.[41] The mechanisms of class and racial stratification within the schools, while sometimes challenged, are more often explained in terms of good professional practice. As part of an attempt to establish a sphere of professional autonomy and influence, the classroom interactions that provide the earliest basis for labeling are largely closed to parents. The processes of grading, advancement, tracking, and other mechanisms of differentiation are similarly protected by conceptions of professional control and expertise, and the testing procedures that have come to invade the schools have been justified by their scientific validity in identifying ability, despite mounting evidence of their biases.[42] The efforts of teachers and administrators to place the schools "above politics" and grant professionals complete autonomy have reduced most contact with parents to the empty rituals of the PTA.[43]

Yet professionalism may have backfired by cutting teachers off from the source of their power. The realization has become more widespread that what teachers want is not always in the interests of children. This has become most obvious in the treatment of black and Hispanics children, but has also emerged in other cases where teachers promoting their own interests have sometimes ignored the interests of children. The resistance of teacher groups to reviews of their own competence, to evaluations based on the performance of their pupils, and to parental participation in many forms has usually seemed self-serving and unprofessional. In these battles, teachers have been caught in the inherent dilemma of public sector professionals: although they resist parental participation in the interests of establishing their own autonomy and expertise, in the end they are dependent on public and parental support for their continued security. In a period of taxpayer revolts and of children perceived as liabilities, this dilemma has become even more acute; more than ever, teachers must rely on parents for financial as well as pedagogical support.

At times, the spirit of antiprofessionalism has generated efforts to abandon any conception of the professional. Ivan Illich's call to eliminate all formal schooling and return to more informal methods of education expresses an extreme antagonism to professionals.[44] Less extreme criticisms abound, from both right-wing critics reasserting parental prerogatives in value-laden areas like sex education and integration and left-wing critics attacking educational inequalities. In teaching, as in other child-related occupations, the extreme attacks distort the ambivalence we should feel toward professionals whose claims of special expertise are not completely illegitimate. Even as some teachers use professional standing to hide incompetence or bias, others seek autonomy as a way of providing an alternative environment where a child may learn skills he or she cannot learn at home. As long as we recognize the legitimacy of some conflicts within the schools, embedded in the distinctiveness of schools and families, it would be inappropriate to destroy all aspects of professional autonomy.

Yet an imbalance between parents and teachers remains, a fact implicitly recognized in the legislation requiring parental participation in such programs as Title I and Head Start. Imperfect as these efforts may be, they at least seek to strengthen the bargaining power of low-income and minority parents in programs that directly affect their children. In forcing professionals to share their assumptions and methods with parents, such measures represent an effort to create new forms of professionalism. In such a relationship there is no *a priori* reason to think that the traditional viewpoints of professionals will continue to dominate, or conversely that parents will obliterate every trace of professional ability and autonomy. In the best of circumstances, the results have been a synthesis of parental and professional expectations, with a greater degree of consensus that has typically been possible in any but the most homogeneous schools.[45] In such a structuring of the power relationships, the possibilities seem all the

149

greater for parents and teachers to work as "partners" rather than as "antagonists."

This is only part of the solution, however. As long as schools combine contradictory roles—providing equality of opportunity and perpetuating class and racial divisions, serving broad social purposes and being used in the interests of private gain—conflicts between parents and schools will endure, and they cannot be resolved simply within the schools themselves. The root of the problems remains the fact of dual and contradictory roles for the schools. As long as they continue, public education will remain an embattled institution, less effective than it could be.

Dismantling the Public Schools

During the 1970s and early 1980s, conflict over public education took on new dimensions. In the face of a long history of faith in education, the charges of overeducation suggested the ineffectiveness of schooling. In contrast to the earlier belief that everyone could benefit from expanding education, doubts arose that the middle class and the poor could both be served by the public schools. New opposition to equal educational opportunity appeared in fiscal conservativism and in the sense that Americans in the 1960s had pushed democratic and egalitarian goals too far. The middle-class fear that their children were no longer guaranteed middle-class positions generated new pressure to limit opportunities available to lower-class and minority students. Throughout the decade, various proposals emerged to place control of education in private hands through vouchers and tax credits, and institutional alternatives to the public schools grew rapidly. Building on these developments, Ronald Reagan's promises to enact tax credits for education and tax credit legislation sponsored in 1981 by Senators Moynihan (D-N.Y.) and Packwood (R-Ore.) have given political prominence to the movement away from public education.

Not all the efforts of the 1970s were attempts to dismantle the public schools, of course. Many changes were traditional appeals for more and improved schooling in order to overcome existing inadequacies. The effort to expand vocational education was one response to the failure of vocational programs.[46] Staying in school longer reflected the uncertainty of economic returns for lower levels of schooling. The new emphasis on preschool programs was based on the assumption that early education could equalize educational opportunities. These developments conformed to earlier trends: a consistent response to both the need for social reform and the need to reshape the schools has been to insist that the schools are basically sound and that more extensive versions of the same institution would be the most appropriate solution.

Yet the 1970s and early 1980s were novel because some reformers have tried to diminish the importance of public education, either by transferring greater power to private hands or by establishing alternative educational institutions outside the schools. The most widely publicized efforts have been the proposals to replace current financing mechanisms. To the extent that public education has trampled cultural and familial values, the voucher and tax-credit proposals—which would provide public funds to parents, to be spent for whatever schools they choose—have much to recommend them.[47] Yet these justifications obscure the likelihood that greater private control over education will exacerbate the inegalitarian patterns of schooling, particularly those based on class and race, as whites and middle-class Americans segregate themselves from minorities and lower-class students. At the same time taxpayer revolts, like Proposition 13 in California and Proposition 2½ in Massachusetts, have reduced funds for public schools, accelerating the flight of middle-class children from them. One result has been increased pressure to use public funds for private schools, coming not from low-income parents wanting access to private education or assuming that tax credits will help their children go to college, but from middle-class parents who have seen access to private schools closed off for financial reasons, from whites seeking to bypass the integration of the public schools, and from those who have come to feel that public policies are biased in favor of nonwhites, the poor, and women. The process forms a vicious cycle: withdrawal of funds from public schooling furthers the deterioration of public education, leaving individual parents with little choice but to seek alternatives outside the public system, which in turn results in increased pressure to use public funds for private schools.

The attempt to change funding mechanisms so as to channel public funds to private institutions is a subtle and powerful way of reinforcing the inegalitarian aspects of schooling, since these funding mechanisms delegate public responsibility as well as funding to institutions that are nominally private.[48] In contrast to public institutions, where democratic access and control is expected, the use of public funds in "private" institutions does not presume democratic control or collective definition of institutional goals. Quite the contrary: public funding for private education has been justified because it will allow parents to pursue their own goals for their own children, lessening any responsibility they might have

151

toward other people's children. If past experience is a guide, efforts to regulate the use of public funds in private institutions will be fought as illegitimate exercises of power over private decision making, as has happened in federally funded institutions of higher education. The pious hope that relegating public responsibilities to private schools can improve the educational system should not blind us to the difficulties this presents for democratic control and the egalitarian goals of schooling.

A second phenomenon of the 1970s, more diffuse but with consequences potentially as grave, has been the tendency to dismantle public schooling by transferring some of its obligations to other institutions. The effort to develop training programs outside the schools—in the Comprehensive Employment and Training Act (CETA) and Youth Employment and Demonstration Projects Act (YEDPA) programs of the Department of Labor, for example—recognizes that school-based vocational programs are failing students and that different (though parallel) institutions have become necessary to prepare them for the labor market. The apparent growth of industry-based training programs toward the end of the 1970s—by some estimates the fastest growing part of all education—also signaled a dissatisfaction of employers with school-based training.[49] The various work experience programs instituted in the 1970s, which release students from school for part-time work, imply that schools are inappropriate places to teach youth work-related norms. Efforts to eliminate compulsory education similarly imply that at least some high school students are better off preparing for their adult roles in nonschool settings.[50] At the opposite extreme, the extension of school-like activities in Head Start and other "developmental" preschool programs reflects the inability of the elementary grades to provide compensatory education and the feeling that an earlier start is necessary to provide remedial education. In less specific ways, the emerging emphasis on the "family as educator" and the "community as educator" suggests a shift to parent education programs, efforts to devise community-based education, and the use of informal educational networks in place of formal schooling institutions.[51]

Like vouchers and tax credits, the proposals to establish institutional alternatives to the schools have considerable merit. They recognize that education takes place in a variety of settings and that school-based programs are not appropriate for all functions and all students. They acknowledge that the schools have become so politically entrenched and hidebound that creating competitive institutions may be easier and more effective than reforming the schools, and they promise greater diversity in education. Like the efforts to return power to private hands, the attempts to shift educational responsibilities to other institutions acknowledge that the conflicts within the schools have become too serious to continue. Partly because they are relatively new and incompletely formed, some of the institutional alternatives now being proposed do present opportunities to reshape the state's relationship to children.

Yet dismantling the schools is potentially reactionary, if only because this effort may eliminate the egalitarian potential of schooling by promoting class and racial divisions and by allowing the major children's institution to slough off its public responsibilities. Since youth training programs established separately from the schools are now for those who have "failed" within the schools, they facilitate class and racial segregation even more than the current educational systems. Work experience programs may be ways of inculcating working-class norms rather than enhancing occupational opportunity. Despite the positive effects of some preschool programs, shifting the emphasis for compensatory education to very young children may allow elementary educators to blame others for poor school programs. The emphasis on "parents as educators" could suffer from the same tendency to dilute the responsibility of the schools and to blame parents for the failures of their children; as we will see in chapter 8, the current efforts to develop parent education programs have shown precisely these biases.

Nor can these alternatives escape the same pressures that confront the schools: the tendency to justify public programs for children on the basis of parental failure and the distrust of other people's children; the mandate that the state not infringe on labor markets; the use of public institutions for private gain and the transmission of privileged positions. Indeed, most of the alternatives to the public schools—especially private schools and proprietary training programs focused only on employment—all accelerate the tendency to value education solely in terms of economic and private goals. Current responses to the dilemmas of public schooling are thus ambiguous: while they may present some opportunities to reform the educational enterprise, they threaten to dilute the public responsibilities and egalitarian hopes of schooling, and they are likely to replicate the conflicts endemic to public education.

We should not minimize the depth of this dilemma. The interest group basis of American democracy has not led to egalitarian outcomes, either in the economy or in education. Nonetheless, popular participation in educational decisions has tended to foster more egalitarian treatment of children—or to curb the worst abuses—not only because political power is more equally distributed than economic power, but also because the ideology of schooling as an equalizer has had some force. The nineteenth-century hope that public education would be a "balance wheel of democracy" hid less noble goals, but that ideology has been so long and so insistently promoted that it remains a powerful argument against the exercise of naked privilege in the schools. The conception of schooling as a path of upward mobility has been given enough content in the twentieth-century developments of public schooling to generate widespread support. Those unfairly treated by the schools—blacks and Hispanics, in particular—continue to maintain their belief in the power of schooling, and they have continually fought to gain access to the schools.[52] While the principle of merit has been used to justify the mechanisms of stratification like tracking and testing, it has also served as a way of attacking some of the inegalitarian procedures of the public schools—the placement of intelligent minority children in special education through biased testing, for example, or the relegation of promising working-class students to vocational tracks of little consequence. As long as there are avenues of democratic access to the schools, there is some chance that the egalitarian promise of public education can be promoted. Where public access is diluted—as is implicit in public funding of private schools—then we can expect the inegalitarian role of schooling, the passing on of the patterns of privilege associated with "private" families, to become relatively stronger.

In a class-divided society, the use of public institutions for private interests has led to continuing corruption of public responsibility. The ideal of universality in public education has been compromised by class and racial segregation. The beliefs that the public schools can prepare a literate and critical citizenry, instill common values, foster communal responsibility, develop a variety of human capacities, and provide some equality of opportunity have been perverted by the reduction of education to its economic functions and by the class biases built into the educational system. To overcome these distortions, we must eliminate class differences and abandon conceptions of public institutions which emphasize private gain.

6

Youth Policy: The Dilemmas of Development and Control

AMERICAN youth appear to be in a terrible state. Juvenile crime, ever increasing, has become more violent, and the perpetrators are younger. Illiteracy has suddenly become a new educational problem, second only to discipline in the schools. Youth unemployment is high and shows little sign of abating, while young people are regularly chastised for their lack of commitment to school and work. Teen-agers are becoming pregnant too often and spreading too much venereal disease. The litany of woes is seemingly endless. The elaboration of institutions for youth in the postwar period—the expansion of secondary and postsecondary education, the constant revisions of the high school curriculum, the initiation of employment and training programs, the expansion and deinstitutionalization of the juvenile justice system—all seem to have gone for nought. Youth is "in trouble," and the search for new initiatives has often taken on a desperate quality.

In this tale of woe, it is hard to disentangle what is serious and what is hyperbole and hysteria. Certainly the problems of youth, like so many other aspects of childrearing "crises," are all too familiar. The large number of young people migrating to mid-nineteenth–century cities, the discovery of adolescence as a period of *Sturm und Drang* at the turn of the century, the misbehavior of youth during the 1920s, the teen-age gangs in the 1950s, and the unruly protestors of the 1960s all generated the same kind of concern. No problem has seemed more constant; a recent Carnegie Council report pronounced that "the 'youth problem' in the United

States is not going away."[1] Time and again the same complaints have been made, the same questions posed, the same resolutions adopted— more control, more schooling (or more "relevant" schooling), more rigorous teaching of the work ethic, improved juvenile justice programs. The constancy of the perceived problems and the responses to them raises fundamental questions about why youth is such a troubled stage of development and why the public institutions to cope with youth have so consistently needed reform.

To answer those questions we must first understand the social construction of youth—that period roughly between age fourteen and the early twenties—as a stage halfway between childhood and adulthood. Since youths are not yet adults, concern for their development has always generated the same humanitarian impulses as has concern for children. But since youths are almost adults, especially in preparing for work and establishing sexual relationships, we often treat them like adults and deny their developmental potential. When applied to other people's children, particularly lower-class and minority youth, this ambivalence is easily converted to hostility and takes institutional form in social policies to control and incarcerate youth rather than to enhance their development.

Americans have created a variety of age-segregated institutions for youth—high school and college, employment and training programs, the juvenile justice system, the draft—and a variety of other youth-specific programs, like those to cope with teen-age pregnancy and runaways. All of them manifest the same uncertainty about how to balance childlike characteristics with adult qualities and responsibilities. Whether to support youth's development and hope their tribulations will pass or to control their bad behavior and hope that well-behaved adults will result has been the inescapable dilemma. So long as society regards youth as a stage of life between childhood and adulthood and creates institutions whose purpose is to move young people from one stage to the other, there will be a youth problem. But it may be possible to avoid the constant recycling of the same problems, the hysteria which goes with each rediscovery, and the sense that a new youth policy is necessary because the last one failed once again.

The Social Construction of Youth

Youth obviously falls between childhood and adulthood, but the need to make a transition from the dependence of childhood to the independence of adulthood does not explain why youth has been perceived as a troubled period. In the early stage of adolescence, youth has always been associated with biological changes, but youth as a problematic stage of development has been a social construction, coincident with biological changes but independent of them since the tasks and choices that youths face are shaped by social and economic institutions.[2]

In colonial America, the category of youth was ill-defined. The transition from childhood to adulthood, signified by marriage and ownership of the family farm or established occupational status, was gradual and could last until the late twenties or early thirties. Momentous decisions were almost nonexistent, and the stresses of transition were unremarkable.[3] During the first half of the nineteenth century, youth as a stage of life became more clearly defined, as young people (especially boys) engaged in periods of semidependence, moving in and out of their homes, school, and work. A growing advice literature, paralleling the literature of domesticity, codified a new public consciousness of youth as a critical stage of development. As Joel Hawes, a nineteenth-century writer of advice to youth, described the period in *Lectures to Young Men*, published in 1832, it was "the forming, fixing period. . . . It is during this season more than any other, that the character assumes its permanent shape and color. . . ." He regarded youth as a period in which young people were "exceedingly liable to be seduced into the wrong paths—into those fascinating but fatal ways, which lead to degradation and wretchedness."[4] Yet the experiences of young people were too varied and too unpredictable, with too much mixing of age groups in families, schools, and work settings, for the conception of youth as a special stage to have widespread applicability.

During the last half of the century, teen-agers began to live at home for longer periods, losing much of their independence. They stayed in school longer and were less likely to enter the labor market.[5] By the first decades of the twentieth century, the retention of young people in age-graded schools and their progression from school into work and then into marriage had become more regular. The vocational purposes of education made schooling the dominant way of preparing for adult occupations. As child labor declined, as teen-agers withdrew from or were pushed out of the labor market, and as years at school lengthened, teen-agers found themselves in age-segregated settings: junior high school, high school, and (for middle-class youth) college; the juvenile court for those in trouble; and youth groups like the Boy Scouts. By the 1920s, the activities of the teen-age years had become ordered in a defined schedule and were therefore more predictable.

The greater uniformity of teen-age experiences was important in the development of youth as a distinct stage, but the expansion of choices facing youth generated the real *Sturm und Drang* of adolescence. By the progressive era, youth had come to be a period of critical decisions, particularly decisions about an occupational identity, including schooling decisions, and a sexual identity, including the choice of a spouse. Occupational and sexual decisions were less troubling before the nineteenth century: boys tended to follow their father's occupations, girls became homemakers, and parents played a major role in the choice of marriage partners. Several developments—the expansion of occupations, the decline of small-scale farming and independent craftwork, the decrease in self-employment and the increase in wage labor—made occupational choice a more conscious decision, especially for boys but increasingly in the early twentieth century for girls too. The concept of romantic love which spread in the late eighteenth and early nineteenth centuries supported the choice of a spouse as a real decision based on an individual's preferences rather than a choice dictated by parents, business alliances, or community concerns. More generally, the shift from a world in which children succeeded their parents to one in which children were expected to become individuals different from their parents generated the conditions of both choice and anxiety.[6] As youth became freer to make their own decisions, a range of now-familiar problems emerged: the "wasted years syndrome" between leaving school and assuming adult employment, delinquency, and fears about teen-age sexuality.[7] These problems were of concern both because they were blamed on adolescents themselves and because their long-range consequences were serious.

The most forceful statement of the new stage came from G. Stanley Hall, whose *Adolescence, Its Psychology and Its Relations to Physiology, Anthropology, Sex, Crime, Religion, and Education* (1904) set the terms for all subsequent discussions of young people. "Adolescence," Hall wrote, "is a new birth," a time of promise and pain, achievement and failure, and of turmoil. In adolescence "the higher and more complete human traits are now born," but the

> momentum of heredity often seems insufficient to enable the child to achieve this great revolution and come to complete maturity, so that every step of the upward way is strewn with wreckage of body, mind, and morals. There is not only arrest, but perversion at every stage, and hoodlumism, juvenile crime, and secret vice. . . . It is the age of sentiment and of religion, of rapid fluctuation of mood, and the world seems strange and new. Interest in adult life and in vocations develops. Youth awakes to a new world and understands neither it nor himself. The whole future of life depends on how the new powers now given suddenly and in profusion are husbanded and directed. Character and personality are taking form, but everything is plastic. Self-feeling and ambition are increased, and every trait and faculty is liable to exaggeration and excess.

Fears for youth, Hall warned, could not be overstated:

> Modern life is hard, and in many respects increasingly so, on youth. Home, school, church, fail to recognize its nature and needs and, perhaps most of all, its perils. . . . Never has youth been exposed to such dangers of both perversion and arrest as in our land and day.

Six years later, Jane Addams echoed Hall:

> We may either smother the divine fire of youth or we may feed it. We may either stand stupidly staring as it sinks into a murky fire of crime and flares into the intermittent blaze of folly or we may tend it into a lambent flame with power to make clean and bright our dingy city streets.[8]

These commentaries were extravagant, but in describing youth as a period of plasticity, with possibilities for igniting either the "fire of crime" or the "lambent flame" of renewal, they reflected both the centrality of decisions open to teen-agers and the adult fears that "perversion and arrest" would result.

Despite the historical trend toward more homogeneous experiences and the tendency to perceive youth as a homogeneous group, the social construction of youth has never been uniform. Class distinctions have always been the rule. The limited conceptions of youth in the early nineteenth century were restricted to the white middle class, and the advice literature of that period focused on middle class boys and girls. The fears over adolescence as a stage of *Sturm und Drang* in the progressive era were similarly class-differentiated: the "wasted years" and juvenile crime of lower-class and immigrant youth were treated by harsh discipline and the juvenile court, while sexual excesses and a lack of discipline associated with middle-class youth could be treated with advice literature, in voluntary organizations like the Boy Scouts, or in school programs. The class-based distinctions have continued to the present: the gangs of the 1950s, juvenile crime of the 1970s, teen-age pregnancy, and youth unemployment are predominantly lower-class issues, while the political and cultural rebellions of the 1960s, the sexual excesses of youth (excluding pregnancy), and the identity crises of college students are all middle-class problems. Adolescence as a time before entering the work force and choosing a mate starts earlier for working-class youth and ends earlier, as they leave school, begin work, or get married at an earlier age; adolescence for middle-class youth extends later, primarily because of extended school and college attendance. The class distinctions in the social construction of youth are not simply descriptions of the tendency of different classes to follow different paths through school and work and to engage in different kinds of "deviant" behavior; rather, the distinctions embody ideas of class-appropriate socialization. The anxiety associated with lower-class rowdiness, which leads to lower-class boys being adjudicated delinquents while their middle-class peers are turned over to their own parents or excused for adolescent mischief, betrays a class-biased conception of appropriate behavior. Conversely, the concern with individuality and independence among middle-class youth—in the social sympathy for their identity crises. In the construction of college as an institution where middle-class youth can play with their independence—has never been extended to working-class youth.[9]

In even more obvious ways, the social construction of youth has been divided by sex as well as by class. The crises of adolescence for girls have always been related to sexual identity and marriage, while the dominant problems for males remain those of occupational decisions. Sexual activities are considered a problem for girls, not for the boys who impregnate them. In the juvenile justice system, unacceptable behavior for girls—for which they are adjudicated status offenders—is likely to be linked to charges of promiscuity, whereas sex-related charges are almost nonexistent for boys (save in the extreme case of rape).[10] The social programs to cope with the problems of youth are similarly sex-typed—pregnancy prevention programs for girls, employment and training programs for boys. The policies are not entirely irrational: the consequences of sexual behavior are more serious for girls, and boys will stay in the labor market more continuously and longer than girls. But as in the case of class distinctions, the differences are more than descriptive: boys participate in teen-age sex and conception as much as girls do, unemployment rates are as high for girls as they are for boys, and labor market participation rates for men and women have narrowed considerably. The distinctions between "male" and "female" problems among youth reflect sex-stereotyped conceptions of how boys and girls should prepare for their adult futures and what activities will dominate their adult lives.

The social construction of youth as an intermediate stage between childhood and adulthood, combined with the sharp distinctions of class, race, and sex, has generated deep ambivalence among adults. Since young people are still children, adult perceptions and social policy can emphasize their unrealized development and the crucial decisions that face them. Yet youth has some of the attributes of adulthood, and compared with children they are themselves in the process of making truly consequential decisions. Even more than in the case of children, whom we presume to be malleable and unthreatening, adults feel uncertain about the potential of youth to reject adult society and its norms. Adolescents therefore threaten adults because youth can cause immediate trouble and their decisions can affect their futures irreversibly; they are represented by James Dean and Sal Mineo in "Rebel Without a Cause" rather than Beaver Cleaver or Charlie Brown.

Ambivalence toward youth manifests itself most obviously in the contradictory treatment of their difficulties. Adolescents are treated as if their concerns are real, yet they are chastised for being spoiled, self-centered, and lazy, and for being unrealistic about life's requirements. Their rights to sexual exploration may be recognized, while their blatant sexuality is considered irresponsible, immature, and immoral (especially for women). They are berated for not being committed to the work ethic, but are condemned to jobs that are low-paying, dull, and lack any motivation other than limited pay. They are told that adolescence is a "moratorium" between childhood and adulthood they should enjoy and then chastised for their playfulness. The idleness of youth, and the self-absorption of a period which is supposed to be a time of decision making, arouse the hostility (as well as the envy) of adults; the sexual explorations of adolescents and the indulgences of "youth culture" constantly generate angry mutterings from their elders, even though adolescence is regarded as a state of trial and experimentation. The ambivalence adults feel toward youth is clearly reflected in wild swings of opinion about them. On the one hand are those who stress the tremendous size of the "generation gap," the difference between parents and their adolescent children, the inappropriateness of "youth culture" and youthful rebelliousness. This group ridiculed the youth movement of the 1960s and has been relatively happy with the return to quiet campuses and careerism in the 1970s and 1980s. The other approach tends to celebrate youth as the hope of the future, the only group with any potential for remaking the world; from this vantage the youth rebellions of the 1960s were welcome, and the subsequent return to apolitical concerns signals passivity rather than normalcy.[11] A high school administrator described the students of the early 1980s in glowing terms: "The crazy kids have graduated. Now we have a new, nicer generation of kids. Everything's nicer." But a teacher retorted: "As much turmoil as the '60s brought this school, at least something was happening, and students were concerned about something besides their navels."[12] If adolescents often seem confused, one of the reasons is that adults have been unable to decide what youth should be.

Not surprisingly, class and racial distinctions pervade our ambivalences and shape our social policies toward youth. The kinds of youth we most readily condemn—those most often charged with being "overeducated," those who find themselves in the various vocational and manpower programs, high school dropouts, girls who are sexually active, and youth within the juvenile justice system—tend to be lower-class and minority. They are precisely the individuals—other people's children—who have always been the targets of middle-class hostility and suspicion, especially the suspicion that they might corrupt other youth. The animosity toward lower-class youth is much more open than the antagonism toward lower-class children. Adults are more willing to see young children as blameless and still capable of being socially formed, worth the "investments" of schooling and compensatory programs. By the time children have become teen-agers, the terms of ambivalence have sharpened. Adults are more likely to see lower-class adolescents as themselves to blame for school failures or for being juvenile offenders, and adults are more ready to see them as full-developed individuals who are unlikely to benefit from social investments like training.

The social construction of youth and the class biases embedded within our attitudes generate yet another uncertainty in the treatment of youth. Some adolescent problems are of obvious concern, like truly criminal behavior and unwanted pregnancies, and these problems are all the more heart-rending because they threaten to destroy any possibilities for a healthy adult life. Other problems are more ambiguous, however, and reflect adult perceptions more than anything else. Often the youthful behavior that irritates adults is forbidden only to adolescents; disobedience, rowdiness, overt female sexuality become status offenses and therefore crimes when committed by juveniles, but not if committed by adults. Much of the adult reaction to youth seems to reflect a concern with obedience *per se*, a reflection that youth are still children who owe obedience to their parents and other adult authorities; the deep loathing of youth culture, especially among conservatives, often interprets youthful rebelliousness as a permanent rejection of conventional adult norms. Invariably, adults complain that bad behavior among adolescents will have lasting consequences: rowdiness will lead to a life of vagrancy and crime, idleness as an adult, and the rebelliousness of the adolescent will create a generation of adult rebels. But the evidence is considerably more ambiguous. The rebelliousness of adolescence appears to be almost universal, but those middle-class youth whose mischief is apt to be overlooked by the police do not suffer permanent harm.[13] The youthful rebellions of the 1960s have not produced a generation of adult radicals, and even teen-age unemployment, which has loomed as a serious problem for more than a decade, is for many youth a form of testing different occupations without serious consequences for adult employment.[14]

We must therefore distinguish two strands of the "youth problem":

those actions of adolescents which have a lasting effect on their lives and are legitimately a target of social policy; and those actions which are more ambiguous but which generate intense hostility among adults. The two strands are worth distinguishing because the hostile side of ambivalent feelings is likely to generate policies that control different forms of obnoxious behavior rather than improve the future chances of young people. Adult anger has fostered a readiness to consider some youth—predominantly lower-class and minority youth—as liabilities, to abandon much of the pretense of considering them "our most precious natural resource and worthy of investment. Anger over intermittent employment among youth has led to condemning their indifference to the work ethic and devising ways to socialize them more completely, rather than to realistic appraisals of what youth gain is from such socialization or serious efforts to improve the quality of jobs available to them.[15] Hostility to school misbehavior has led to demands that youth "work harder," rather than to efforts to understand why they are so bored in school. Hostility to youthful crime rates has led to an ever-expanding juvenile justice system and calls for harsher punishment, rather than to efforts to understand and reverse the conditions that lead some teen-agers to abandon the conventional progression through school to work. In each instance, anger has led to policies that are essentially punitive and controlling—as if youths were already adults who cannot be rehabilitated—and away from public efforts that could comprehend the sources of the problems and reconstruct the options available to youth.

If we understand youth as a developmental stage and the "youth problem" as a dual problem—in part a response to the reality of unemployment, juvenile crime, and teen-age pregnancy, and in part a response to youthful "acting out"—then we can understand the dominant tendency to treat the problem with various educational solutions. Educational programs represent a rational response to some "real" dimensions of the youth problem: they can be effective in giving young people a sense of purpose, in providing them with alternatives to acting out, and in giving them the economic means and social status necessary for adult roles. If training programs work as designed—if they in fact impart skills and lead to increased employment opportunities, earnings, and status—then they combine rehabilitation and control, the state's twin goals; in "saving the child" they avoid the threats to social peace that unsatisfied and disillusioned workers present. But even if programs fail to make good on their vocational promises, they may still be appropriate if they merely occupy students, keep them out of trouble, and try to teach them appropriate behavior. As a response to fears that youths will be disruptive and become poorly socialized adults, using the schools and training programs as "warehouses" appears to be an appropriate (if illegitimate) response. This has led to the simultaneous enlargement of two different and partially contradictory functions of youth institutions—training, or preparing students for the labor market, and warehousing, or keeping them out of the labor market—as responses to different aspects of the "youth problem."

In fact, the essential basis of American youth policy since the early twentieth century has been the creation of public institutions for youth, designed simultaneously to keep them out of trouble and to prepare them for their occupational roles. At the turn of the century the expansion of the high school, the development of various training programs like vocational education, cooperative education, and continuation schools, and the creation of the juvenile justice system were all responses to the "youth problem": these institutions were highly age-segregated, as befitted a separate stage of development; they were segregated by class and race, conforming to the expectations of what different groups of youth most needed; they combined programs of training with mechanisms of controlling behavior, the precise mix depending on the institution and the class background of those in them; and they reflected the assumption that training is more appropriate for young people than adult activities are (employment or family). Ever since then, the basic approach to youth problems has been the expansion and the elaboration of training programs, justified as simultaneously preventing youth from flooding labor markets unable to absorb them, keeping them off the streets, and imparting values and skills of vocational relevance. Which of these would dominate has never been clear, and in practice has often depended on class and racial biases.

Just as youth are intermediate between childhood and adulthood, so too are youth institutions pulled between adult institutions and practices that are more clearly applicable to young children. The treatment of work in youth institutions provides a good example: although adolescents spend their time preparing for employment, they do not engage in serious employment. At the same time as many reformers have pushed for more work-oriented activities—work-experience programs, vocational and career education, training programs outside the schools like Job Corps and Youth Employment and Demonstration Projects Act (YEDPA)—the trend since the child labor legislation of the progressive era has been to eliminate youth from employment, to lengthen the period of preparation, and postpone "adult" employment. The result is that, even though labor force participation rates for adolescents are currently high, the employment they have is by and large "youth" employment—in fast-food restaurants, gas stations, as babysitters and errand boys—trivial, demeaning, unstable, and without any future. The attempts to incorporate work into the school curriculum have similarly amounted to "playing at work" rather than real employment. The responses to teen-age delinquency provide another example of institutions being torn between conceptions of adulthood and childhood: the juvenile justice system has been constantly pulled between adult forms of control—involving due process and prison sentences—and forms intended to consider the age of youthful offenders, to treat them more like children growing up than fully formed adults.

To some extent the ambiguities of youth institutions are inevitable, given the social construction of youth as a transitory stage. However, the precise forms of the resulting conflicts, the class and sexual biases, and the hostility toward disobedience that they reflect are not inevitable. In both the training and employment programs and in the juvenile justice system, which we examine in the next sections, ambivalence toward youth and the class divisions among youth have undermined the ability to solve the problems of youth.

Employment, Training, and Warehousing

Twentieth-century Americans have been ambivalent about whether young people should work or should be in school. However, all have agreed that unemployment is far worse than either employment or schooling. The fear has invariably been that unemployed young people may become delinquents and develop attitudes that inhibit adult success, that their experiences may led to disenchantment with the work ethic. The lament for wasted social resources has been particularly strident, as concerned with the loss of taxpayers' "investments" as with the possible devastation of the youth involved:

> All unemployment is wasteful. When it is concentrated among youth, as in the current context, it has particular human, social, and economic consequences. It implies not only a current loss of valuable human resources, but also lost returns on human capital investments which will doubtless extend well into the future.[16]

Like the creation of youth institutions, the concern for youth unemployment and efforts to reduce it through training programs date from the progressive era. Early twentieth-century surveys of youth in the labor market found them overwhelmingly in unskilled, poorly paid, seasonal jobs with high turnover rates, poor working conditions, and few opportunities for advancement—"blind alley" jobs, generating the "wasted years syndrome." The economist Paul Douglas wrote in 1921 that young people drifted from "job to job, from industry to industry, still unskilled and exposed to all the social and industrial evils which threaten adolescence." As a consequence, adulthood found the working-class youth among "the class of the permanently unskilled with the attendant low wages and unemployment of his class."[17]

In response, a host of school-based programs were established to keep youth in school and to provide them with employment skills—vocational education, continuation schools, and cooperative education. The forerunner of current training programs, education for work was designed to provide working-class youth with economically relevant training, and thus a rationale for staying in school. In practice, the training had little economic relevance; vocational programs played a limited role in keeping youth in school longer, and there was little evidence that the school-based training led to higher wages. Instead, the new orientation to teaching work in school had its greatest impact within the school itself, serving to segregate youth by class according to their "evident or probable destinies."[18]

During the Great Depression, the approach to youth unemployment was temporarily modified, though the rhetoric about training remained what it had been. Youth benefited from the New Deal institution of public employment, largely as an afterthought because the unemployment of adult breadwinners was more pressing. Although the youthful versions of adult programs, such as the Youth Conservation Corps, provided some actual employment, they were justified more in terms of the training they provided than for the employment opportunities they created. Just as was true for adults, the employment programs of the depression were considered temporary expedients, however; once the crisis of the depression was over, the elaboration of training programs divorced from employment continued as the dominant solution to the problems of youth.[19]

The dominance of training solutions again became apparent during the 1960s. In response to "technological unemployment" and the persistence of high unemployment among urban blacks—James Conant's "social dynamite"—vocational education was rejuvenated in the Vocational Education Act of 1963 and then in the 1968 amendments. Yet because vocational education has had on the average very little economic return, its promise to reduce unemployment and integrate minorities into the economic mainstream was empty.[20] The development of various manpower programs during the 1960s expanded the variety of training programs outside the schools, but like vocational education their results were mixed. One program—the Job Corps—provided stipends for young people in training, but this "employment" lasted only a few months and proved to have little value in obtaining subsequent employment.[21] Whatever the causes of failure in the various programs of the 1960s, they were clearly more effective as warehousing mechanisms—containing "social dynamite" by keeping working-class and minority youth in institutional settings—than as training.

During the 1970s a confluence of special factors drove teen-age unemployment to historic highs. In 1975, the peak year for adult unemployment, 19.9 percent of those aged sixteen to nineteen who were looking for work were unemployed, compared to 7.3 percent of those twenty and over. Between 1975 and 1980 nearly 50 percent of all unemployed persons in the United States were between sixteen and twenty-four. Despite the widespread assumption that youth unemployment almost always involves short terms between jobs, as youths move from job to job, most youth unemployment occurs among young people who cannot find jobs for long periods of time; more than 50 percent of unemployed male teenagers tended to be out of work more than six months. Teen-age unemployment, always bad, has increased since the 1950s; not only has overall unemployment increased, the ratio of youth unemployment to adult unemployment went from 2.5 in 1954 to 3.3 in 1978.[22]

Not surprisingly, the situation has been the worst for youth from low-income families and especially for low-income nonwhites. In March 1978, the unemployment rate for low-income white youth was 25.5 percent; for low-income nonwhite youth it was 48.8 percent. The unemployment rate for black high school graduates was almost three times the rate of their white counterparts. The increase in youth unemployment has been most serious for nonwhites: since 1954, white teen-age unemployment rates have increased slightly, but they have doubled for black teenagers. The unemployment rate was 19 percent between 1955 and 1959 for nonwhite male youth, and 34 percent in 1977–78 for the same group. For nonwhite females between sixteen and nineteen, unemployment was 23 percent between 1955 and 1959, and 38 percent in 1977–78. Evidently, black and Hispanic teen-agers suffer the additional barriers of discrimination.[23] Despite the gains that blacks have made in the postwar period—in narrowing educational differences with whites and in the increased returns to schooling—these gains appear to have benefited experienced and well-educated blacks more than adolescents. While the efforts of the federal government to reduce employment discrimination have not yet had any clear effect in labor markets,[24] even these efforts have focused on older workers. The result is that unemployment among minority youth remains one of the most intractable social problems. As one commentator put it, "Unemployment is a tragedy for Black youth and a disaster for Black young women."[25]

The "crisis" of the 1970s represented an escalation of chronically high rates of youth unemployment during the postwar period, rather than a new and unexpected phenomenon. Throughout the postwar period the unemployment rates for teen-agers have been between 2.5 and 4.5 times as high as adult unemployment rates, This implies that the youth labor market is structurally different from the rest of the labor market. Employers prefer to hire older workers, and for most jobs—especially jobs with career potential—they will not seriously consider teen-agers except in periods of labor shortage.[26] They often consider young workers erratic and unreliable, less well socialized to the workplace. In an economy with a chronically high level of unemployment, where it is usually possible to hire a slightly older worker, there is no reason for an employer to run the risks involved with younger workers, and the employment rates of adolescents suffer. The reasons given vary: some employers cite child labor laws as barriers to hiring young people; others blame the minimum wage and other costs of employment, including Social Security, fringe benefits, occupational health and safety regulations, which induce employers to hire individuals whom they consider less transient.[27] Although the evidence on the effects of labor laws and the minimum wage is mixed, conservatives have nonetheless made them a central issue by demanding a subminimum wage for teen-agers.[28]

Finally, youth appear to be harshly affected by the increasing levels of certification required for more and more jobs. While the estimates are loose at best, one-third of all jobs in 1950 did not require a high school diploma; in 1970, 92 percent of all jobs required a diploma.[29] The fastest growing occupations in the postwar period have been professional and government positions, most of which require high levels of education. One implication is that the increasing educational requirements for most occupations (particularly for stable occupations) may have prevented teen-agers from being considered for an ever-increasing proportion of jobs, and crowded them into the unskilled, poorly paid positions in the service sector—jobs in fast-food restaurants and service stations, as busboys, waitresses, and babysitters—conventionally open to teen-agers but which contain no career paths and encourage unstable work.[30] A growing number of positions are closed off to youth because of educational requirements, while the available jobs are increasingly the "dead-end" jobs that have always been criticized for contributing to the instability of youth.

Youth unemployment thus results from both personal factors, particularly the low educational levels of youth involved and perhaps a lack of information about labor markets,[31] and labor market conditions, including discrimination against youth, racial discrimination, the inflation of educational requirements, and increasing numbers of secondary labor market jobs with poor working conditions. While the causes are complex, the solutions to youth unemployment have followed a predictable and simplistic pattern: rather than dealing with labor markets the solutions propose another set of educational solutions. In the 1960s and 1970s various programs were developed to make the schools more "relevant" to work and to ease the transition between school and work.[32] Vocational education programs proliferated, first under the Vocational Education Act of 1963 and the amendments of 1968, and then under the Vocational Education Act of 1976. Career education burst forth upon an educational establishment eager for quick solutions in the mid-1970s, with the immodest goal of reorienting all of schooling around the quest for work.[33] Work experience programs proliferated at the high school level, intending to allow students to explore "career options." Their most obvious effect was to affirm how bored many youths were in school and to persuade some students that pumping gas and serving hamburgers do not provide the basis for a fulfilling life. In terms of expanding occupational choices and improving occupational futures, the work-experience programs showed few positive returns.[34] The expansion of two-year colleges continued, with the majority of them explicitly vocational in their curriculum and purpose. The programmatic changes in schools, despite their small impact, were still notable for their single-minded emphasis on the vocational purposes of schooling to the exclusion of all others.

The second strand of current youth policy draws upon the employment initiatives of the Great Depression and was developed as an explicit alternative to school-based programs. The manpower programs of the 1960s were revived as "employment and training programs" in the 1970s, in the Comprehensive Employment and Training Act of 1973 (CETA) and in the Youth Employment and Demonstration Projects Act of 1977 (YEDPA) which was explicitly intended to reduce the high levels of youth unemployment. Touted as an effective alternative to education for work programs, youth employment and training programs share the assumptions of the traditional vocational education solutions: they are efforts to cope with unskilled young people who have no real place and may engage in antisocial behavior, and they assume that training will be sufficient to insure later employment. Despite their origin as responses to high unemployment rates, the specific programs that absorb youth have stressed training rather than employment. Although 43 percent of the individuals in general CETA programs in 1978 were in public service employment positions, only 24 percent of the youths were in those programs; the other 76 percent were enrolled in CETA Title I programs which provided training and counseling but little employment. Only about 230,000 public service employment positions were open to those under twenty-two, a small fraction of all youth who were in some kind of program and less than 10 percent of those who might be unemployed at any particular time.[35] Moreover, about 80 percent of employment positions available to youth were summer jobs, so temporary that they were neither serious employment nor training. These jobs are best understood as efforts to keep troublesome adolescents off the streets during the long summers. Even YEDPA, created in response to the perception that the amount of employment available to young people is chronically inadequate, failed to change the thrust of federal policy both because of its relatively small size—less than 200,000 enrollees in 1978—and because two-thirds of the positions created were in the Youth Employment and Training Programs (YETP), which provided training and ancillary employment services but not employment.[36]

The changes proposed by Ronald Reagan early in his administration reinforced the dominance of training over employment programs. In the search for ways to slash social programs, expensive public employment programs were completely eliminated, with the clear message from the administration that the Department of Labor would abandon its "income supplement" and "income maintenance" programs in favor of training. In turn, CETA training programs were themselves substantially cut and combined into a single grant, so that youth programs have to compete against adult programs with stronger political constituencies.[37] In every way, the Reagan proposals have reflected extreme versions of the assumptions which have always governed youth policy: programs for youth should be subordinate to programs for adults, public efforts must remain subordinate to private labor markets, and training rather than employment opportunities are the appropriate public response to youth problems.

The continuing strength of training as the core of youth policy assumes again that unemployed youths lack only the skills and the socialization necessary for the occupations available. For some young people this assumption may be true: those individuals who come out of public schools illiterate and incompetent in every way appear to be helped substantially by some training programs. Nonetheless, the value of training programs has not been generally established since many programs create no advantages for their graduates whatsoever; for other programs the advantages in terms of earning levels and employment rates dissipate after a few years.[38]

To some extent, then, the conservative attacks on CETA and YEDPA make sense: the programs have done little to modify the conditions of the labor market for youth or adults. Programs may not have been consistently implemented or in place for long enough periods, and evaluation methods may still be inadequate. However, the dismal experience with manpower programs of the 1960s suggests another possibility which has long plagued vocational education and which European countries have been willing to recognize: it makes no sense to train individuals without ascertaining whether there are jobs to absorb them and without coordinating training with the available jobs.

The problem, however, may be even deeper: the task set for training programs may well-nigh be impossible. The programs take lower-class youth whom the schools have failed to train, and they attempt to do in relatively short periods of time what the schools have not done over a period of at least ten years. Their supposed advantage is that, by being more closely connected to work and with the threat of unemployment more tangible, the incentive to learn is greater. Yet each of these assumptions is uncertain. Training programs that are not coordinated with specific and permanent jobs may be no more relevant to employment than are school-based programs. The threat of unemployment may be palpable enough, but the threat may be irrelevant if a training program cannot guarantee a meaningful position upon successful completion. With an increasing number of decent jobs requiring formal educational credentials to enter them, dropping out of school and entering a training program may itself be destructive of future employment opportunities. Moreover, since the training programs are explicitly directed at lower-class youth and are based on the assumption of personal failure, the labeling associated with this kind of intervention may serve to undercut employment possibilities. It is thus difficult, despite pious hopes, to see why training programs should work where schools have failed.

Since employment and training programs provide so little employment, since so much of the employment is short-term, and since the effects of training are so minimal, their real function remains that of warehousing. In this they have been relatively successful: the various employment and training programs involved close to three million youth in 1977 and reduced the youth unemployment rate in 1976 by about four percentage points, compared to what it would have been in the absence of such programs.[39] If nothing else, the programs provided places for thousands of young people no longer in school and yet with no "adult" positions to enter, serving to keep youth out of the way and out of trouble until they mature. Yet the warehousing role remains illegimate. Supporters of training programs cannot admit that their essential function is to keep youth off the streets and out of the labor market, and so they continue to promote them as solutions to unemployment, poverty, discrimination, and delinquency. Only conservatives have been willing to condemn programs like CETA and YEDPA for their ineffectiveness, and they have done so largely out of hostility to all social programs for the poor. Thus neither the conservative onslaught nor the dismal results of vocational and training programs has seriously challenged the view that youth as a developmental stage should be treated with educational solutions, and the obvious alternatives—changing the options available to the young—remain largely untried.

The historical popularity of educational solutions also reflects the restrictions on the state's interference in "private" labor markets. Education and training programs have always been legitimate, since they produce skills which employers use and which they might otherwise have to provide themselves. To address employment problems more directly—to guarantee reasonable levels of employment for young people or to guarantee that successful completion of an educational program would be rewarded with meaningful work—would require a level of government influence over "private" labor markets which is impossible in a capitalist society, and has not been acceptable to either liberals or conservatives. To go further and address the quality of jobs available to youth—to prevent discrimination against young people and against black and Hispanic teenagers, to shape the jobs available so that they include more rewarding kinds of work than pumping gas and pushing fast food—would require public interference with the conditions of employment which has always been resisted in the name of protecting the prerogatives of private firms.

The few efforts in the postwar period to intervene in labor markets directly have all been strenuously opposed. Efforts to reduce discrimination against minorities, for example—critically necessary to attack the most persistent part of youth unemployment—have had little success since the passage of the 1964 Civil Rights Act, but even those efforts have been focused on adults rather than youth. Attempts to upgrade the quality of jobs available to youth have never been incorporated into government policy, even though the "quality of work" has periodically appeared on the social agenda.[40] Public service employment has been limited because of the public expenditures involved, because of fear that it might dilute private labor market incentives, and because production of goods and services with public employment might interfere with profit-making opportunities in the private sector. As a result, public employment has been resisted as a step on the road to socialism, and has been consistently pushed into activities that would not compete with the private sector. The absurdity of this restriction is sometimes obvious: at the same time that youth unemployment levels are high, some areas (especially central cities) suffer from dilapidated housing, housing shortages, and poor public facilities, but the mobilization of human resources to meet obvious social needs has been resisted as encroaching on the prerogatives of the housing and construction industries. The limits on the state facing a capitalist labor market has thus forced youth policy into indirect and inappropriate solutions, since the more forthright approaches to the underlying employment problems have been politically limited. Ironically, the inability to intervene in labor markets has been the death of education and training programs because it has made it impossible to coordinate training with available jobs and because the structural problems of youth labor markets—especially discrimination and the inadequacy of employment opportunities—have often made training irrelevant.

If employment and training programs have had any effect on youth unemployment, their effect has been similar to the role of the schools. The training they give has uncertain effects on future earnings and employment, but by their very size the programs reduce the amount of unemployment. This may be reason enough for their continued existence, but as a solution to persistent "youth problems," the training programs add little to our youth policy except to generate a "back-up" institution to the schools. In the process, they have inherited the structural problems of school-based programs—particularly the dilemma of trying to provide real opportunity for lower-class and minority youth in an inegalitarian and class-divided society—with the added problems of taking young people already designated failures and trying to generate quick results without the ability to shape employment opportunities. The real promise of education and training programs has thereby been corrupted: the links between employment and training have been broken, and the opportunity to create more and better employment for youth has been undermined by the emphasis on training.

The Juvenile Justice System: Control over Rehabilitation

The similarities between training programs and the juvenile justice system are striking. Both originated in their current form during the progressive era. Both represent responses to the most intransigent youth problems, unemployability and delinquency, respectively. Both are "back-up" institutions to the schools, while both are simultaneously influenced by their adult counterparts, manpower programs and the adult criminal system. The two problems they address are related, since unemployment leads to crime and criminal records reduce employment prospects. Finally, the dilemmas of how to treat youth—the conflicts between training and warehousing, between rehabilitation and control—are present in both. Even more than in employment and training programs, however, youth within the juvenile justice system are more overtly threatening, the class biases of the system more powerful, and the slide from child saving and rehabilitation to social control and protecting the community all the faster.

The dilemmas of the juvenile justice system have never been more apparent than in the 1960s and 1970s, when an explosive rise in juvenile crime became the focus of intense concern. The statistics are staggering: between 1950 and 1975 the annual number of arrests of those under eighteen rose from 35,000 to over three million. Over half the arrests for serious crimes—murder, robbery, rape, auto theft, and burglary—now involve juveniles, so that delinquency no longer represents the minor crimes of adolescence, like alcohol use or petty vandalism.[41] Even more than youth unemployment, juvenile crime has become the clearest indicator of a "youth problem." Yet juvenile crime remains ill-defined; even as juvenile crime grows more serious, it still includes a preponderance of status offenses—truancy, incorrigibility, general disobedience. Our ambivalence toward youth has generated a continuing uncertainty: does juvenile crime represent a downward extension of "adult" crime, or is it the temporary rebelliousness or "acting out" of adolescence manifested in status offenses? If juvenile delinquents are criminals in the adult sense, then they ought to be segregated from society, incarcerated, and controlled. If they are merely rebellious, then gentler handling is appropriate, directed toward smoothing the transition to adulthood. This uncertainty has led to inconsistent treatment of juvenile offenders, creating a system that neither rehabilitates them nor protects the community from their increasingly serious acts.

A second dilemma, apparent as well in the other aspects of "youth policy," is even more insistent within the juvenile justice system: as an institution of last resort, the juvenile justice system gathers together those adolescents who have failed in more conventional institutions—schools and manpower programs—and makes a last effort to prepare them for adult roles. Unfortunately, the juvenile justice system has little at its disposal besides the power of incarceration. It is especially helpless in dealing with the education and unemployment problems that affect juvenile behavior, and the coerciveness of incarceration undermines therapeutic efforts and attempts at training. Indeed, the persistent failure of rehabilitation poses the question of whether it is logically impossible, because the conflicting impulse to control and the burdens of being an institution of last resort present insuperable barriers.

The assumptions and structure of the current juvenile justice system took shape in two phases.[42] The juvenile asylums of the mid-nineteenth century, which took children out of their homes and placed them in large institutions, invariable originated with a rhetoric of benevolence and rehabilitation as a way of protecting poor youth from their home environments. Just as invariably, they shifted toward incarceration as an end in itself, to protect communities from potentially delinquent youth. In the second phase, the special treatment of children was expanded and institutionalized in the juvenile court movement around the turn of the century. The underlying rationale restated the earlier claims of benevolence: the juvenile court could more readily deal with youth in informal ways suited to their individual circumstances, in contrast to the harsh treatment or neglect they received in the adult criminal system. The juvenile court system was to be the family enlarged, designed to provide the familial understanding and guidance presumed absent from the homes of the lower-class youth.

The assumed benevolence was suspect, however. The "coercive predictions" of which children were likely to become criminal overwhelmingly brought lower-class, minority, and immigrant children into the court. In practice the court served to remind such children (and their parents) of their inferior position, and of the importance of "good"—that is, native middle-class—behavior. Rehabilitative efforts to transform potentially dangerous individuals into productive citizens remained a central rationale of the juvenile court, but the disparities between means and ends were enormous: the caseload of court officers was too large, coercion undercut efforts to establish personal relationships, and the obvious class and racial biases of court workers fueled the hostility between court and clients and eroded the ideal of familylike relationships. Rehabilitation justified arbitrary and widespread efforts to control certain kinds of children, rather than a goal that could be seriously attained.

The legacy of the juvenile court has thus been complex and contradictory. Impulses to control the behavior of poor and minority children have coincided with a benevolence deeply felt by reformers. The tension was evident right from the beginning. Reflecting on the origins of the juvenile court, Julia Lathrop, the first chief of the Children's Bureau, wrote that the court

applied not to all children but only to a neglected minority—those who committed or were charged with offenses against the law. Their sufferings made an appeal to both commonsense and pity, while their menace to the order of the society which disregarded them could not permanently be ignored.[43]

In practice, protecting the community dominated. Rehabilitative efforts were compromised by the court's limited resources, by its imperfect understanding of rehabilitation, and by hostility toward lower-class clients. The blurring of delinquency, involving real crimes, and dependency, involving status offenses, reflected the same conflict: the rehabilitative function called for extending the court's influence as far as possible, well beyond those youths who had committed obviously criminal acts, but the nature of that influence was coercive and controlling. Even probation—the retention of juveniles in their own homes under the watchful eye of the court—expanded the court's scope so as to create a new coercive form rather than reduce the punitiveness of the justice system; more youth became subject to the legal system than ever before. With this kind of tension, it is not surprising that the juvenile court could do little to rehabilitate adolescents.

Until the 1960s, when youth crime and unemployment rates burgeoned, the juvenile justice system itself remained relatively invisible. The new sense of "crisis" in the 1960s was bluntly expressed by the President's Task Force on Juvenile Delinquency in 1967:

> The great hopes originally held for the juvenile courts have not been fulfilled. The system has not succeeded significantly in rehabilitating delinquent youth, in reducing or even stemming the tide of juvenile criminality, or in bringing justice to the youthful offender. To say that juvenile courts have failed to achieve their goals is to say no more than what is true of criminal courts in the United States. But failure is more striking where the hopes are the highest.[44]

The task force emphasized prevention and diversion—ways of handling juveniles without bringing them into the juvenile justice system itself, through service programs and youth bureaus. At the same time juvenile justice became linked to calls for more vigorous policing. Under the Omnibus Crime Control and Safe Streets Act of 1968 and expanded federal funding, the capacity of the police to arrest developed faster than any other part of the juvenile justice system. The resulting increase in the rates of detention was far greater than the increase in juvenile crime rates.[45] This development not only contradicted the emphasis of the 1967 task force report on decriminalization and diversion, but it also undermined the capacity of the system to do anything at all with the juveniles in its charge.[46] Ironically, increased policing of juveniles contributed to the paralysis of the system: it could neither keep kids off the streets nor could it provide any meaningful approaches to rehabilitation.

Under pressure to deal with rising rates of juvenile crimes, Congress passed the Juvenile Justice and Delinquency Prevention Act in 1974. Despite a finding that federal intervention had been inadequate, the 1974 act provided relatively little funding for special rehabilitative programs, compared to the funds already available through the 1968 act for policing. By ignoring the trend toward more policing, the existence of larger and more numerous detention facilities, and the structural causes of juvenile crime, the 1974 act reinstitutionalized the kind of juvenile justice system in place since the progressive era. Rehabilitation and prevention were stressed in the new legislation, but in practice policing functions continued to dominate.

Partly because of the constant emphasis on controlling elements, adolescent contact with the first line of the juvenile justice system—the police— is more widespread than is generally realized. In one sample, 88 percent of all boys and girls reported committing at least one delinquent act in the previous three years, while 20 percent of the sample reported contact with the police.[47] Such contact is evidently much more widespread than subsequent processing: of the 20 percent only 4 percent turned up in official police records, 1.9 percent were referred to juvenile court, and 1.3 percent were found "delinquent" and declared wards of the court. These data confirm a widespread suspicion: adolescent behavior involves a nearly universal rebelliousness, much of which is technically considered delinquency but which is undetected or ignored because of the considerable discretion of the police, court workers, and teachers in dealing with youths.

The discretion of those in the juvenile justice system in turn permits class and racial biases to operate. In one study 26.5 percent of boys of higher socioeconomic status had contact with the police, compared to 44.8 percent of lower-status boys; 28 percent of white boys compared to 50 percent of black boys had at least one contact. To some extent differential rates of policing in white and black communities, and in wealthy and poor neighborhoods, explain differentials in rates of apprehension. Once apprehended, nonwhites and those of lower-class status are more likely to have a court penalty, rather than having their cases informally disposed of.[48] This confirms that the juvenile justice system responds to juveniles themselves, not just to the acts they commit; the judgment of "predelinquency" is more common for minority and lower-class boys and stands as a special warning about appropriate behavior.

Sexual bias within the juvenile justice system also works to reinforce patterns of behavior considered appropriate. Girls overwhelmingly are detained and incarcerated for status offenses—being beyond the control of parents and in need of supervision, running away, incorrigibility, and, as

177

has been true since the system's origins in the nineteenth century, sexual activity. Even nominally criminal acts—shoplifting or prostitution—may be charged as status offenses rather than delinquency. One study, for example, found that over 80 percent of girls incarcerated were found guilty of status offenses, while only 18 percent of male incarcerations were for status offenses. This difference reflects an obvious double standard: in boys independence is tolerable, even encouraged, but in teen-age girls it indicates some form of deviance and is punished as such by the juvenile court.[49]

If the juvenile justice system succeeded in turning youth from destructive paths into meaningful employment and responsible adult life, then its biases and its denial of rights to adolescents might not be quite as objectionable. This basic assumption has generated a staggering variety of "rehabilitative" programs. In general, they replicate the activities of current employment and training programs, providing counseling, work experience, information about labor markets, and encouragement to return to conventional schooling programs.[50] Unlike programs for nondelinquents, however, the strong assumption that psychological factors are responsible for delinquency has led to a preponderance of therapeutic and counseling programs rather than work-related training programs.[51] Unfortunately few of these programs have been effective in changing the values and attitudes of the youth enrolled in them, in changing their delinquent or "predelinquent" behavior, or in assuring them access to employment with any advantage in terms of earnings or job conditions.[52] In fact, one longitudinal study found that boys enrolled in an intensive "delinquency prevention" program suffered as a result; compared to a control group, they reported more drinking problems, held lower-status jobs, reported more stress-related disease, and tended to die younger, without any compensating differences in crime rates.[53] The implication is that the labeling and the coercion that are inevitable parts of such programs outweigh whatever good they may do.

The consistent failure of programs within the juvenile justice system raises the question of why rehabilitation seems so elusive. One reason involves the system's priorities: the greater willingness to fund policing and incarceration has consistently dominated the efforts at deinstitutionalization and rehabilitation. A second reason involves the role of the juvenile justice system as a back-up to the schools: those individuals for whom the incentives of the schools are insufficient to motivate acceptable behavior are left for the juvenile justice system to rehabilitate.[54] This increases the difficulties of training; the promise of future employment is even weaker than it is in the schools, since youths with a police record have a harder time finding employment. The time span of juvenile programs is insufficient: if a decade of schooling has failed to instill appropriate behavior, the expectation that a six-month program can accomplish the same task is absurd. The incentive unique to the juvenile justice system—the threat of incarceration—turns out to be ineffective and self-defeating.

Above all, the relationship between juvenile programs and employment is insufficient. Given the strong relationship between unemployment and juvenile crime rates—with periods of high unemployment increasing juvenile crime[55]—the inability of the juvenile system to do much about unemployment rates dooms existing programs to marginal effectiveness. Within this constraint, the emphasis of existing programs on psychological factors rather than employment problems is a further weakness. The experience of the schools is instructive: the school as the mainstay of our "youth policy" has worked best when it delivers on its vocational promise, when students can be reasonably assured that good performance leads to decent employment opportunities. When the relationship between training and employment has broken down—when the economic rate of return to schooling has fallen, or when the jobs are worse than students have come to expect—then enrollments have fallen and dissatisfaction with the schools has increased. This experience implies that, to be successful, juvenile rehabilitation programs must guarantee that successful completion will substantially increase employment stability, earnings, and other social goods. This is precisely what juvenile programs cannot guarantee because they are not connected to existing labor market opportunities and because the adolescents they treat are at the end of the queue of potential jobholders. Their task is made even more difficult during periods of high unemployment—like the 1970s and the early 1980s—since unemployment rates both increase juvenile crime and make job placement all the more difficult, especially for youth and for those who have a criminal record. If the juvenile justice system cannot offer youthful offenders a future in the form of employment, then it has essentially nothing to offer.

The juvenile justice system is thus caught in the worst of all possible dilemmas. It is unable to deliver on the promise of rehabilitation, and yet it is stuck with the duty to control youth and must therefore incarcerate many of them. But since it can not give up on the hope of rehabilitation, incarceration is gentle—usually short-term, in minimum-security facilities or community placements, or on probation—and fails to protect the community from those who are truly violent. Given the system's structural problems, the various reforms that have been proposed in the last two decades seem inadequate. New proposals to limit the number of youth brought into the formal part of the juvenile justice system, through pro-

179

grams of diversion and community-based work programs, might reduce the system's harshness. But they are also likely to expand its scope (as probation did earlier), particularly since attempts to divert youth from the juvenile court and into alternatives like youth service bureaus will lead many to assume that the alternatives are extensions of the existing justice system. Diversionary programs also meet tremendous resistance since community forces—including the police, teachers, and neighborhood residents—have rarely supported noncustodial programs, preferring that troublesome juveniles be kept off the streets and out of their communities.[56]

A second reform—decriminalization—proposes to eliminate as crimes all status offenses on the assumption that the benevolent intentions of *parens patriae* have broken down and that status offenders have been consistently denied constitutional rights. The Juvenile Justice and Delinquency Prevention Act of 1974 moved toward decriminalization by requiring that status offenders "shall not be placed in juvenile detention facilities or correctional facilities, but must be placed in shelter facilities" and by emphasizing "educational programs or supportive services designed to keep delinquents and encourage other youth to remain in elementary and secondary schools or in alternative learning situations." Yet the separation of status offenses from real crimes remains incomplete, partly because resistance at the state and local level reflects a continuing desire to see troublesome juveniles out of the community. As long as status offenders are brought into the juvenile justice system in any way, they are still considered offenders and outcasts: the differences between "shelter" facilities for status offenders and "correctional" facilities for delinquents are in practice unclear, especially to juveniles held against their will. The process of decriminalization has not reduced the scope of the court's control, nor has it resolved the central issue of what to do with youth in the juvenile justice system.[57]

Diversion and decriminalization have been part of a persistent tendency to "deinstitutionalize" the juvenile justice system. The juvenile court and the parole system established in the progressive era and the half-way houses, shelters, youth service bureaus, and community-based treatment programs established more recently have all been attempts to prevent the incarceration of juveniles in more formidable institutional settings. But neither the number of institutional spaces nor the number of youths incarcerated has declined through almost a century of deinstitutionalization efforts. The effect of deinstitutionalization has primarily been to establish new programs—new institutions, in effect—rather than to reduce the scope of the juvenile court.[58] In the absence of any real ability to help troublesome juveniles and with persistent pressure to control unruly youth, deinstitutionalization remains contradictory, a recurring expression of the hope of treating adolescents informally and benevolently rather than a clear program.

At the same time, the basic principles of the juvenile court have come under attack. The juvenile system has been under pressure to drop its benevolent and rehabilitative aspirations and treat juveniles as adults. The increase in adolescents who appear to be "hardened criminals" engaging in murder, armed robbery, and rape has allowed many to abandon the usual view of juvenile offenders as youngsters momentarily gone wrong and to consider them as adults. Relative to the present model, this view represents an abandonment of the hope of rehabilitation (slim as that hope may be) and the advocacy of an extreme version of control.

From a different ideological perspective, the movement to extend the legal rights of adults to juveniles also reflects an abandonment of basic principles, specifically the assumption embedded in *parens patriae* that the juvenile court acts in the best interests of the child. In providing due process rights for the first time in 1966, the Supreme Court outlined the special horror of the juvenile court: "There may be grounds for concern that the child receives the worst of both worlds: that he gets neither the protections accorded to adults nor the solicitous care and regenerative treatment postulated for children."[59] One year later, the Court formally rejected the contention that the informality of juvenile court proceedings was justified by the helpful and nonpunitive nature of the treatment, since the evidence indicated that industrial schools and other detention facilities were really prisons rather than rehabilitation centers. *In re Gault* (1967) established a variety of due process rights for juveniles accused of delinquency, including notice of charges, notice of the right to counsel, the protection against self-incrimination of the Fifth Amendment, and the right to confront one's accuser and other witnesses.[60] While these are important rights, the extension of due process to juveniles—like the efforts to try adolescents as adults—also signals resignation to the fact that the juvenile court cannot be the tender and forgiving parent substitute of its early ideal.

At least some of the reforms which have been proposed are consistent with the benevolent goals that underlie *parens patriae* and the juvenile justice system. Diversion and deinstitutionalization are intended to facilitate placements appropriate to the offenses juveniles have committed, placements that provide a greater hope for rehabilitation; decriminalization recognizes that many offenses of juveniles are not worth social notice in the first place, especially if the consequences of that notice are harmful rather than helpful. Other reforms, especially the extension of juvenile rights, are necessary antidotes to harsh impulses toward youth. These reform efforts—as well as efforts to generate more funds for rehabilitative programs rather than policing and to teach real skills to those without them—are laudable attempts to resurrect the old ideal of acting on behalf of youth.

But on the whole, the trends of the last two decades have reaffirmed the essential duality of the juvenile justice system. Whether its charges are to be considered adults or children with claims to special treatment, whether its mission is the protection of society or the development of wayward youngsters, have never been fully resolved. The reconciliation of these conflicting goals is possible only if rehabilitative programs are successful in transforming troublesome youth into productive and law-abiding citizens, in which case youths are saved and society is protected. But given the failure of rehabilitative efforts, the hope of reconciling these conflicting pressures has been constantly thwarted. As the institution of last resort, the aura of failure and the processes of labeling and stigmatization are all the more intense, the racial and class-based hostilities all the more powerful, and the pressures to control unruly youth more extreme than they are in any other setting. Yet the mechanisms of control are themselves imperfect because the juvenile system is constructed more to deal with "predelinquents" and status offenders than with the "hardened criminals" who emerged in greater numbers during the 1970s, and thus they are unable to keep violent juveniles from terrorizing their communities. The result is an institution faced with conflicting pressures but without the means at its disposal to reconcile them, driven to inappropriate punishment of some juveniles and inappropriate release of others, and constantly in the process of reform without success.

Resolving the "Inevitable" Youth Problem

As long as youth is structured as a stage of life between the dependence and irresponsibility of childhood and the independence and responsibility of adulthood, we will remain ambivalent about youth themselves—wishing they were less childish, but not wanting to push them into adulthood too quickly, unsure of whether to train or control them, to ignore their bad behavior or to suppress it. Since the decisions of youth determine adult status and seem irreversible, they will continue to be anxiety-ridden and tumultuous. Adolescent tribulations are therefore built into our conceptions of youth and the public institutions that contain them.

Yet the problems of youth have been exacerbated by two aspects of

American society which are neither inevitable nor unchangeable, though they are deeply rooted: the nature of class and racial divisions and the structure of capitalist labor markets. Despite the occasional manifestation of public concern over adolescent identity crises or student rebelliousness, the "problems of youth" on the social agenda have largely been problems like school failure, unemployment, and juvenile delinquency associated with lower-class youth. These problems are themselves caused by class divisions: class and racial discrimination consistently operates to the detriment of lower-class and minority children, so that by the time they are adolescents the cumulative weight of poor school performance, higher unemployment rates, poor prospects for stable future employment, and despair has generated the complex of problems we associate with troubled youth. Yet the class biases in the social construction of youth impede the resolution of those problems. For lower-class youth, public responses often assume that the "evident or probable destinies" of such individuals are unskilled, unstable, and underpaid occupations. The incomplete efforts at training youth in school-based vocational programs and in employment and training programs, the willingness to abandon training in favor of warehousing, and the preference for control over rehabilitation are all class-biased—and ineffective—responses to class-based problems.

The problems of American youth are also linked to the deficiencies of employment under American capitalism. Increasing levels of unemployment and the special structure of the youth labor market have meant that youth—particularly lower-class youth with few prospects of continuing to college and middle-class occupations—have little of serious significance to occupy them. The hopelessness of unemployment and the juvenile crime it fosters are the most obvious manifestations of this "waste of human resources," publicly recognized because they are so threatening. Without the ability to change the level and the composition of employment itself, all other policies are doomed to remain incomplete. The history of efforts to mount training programs, from the vocational programs of the progressive era to the initiatives of YEDPA and the revised Job Corps, is one of skills unutilized because of the lack of available occupations, of training that is not coordinated with employment—efforts that have all failed to confront labor markets directly. Until this becomes possible, our implicit youth policy can at best try to contain the dissatisfactions of youth and will necessarily continue to be in a state of perpetual crisis and reform.

Paul Goodman's judgment of the "youth problem" of the 1950s has held even more forcefully into the 1980s:

> The majority of young people are faced with the following alternative: either society is a benevolently frivolous racket in which they'll manage to boondoggle, though less profitably than the more privileged; or society is serious (and

they hope still benevolent enough to support them), but they are useless and hopelessly out. Such thoughts do not encourage productive life. Naturally young people are more sanguine and look for man's work, but few find it. Some settle for a "good job," most settle for a lousy job; a few, but an increasing number, don't settle.[61]

If we cannot provide meaningful employment, "man's work"—for men and women—then the other elements of our "youth policy" will all be ineffective: educational programs unable to deliver on their vocational promises will degenerate into warehousing institutions, remedial training programs will similarly be ineffective, and the rehabilitative programs of the juvenile justice system will become controlling mechanisms coping with the symptoms of youth problems but not the causes. But of course meaningful employment is precisely what the American economy cannot provide: capitalist firms thrive on a modicum of unemployment, and the generation of unskilled, meaningless work has followed the imperatives of cost minimization and capitalist control over the labor process. Until these practices and the structure of work which proceeds from them are substantially revised, we can expect conventional youth policies to be ineffective.

In the end, the problems of youth are the problems of adults. The critical decisions of the adolescent years—occupational decisions and sexual decisions—describe the first efforts to grapple with the problems of work and love with which all adults must struggle if they are to live active and thoughtful lives. To some extent, therefore, the confusions of adolescence reflect the confusions that adults experience, and the sense that the "youth problem" has gotten worse may reflect this fact. With the economic world in turmoil and future employment opportunities unclear, the occupational decisions of youth must be even more troubled; with changing sexual norms and changing sex roles, the choice of sexual identities is more open than it has ever been, with less guidance from established norms. Yet the problem of youth is not the existence of choice and the necessity of grappling with alternatives, but rather the sense that the available options are insubstantial. We can give nothing to young people if we do not offer a world in which adults can live decent, productive, and rewarding lives, in which they can work and love in satisfying ways. Working toward these goals would not eliminate the stresses of youth, but at least they would be goals worth striving for. If the opportunities we provide young people are either illusory or insubstantial, then we can expect their own turmoil to reflect the poverty of what we offer.

7

Welfare Policy and the Needs of Other People's Children: The Limits of Redistribution

THE ugliest blotch on the myth of American affluence has been the persistence of poverty. In urban slums, in Appalachian hollows, on Indian reservations, in the backwaters of the South, poverty has been a constant reminder that the American form of capitalism, powerful though it may be, has left many people out. More than 11 percent of all individuals and almost 16 percent of children were "officially" in poverty in 1978, and racial differences make the official figures still more grim: 27 percent of Hispanic children and 41 percent of black children were poor.[1] Despite extensive efforts in every period of social reform to reduce childhood poverty—most recently in Lyndon Johnson's War on Poverty—children continue to be the most impoverished group in the population, and the prospects for improvement are disheartening.

Poverty has been a continuing thorn for Americans brought up on the expectation that hard work and a munificent environment would bring individual and social wealth. These optimistic expectations have been challenged ever since the progressive era, as Americans began to acknowledge that poverty could be caused by economic and social institutions rather than individual failure. Yet that acknowledgment has been slow and grudging. Americans still prefer to ignore poverty or to embrace the ethic of private responsibility that blames individuals and families for their own poverty.[2] Unequal earnings continue to be seen as a legitimate reflection of unequal skills and effort, despite the poverty they imply. This has been the dark side of the American dream: while individualism and hard work could lead to success, individuals could also fail. In either case, the process has been considered both "private" and individual. Only during the most severe periods of social instability—the 1890s, the Great Depression of the 1930s, the 1960s—has the assumption that opportunity is individually determined been widely opposed by one that attributes poverty to structural conditions beyond individual control: discrimination, unequal access to education and to job opportunities, and an economic system that fails to provide enough jobs for those seeking them.

The issue of responsibility for poverty has generated the major conflicts in social welfare policy and has divided conservatives who stress the individual and private roots of poverty from liberals who assert its social and public causes. Still, from every ideological perspective, childhood poverty has always been treated as a special horror. Americans have been outraged by reports of children abused by poverty, even when they are indifferent to the plight of poor adults. As John Spargo, a progressive era reformer, wrote in *The Bitter Cry of the Children* (1906):

> Poverty, the poverty of civilized man, which is everywhere coexistent with unbounded wealth and luxury, is always ugly, repellent and terrible either to see or to experience: but when it assails the cradle, it assumes its most hideous form.[3]

Childhood poverty has been especially hideous from an instrumental perspective: liberals and conservatives alike have complained that poverty entails a waste of human resources, stunting the development of little children and generating social burdens rather than productive citizens. Poverty among children is also special because individual failure as the cause of poverty cannot be extended to the young.[4] Instead, children, the innocent and blameless, are the victims of other people and other institutions—their parents and economic conditions, and more recently, "government bureaucrats" and "do-gooders."

Despite a consensus that childhood poverty is economically inefficient, as well as immoral and cruel, efforts to eliminate it have invariably been incomplete. The hostility to "other people's children" and instrumental rationales for public spending on children have limited and distorted public efforts to reduce poverty. The assumption that poor parents have failed their children as a precondition for public support—*parens patriae*, once again—means that poor parents are invariably condemned as immoral, and their children are made to suffer the consequences of reduced support. Indeed, that is a fundamental characteristic of the American approach to poverty: the young are punished for what are considered the transgressions of their parents and the failures of private responsibility. Because it is difficult for Americans to view children distinct from their parents and almost impossible to develop public policies that would do so, public policies are caught in the dilemma that supporting poor children requires assisting their parents as well, contrary to the political demands that public aid should not undermine labor markets, the work ethic, and the prevailing conception of family income as "private." In practice, the short-run needs of the labor market have usually prevailed over longer-run interests in preventing the "stunted development" of future workers. When the welfare of children conflicts with economic constraints, children lose.

As a result, childhood poverty remains higher than for any other group. In 1978, 17.2 percent of children under five and 15.5 percent of children between five and seventeen were below the official poverty thresholds, compared to 8.7 percent of those eighteen to sixty-four and 13.9 percent of those over sixty-five. Children therefore constitute a large fraction of the poor: 40.5 percent of those defined as officially poor in 1978 were under eighteen. Moreover, these figures conceal as much as they reveal. The official poverty line, intended to reflect a level of income necessary for survival, is based on the Economy Food Plan (now the Thrifty Food Plan) of the Department of Agriculture, designed for "temporary or emergency use when funds are low"; the department estimates that only 10 percent of the people using the plan can manage to eat an adequate diet.[5] The official poverty standards are thus too low for continued survival. A more realistic alternative is to use half the median income as the poverty standard, since interview data indicate that many people consider this to be a better conception of poverty. By this measure, 19.7 percent of individuals and 24.5 percent of children were poor in 1974, compared to official figures of 11.2 percent and 15.1 percent. With more acceptable definitions of poverty, then, one-quarter of all America's children are poor. The special plight of minority children is even more obvious: perhaps 40 percent of Hispanic children and 60 percent of black children are poor.[6]

There has been some decrease in the incidence of poverty in the past two decades, partly as a result of the economic boom during the 1960s and partly because welfare programs were expanded. But the progress of children in moving out of poverty lags behind that of other population groups. Between 1966 and 1970 the incidence of official poverty for the elderly dropped from 28.5 percent to 24.6 percent, while for children it fell at a somewhat lower rate from 17.4 percent to 14.9 percent. Between 1970 and 1978, while official poverty among children was increasing to 15.7 percent, the incidence for adults aged eighteen to sixty-four decreased slightly from 9.6 percent to 8.7 percent, and the incidence for the elderly dropped dramatically, from 24.6 percent to 13.9 percent. The social welfare programs of federal, state, and local governments have thus been much less effective in moving children out of poverty, compared to most other population groups. The programs that transfer funds to the poor vary considerably in their generosity, and children are most affected by the least generous program, Aid to Families with Dependent Children (AFDC). Furthermore, because of limited state coverage and various restrictions, the AFDC-U program for two-parent families with unemployed fathers reaches very few children, and so the 42 percent of officially poor children in two-parent families have been helped very little by welfare programs. As a consequence, in 1972 only 23 percent of poor families with children were made "nonpoor" by government programs, compared to 63 percent of families with an aged head.[7] Clearly the power of transfer programs to reduce poverty among children has been weak.

Here, then, is one way of viewing the welfare "mess": generations of reformers have addressed the "hideous form" of childhood poverty, but public programs have made little difference. The tremendous expansion in welfare programs during the 1960s was limited in moving children out of poverty, and even the small progress in alleviating childhood poverty was reversed in the 1970s. The weakness of the economy during the 1970s and the growth of single-parent families have increased the number of children who need public aid even to survive, yet resistance to providing the benefits necessary for decent living standards has intensified. In a period of fiscal retrenchment and taxpayer revolts, public opinion polls suggest that welfare programs are the most favored areas for cuts in government spending,[8] and conservatives have singled out welfare programs and social services to the poor as the most flagrant of all government "give-aways," supposedly responsible for federal deficits, inflation, declining productivity, and a host of other evils. The contrast between these conservative reactions and the rhetoric that has historically condemned childhood poverty is enormous and testifies to the difficulty of principled politics on behalf of other people's children.

The welfare system illustrates, better than any other children's institution, a central limitation of *parens patriae*. Although public institutions promise to provide for children when their parents cannot, it proves impossible (except in extreme conditions) to separate children from their parents, either physically or conceptually. Providing for poor children therefore means providing for their parents at the same time. But we are unwilling to support poor adults, who despite all evidence to the contrary remain suspected of sloth, dissolute living, and the destruction of American values.[9] Rather than support their parents we choose to minimize our responsibilities to poor children. The result is the steady abandonment of poor children, despite the abundance that surrounds them. As one welfare rights organizer and welfare recipient declared:

> When I see money being wasted—sending men to the moon to play golf, dumping nerve gas in the ocean, burning potatoes, killing off hogs, mutilating them, just getting rid of them—and then I see hungry and raggedy children running around, this is the kind of country we live in, and this is what just burns me up. I feel the only way changes will be made, especially in the welfare system, is through poor people, welfare people organizing and raising a lot of hell . . . which is all we can do.[10]

The Structure of Aid to Families with Dependent Children

Welfare at the onset of the 1930s was a ramshackle affair. In the mothers' pensions begun in the progressive era and in the private charity based on nineteenth-century principles of "scientific philanthropy," welfare efforts were designed to support the "deserving" poor, especially widows and children who found themselves poor through no fault of their own. The greatest fear of philanthropists, public officials, and charity workers was that the dole would "pauperize" recipients, causing them to abandon efforts to work themselves out of poverty. To guard against this possibility and reinforce work norms, the "undeserving" poor and the "employables" received no support. Even those judged "deserving" received meager support, accompanied by invasions of privacy, curtailment of rights, and moral exhortations. The degradation of welfare recipients guaranteed that there would be no incentive even for "unemployables" to go on welfare.[11]

Neither these assumptions nor the methods of providing welfare were able to cope with depression levels of unemployment and poverty, a fact as apparent in the 1890s as in the 1930s. But in the Great Depression, individualistic conceptions that blamed poverty on the poor were considerably less tenable. As the unemployed became increasingly strident in their demands and as civil disorders increased, the Roosevelt administration moved to establish a federal relief program for "all needy unemployed persons and/or their dependents" through the Federal Emergency Relief Act (FERA). Federal aid defused civil disorders, but the source of FERA's effectiveness was also its most vulnerable point. Extending aid to all who needed it was unacceptable to a wide range of people who wanted to tie relief to work. The most immediate efforts to transform public assistance into work programs, making aid contingent on job participation, were the Public Works Administration, the Civil Works Administration, and the Social Security Act of 1935, which resurrected the division between employables and unemployables. For employables—or, more accurately, those who had been employed—a system of social insurance was instituted, including unemployment insurance and an old age security system conditioned on prior wages. For unemployables—principally the aged poor, the blind, and children—the legislation established federal grants to support state and local efforts rather than the comprehensive plan that had been the basis of FERA. For children, benefits were restricted to those deprived of economic support "by reason of the death, continued absence from the home, or physical and/or mental incapacity of a parent" (usually meaning a father).[12]

The structure of federal grants allowed the states to reproduce the old systems of mothers' pensions, with all the inequities and inadequacies of those programs: states were allowed to set levels of support which were often pitifully low and which varied drastically around the country; the moral judgments used in distinguishing the "deserving" from the "undeserving" poor persisted; and dependent children who were poor despite the presence of their fathers were not helped. A variety of techniques developed during the 1940s and 1950s to discipline the welfare population and to insure that public assistance would not undermine local labor markets. Aid levels were invariably set below the minimum wages available in local areas. State and local administration allowed support levels and eligibility standards to vary among states and within states. The low-wage agricultural labor markets of the South were accompanied by the lowest levels of public assistance in the country, and in seasonal labor markets (as in agricultural areas), welfare recipients found themselves cut off the rolls when seasonal work began.

Closely allied to concerns that local labor markets not be undermined were the "employable mother" and "unsuitable home" provisions. "Employable mother" rules required that mothers receiving AFDC grants go to work when "suitable" employment was found and when provision for day care existed. "Unsuitable home" restrictions drew upon nineteenth-century assumptions that charity should not support those homes in which the mother was so dissolute, immoral, or otherwise incompetent that the home was "unsuitable" for children. Both restrictions were used against black mothers more than white mothers, and in the South more than in the North. Both shifted decisions about whether a mother should work and about how best to care for her children to caseworkers and welfare administrators. The unsuitable home restriction provided a rationale for examining the sexual conduct of AFDC mothers and allowed moral judgments by caseworkers to have serious material consequences; although formally terminated in the late 1950s, it continued to influence local practices through the 1960s. Other restrictions, especially the "substitute father" and "man in the house" regulations, were similarly used to eliminate from the rolls those families that had an able-bodied man, and served as the excuse for unannounced visits and infamous "midnight raids" to see if there were any men in the house.[13]

The 1940s and 1950s were thus a period of extreme local discretion coupled with repressive practices to keep families off the AFDC rolls and prevent children from receiving aid. Despite some demographic changes that should have expanded the rolls—increases in the number of small children and female-headed families, and migration from low-eligibility southern states to the urban North—the growth in the number of families on welfare was a modest 17 percent between 1950 and 1960. While it is difficult to determine causality, the various discretionary methods combined with continuing popular views about the kind of people who "go on welfare" undoubtedly had a sizable impact, both by discouraging potential welfare recipients from applying and by providing the grounds for denying eligibility to those who otherwise qualified.

The turmoil of the 1960s—the militancy of the poor, the frantic efforts to reform AFDC, and above all a huge expansion in the AFDC rolls and levels of support—replaced the stable conditions of the 1950s. At least part of the growth in AFDC families was demographic: an increase in female-headed families of 30 percent between 1960 and 1970 meant that the population most eligible for AFDC expanded relative to the population as a whole. But this growth was small compared to the increases in the AFDC rolls and overall spending levels, which are comprehensible only as a response to increased militancy during the decade. Once again, as they had in the 1930s, the poor found themselves with political clout. The civil rights movement, the threat of social disorder created in the ghetto riots, legal advocacy by poverty lawyers, and organizations like the National Welfare Rights Organization institutionalized and legitimized the struggle for expanded welfare benefits and made poor people aware of those benefits. Some of the worst administrative abuses were curbed, including some of the discretionary power of caseworkers. Legal strategies during the 1960s slowly established welfare as a right with certain legal and procedural safeguards. As a result, participation rates jumped during the late 1960s from around three-fifths of those eligible in 1967, indicating a large pool of families either unaware of welfare, unwilling to apply, or wrongly denied benefits, to almost 100 percent in 1971.[14] Simultaneously, another result of the militancy of the 1960s was the enactment of new programs to distribute specific goods to the poor—principally food stamps and Medicaid. By 1975, when total AFDC payments were $9.2 billion, subsidies under the food stamp program equaled $4.4 billion and Medicaid subsidies were $12.3 billion.[15] Some of the subsidies went to those ineligible for AFDC payments, but the additional resources available to the poor from in-kind programs were substantial.[16]

These developments did not go uncontested, as efforts to limit the expansion of welfare costs by reducing welfare rolls emerged. The 1962 amendments to the Social Security Act expanded social services rather than income, allegedly to help the poor break out of the cycle of poverty by transforming their attitudes. This approach, the result of the "culture of poverty" thesis then in vogue, quickly proved to be a failure. In 1967, another set of amendments stressed self-support, allowing or requiring the poor to work their way out of poverty. One part of "workfare" was the Work Incentive Program (WIN), which required "employables" receiving AFDC payments—those who were not aged, incapacitated, or required to be in the home to care for children under six—to register for training and employment programs. The other part focused on disincentives in AFDC: grants formerly had been reduced one dollar for every dollar of earned income, eliminating much of the material incentive for welfare recipients to work. The amendments changed this practice, permitting recipients to keep the first thirty dollars per month of earnings plus one-third of the remainder. Paradoxically, both of these changes exacerbated the problems of welfare. WIN proved ineffective in moving individuals off the welfare rolls. Instead it added another layer of complexity to the welfare program, served as a source of harassment, and often reduced resources available to welfare recipients; it was symbolic rather than substantive, an attempt to assure taxpayers that steps were being taken to reduce the welfare rolls.[17] Whether the "thirty and one-third" rule has had any real effect on the rolls is unclear, but the rule allowed those on welfare to increase their earnings and still remain on welfare. This resulted in some welfare families having higher incomes than families of low-wage workers with earnings too high to qualify for welfare, worrying those concerned about undermining the work ethic and causing political controversy among the "working poor."

Concern with the size of welfare costs and the effects of welfare on work incentives was therefore present throughout the 1960s, even though other forces led to expanding aid for poor children. But once political pressures and the threat of urban riots subsided, opposition to welfare asserted itself with full force. The changes in AFDC during the 1970s were largely attempts to undo the results of the 1960s, by reducing the costs of welfare, by reaffirming the importance of work, and by reasserting the distinction between the deserving and undeserving poor. In response to pressure from the states, themselves under increasing budgetary constraints, HEW revised regulations affecting eligibility procedures, fair hearings, and the methods used to adjust overpayments, returning considerable power to the states and diluting federal ability to control the worst state abuses. HEW also adopted the Quality Control System (QCS) to exert more direct pressure on the states to reduce their rolls.[18] Under this system, each state analyzes a sample of AFDC cases to determine the extent of eligibility, overpayments, and underpayments, and federal aid is reduced for failure to attain specified error rates. Often viewed simply as a way of detecting frauds, in practice the QCS introduces more restrictive eligibility policies. Because the AFDC system is so complex and eligibility and payments standards are ambiguous, simple mistakes are much more common than fraud.[19] The only way a state can reduce its error rate is to use procedures that are restrictive, thereby reducing the number of "qualified" applicants and the levels of support.

The administrative rationalizations of the 1970s followed earlier patterns of trying to reduce welfare rolls by controlling fraud and tightening procedures, but they also reflected an admission that the welfare population would not "wither away," as had been the hope since 1935. Most dramatically, the composition of AFDC has changed. During the 1960s, the AFDC population became overwhelmingly composed of children and their single mothers rather than widows, the "deserving poor" who were 61 percent of the first Aid to Dependent Children recipients. The new clientele reflected long-term increases in divorce, separation, and children born to single mothers, as well as employment discrimination against women. The result has been the emergence of a persistently large welfare population, one that is "permanent" in the sense of needing transfer payments, even though large numbers shift on and off welfare over time.[20] The predominance of single mothers on welfare has been particularly distressing to those who attribute the increase in population to declining restraints on moral behavior and who view the problem of welfare as moving people off the welfare rolls and into work; the dilemma of whether to force mothers of young children to take jobs has been troublesome, since it so evidently contradicts the domestic ideology.

One reaction to the high costs of welfare and the number of single mothers on AFDC has been an attempt to shift the public costs back to private incomes—in this case to absent fathers. The Child Support Enforcement Program, legislated in 1974, requires a welfare mother to cooperate in locating the absent father or risk being denied eligibility. While the enforcement program has been defended for encouraging paternal responsibility and reducing welfare costs, it benefits neither mothers nor their children. All revenue recovered from absent fathers goes to the public treasury, so there is no financial benefit to mothers or children from participating and no incentive for fathers to comply. Indeed, the program may in fact decrease support to children. The poorest families tend to form kin networks to help their members through hard times, and through them fathers and other paternal kin contribute to the nurturing and support of children in a variety of ways. By ensuring that financial contributions from these sources will be routed to state and federal treasuries rather than to poor children, the Child Support Enforcement Program discourages a father from maintaining contact with his children and may disrupt kin networks. As usual in the welfare system, the procedures of the Child Support Enforcement Program violate the privacy rights of AFDC mothers and dilute their control over their own lives. Caseworkers rather than mothers make the decision to pursue fathers, despite the possibility that fathers may beat their wives and children in retribution.[21] The Child Support Enforcement Program has collected more money than its administrative costs, but once again increased efficiency of the AFDC system has been bought at the expense of its beneficiaries: while taxpayers gain, poor children and their mothers lose.

Another recurrent "solution" to the welfare costs has been to try to move welfare parents into the labor force. From WIN, instituted in 1967 to register eligible welfare recipients for jobs, to the elaborate program of public sector jobs in Carter's welfare reforms, to Reagan's workfare proposals, the impulse to convert "liabilities" to "assets" by forcing or encouraging welfare recipients to work has been constant. As part of the effort to insure that welfare programs would not undermine work incentives, these efforts have regularly been justified by harsh rhetoric and the promise of cutting off aid; Jimmy Carter assured the 1976 Democratic Platform Committee:

> No one able to work, except mothers with pre-school children, should be continued on the welfare rolls unless job training and a meaningful job were accepted. . . . If they decline the job, they should be ineligible for future benefits.[22]

Yet the efforts to move welfare recipients into the labor force have never helped more than a tiny fraction of welfare recipients; with high unemployment rates and a welfare population composed largely of children, their mothers, and the disabled, there is every reason to think that work requirements can never substantially reduce welfare costs.[23] Instead, work requirements are part of a long series of rhetorical commitments to maintaining work incentives and administrative devices to harass recipients. Their only real result has been to enlarge the category of mothers considered suitable for employment—from mothers with children over eighteen, to mothers with children over six, to mothers with children over three under Reagan's proposals—contradicting the original impulse of mothers' pensions that mothers should not be forced to work.

State practices, federal legislation and regulations, and litigation during the 1970s all reveal a pattern of restrictiveness toward welfare recipients. But two irreversible changes during the 1960s have affected subsequent developments. First, the introduction of poverty lawyers and legal tactics into battles over welfare meant that much of the local discretion—the "discretionary paternalism" that had always been part of charity efforts—was successfully fought and replaced by more precise standards and administrative controls. The attempts to cut down welfare costs in the 1970s took the form of greater administrative hurdles, additional requirements (such as work requirements and the duty to cooperate in locating absent fathers), and managerial techniques like the QCS rather than arbitrary and capricious decisions at the local level.[24] Second, in the course of the 1960s, the poor became more aware of welfare programs, and the proportion of those eligible for AFDC who actually receive it increased to almost 100 percent. Subsequent modifications of eligibility standards and intake procedures could eliminate only those families on the margin of eligibility. It was no longer easy to exclude a large number of eligibles by exercising unlimited discretion, by failing to inform potential recipients of programs, or simply by discouraging them from filing applications. Ironically, the advent of highly rationalized administrative procedures to reduce the welfare rolls came at precisely the time when the impact of purely administrative changes was smaller than it had ever been, as changes in the welfare rolls have become increasingly dominated by economic and demographic shifts rather than administrative practices.[25]

Nonetheless the restrictions of the 1970s may have made their impact on the welfare rolls, though the evidence is ambiguous. Between 1971 and 1975, the population most eligible for welfare assistance—female-headed families in poverty—increased 13.5 percent, while individuals on the AFDC rolls increased by only 6.9 percent.[26] The most devastating manifestation of the restrictiveness of the 1970s, however, has been the reduction in real payment levels. Compared to real increases in average monthly payments of 15 percent between 1963 and 1967 and 9.2 percent between 1967 and 1971, the average payment per recipient increased only 5 percent (in real terms) between 1971 and 1976; real payment levels remained approximately constant through 1978, and thereafter began to decline under the impact of inflation, as actual payments remained the same.[27] Unlike Social Security payments, which are indexed to keep up with inflation, or unemployment insurance payments, which are a fraction of wages and therefore increase as wage levels increase, there are no automatic mechanisms to adjust AFDC payments to inflation. As taxpayer revolts make increases in welfare support levels more unlikely at both the federal and state levels, welfare grants will continue to fall behind the rate of inflation more and more.

The election of Ronald Reagan has accelerated the reversals begun under Richard Nixon. The conservative mood of the country made it fashionable to reconstruct the old categories of the deserving and undeserving poor, to define the deserving poor as narrowly as possible, and to heap abuse on all others. Martin Anderson, a leading conservative critic of the welfare system, and domestic policy adviser to Ronald Reagan, expressed this distaste for the undeserving in words similar to Jimmy Carter's:

> Our welfare programs should be guided by the simple principle that a person gets welfare only if he or she qualifies for it by the fact of being incapable of self-support. If they don't qualify, they should be given reasonable notice, and then removed from the rolls.[28]

But where Carter at least tried to reform AFDC and increase funding, Reagan has acted more decisively in reducing funds and abandoning the postwar reform agenda. In legislation taking effect in fiscal year 1982, the AFDC program suffered funding cuts of 15 percent (in a period of about 10 percent inflation). In a period when poverty rates were beginning to increase due to higher unemployment rates caused by the recession that began in the middle of 1981, approximately 11 percent of AFDC families were to be eliminated from the rolls. The changes include new limitations on eligibility and reductions in the work incentives instituted by the 1967 amendments. They also allow states to select other options that would further reduce the welfare rolls, reduce payments, and force welfare recipients into various versions of "workfare" (now called "work supplementation programs" or "work incentive demonstration programs").[29] Furthermore, the Reagan administration has proposed converting the existing funding mechanisms to block grants, a change that would return more power to the states and reduce federal funds even further. Such changes would be consistent with Reagan's intention to "take the country back as far as the Constitution," before the federal government became involved in funding a variety of programs like welfare that had once been the responsibility of state and local government.[30] In many ways the reduction of federal funding, the reintroduction of greater state discretion for administration and eligibility, the greater state responsibility for funding, and the restitution of "workfare" programs portend a return to the pitiful funding and the administrative abuses of the 1950s.

In the ups and downs of the past two decades, the AFDC system both improved and remained inadequate—and may become still less adequate. The proportion of the poor receiving aid increased dramatically and levels of support increased, at least during the 1960s. There was some progress in reducing poverty, and transfer payments prevented a deterioration in poverty as unemployment increased during the 1970s. The food stamp and Medicaid programs greatly expanded the resources available to the poor. Some of the worst administrative abuses and violations of the rights of welfare recipients were reduced, though by no means eliminated. Yet the coverage of the poor remains incomplete, the effectiveness of the welfare system in moving families with children out of poverty remains low, and too many children remain poor. Furthermore, the welfare system is still beset by the same tensions, and so the progress of the 1960s now seems fragile given the hostility toward the poor in the 1980s. Evidently, Americans have failed to resolve the basic dilemma first apparent in the mid-nineteenth century: whether poverty should be considered a public problem requiring expanded state involvement, or a private and individual problem for which the state should accept minimal responsibility. The dilemma remains all the more acute for children, for no matter how Americans view poverty among adults, it is hard to blame children for being poor or to condemn them to the category of the "undeserving."

Constraints on Public Assistance for Children

In the cycles affecting welfare over the past fifty years, we can see the two different forces of the liberal democratic state operating simultaneously. On the one hand, democratic pressures and the threat to social stability from those unable to earn a subsistence wage, during the Great Depression and the 1960s, forced the expansion of public assistance. Once these threats subsided, assistance programs suffered periods of retrenchment and greater restrictiveness, as they did during the 1950s, and again in the 1970s and 1980s. The cycles themselves suggest that, given the inability of the poor to develop a permanent and powerful interest group, the power to threaten social peace—"raising a lot of hell"—has been considerably more potent than moral arguments on their behalf.[31] The cycles also reveal the second force acting on the state—the continuing influence of nineteenth-century liberalism, which views economic conditions as the product of private decisions and individual initiative. In this view, any gain that is not achieved through individual initiative in the private market is wasteful and unproductive. When public assistance is necessary, it must always be less than can be gained in the labor market. This argument, rooted in the tenet of nineteenth-century liberalism that required that the state not undermine private labor markets and that market incentives remain intact, has been more consistently argued, and argued from a wider range of ideological viewpoints, than the impulse simply to reduce welfare spending. It continues to be a prime concern among modern liberals as well as conservatives in the desire to reduce the work disincentives implicit in the welfare system.[32]

These two sets of forces are necessarily antithetical. If the poor gain high welfare benefits, the costs of welfare and its potential for undermining labor markets increase. Conversely, mechanisms to reduce welfare costs and to force welfare recipients onto labor markets with few job opportunities reduce support for the poor. This antithesis has been recognized in conservative and liberal discussions as the "great trade-off" among grant levels, costs, and work disincentives, and in neo-Marxist analyses as a contradiction between the state's role in supporting capitalist institutions (like labor markets) and its role in legitimizing the social system by limiting poverty.[33] No matter what the vocabulary, the contradictory pressures on welfare policy—the need to provide a decent subsistence for the poor versus the need to limit support so that a pool of inexpensive labor is available and labor market incentives are maintained—are deeply rooted in the social and economic system. Gains in public assistance have therefore been open to reversal, are always politically controversial, and have been achieved not through moral arguments or within the context of traditional interest group politics, but through various forms of protest.

Children are affected by the contradictory forces within the welfare system as a whole, since the benefits available to them have gone up and down with its restrictiveness or expansiveness. But another set of tensions affects children and helps explain why children are so shabbily treated. A basic assumption of most public assistance programs that benefit children is that *children* should be supported, not poor individuals or poor families.

The AFDC system, the earned income tax credit for the working poor, and some proposed revisions like Nixon's Family Assistance Plan have been aimed at families with children and have by design left out childless households. Yet the government's inability to separate children from their parents and the public unwillingness to support certain kinds of parents have led to practices that remove innocent children from the rolls—the "unsuitable homes" and "man in the house" regulations, and more recently, the Child Support Enforcement Program, which in part refuses support to children whose mothers are considered "immoral." Such practices ignore the possibility that these children might be precisely those most in need of assistance, and they deny that the "immorality" of the mother ought not affect the welfare of the blameless child. In effect, poor children are not considered innocent: the state requires them to bear some of the burdens of their mothers' presumed sins.

The state's attitude toward fathers has been no better. One goal of welfare systems, from mothers' pensions to the present, has been to preserve the family, generating the concern that welfare programs not include incentives for the father to leave. Yet in practice the imperative has been stronger not to support able-bodied fathers, who are presumed to have no legitimate reason (as mothers might) for staying out of the labor force. Until 1962 AFDC extended aid only to families with the father absent. Even now the AFDC-U system, which extends aid to families with an unemployed father, has been adopted in only twenty three states and the District of Columbia, and because of serious restrictions accounts for only 3.7 percent of families and 5.1 percent of all welfare recipients.[34] The "man in the house" and "substitute parent" regulations and the Child Support Enforcement Program are other devices to insure that able-bodied men are not inadvertently supported. As a consequence, children with both a mother and a father fare the worst under present programs; they are only half as likely to be moved out of poverty, compared to children with an absent father. Every reform proposal has mimicked the current welfare system by maintaining differentials between families with an able-bodied man and female-headed families, providing incentives to form female-headed families. The incentives for splitting up families are not accidental, however, but reflect the constraint that public assistance not undercut labor markets by supporting able-bodied men.[35] Children are again penalized for the "sins" of their parents, in this case the "sin" of remaining together.

The inability to break the link between parents and children and the strong tie between income support and employment are clearest in the treatment of different kinds of poor children. Children whose parents

199

have insufficient independent income are supported at very different levels under social insurance programs—primarily Old Age, Survivors, Disability, and Health Insurance (OASDHI or Social Security) and unemployment insurance—and under public assistance programs (primarily AFDC, with a few children supported by Supplemental Security Income). In theory, social insurance programs are distinguished by their connection to employment: wage earners and employers contribute part of earnings, and benefits are presumed to represent previous earnings. In practice these programs are a mixture of insurance and assistance: benefits are not precisely tied to past earnings, and there is some redistribution from high earners to low earners in insurance as well as assistance programs. Despite the fact that the difference between social insurance and welfare programs is imprecise, it remains strong enough in the public consciousness so that social insurance benefits are considered to be "earned rights"; the stigma attached to welfare dependency is relatively absent from social insurance programs, and many citizens opposed to welfare spending support social security and unemployment insurance.[36] As a result, the payment per child in 1979 under Social Security was $205 per month for the child of a deceased worker, $120 for the child of a retired worker, and $95 for the child of a disabled worker; the average family under unemployment insurance received $386 per month; while the average family on AFDC received $271 per month and the average recipient received $93.[37] This differential treatment reflects a class bias: unemployment insurance and Social Security benefits go to families that have had a regular connection to employment and are therefore part of the working class. AFDC benefits, with lower support levels, go to a marginal class with a much less regular connection to production. Children are again differentially treated according to characteristics of their parents, in this case their class status.

A further ambivalence embedded within the AFDC program concerns the mother-child relationship. In the mothers' pension movement and in the Social Security Act of 1935, the purpose of providing aid was to enable the mother to devote full time to the care of her children. Yet a contrary view of the mother's role has always been present as well: that she ought to get to work as quickly as possible, to become self-sufficient rather than dependent on government benefits. This view has gained prominence as the "employable mother" rules in AFDC have been institutionalized in the WIN program and in the expanded category of "employables." Now only mothers with children under six are clearly thought to be necessary in the home, and mothers with school-age children are generally considered "employable"; and Reagan has proposed that mothers with children over three be eligible for "workfare." Of course, attitudes toward maternal employment have changed drastically since 1909. But rather than expanding the options available to poor women, these changing attitudes have been used against them, restricting their decisions by forcing them into the labor market. In contrast to the nonwelfare population, the decision to work or not has been taken out of the hands of welfare mothers and has been made by welfare regulations and caseworkers. The "workfare" impulse and the imperative to get mothers back to work thus undercuts the original purpose of AFDC: to provide resources so that children can have the benefit of their mother's presence.

The ambivalence toward maternal employment and the reluctance to support able-bodied but underemployed fathers provide two examples of how the welfare system, originally intending to "support the family" by providing basic resources, in fact undermines families by taking decision-making power away from parents and by providing requirements and incentives contrary to family ideals. Other examples exist, like the Child Support Enforcement Program, which theoretically "supports" family units by insuring that fathers will not abandon their families, but in practice may disrupt extended kin networks and may expose the mother to violent retaliation. In these destructive practices and in the failure of welfare programs to reduce poverty substantially, one fundamental issue dwarfs all others: the treatment of poor children is dictated by considerations unrelated to their welfare. Instead, the interest of taxpayers in reducing welfare costs, a punitive attitude toward unemployed fathers (and, increasingly, unemployed mothers), and moralistic attitudes toward welfare mothers have dominated. In the process, the imperative that public welfare protect those children most in need of the state's assistance has been destroyed.

The Welfare "Mess" and the Poverty of Reform Proposals

The permanent expansion of the welfare system combined with its high costs and its ineffectiveness in eliminating poverty created a sense of perpetual crisis and constant reform during the 1970s. Yet while everyone agreed that the welfare system was seriously flawed, few agreed on the nature of the welfare "mess." Conservatives were most worried that costs were too high, fraud was too widespread, and work values were undermined by the welfare system. Liberals tended to be more concerned about inadequate levels of support, the denial of personal freedoms, the stigma and loss of dignity associated with being on welfare. For those whose prime interests were administrative, the multiplicity of programs and the sheer ungovernability of many of them were the most important problems. For others, the variations in support levels among states and even among welfare jurisdictions within states remained one of the most critical issues.

Yet during the 1970s some consensus emerged on at least two issues. One involved the administrative complexity and irrationality of the welfare system, which have led not only to high administrative costs but also to a system insensitive to recipients' needs and impervious to reformers' efforts. The second issue reflected the concern with work incentives, particularly with the disincentives to work embedded in the current system. As a result many reform proposals were aimed at reducing the marginal tax rate, the rate at which increased earnings of welfare recipients are "taxed away" through reduced grants. Despite mounting evidence that the disincentive effects of welfare plans are much smaller than many have believed,[38] anxiety over work disincentives remains virtually undiminished. Indeed, aside from simply cutting costs, it is now the dominant issue in welfare politics, particularly in the "equity" argument that nonworkers should not have incomes that approximate worker incomes.[39]

General agreement on the issues of work incentives and greater administrative rationality have not produced a consensus on the reforms best suited to achieve these goals. Rather, a variety of reforms were proposed during the 1970s, each revealing how intractable the problem of welfare had become. The least disruptive of these was an "incremental" approach, which would integrate assistance programs after eliminating their worst features: extending AFDC-U for families with unemployed fathers to states that did not have it, establishing a national minimum level of AFDC support, replacing food stamps with cash grants, and instituting a system of national health insurance to replace Medicaid and Medicare. The incremental approach had the advantage of practicality;[40] but for those wanting to eradicate the inadequacies of benefit levels, the abuses of discretion, the administrative complexity, the stigma, and the futile application of work requirements where no jobs existed, it had little appeal.

Under the assumption that the welfare system was too seriously flawed to be much improved by tinkering, another set of proposals would have replaced the current system with a program of cash assistance based on earnings. Usually integrated with the federal income tax system, most of these proposals took the form of a negative income tax.[41] By centralizing welfare administration and by instituting precise determination of grants, proponents argued that many current abuses would be reduced: ineffective mandatory training and employment programs like WIN would be replaced by a relatively low marginal tax rate and a low guarantee level to motivate employment. A negative income tax would integrate the welfare system with the tax system to reduce the stigma associated with welfare and reduce the sharp moral distinctions between "deserving" and "undeserving" poor. But negative income tax plans cannot escape the deeper constraints that limit the welfare system, and as a result the same wrangling over benefit levels and marginal tax rates dominated the debates over different negative income tax proposals. In addition, in a decade of escalating unemployment rates it is unclear how the work incentives implicit in low guarantee levels and low marginal tax rates could be effective in moving families out of poverty. Despite their advantages in rationalizing and making more uniform the current welfare system, negative income tax plans were not the major departure from past tradition that their advocates often claimed.

A third proposal for restructuring welfare emerged during the 1970s, which called for more fundamental changes than the previous two approaches: a "three track" system that recognized that the poor do not constitute a homogeneous group and included three programs directed at different groups. President Carter's Program for Better Jobs and Income, presented in 1977, is an example of a three-track system. "Unemployables"—the aged, disabled, and single parents with children six and under—would have a relatively high guarantee level (approximately 65 percent of the poverty line) with benefits reduced by fifty cents for each additional dollar of earnings. "Employables" would have a much lower guarantee of less than half the poverty line, and would therefore have to work to earn an adequate income; however, for those unable to find jobs in the private sector (including "regular" government jobs), the program would have provided one public job per family at the minimum wage. Finally, for the working poor—those who have regular employment at low wages—an expansion of the existing earned income tax credit would have supplemented their earnings.[42] Like other three-track proposals, the Program for Better Jobs and Income was designed to preserve income differentials between those who work and those who do not. Like its antecedents, it maintained the integrity of the private labor market by ensuring that public service employment went only to those unable to find a job in the private labor market, by making the income associated with public employment lower than that in private employment, and by aiding the working poor through an earnings subsidy rather than through cash grants requiring no employment. But unlike other proposed reforms, the three-track approach deals forthrightly with the inadequacies of the private labor market; it faces squarely the fact that many jobs available do not pay enough to prevent families from slipping into poverty and the fact that there is not enough employment for all those in the labor force.

Yet as progressive as the three-track plans are, they do not overcome basic structural problems. Children would be affected by the imperatives of the labor market in the continued ambiguity over whether mothers should work or not and in the differential treatment of those who do not work. Children six and under are more likely to be in families of "unemployables," as long as mothers with young children are considered "unemployables." Although the basic benefit levels for them would be higher than for children of "employables," the support levels proposed by Carter were still grotesquely inadequate—65 percent of the official poverty standard, a standard that has itself been designed to cover only short-term emergencies. Thus, as is currently true, "unemployables" would be forced to work or to pool incomes in kin networks in order to survive. In the resources available to them and in the strain on their mothers, these children—the youngest and most vulnerable children—would still suffer relative to the children of "employables." As always, the welfare of children remains subordinate to the goal of maintaining the status of employment.

A second potential problem involved what is in many ways the most progressive aspect of the three-track proposals, the program of public service employment. With such a program, welfare would begin to transcend its role as a mechanism for merely redistributing income and would begin to provide a clear alternative to labor markets as a way of generating goods and distributing income. But a strong caveat is necessary: public employment is subject to the same constraints as all other public programs, and in a welfare context it could easily be transformed into work relief rather than being a mechanism of economic independence. Since the jobs created under such a program would be neither in the private sector nor in the conventional public sector, they would be considered the least valuable. Employers and labor unions would press to eliminate from public employment any work that could be contracted to private employers, such as public works.[43] Wages for those participating would be politically determined rather than determined by market forces, generating intense political battles. (For example, the AFL-CIO opposed Carter's Program for Better Jobs and Income on the grounds that the public service-wage—set at the minimum wage—was lower than the prevailing wage in local labor markets and would thus undermine wages.) With the wage rate set lower than that available in the private labor market, but higher than what nonworkers get in direct grants, public service employment would appear like work done to qualify for a grant rather than work performed because of its value in a market sense. These conditions constitute a set of incentives to create "make-work" programs rather than programs where output and jobs are inherently valued. Finally, work requirements in the context of welfare programs have been associated with some of the worst treatment of welfare recipients, and therefore public service employment is too closely connected to past "workfare" efforts to be supported by recipients themselves. Even three-track proposals, then, were unable to escape the dilemmas inherent in the welfare system, despite their complexity and their efforts to address the different sources of poverty and the inadequacies of the private labor market.

Despite the pressure for reform, none of the proposals advanced during the 1970s proved politically acceptable. Nixon's Family Assistance Plan failed because of inadequate benefit levels; Carter's Better Jobs and Incomes plan was politically dead almost as soon as its details had been unveiled, unacceptable to too many interest groups despite being the result of the most thorough study of reform alternatives ever made. There is no greater testimony to the difficulty of reforming welfare than the inadequacy and political unacceptability of every major approach to reform considered during the 1970s; there is no better evidence of the inability of our political system to act on its deepest convictions.

In retrospect, the reform impetus of the 1970s failed to consider the rising tide of anger at welfare programs. That rage reflected racial hostility toward blacks and Hispanics, but it also reflected the deterioration of economic conditions and the frustration of many Americans with a government unable to resolve its problems. The failure of costly welfare programs to reduce poverty substantially generated hostility toward the whole enterprise and allowed Americans to see in the welfare system everything wrong with public programs: excessive government intervention into private life, outrageous expenditures on people who did not work, public support for "immoral" and "deviant" ways of life. With the election of Ronald Reagan, the ever-present hostility toward the poor has become permissible, even fashionable. The "solution" has been not to propose any real reforms but to reduce transfer payments and social programs, to abandon the effort at federal policy making in favor of state discretion, and to act as if poverty is both trivial and unworthy of public attention. In the retreat to defining childhood poverty as the responsibility of parents, the Reagan proposals create the conditions for more misery, the progressive alienation of the poor, another round of urban riots and another stage in the repeating cycles of crisis and reform.

No one can be complacent about the welfare system. Welfare reform has been on the national agenda almost constantly for two decades, and serious efforts to alleviate poverty through government programs stretch back to the progressive era. The same debates over levels of support and over fears of fraud and "pauperization" have been constantly recapitulated. The same kinds of practices keep reemerging, including distinctions between the "deserving" and the "undeserving" poor and between "unemployables" and "employables." The hope that the welfare population will "wither away," particularly with the initiation of work programs, constantly reappears. Yet the structure of American capitalism guarantees a relatively large welfare class; the causes include the persistence of business cycles and periodic high levels of unemployment, an upward trend in the unemployment rate and high levels of underemployment, and increased numbers of female-headed families unable to support themselves because of discrimination. Given these conditions, the central preoccupations that keep recurring—to minimize the welfare rolls and to maintain work incentives—ignore the causes of poverty and guarantee the inadequacy of welfare programs.

Redistributive programs—programs like AFDC that redistribute income from the majority of taxpayers to a vulnerable minority—cannot eliminate poverty, under any conception of poverty. Under conditions in which the state can alleviate poverty only by taxing away the "private" earnings of individuals and corporations, providing for the poor will always generate resistance. At best, the poor can make limited advances during some periods, especially when they exercise the threat of social disruption; in other periods, redistributive programs are cut back. In a society where incomes are considered private and where other people's children are viewed with such hostility and distrust, redistributive systems lurch back and forth between levels of insufficiency and levels of disaster, fundamentally inadequate to the tasks of eliminating poverty.

For real reform, it will be necessary to move beyond merely redistributive mechanisms of income support. To alleviate the poverty of female-headed families, which constitute such a large proportion of poverty, policies should deal directly with the sexual and racial discrimination and unequal skill levels that cause women to have insufficient earning power.[44] Those concerned about the proliferation of unstable, low-skilled jobs have advocated programs to stimulate the transformation of such jobs into more stable, skilled positions, a policy that would reduce the group moving in and out of poverty. Programs to deal honestly with insufficient employment—for example, public employment without the compromises and constraints that now tend to turn such employment into short-term, unskilled work of marginal value, and public employment that provides the basis for regional development and economic growth—ought to be part of any system of income supports. But these alternatives would interfere with "private" labor markets as they currently operate, and none of them have been taken seriously as welfare reforms. Real solutions—ones aimed at the roots of poverty—must await the relaxation of constraints on the state in a capitalist economy.

In the meantime, the early promise of the welfare system—to support those children, themselves blameless, who are impoverished and unlikely to develop "to the full limit of their potential"—remains empty. Even the instrumental argument that the present costs of providing for poor children will yield future returns has failed to have much weight. In practice, the welfare of poor children is determined by more immediate calculations: children are denied aid if adequate support might threaten the integrity of labor markets, the solvency of the public treasury, or the moral standards of the community. In the process, the promise of *parens patriae*—that the state will provide for children whose parents cannot provide—is effectively vitiated. Instead, we so desperately distrust and dislike lower-class adults that we are willing to let their children suffer as well.

8

The Frontiers of Public Responsibility: Child Care and Parent Education

OF ALL the public programs that treat children and youth, child care and parent education most clearly portend changing relations among families, children, and the state. Pressure to expand government programs to young children, for whom the dictates of maternal care and private responsibility have been strongest, raises questions about familial privacy, parental decision making, and state responsibilities for childrearing. Child care generates new possibilities for opening up the boundaries of the closed nuclear family, establishing social responsibilities for children, and changing sex roles—all of which represent potentially richer (though controversial) conceptions of family life. Both child care and parent education present opportunities to replace *parens patriae* with different justifications for public programs, to change our hostile attitudes toward maternal employment, and to devise new conceptions of professionalism which avoid the dangers of "professional childrearing." The possibilities may not be realized, of course. Developing new models of public responsibility has generated intense conflict, from conservatives interested in constricting public responsibility, from professionals who want to maintain their own power, and from antifeminists who interpret any support for maternal employment as "undermining the family." Nonetheless, the possibilities for revising conventional patterns are richer in this area both because public policies toward young children have not been institutional-ized or rigidified and because the expansion of maternal employment has forced a reexamination of the traditional domestic ideology.

Child care and parent education have much in common. Both have gained attention by promising a bewildering array of private and social benefits: freeing parents, especially mothers, from the most rigid con-straints of childrearing, improving parenting skills, broadening the social-ization process for young children, and enhancing cognitive development. They have also been controversial because they are viewed as threatening the sanctity of the home. Their popularity has been stimulated by child development research and attempts to enhance cognitive learning. Both have tended to "professionalize" the rearing of young children by bring-ing experts into advisory and childrearing roles. They reflect the pressures and ambiguities experienced by women in the work force. The question posed by Aid to Families of Dependent Children—whether state policies should support mothers of young children at home or encourage them to work—is apparent in debates over both subsidized child care and parent education. Each has been shaped by an emphasis on preparing children for success in school, and each reflects an historic dichotomy between provisions for poor children and those for the more affluent. Both are in a critical stage of development, somewhat like the schools in the early nine-teenth century: while most child care and parent education programs are now privately funded and provided on an *ad hoc* basis, public subsidies have increased and advocates are hoping to extend such programs to more children.

While child care and parent education pose similar questions about state policy, their recent development has pointed them in very different directions. Child care assumes that women are no longer full-time moth-ers, and that family-based childrearing is neither the only nor necessarily the most appropriate setting for children. In contrast, parent education programs emphasize care by parents, especially mothers, and assume that public programs should focus on the quality of family-based care. Parent education is promoted as an alternative to child care because it is cheaper, more effective in teaching young children, and more respectful of the parent-child bond. Child care provides supplementary childrearing ser-vices, usually with the effect of alleviating childrearing responsibilities for mothers and facilitating maternal employment. In contrast, parent educa-tion provides information and often strengthens conventional sex roles. Thus each offers a distinct alternative to the question of how to "support the family."

The dichotomies between child care and parent education are not inevitable. The two can be compatible, as now happens when parents use child care and also seek advice from professionals or parent groups, and when programs provide both part-time care and parent education. Head Start offers one example of integrating child care and parent education, providing extrafamilial care and a forum for parents to organize and discuss their common problems. Parent-participation nursery schools in California provide another model, offering half-day care and required attendance at parent education sessions.[1] Although more complicated when full-day care is necessary and single working parents are involved, similar combinations of day care and parent education are conceivable.

Yet while integrating child care and parent education is possible, the divisions between them remain sharp and include many of the same dilemmas confronting other children's institutions. What roles women should play in the home and labor force, what kinds of settings are most appropriate for children, what resources are necessary for strong family life, how the state can enhance development and still allow families choice and privacy—these remain essential questions in the evolution of all children's institutions. Child care and parent education articulate these questions in sharp and intense ways; their historical development and present condition suggest the possibilities and the constraints we face in answering them.

Continuities in Child Care

The central dilemma of child care has always been obvious: child care involves rearing children by individuals other than mothers, contradicting the dogma of domesticity and supporting maternal employment. As compensation for this undeniable fact, advocates have historically proclaimed a host of benefits for child care: the enhancement of cognitive and social development, care "superior" to that found in inadequate homes, the reduction of child abuse and neglect. Almost always the presumed benefits have been justified on the traditional grounds of *parens patriae:* the state can do what parents are failing to do or are doing badly. Public funding for child care has always been grudgingly given because the ruling assumptions have been that the well-organized family should neither need nor want extrafamilial care and that mothers should rear their own children. Public support has therefore been justified only by national emergencies—such as the job creation program for teachers during the 1930s or the effort to mobilize women workers during World War II—or when social problems have reached crisis proportions, as in the efforts to increase child care during the 1960s to reduce welfare costs and provide compensatory education. Otherwise public policy has continued to insist that mothers should rear children, even as the number of working mothers with young children has increased dramatically in the postwar period. The result has been to keep child care underfunded, chaotic, and disreputable.

Since the late nineteenth century, the child care movement has consisted of two separate elements: one including day nurseries and welfare-related programs; the other, nursery schools and education-based programs.[2] At the turn of the century, most day nurseries were extensions of private philanthropy associated with settlement houses and directed at children from low-income families whose mothers worked. Their primary concerns were to protect children from parental neglect, to teach children and parents socially desirable domestic and occupational skills, and to impart American habits to immigrant families. The families of children in day nurseries were considered inadequate, as summed up by one nursery worker who noted, "we gave many of them more abundant food and much better care than their poor homes could afford."[3] The ideology of domesticity reinforced this view: mothers who could not or chose not to rear their children full-time were by definition inadequate. The major reform efforts to aid mothers during the progressive era concentrated on keeping children in the home, for example, by providing financial aid to "deserving" mothers through mothers' pensions. By the end of the progressive era, the day nurseries had become stigmatized as serving the most pathological families and children of the "unworthy poor"—a special irony since working for income was in other circumstances a statement of how "worthy" a poor person was. Whatever possibilities that had once existed for day nurseries had been undermined; vacancy rates and staff turnover were high, care was poor, and few people offered day nurseries as models of extrafamilial child care.

The education-based element of the child care movement contrasts sharply with the welfare orientation. Based in nursery schools and tied to child development research, this element has stressed socioemotional development and (to a lesser extent) cognitive growth of the child, rather than the mother's employment. As they evolved in the 1920s, nursery schools were part-day rather than full-day, and were directed at the developmental enrichment of middle-class children. Conceived as extensions of the home and complements to mothering rather than "mother substitutes," nursery schools assumed full-time mothering and the adequacy

211

rather than the inadequacy of the families they served. They thereby avoided any conflict with social ideals of women's roles, as well as the stigma associated with poor and "deviant" families. Nursery school people regarded day nurseries with contempt: the day nurseries suffered the disadvantages of inadequate resources, a clientele of the "undeserving poor," and the stigma of social welfare goals rather than the more respectable efforts to educate young children. Even though nursery schools were never widespread, they provided a strong institutional image of what the education of young children ought to be, an image significantly different from that provided by day nurseries.[4]

Whether in philanthropic day nurseries or tuition-financed nursery schools, child care through the 1920s was almost exclusively private. The Great Depression introduced the first major change in these arrangements with the establishment of nursery schools as part of the Works Progress Administration (WPA), started primarily to provide employment for unemployed teachers. In contrast to the day nurseries and the nursery schools, the WPA nurseries cut across class lines. Since they were administered through state departments of education and local school boards and often staffed by primary school teachers, they developed an explicitly educational orientation and gave child care a legitimacy it had never previously had.[5] But the WPA nurseries did not provide a permanent model: public funding was tied to the depression crisis, and as that ended so did the nurseries.

World War II expanded federal funding, as day care centers were established to facilitate the employment of women in defense-related industries. In the memory of child care advocates, the war years were a Golden Age, when child care was available to a large number of children without income restrictions. Certainly more children were cared for through federal support, under better conditions, than ever before. But even at the height of the Lanham Act program in 1945, there were spaces for less than 10 percent of those estimated to need child care. Support still was meager, and distrust of maternal employment remained high. Once the war emergency ended, federal funding for child care stopped almost immediately. In the postwar efforts to return men to employment and women to the home, there was no pretense that what had happened during the war might be appropriate in normal times.[6]

After a hiatus in the 1950s, interest in child care increased with the surge of women employment, with new research in child development asserting the importance of the preschool years and with the compensatory efforts of the War on Poverty. Head Start was the centerpiece of those efforts, linking the two historically divergent elements of child care:

it aimed at poor children and families in need of support, as the day nurseries did, but its focus on cognitive development was more consistent with educational goals than reducing welfare rolls.

Other federal funding initiated in the 1960s was directly linked to welfare reform: welfare mothers would be brought into the labor market while their children were taken care of in day care centers. The major sources of funding came through AFDC and the Manpower Development and Training Act, both of which provided for child care as a necessary expense related to training or to employment required for receiving welfare payments. Programs proliferated: by the 1970s there were more than 200 programs that provided federal funds for child care.[7] Many of these programs have since been consolidated in Title XX of the Social Security Act, which is somewhat broader than other welfare-based programs: families with incomes up to 115 percent of a state's median income are eligible, a range that includes middle-income families. In practice, however, Title XX has made little difference to publicly subsidized child care. Limited funds have restricted eligibility to the poorest families, and the priorities of Title XX have continued the tendency to link federal funds to the reduction of welfare dependency. As a 1977 HEW report put it, "general day care is essentially targeted towards the employability of the parent rather than the needs of the child."[8] As a result, child care under government subsidy remains largely a welfare program designed to get the poor into the work force, indicating that the domestic ideology can be violated only to reduce welfare costs. Only one source of federal funding acknowledges that middle-class mothers use child care: by means of the child care credit of the personal income tax, the federal government subsidizes one-fifth of child care expenses in a way that places few restrictions on the kind of child care utilized.

Through the various programs, federal subsidies are substantial, amounting in 1978 to perhaps $1.75 billion in direct subsidies and $500 million through the income tax system.[9] Yet federal support has a ramshackle air because of the numerous programs created since the 1960s. Head Start, Title XX, subsidies through the income tax, funding through the AFDC, and smaller programs have different standards, purposes, and recipients, and none is coordinated with privately funded child care. Efforts to expand and coordinate federal support for child care during the 1970s often acknowledged the legitimacy of extrafamilial programs, and tried to break away from the historic divisions within child care—between care for the affluent and the poor, between custodial functions related to welfare programs and educational functions, between aiding maternal employment and resisting it. Yet so powerful have the historical continuities in child care been that it has been almost impossible to restructure the conceptions that underlie government subsidies.

First and foremost, public participation has continued to reflect the domestic ideal that mothers should not work, unless their families would otherwise be on welfare. This concept has been almost impossible to overcome, even though the level of maternal employment has skyrocketed, and sustained criticism of traditional concepts of mother-child bonding has mounted. The dominant federal programs for child care remain linked to welfare, and, in the special case of Head Start, to compensatory education. Antifeminist attacks have stymied the three major efforts to legislate comprehensive child care programs: the Comprehensive Child Development Act of 1971, vetoed by Richard Nixon with the comment that the act would "commit the vast moral authority of the National Government to the side of communal approaches to child rearing over against the family-centered approach"; the Comprehensive Child and Family Services Act of 1976, defeated by a smear campaign from the antifeminist right; and the Child Care Act of 1979, in which antifeminist sentiment was one of several elements causing its sponsor to withdraw the bill. Despite changes in the facts of family life, it has still proved impossible to overcome old assumptions about the proper roles of women.

Since public child care programs have always been forced to endure the public's hostility toward women working, their strongest defense has come under the familiar doctrine of *parens patriae*—as necessary for "abnormal" parents and children. Underlying the "pathology" model of intervention has been a distrust of women working and of families so poor that both parents need to work; of women who have no husband in the house; and of lower-class families who are sometimes suspected of not being able to handle their parental responsibilities. From the nineteenth-century day nurseries to Head Start to current Title XX centers, the fear has persisted that children in extrafamilial care have parents who choose not to give them adequate care at home. So strong has the "pathology" model been that even supporters of child care have resorted to justifying care in terms of health needs and compensatory care or, in its most flagrant manifestation, using horror stories about child abuse and neglect to mobilize public support for child care.[10]

Hostility toward women working, with the exception of mothers on welfare, and the assumption of parental inadequacy have meant that the conception of proper care for young children has always been class-biased. From the day nurseries to Title XX programs, it has often been assumed that the unfortunate children of the poor are better served by charitable and governmental institutions than by their own parents and that it is reasonable to keep standards of care low. If child care is to reduce government outlays, then child care expenditures can not exceed the costs of maintaining a mother and child at home. As opposed to the "custodial" model for the poor, the "developmental" model for middle-class children requires more funds, trained child care workers, and planned curricula. The two models have in theory begun to merge with the inclusion of educational goals in Head Start and Title XX, through attempts to establish a special child care credential, and in efforts to universalize child care by attaching it to the public schools. However, the historic division between welfare and education remains, manifest in conflicts between social workers and educators over who should receive public funds.[11] The distinction continues between public support for "custodial" care tied to welfare costs and private funding of "developmental" care for middle-class children, and in the extreme class and racial segregation of child care.

The dilemmas of childcare professionals in public institutions are especially apparent. The conflicts among groups of professionals, especially between social workers connected to the welfare model and educators emphasizing "developmental" care, illustrate the close connection between institution building and the status of professional groups: winning control of child care means expanded power, control, status, and jobs, and so the battles among professionals are self-interested as well as ideological. But child care also provides a good example of the constraints on professionalization in public institutions. The conflicts between parents and professionals over the care of young children have been perennial, though they have often been muted. The veiled contempt for the parents of children in day nurseries and the feelings among child care workers that they are superior parent substitutes continues, especially in child care settings designed to care for "deprived" children or in compensatory programs such as Head Start; the "pathology" model by its very structure holds up professionals as superior to parents. At the same time, parental resistance to the professionalization of parenting has impeded the efforts of child care workers to become more professional. The antipathy to federal child care subsidies as "rearing children by the government,"[12] which emerged most powerfully in a smear campaign against the Child and Family Services Act of 1975, expresses a fear of professional influence over young children, widespread even though it has been most stridently expressed by the antifeminist right. The efforts of child care workers to increase their credentials and pay have so far been stymied, partly because of taxpayer resistance to higher costs but also because of a feeling that advanced degrees are unnecessary. Similarly, the American Federation of Teachers' proposal to run child care within the schools has met considerable resistance from those who feel that the model of professional teachers is inappropriate for young children.[13] More than in any other area, the notion of "professionalized childrearing" for young children seems both dangerous and a contradiction in terms.[14] The result has always been considerable uncertainty about the roles professionals should play in child care, and low status for child care workers.

Finally, as in other children's institutions, public child care policies have historically been shaped by considerations unrelated to the interests of children. The WPA day nurseries of the 1930s were motivated by a desire to employ teachers. The Lanham Act centers during World War II were instituted because of the pressures of war-related employment. The child care programs of the 1960s emphasized welfare savings more than the well-being of children, and debates over the role of the public schools in child care have been initiated by teacher unions primarily concerned with jobs in a period of declining school enrollments. Through all the debates about child care, the motivating concern has been a social crisis external to children and families. The desires of mothers for child care so that they can expand their social roles have been pointedly ignored, for fear of legitimating that choice. Indeed, since increased interest in child care in the postwar period has been so clearly stimulated by changing sex roles, the inattention to maternal employment in federal policy has been astonishing. The possibility that professional child care might be beneficial to children—to all children, not only those "educationally deprived"—has similarly been ignored. The results have been, once again, to generate children's institutions pulled by conflicting demands. While expanded subsidies to child care have proved of immense benefit to some children and parents, begrudging and often hostile attitudes have kept child care on the defensive, trapped by its class-divided history and by ambivalence toward working mothers.

Alternative Futures for Child Care

In many ways, the state of child care in the early 1980s is similar to that of the schools in the early nineteenth century. Like schooling then, child care is now provided through a welter of organizations, uncoordinated and often contradictory in their goals, and is funded through a mixture of private fees and public subsidies for the poor. Like the history of schooling, the purposes of child care have been pulled between two poles, that of controlling the poor (in this case, controlling welfare dependency) and that of developing the child and providing more equal access to chances for future success.

The disorganized condition of child care—its confused goals, limited public funding, and the historic tension between child care for the poor and that for the affluent—may remain. The events of the 1970s—the veto of the Comprehensive Child Development Act of 1971 by Richard Nixon, the collapse of the 1976 Comprehensive Child and Family Services Act (sponsored by Walter Mondale and John Brademas), the withdrawal of Alan Cranston's Child Care Act of 1979, and the antifeminist backlash and taxpayer revolts—have added to the uncertainty and chaos. But the pressures toward expansion and coordination are also powerful: the continuing trend in maternal employment, the sheer number of children involved, and the demands for a conscious family policy which incorporates child care are all sources of pressure for a more coherent approach.

Achieving a consensus broad enough to expand and rationalize federal support will first require the resolution of three dilemmas which have marked the entire history of child care: our attitudes toward maternal employment, the confused purposes of child care, and the roles of professionals. The collective uncertainty about these three issues has contributed to the chaos of child care in the postwar period and to the heated debates of the 1970s and 1980s. Some of the debates have been empty, of course. Discussions about "custodial" versus "developmental" child care have often focused on the credentials of child care workers rather than on interactions in child care settings, failing to recognize that the two are not the same. Turf battles among professionals have promoted self-interested arguments masquerading as debate. The literature examining the data on child care use has done a poor job of deriving from the available "facts" guidance for federal policy.[15] As is always the case where the family is involved, assessments of child care are often clouded by nearly hysterial reactions and mythical constructions of the family. But the basic issues are still momentous: the balance between state and parental responsibility for young children, the organization of families, and what the state's role should be in changing sex roles. The debates are also critical because, given the current fluidity of child care, their resolution will shape child care institutions for the foreseeable future.

The first and most obvious issue to be resolved involves the roles of women. The most vociferous opposition to child care has always come from those espousing domestic ideals about women's roles, sometimes expressed in psychological terms as the child's requirements for a full-time mother.[16] If the traditional notion of domesticity continues unrevised, then child care will continue to be seen as a "mother substitute," inevitably inferior to mothering, suggesting that children in child care are apt to be both pathological and deprived. Under these circumstances, we will continue to rely on social crises to justify state support.

Revising old assumptions about maternal employment may become easier, as mothers with young children continue to go to work, as employment among middle-class women dilutes the class bias directed against employment among working-class women, and as evidence accumulates contradicting the notion that maternal employment damages children. The benefits of working for mothers are becoming more widely appreciated, and the beneficial effects of child care on children—including reduced isolation, contact with a larger number of peers, and the possibilities for more varied and richer attachments to different adults—have also been confirmed.[17] These accumulated experiences provide a basis for revising the conception of child care as a "mother substitute" and posing an alternative in which child care is another, normal way of rearing children. In this revised view, child care has some clear advantages over family-based childrearing—freeing women for expanded roles, giving children other adult figures and more interaction with peers—as well as some of the same problems that plague home-based care, like the problems of inadequate resources, of the emotional energy of caretakers, and of how "best" to rear children. Some dilemmas of childrearing are inescapable no matter what the setting, but a revised conception which accepts maternal employment and child care as normal avoids adding the additional burdens of the "pathology" model.

The second issue that must be resolved involves the purposes of child care. Debates over child care still tend to start with an old question: whether the basic purpose of child care is to free mothers or to stimulate the child's development.[18] This way of framing debate forces us to chose one purpose or another and results in forms of child care which must ignore either the mother or the child. This conventional debate fails to acknowledge that the two goals are not necessarily antagonistic. Every institution that cares for children can serve both "custodial" and developmental functions, as good child care always does. The appropriate issue, therefore, is whether child care is designed so that the two roles are performed well rather than badly, so that, for example, the schedules of child care facilities are supportive of parents working and so that an educational and developmental component is a conscious aspect of child care facilities rather than the haphazard result of hiring teachers with credentials.

The traditional debate also ignores the variety of other purposes for child care. For some families, child care facilities have become ways of lowering the boundaries of the isolated nuclear family and building "extended families";[19] in other settings, parents organized around child care have engaged in other political and community concerns.[20] We can see these expanded conceptions of child care implemented in a variety of settings: when parents develop cooperative child care programs that begin to involve more activities than child care; when child care information and referral services expand their concerns to other child-related issues, such as housing, recreation, and safety; and when networks of child care providers and users are established on the basis of preexisting community ties.[21] Similarly, one can imagine child care at workplaces as a way of integrating family life and work life, rather than simply as a mechanism for reducing labor turnover and production costs to employers.[22] Other parents have self-consciously tried to use child care to socialize their children in new ways, to develop the "new woman" and the "new man."[23] All these represent the potential for child care to serve a variety of concerns about childrearing, but the possibilities for these other kinds of goals are dim if the debate between "welfare" and "developmental" purposes continues to dominate discussion. The alternative is to recognize that, like all rich and enduring institutions, child care can serve many legitimate purposes. The issue then becomes how to reconcile and combine the goals of parents, caretakers, and society, rather than how to exclude some of them.

The third issue that must be addressed involves the relation of child care workers to parents. One of the current uncertainties of parents about child care stems from a distrust of others who may have alien values taking care of their children. As one father described a nearby child care facility:

> I would not be comfortable living like [the caretakers]. Instead of a living room set, they'll have a couple of chairs, no T.V. . . . the way those people dress the kid, I think that affects the kid. . . . Those who were running the day care center, that's just not my type of social life . . . you know, the guys had long hair down to here . . . several of the kids were half-dressed. That may be fine for them, but not for me.[24]

This distrust is powerful enough to lead many working parents to rely on a patchwork of care by relatives and odd working hours in order to avoid child care by "outsiders."[25] As in the case of the schools, some of those differences are inevitable whenever parents share childrearing with others. Some differences are legitimate and even beneficial to children in presenting them with alternatives, and some parents welcome child care providers doing for their children what they themselves cannot do.[26] But some of the distrust of child care—the fear of long-haired child care providers, for example, or discomfort at the lack of a television—is probably unnecessary and a reflection of how unwilling many parents are to weaken the barriers of the private family. The distrust of child care workers as alien influences may dissipate, as child care becomes more widespread and more acceptable. Of course every family undoubtedly comes to its own resolution of this problem, but it remains a public issue when child care providers exacerbate unnecessary fears and constrain parental choices.

Another strand of uncertainty about child care workers involves distrust of professionalism itself. Those who have railed against the "professionalization of parenting" and "rearing children by the government" have some basis for their fears. Since professionalism has depended on special status and control over institutions which then distance professionals from parents, the conventional model of professionalism might lead in child care to the treatment that too often typifies the public schools: racist, class-biased, sexist, often explicitly controlling, often behaviorist in approach and pedagogy, and in so many ways unsuitable to the rearing of small children. One alternative has been to try to develop new conceptions of professionalism, in which professionals ally themselves with parents and in which parents have an important voice—the model of parent-controlled child care.[27] Part of this model has been the effort to develop child care professionals—Child Development Associates—whose competencies are developed through experience and verified on the job, rather than taught in school-based programs which may have little relevance to practice and which can only exacerbate the problem of distancing.[28] Another part of the effort to develop "new professionals" has been the effort to insure parental decision making in child care facilities, on the theory that giving parents power is necessary to limiting conventional power of professionals and to making parents and child care workers "partners" rather than "antagonists."[29] The alternatives to conventional notions of professionalism and the concepts of parent participation are still underdeveloped; they are novel, unfamiliar, often resisted by professionals, and limited in application. But the efforts that are being taken are promising ways to resolve the inherent dilemma of professionals, by developing models that invite parental participation while still harnessing special skills.

Resolving the debates about maternal employment, the purposes of child care, and the relationships between parents and professionals will not be easy. The need to make politically "realistic" arguments have forced most child care advocates to stress the traditional rationales for state intervention, the value of child care in reducing welfare costs, for example, or in reducing child abuse. The necessity of framing arguments in instrumental terms has tended to reduce child care to just another social service available to families in need—*parens patriae* in still another form. For every child care advocate pressing for more radical innovations, numerous others are attempting to establish conventional notions of the state's role in child care: conservatives arguing that women belong in the home (and that child care is a communist model), education professionals attempting to require traditional credentials for child care workers, fiscal conservatives arguing that child care is not worth public subsidies and that publicly subsidized programs should be explicitly "custodial."

Given these pressures, one politically likely result is that child care will be expanded and routinized only if control is granted to public school systems. As the history of the kindergarten suggests, publicly funded early childhood programs for "normal" children have typically been legitimate only in the public schools, and developing an alternative institution has been extremely difficult.[30] Public school control would lead to child care following the more conventional concept of the state's relationship to the child: it would require traditional education-based credentials for child care workers; it would dilute parental control and new concepts of professionals working with parents; it would make child care bureaucratic and relatively less flexible; and it would almost certainly emphasize schoollike activities, eliminating the more "utopian" and community-oriented concepts of child care and ignoring the variety of purposes and models which now characterize child care.[31] The fact that some other views of child care exist and have attracted widespread support from parents and providers weighs lightly against this political reality: the concept of how the state ought to relate to children is so deeply rooted—in the dominance of the private family and *parens patriae*, in the correlative concepts of professionals, in limits on public spending—that changing even one small institution like child care involves battles over the basic nature of the state.

Still, compared to other institutions for children, the alternative futures for child care are more varied and seem more attainable. Child care presents an opportunity to reshape the relationships among families, children, and the state, and to redefine the nature of public responsibility. While government support for child care has always been justified in the terms of *parens patriae*, child care advocates have insisted that child care is a normal activity for normal children, for which public funding and regulation is appropriate. Even though governmental funding has been limited in the past to crisis situations, child care presents a way—indeed, one of the major ways—to revise traditional sex roles and concepts of parenting. While child care professionals have often been hostile to parents of the children in their care, and parents have distrusted the professionalization of childrearing, new models of professionalism which incorporate parents present radical alternatives to traditional conceptions. More than any other institution, child care presents opportunities for diminishing the isolation of the nuclear family and developing communities of mutual responsibility for children, which would include a concept of public love and concern for other people's children. To be sure, the battle among alternative conceptions of child care has been and will continue to be bitter, since fundamental issues are at stake. The fact that child care as an institution is relatively unformed makes the possibilities for challenging traditional assumptions all the more real; the importance of child care in the structure of the family and the rearing of children makes the challenge all the more worthwhile.

Parent Education and the New Domesticity

The questions of who should care for young children and how they should be reared have also been at the heart of efforts to revive parent education.[32] The 1970s saw a succession of charges hurled at parents, mothers especially, that they have selfishly chosen to follow their own desires to the detriment of family life and that they no longer know how to parent. Academics and journalists have developed several explanations of parental indifference and incompetence: the decline of extended households and geographic mobility have shattered the opportunity to learn parenting from one's own parents and grandparents; the small size of families has freed parents to ignore their children; childrearing has become too complex for parents living in a highly bureaucraticized and competitive world. At a deeper and more hostile level, conservatives have charged that parenting (particularly mothering) has been devalued by the women's movement, by overpopulation, and by the high cost of children. In turn, parental incompetence has been blamed for every imaginable social problem: poverty, juvenile delinquency, poor school performance, child abuse, moral failure, and the decline of Western civilization.

One solution, championed by both conservatives and liberals, has been formal parent education—a proposal backed by childrearing experts contending that childrearing is the most complex of tasks and that parents need expert advice to raise their children through the early years without trauma. Indeed, for scores of academics and Washington policy "experts," parent education became a new panacea during the 1970s: advocates claimed that parenting programs would help poor children and dignify the citizen-mother whose role was in jeopardy; parent education would both "save the children" and "support the family." At a time when sharp attacks on social spending were mounting, parent education was touted as a cheaper alternative to school-based programs and "developmental" day care. In costing less and promising more, the advantages of parent education have been obvious, especially in an atmosphere of fiscal crisis, taxpayer resistance, conservative moralism, and disillusionment with liberal programs.

Despite its apparent novelty, parent education builds on a history of both private and public efforts. The most direct antecedents of formal parenting programs date from the progressive era. The National Congress of Mothers, the forerunner of the PTA, was established in 1897 to provide parents with contemporary scientific thought and advice about childrearing. In order to achieve a more enlightened motherhood, women's organizations served as moral and scientific "missionaries" to lower-class families and helped organize middle-class women in the cause of "educated motherhood."[33] The Children's Bureau, founded in 1912, built upon similar assumptions; limited by its mandate not to organize mothers or to intervene directly into the lives of children, the bureau investigated the living conditions of poor children and offered advice on health, child development, and baby care. But aside from the administration of limited maternal and infant health legislation during the 1920s, the bureau reflected the view of childrearing as an individual and private concern rather than espousing new notions of public responsibility.[34]

The 1920s were years of tremendous growth for the parent education movement, through organizations like the PTA, the Child Study Association of America, the National Council of Parent Education, the American Home Economics Association, and the American Association of University Women. Parenting courses were established in colleges, high schools, and even in grade schools. At the same time, the emphasis of the movement shifted away from its earlier social welfare and settlement house concerns. Parent education took on a much more middle-class focus (as had child care); interest in parenting programs as mechanisms of social reform disappeared, in favor of a more passive view in which experts confined their teaching to principles of child psychology and children's health.

Parent education continued to expand during the early 1930s, funded through FERA and WPA, providing employment and a cheap palliative for the economic and family crisis of the depression. Parent education was a way of showing support for the nuclear family under the stress of unemployment, at a time when collective solutions appeared as threatening alternatives to private ones. The family life adjustment program, begun in the late 1930s, continued into the early 1950s, and other federal funds were available through community mental health programs, vocational training programs, land grant colleges, and state extension services. But there was little new in these efforts, and some of the promising federal programs were allowed to die. By the 1950s, with familial togetherness the new ethic and little political interest in social welfare, parent education as a formal movement ceased to attract much attention. In contrast, interest in parenting materials, like the childrearing manuals of Dr. Spock grew enormously, but the presumption of private responsibility for childrearing rendered formal, publicly subsidized parenting programs obsolete.

Formal programs of parent instruction began to be seriously proposed once again near the end of the 1960s, partly in response to the apparent failures of the War on Poverty. The negative findings of the 1970 Westinghouse report evaluating Head Start deflated the dreams that compensatory preschool programs could resolve the school problems of the poor.[35] But the Westinghouse report raised hopes of a different sort: the finding that parental participation led to more lasting cognitive gains was transformed by child development experts into a call for action, arguing that the federal government ought to emphasize the parent as the principal influence on the child. Developmental psychologists scorned the "naive environmentalism" of Head Start and began to emphasize the familial context in which children's sustained cognitive development normally occurs. From this vantage, early education alone—as in the compensatory programs of the 1960s—was inadequate, because it neglected the family context. The only effective way to improve the school performance of poor children, the argument continued, was to teach parents (more particularly, mothers) how to develop the intellectual promise of their children in the home during their early years.[36] Parent education programs proliferated, some of them relatively large and federally funded, many of them small experimental programs, and still others little more than informal discussion groups.

Despite the uneven development of parent education and the rich variety of parent education programs, its basic assumptions have remained virtually unchanged since the progressive era. The fear that parents—especially poor parents—cannot raise their children adequately is a venerable one, repeated whenever there has been a sense of family crisis. Experts' fear of the damage done to children by ignorant parents revived once again the image of the vulnerable child. The proposal to resolve problems of the greatest complexity—poverty, educational deprivation, adolescent unrest, the disruption of families—by parent education reflects the notion that properly trained parents can by themselves shape their children. The ideal of the full-time mother is a reversion to older domestic ideals confining women to home-bound roles, and the importance of education and the latest research developments in helping women fulfill their true potential as mothers revives from the progressive era the concept of "educated motherhood." Conservatives have seen in parent education a way to cut back costly social services and to reassert childrearing within the private family. Liberals have found it a way to provide resources—in this case, informational resources—to parents. Above all, by implicitly blaming parents for the perceived failures of childrearing, parent education has always directed attention away from more fundamental social and economic causes of family distress.

These assumptions, along with the need of the new Office of Child Development (OCD) for programs to ensure its organizational identity and survival,[37] underlay the creation of the federally sponsored parent education programs of the 1970s: the Parent and Child Development Centers (PCDCs) for parents of children under three; Home Start, for parents of children from three to six; and Education for Parenthood (EFP), to teach parenting skills to teen-agers in grades seven to twelve. The PCDCs began with three pilot projects in 1971, designed to test the relative merits for poor parents of center-based and home visiting systems. Each of the settings emphasized teaching mothers the rudiments of child development and alternative ways of coping with specific behaviors, and familiarizing them with toys and materials to stimulate their children's development. The PCDCs have been explicit in promoting parent education as a superior substitute for compensatory education and in advocating the "new domesticity," the view that the poor mother ought to be at home devoting herself full-time to the intellectual development of her children.[38] Their goals were nothing if not grand:

> By sharing the lore of child development with parents, especially mothers, in low-income families to enable them to become effective agents of their own children's social, emotional and intellectual development during the years from birth to three, it was hypothesized that much of the environmentally based, cumulative disadvantagement of low-income children could be prevented.
> Other benefits were also expected to accrue to participating parents, children and families, including: the acquisition of a wide range of social skills and intellectual competencies on the part of mothers; more positive attitudes and motivations; increased potential for employment of mothers when infants reach

school age; involvement of fathers and their increased understanding and psychological support of mother in the child-rearing tasks; greater family solidarity; positive effects on older children and on subsequent infants born to participant families.[39]

While OCD felt that these goals had been realized, it is difficult to judge the validity of that conclusion. The reliability of program evaluations which do not consistently monitor home activities is suspect, and OCD's evaluations downplay their costs, a crucial consideration given the fact that the PCDCs cost more than other forms of parent education or center-based programs.[40] The PCDCs may well have benefited many parents and children, but they have not been the panacea they had promised to be. It has proved extraordinarily difficult to establish new PCDCs—a reflection of both their costs and their lack of acceptance—and there has been no suggestion that they could be expanded to cover a significant proportion of poor children.

It is easier to judge a much less rigorous program such as Home Start, begun in 1972 with the intent of replicating the benefits of Head Start but without removing children from their homes. Home Start has operated by sending "home visitors" into family settings, to teach poor parents—almost always mothers—to become "child development specialists," to serve as a "sympathetic listener, a helper, advisor, and *friend* to the entire family being serviced," and to encourage poor mothers to adopt "a positive 'preventive' approach . . . so that the atmosphere and attitudes conducive to a happy home environment are encouraged." Like the PCDCs, the hopes for Home Start were enormous: it represented an alternative to center-based programs that was cheaper and supposedly more effective in stimulating cognitive development, more flexible, and with more father involvement. Still more heroically, Home Start was expected to strengthen the allegedly declining family spirit among the poor by getting all family members to recognize their mutual responsibilities and so revitalizing family life that no one—no mother—would ever want to leave the family hearth.[41]

Home Start embodied pedagogical conceptions so anachronistic that it is remarkable they were advanced as original in the 1970s: the home visitors bore an alarming similarity to the "friendly visitors" at the turn of the century who dispensed love, religion, and advice as cure-alls for poverty. The magnitude of their tasks was enormous: with only ninety minutes of advice per week, home visitors were expected to teach poor women how to rear their children so that they could compete with middle-class children, without alleviating the economic deprivations that defined the Home Start population. The Home Start strategy sought to overcome economic problems by changing attitudes and ignoring the harsh causes of poverty. The "happy home" approach smacked of trying to convince the poor to adapt to poverty, holding out the hope of a better future for their children as consolation for their present troubles. Given the startling gap between ends and means, it is not surprising that so few Head Start programs adopted a Home Start component (despite pressure from OCD), and that the majority of parents refused to switch out of Head Start.[42]

Like the PCDCs and Home Start, the Education for Parenthood program promised everything: EFP would teach teen-agers parenting skills, and by imparting greater appreciation for the difficulties of being a parent would also improve teen-agers' relations with their own parents, make them more deferential to their elders and more conscious of their future responsibilities. By teaching positive attitudes toward family life, EFP would slow the "decline of the family" and reverse "antichild" sentiments. In theory it reached boys as well as girls, included the affluent as well as the poor, and was flexible enough to be adapted to local needs. Above all, EFP was promoted as easy to implement and cost-effective, especially in view of claims that it was truly "preventive" because it reached prospective parents early in their development.[43] Yet the evaluations indicate that, while participants felt positively about EFP, there was almost no discernible change in their attitudes toward parenting. Still more tenuous is the assumption that the minor differences that showed up would persist long enough to improve parenting practices, and then affect the cognitive and social development of the next generation. Students enrolled in the program were predominantly female (79 percent in one evaluation and 85 percent in another), with minority and lower-income pupils overrepresented. Despite its claim to universality, then, EFP had a target group precisely the same as the other parent education programs: those whose children were likely to do the worst in American society, the poor and minority groups in particular. Whatever parenting "skills" EFP emphasized, the general attitudes it consciously and unconsciously imparted reflected the outmoded ideology of domesticity and the misguided ideal of overcoming poverty by educational approaches.

In recapitulating earlier historical developments, the dominant federal parenting programs of the 1970s illustrated once again the pernicious conventions of the state's relationship to children. The programs proposed simple solutions—home visitors, expert advice, high school courses—to problems that are among the most complex and intractable in our society. They represented a substitute for more direct efforts to eliminate poverty, racial discrimination, and class divisions. By calling up an older ideal of "educated motherhood," they returned to earlier conceptions of sex roles, rather than trying to revise ideas of what mothers and fathers might be. In focusing on the failures of parents and suggesting educational solutions, these parent education programs drew attention away from the social and economic causes of childrearing problems and substituted a notion of the "happy home," adjusted to the conditions of poverty, as the goal of social policy. In blaming parents, they defused the need for more thorough reforms of social institutions and absolved the state from complicity in the continued failure of poor and minority children.

The formal parent education programs of the last decade also illustrated several dilemmas of childrearing professionals. In espousing the "new domesticity," they advocated full-time mothering as the best antidote to all the evils of society, while promoting the expertise of professionals and the need to teach mothers how to mother. In asserting their expertise over "deficient" clients, they reinforced the potentially antagonistic relationship between professionals and parents, undermining what good parent education can do and driving away parents as the Home Start experience illustrated. Finally, parent education programs perpetuated—as professionals always have—the belief that there are "scientific" and educational solutions to problems that are economic, social, and ethical. Child development specialists have useful insights and information to offer, representing a breadth of experience and a wealth of knowledge that no individual parent can possibly attain. But the fact that behavioral science during the twentieth century has followed a course of trends, fads, new discoveries in theory and method undermines the notion that its truths can be precise or value-free. To assert the scientific validity of childrearing expertise has often backfired, with parents and citizens resisting all aspects of professionalism rather than submit to demeaning treatment.

The failures of parent education have been frustrating because there is considerable appeal to the simple notion of parent education. In every family, there are moments of panic when parents find themselves confused about what their children are doing and want greater insights into their roles as parents. The volume of childrearing literature currently available is testimony to the desire of parents for information. Between 1970 and 1974, 148 new books on childrearing were published, five times as many as between 1960 and 1964 even though the number of young children decreased. About 23 million books on parenting were bought between 1970 and 1974; there are currently more than two hundred "popular" childrearing books in print, all supplemented by magazines and informal discussion groups.[44] Some parent education programs give certain kinds of information to new parents; though the amount of technical information which new parents need is probably rather small and quickly learned, this is still a valuable function. Some parent education groups provide a forum for parents to share their experiences and to be comforted about their inevitable fears, making childrearing a less lonely and less individualistic task. In this process professionals can be by turns reassuring, informative, and challenging, though the success of such groups requires professionals who are comfortable as partners with parents rather than didactic and paternalistic superiors.[45]

Other potential functions for parent education have been unexplored because of political difficulties. One possibility, most obviously expressed in the EFP program, is that parent education can revise stereotypes about men as fathers and women as mothers; this goal obviously requires the schools to revise the sexual stereotypes that now permeate them. Parent education also has the potential to give teen-agers realistic perceptions of parenting and to enhance their understanding of sexuality as a way of reducing teenage pregnancies. However, this possibility is susceptible to undermining the conventional resistance to sex education for adolescents. Above all, parent education—like child care—has seemed promising as a way of organizing parents around issues related to children and family life. Certainly the historical antecedents of parent education—especially the settlement houses—had political as well as educational goals in mind when they reached out to new parents. Politically conscious forms of parent education seem difficult to implement, however. The political perspective of the settlement houses has been lost, eroded by the political neutrality of professionalism and eliminated as part of the general pressure to disenfranchise the poor. The possibility of the federal government establishing public programs which might mobilize politically on behalf of children—especially on behalf of poor children—seems remote indeed; if anything, the pluralist state concentrates its energies on reducing the representation of any group which might challenge interest groups in power.[46]

The problem, then, is not the conception of parent education *per se* but the particular assumptions that have motivated state-sponsored parent education programs. There are some parent education programs which teach parents what they need to know, which are supportive of parents, and which provide a forum for the common worries of young parents; beyond that, we can imagine parent education being actively used to revise our myths and stereotypes about family life and to express political concerns for children. Yet until we develop new conceptions of the state's relation to families and children, the realization of these prospects are not likely. Instead we have parent education programs that are grand in their promises but meager in their results, condescending to the poor, and restrictive for women. Rather than simply providing information and companionship, formal parenting programs have been distorted by their aspirations for unattainable goals. Rather than developing programs in which parents can draw on expertise, parent education has assumed that parents are incapable and subjected them to the authority of child development experts. Under the guise of "strengthening the family," it may in practice stand as the most dramatic intrusion into the daily interactions of parent and child. Federal parent education programs have thus become part of the conservative approach to social and familial problems, blaming a variety of problems on childrearing techniques rather than on the social and economic context of family life. Given the assumptions that dominate the state's program, parent education is unlikely to be of much help to children or to parents.

The Future of Public Responsibility for Young Children

The similarities between federally sponsored child care and parent education go beyond the fact that both involve young children. Unfortunately, these similarities reflect assumptions, common to most children's institutions, which have worked to the detriment of the programs. The assumption of *parens patriae* means that subsidized child care and parent education depend upon notions of pathology among the poor; both are motivated by welfare considerations (especially forcing welfare mothers into the labor market), buttressed more recently by efforts to provide compensatory education. As in other institutions, the segregation of poor children, undesirable by itself, has forced programs to struggle for their existence and legitimacy. The continuing attachment to domesticity, the view that mothers should stay home, has undermined the potential of child care as a potentially richer childrearing environment rather than an inferior "mother substitute"; and domesticity has prevented parent education from revising traditional sex roles by teaching fathers as well as mothers about parenting.

Child care and parent education have both gained support from child development research and the growing prominence of childrearing professionals. But, as is true elsewhere, professional expertise has had ambiguous consequences. While it sometimes provides important advice, its message is often confused, subject to fads, and raises the specter of "professionalized parenting." The tendency of professionals to preach at parents, to assume that their expertise overrides that of parents, and to keep parents at a distance gives substance to fears of "rearing children by the government"—even as the rhetoric is often employed to constrain public responsibility for children. The evidence of insensitive bureaucrats, class and racial bias, and professional self-interest in children's institutions cannot be ignored. The child care and parent education programs of the state thus display the same corruptions of public responsibility so evident in other children's institutions: stinginess in funding, inconsistent implementation, the segregation of poor children, and professional and bureaucratic insensitivity.

In the process, the potential of child care and parent education has been undermined, again in ways common to other institutions. But because child care and parent education are less institutionalized and rigid—despite their lengthy history—than are the public schools, juvenile reform institutions, and welfare system, the potential for new modes of responsibility are greater. Child care and parent education can provide much-needed services to parents. Both present different kinds of opportunities to revise the sexual stereotypes that have constrained all women and impoverished the lives of all children. Both present opportunities for loosening the boundaries of the private families in ways that could be beneficial to children and parents. Child care raises the possibility of new relations between parents and children in which the burdens (and the joys) of childrearing are shared, relations that would allow parents to see their children as part of the community of children. Parent education can be an antidote to the isolation of the private family by allowing parents to understand that their problems are general rather than individual. Both child care and parent education can provide mechanisms for political organization. In these ways, early childhood programs can be on the frontiers of changing conceptions of family life and parenting; they can also illustrate more broadly how to revise the state's relationship to children.

But to achieve these ends, it will be necessary to accept the validity of maternal employment and the advantages of shared childrearing so that child care and parent education programs can be free from ambivalence and anachronism. Only then can programs for young children be discussed in terms of how they enhance the lives of children and parents. Without revising *parens patriae* as the basis for government programs, the stigma attached to young children in public programs will continue, and class and racial segregation will remain. So too will a different conception of the professional's role—as partner in the childrearing process, as a consultant whose most basic knowledge comes from parents—be necessary. This in turn will require a change in the understanding of what parents and experts can each do, and what "expertise" means. It may require in addition that decision-making power in public programs be restructured in order to include parents. Unless this kind of change comes about, conflict inherent in the relations between professionals and parents will only worsen.

Finally, there must be a different and more limited understanding of what social programs for young children can do. Because of the power of myths about the family—that it is private, that parents determine their children's lives, that only in the most severe circumstances should the state "interfere"—and because of interest group politics and instrumental justifications of public policy, advocates and reformers have invariably been forced to claim more for children's programs than they can possibly accomplish. When the programs fall short—as they inevitably do—the public turns on them, rejecting them as misguided, intrusive, and wasteful. Even modest claims of enhanced cognitive development in children's programs may be inappropriate, not merely because program goals extend to social and emotional development, but also because early childhood programs are still only *part* of the child's environment. Just as parental determinism is inaccurate, placing the responsibility for cognitive and emotional development solely on early childhood programs is inappropriate in a world where so many institutions affect a child's development.

The highly inflated expectations that have repeatedly been claimed for child care and parent education—indeed, for all children's institutions— are absurd: there are no cheap educational solutions to poverty, discrimination, and the deep and corrosive divisions of class, and no real substitutes for direct efforts to eliminate structural inequalities. In the development of child care and parent education to "shore up the family"—in this case, to enhance the capacities of parents—it should be sufficient to see whether a program reduces the strains associated with parenting in ways that simultaneously enhance the parent-child bond and the child's connections to peers and adults outside the family. To impose other requirements for public involvement is ultimately self-defeating.

PART THREE

BEYOND CHILDREN'S INSTITUTIONS

9

The Search for a Family Policy

T HE ATTEMPTS to improve children's lives have usually emphasized children's institutions on the assumption that creating public institutions external to families is the most appropriate way to help children. Elaborating children's institutions reflects, most obviously, the beliefs that children have special developmental needs and that they can be reshaped in ways adults cannot. The unwillingness to blame children for the conditions of their lives (especially poverty) and the desire to keep innocent children separate from adults who might corrupt them has made it easier to provide separate institutions and public funds for children. The elaboration of children's institutions also reflects the ideological power of families and firms as private institutions: Americans have resisted direct intervention into families to enforce childrearing responsibilities and direct intervention into the economy to change the structural inequalities underlying family life. Instead, they have created children's institutions standing *in loco parentis*, doing for children what their parents cannot do and promoting equality of opportunity rather than equality itself. As a result, all of the implicit promises to children—to allow all children to start life with a reasonable chance of success, to protect them from the worst aspects of poverty and the most dangerous influences—have been freighted upon children's institutions.

During the last decade, a relatively novel approach to the "family crisis" has emerged in various attempts to articulate a comprehensive family policy. Many of these efforts have been incoherent, and others have been self-serving.[1] The attention of politicians such as Jimmy Carter to family issues has often seemed an effort to generate an aura of concern and public generosity and so become associated with issues that all Americans can support. In this assumption, politicians have been badly mistaken: the deep political divisions over what "the family" should be and the disagreement over which policies "strengthen the family" mean that family issues are divisive rather than unifying, as the political controversies and rhetorical excesses of the disastrous 1980 White House Conference on Families showed. Family issues have also been saleable, and the writings of academics and journalists about family policy have often seemed an effort to follow a trend, potentially one with political power. As a result, much of the writing on family policy has consisted of familiar issues relabeled: income transfer programs, child care, and social services have become "family support programs"; efforts to promote the equality of women have been lauded for their role in "recognizing the diversity of family forms" and "supporting the family"; and the careful analysis of legislation—which ought to be part of every rational and self-conscious public policy—has been formalized as "family impact statements."

As family issues have become popular, every group and every cause has tried to become included: the aged and homosexuals have insisted that their households be considered "families," and the handicapped received special attention at the White House Conference on Families. In these efforts the term "family" has become unspecific and therefore meaningless, and family problems have expanded to include the entire range of human difficulties. In the process, the historic connection of families to childrearing responsibilities and the special attention in periods of family crisis to the problems of children have been lost.

Despite its vagueness, there are valid reasons for the interest in family policy. One obvious reason involves the scope of the state itself. The expansion of the state in the postwar period has made it impossible to ignore the influences of the state on children through their families. Macroeconomic policy, the income tax structure, antidiscrimination policies, and other employment-related programs have assumed major importance. The range of postwar programs has become staggering: an array of social services; nutrition, health, and housing programs; grants to state and local governments for a variety of programs from sewage plants to recreation facilities; loans for small businesses, minority businesses, and export firms; guarantees for savings deposits, home mortgages, farm prices, and Chrysler; and new public enterprises such as Amtrak and Conrail. These instruments of social and economic policy have generated new consequences for families and children, bewildering in their variety and often contradictory in their effects. As Alva Myrdal, the Swedish sociologist, recognized four decades ago, state expansion has created an implicit family policy; the critical issue is whether that policy will be conscious, consistent, and principled, or whether it will remain unconscious, chaotic, and ambiguous in its effects for children. In Daniel Moynihan's summation:

> No government, however firm might be its wish, can avoid having policies that profoundly influence family relationships. This is not to be avoided. The only option is whether these will be purposeful, intended policies or whether they will be residual, derivative, in a sense concealed ones. . . . A *nation without a conscious family policy leaves to chance and mischance an area of social reality of the utmost importance, which in consequence will be exposed to the untrammeled and frequently thoroughly undesirable impact of policies arising in other areas.*[2]

In responding to the size of the state and the complexity of programs, the calls for a coherent and consistent family policy are no different from the efforts—so far equally unsuccessful—to develop a consistent energy policy, a coherent defense policy, or a sensible transportation policy.

Recognizing that the state has some kind of family policy, even if confused and incoherent, has been the most novel aspect of current debates and has stimulated the most bitter conflict. For conservatives, the state itself is to blame for the turmoil of families. In their view the United States is on the brink of socialism, and the state has become so large as to intrude on every family and every firm. The scope of state programs should be reduced, with social responsibilities "reprivatized" by giving public responsibility back to parents or to small-scale, voluntaristic organizations such as churches and community organizations. Conservatives have also embraced a nineteenth-century conception of the family and sex roles, and so have vigorously opposed governmental efforts to eliminate sex discrimination.[3] At a time of fiscal limitations and widespread hostility to the state, the conservative plea to "get government out of the family" has achieved an extraordinary popularity. To follow it, however, means retreating to the conditions that called state action into being in the first place—the tenets of nineteenth-century liberalism and the dreadful consequences of *laissez-faire* capitalism.

A more moderate approach has emerged in the efforts to make existing policies more coherent and consistent, on the assumption that the chaos created by "chance and mischance" is the most serious flaw in policies for families and children. One element of this approach involves the efforts, especially prominent in social services, to coordinate existing programs. Administrative reformers have complained about "gaps and overlaps," about children who fail to receive needed services because of no information, perverse eligibility requirements, or other administrative problems that cause children to "slip between the cracks" of the existing programs. Like family policy generally, the intentions of the coordination literature are admirable, though findings remain hazy and recommendations vague.[4] Another element, more clearly tied to rhetoric about families, has been the attempt to generate "family impact statements" modeled on environmental impact statements. These exercises would examine the consequences of public programs for families, to detect inconsistencies and results contrary to prevailing norms. Family impact statements promise a great deal, especially in recommending that all public programs be evaluated for their influence on families and children and in providing a political forum for children's advocates. Unfortunately, the efforts so far have been confined to analyzing single issues—for example "flexible working schedules" foster care, and teen-age pregnancy—and have failed to articulate what a family policy might be except to proclaim the truism that "all levels of government have policies and programs that affect families deeply."[5] To be sure, the emphasis on coherence and consistency in public policies might yield some valuable results. However, by emphasizing traditional income support programs and social services, proponents of family impact analysis hold a narrow view of what affects families; by emphasizing consistency and coordination, they embrace a narrow conception of the underlying problems and avoid the politically difficult issues of structural inequalities and moral values.

Modern liberals have been the most far-reaching in their conception of family policy. In their view a comprehensive family policy would unify those state actions, now haphazard and uncoordinated, which affect families; but it would also require the federal government to implement its programs thoroughly and consistently—for example, to fulfill the mandates of full employment embedded in the 1947 Employment Act and the 1978 Humphrey-Hawkins Act and the guarantees of "decent housing for all" in the 1949 Fair Housing Act, as well as eliminate poverty and discrimination in their various forms.[6] In recognizing the public basis of family life, the impact of structural inequalities on children's institutions, and changes in sex roles, liberal proposals go beyond the symptoms of problems to their sources.

Implicit in the liberal position is a second powerful reason for the interest in family policy. Many who have called for a comprehensive family policy have realized that creating institutions for children while ignoring the conditions of their families has not worked very well. Distinguishing children from their parents while simultaneously blaming parents for their children's problems—the assumptions of failure underlying *parens patriae*—has had too many negative consequences; the stigma attached to children in compensatory education and the low levels of income support in AFDC are two of many examples. The hope that we can achieve equality of opportunity in an unequal society has been consistently thwarted by those interpreting public institutions in terms of private gain: whites denying minorities equal access to schooling, middle-class parents vying to keep their children's schools superior, employers subordinating the welfare of children in AFDC to labor market needs. Class and racial biases make it nearly impossible to shape children's lives *de novo* in public institutions. Assumptions about what kinds of socialization are appropriate and fears of other people's children and what they are likely to become govern every institution, converting benevolent intentions into controlling impulses. Acknowledging just how inadequate children's institutions have been has led some liberals to promote a comprehensive family policy aimed at addressing the structural inequalities of family life directly, since children's institutions cannot possibly work as they should if family life is ignored.

Even at its best, however, liberal family policy falls short, for it fails to consider the nature of the state, its constraints, and the kinds of changes necessary to overcome those constraints. Promoting full employment as a cornerstone of family policy makes little sense without understanding why the United States has so consistently failed to achieve full employment. Calling for the elimination of poverty in a period of taxpayer revolts and hostility to the welfare system may be noble but it is also futile without considering the reasons why redistributive programs have always been incomplete. The call to expand social services ignores the negative consequences of *parens patriae* and professionalism. The very idea of a unified family policy assumes that the conflicting policies toward children and families and different interest groups can be reconciled and neglects the deep class and racial divisions of American society. We are thus left with the continuing dilemma of modern liberalism: while the state must be used to enhance the lives of families and children, there is little reason to believe that the state as presently constructed can achieve this goal.

Given the limitations of children's institutions, a coherent family policy—one that would attempt to fulfill society's historic promises to children by modifying the conditions of families—is a progressive and necessary step. However, this step requires going beyond the internal dynamics of family life. A family policy that concentrates on the problems of violence and child abuse, teen-age sexuality, and the breakdown of affectionate relations takes the state into areas where it is least effective and is potentially the most intrusive. Public education programs, the most widespread way of dealing with these issues, have very limited influence. Punishments and prohibitions are even worse: harsh punishments for child abuse may formalize society's outrage, but they have little effect on par-

239

ental behavior; government regulation of divorce has historically had little impact on divorce rates. Public policies designed to improve relationships within families raise the threat of public officials in every bedroom. Nor can family policy attempt to be all things to everyone, trying to incorporate every conceivable living arrangement and every possible government influence on families and children. Rather than reaching inside the families, the most appropriate family policy should attempt to benefit children by modifying the external conditions that affect the ways families live, beginning with the problems underlying every period of family crisis: unemployment and macroeconomic conditions, changing sex roles, racial discrimination, and class divisions. Understanding why the state has been unable to resolve these recurrent issues is the first and most important step in evolving a coherent and progressive family policy.

Family Life and Macroeconomic Policy

To many people concerned about children and families, debates about macroeconomic policy seem irrelevant and technically bewildering. Yet the health of the economy, particularly as reflected by unemployment and inflation rates, has always been central to family life, and Americans have been quick to see the connections. The earliest complaints of urban disorders invariably mentioned unemployment and "shiftlessness"; the recessions that have regularly plagued market-based economies have made family life more difficult, and unemployment has been an essential issue each time Americans discover that the family is "in trouble." However, a recognition that the state's role in the economy is also vitally connected to families has usually been missing. Even as the development of more powerful macroeconomic policies in the postwar period promised an end to business cycles and unemployment—a promise never totally fulfilled—a curious dichotomy has persisted: macroeconomic policies are recognizably important to families, especially poor families, yet the state's role in the economy is ignored in most discussions of family policy.

Until well into the twentieth century, the state played only a limited role in managing the economy. The Great Depression of the 1930s provided the motivation for a much more aggressive governmental role in economic management, a role that was later formalized by Keynesian economics. By the late 1930s, a coalition of liberals and labor leaders had come to support Keynesian policies, which called for a larger and more systematic role for the state to moderate business cycles and prevent recessions, emphasized state management in place of the unregulated market, and ranked full employment as the goal rather than maximum profits. Opposition to Keynesian policies quickly emerged, especially from organized business concerned about state intervention into private enterprise and fearful that Keynes's emphasis on low unemployment would increase their labor costs. The Employment Act of 1946, the major Keynesian legislation in the immediate postwar period, reflected these competing pressures: initially drafted to assure "full" employment, it wound up providing advisory but not administrative agencies and setting vague goals of "maximum" and "high" employment rather than full employment. The act committed the government to very little, but it nonetheless marked a symbolic turning point. With it, the state accepted an active role in managing the economy to prevent recessions.[7]

Conflicting interests continued to shape the state's Keynesian policy, which was activist but oriented to business and military interests and regressive in its distributional impact. Economic policy after World War II emphasized military spending rather than social welfare programs, growth as the cure-all for social problems rather than redistribution and social services, and tax cuts and subsidies favoring upper-income families and business rather than spending on social programs and progressive tax cuts. But the most important modification of Keynesian principals came as a result of the preoccupation of the business community with costs and inflation. The discovery in the 1960s of a trade-off between unemployment and inflation—implying that a high level of unemployment was necessary to curb inflation—clarified the policy choices as well as the political divisions in macroeconomic policy. In the interests of lower wages and higher profits, business has preferred low rates of inflation to low unemployment rates, while labor and advocates for the poor have advocated low unemployment as a way of increasing real wages and redistributing income. The battle over a trade-off between unemployment and inflation has thus represented a form of class struggle between capital and labor, now taking place within the state rather than within the firm.[8]

Macroeconomic policies in the postwar period have thus been constantly torn between contradictory goals, with very different economic interests at stake. To be sure, the development of macroeconomic policies has allowed some groups previously without influence over the economy— especially labor and the poor—to participate in setting economic goals. But at the same time, the implementation of Keynesian policies has been conservative and business-oriented because of the influence of corporate power. The acceptance of Keynesian macroeconomic policy making across a broad ideological spectrum made the state the guarantor of economic well-being, but the continued insistence on the prerogatives of private firms limited the state's ability to pursue full employment single-mindedly. As a result of these dual pressures, the promises of Keynesian policy have never been fulfilled: the chronic inability of the American economy to achieve full employment (except in war time) has kept large numbers of families susceptible to the ravages of unemployment.

During the 1970s two novel problems emerged, indicating an economy in severe distress and increasing the constraints on the state's ability to manage the economy: fiscal limitations and the inadequacy of Keynesian policies. The postwar increases in federal spending, in the federal deficit, and in state and local government spending magnified the central dilemma of macroeconomic policy: by 1980 the state accounted for slightly over 20 percent of the Gross National Product in an economy still considered "private." Public spending began to meet taxpayer resistance as early as the late 1960s and accelerated thereafter. Taxpayer revolts began at the state and local levels, and then extended to the federal level in Ronald Reagan's attacks on social spending. Taxpayer revolts by themselves constrain the power of the state to control the economy: the political pressure to reduce federal spending and to eliminate the federal deficit will make it more difficult for the federal government to combat unemployment through conventional Keynesian tax and spending policies. Unfortunately, any limitation on macroeconomic policy will fall disproportionately on the poor, on minorities, and on children because of their vulnerability to business cycles, unemployment, and poverty. In the constraints imposed by taxpayer revolts, we can see the flowering of another dilemma inherent in macroeconomic policies: the very idea of macroeconomic policy assumes that public control of the economy is necessary for the welfare of all, but the conception of incomes as private and the resistance to taxation for social programs and other people's children thwart the full implementation of macroeconomic policies.

Taxpayer revolts and budget cutting under Ronald Reagan have constrained macroeconomic policy in still another way. If the fury of the conservative budget-cutters were directed at all kinds of government spending—that is, if defense and nondefense spending, direct subsidies to the poor and tax subsidies to the rich, grants for social programs and grants for corporations were equally reduced—then the level of government spending might decrease but its composition would stay the same. But taxpayer revolts have not been neutral: conservatives have been most hostile to social programs, and contrary to much of their rhetoric they often seem more interested in the composition of spending than its level.

Ronald Reagan's proposals have decreased social programs, especially those for children, but they have also increased defense spending enormously. In every economic forecast, the Reagan program will lead to increased budget deficit. This shift away from programs that decrease unemployment with little or no effect on inflation toward defense programs with smaller effects on unemployment and much larger inflationary effects threatens to make a shambles of the economy by increasing inflation and perhaps increasing unemployment at the same time.[9] Thus the peculiar "fiscal conservatism" that allows defense spending to get out of hand will skew macroeconomic policy at the same time as it skews the composition of public spending.

The second problem to emerge in the 1970s was the possibility that Keynesian policy was no longer adequate to the task of managing the economy. This was a special irony since it occurred after Richard Nixon declared that "We are all Keynesians now," conservatives as well as liberals. "Stagflation"—the simultaneous existence of high inflation and unemployment—placed the state in a position of meeting irreconcilable goals: unemployment could be reduced to tolerable levels only by risking high inflation; inflation could be reduced only with unemployment rates reminiscent of the depression.[10] Persistent inflation, high even in recessions, is a relatively novel economic problem, with has complicated the material conditions of family life. Although "creeping inflation" was sometimes a concern during the 1950s, widespread consciousness of inflation came only in the late 1960s, with the inflation started by the Vietnam War. In the 1970s a "permanent" inflation rate of about 10 percent seemed to become established, and inflation eroded the real earnings of the average worker between the late 1960s and the early 1980s.[11] While inflation was made a political issue by middle-class families facing new economic insecurities, its harshest impact has been among poorer groups less able to adjust. These are the aged living on fixed pensions; welfare recipients, whose support levels are set politically; working-class and lower-class people, particularly those with low levels of schooling who typically have relatively small increases in earnings over their working lives compared to managerial and professional employees; and the poor without savings to cushion inflation's impact.[12] Stagflation thus placed the poor in a special bind: whether macroeconomic policy chooses low inflation with high unemployment or low unemployment with high inflation, the poor suffer more than other groups.[13]

The intransigence of stagflation in the 1970s suggested that Keynesian policy itself might be the issue. Put simply, Keynesian policy views economic problems—specifically, business cycles and unemployment—as problems of insufficient demand and proposes macroeconomic policies as solutions such as increased public expenditures, tax cuts, and increases in the money supply to stimulate investment. Between 1930 and the 1960s, such policies worked fairly well; family incomes increased and the economy was more or less under control. But the economic problems of the 1970s and 1980s, especially inflation, are due more to supply than to demand problems. They have been caused by increased costs for natural resources such as oil, the growth of monopolistic corporations and unions that can automatically pass on wage and price increases, the growth of service and governmental sectors with low productivity increases, the soaring costs of health care, the costs of antipollution mechanisms, and low productivity—factors that increase the prices at which goods and services are offered and that make inflation, once started, difficult to stop. Under these conditions, demand-side policies can have relatively little effect on inflation, and they can reduce inflation only at the cost of increasing unemployment. The only appropriate approach is to develop a set of supply-side policies—that is, policies that shift the aggregate supply curve of the economy—not to continue to rely solely on demand-side policies, which are by themselves incomplete.[14]

Yet the macroeconomic policies generated during the early 1980s have displayed a mixture of confusion and ideological monopolization which has made it impossible to develop a coherent macroeconomic policy appropriate to the times. Conservatives, the first to recognize the importance of supply-side changes, overwhelmed moderates and liberals in shaping supply-side economics to their own ends.[15] Consistent with their ideology of *laissez-faire* capitalism, they have promoted a series of traditional conservative programs in the new vocabulary of supply-side economics: tax credits for corporate investment and overall corporate tax reductions, to stimulate productivity and growth; income tax reductions for the rich, to stimulate savings, investment, and production; reduction in federal regulation of pollution, workplace hazards, and employment discrimination, as ways to reduce corporate costs and presumably increase supply; reduction of social programs, to increase work incentives and reduce "unproductive" spending; and elimination of the federal deficit—a goal in practice undermined by their allegiance to increased military spending—despite evidence that this would have no effect on inflation whatsoever.[16]

Despite its sweep, the conservative macroeconomic agenda ignores other policies that would also operate to increase output and decrease inflation—that is, to shift the aggregate supply curve—but that require different forms of government management of the economy rather than the *laissez-faire* approach of conservatives. Efforts to restrict the price-setting power of corporations and unions and to restore competitiveness into the economy by antitrust efforts would slow the rate of inflation; wage, price, and profit controls might be necessary to retard the wage-price spiral in some sectors of the economy. Measures to alleviate supply bottlenecks would require the development of coherent energy and raw material policies, directed by public goals rather than private profits. The concentration of inflation in specific sectors of the economy—food, health care, energy, and housing—suggests that a coherent supply-side policy should address the problems special to these sectors, which in turn might require "sector-specific" policies such as hospital cost containment. The decline of once-powerful industries such as steel and automobiles may also require the development of sector-specific approaches, rather than the general tax incentives of the Reagan administration. Other mechanisms exist to shift the aggregate supply curve by increasing employment directly, of which public employment is the most obvious. There is no dearth of more "liberal" supply-side policies, but so far the efforts to develop them have been undermined by the conservative view that the state is the root of all evil and that a general decrease in state activities and reliance on markets and profit incentives is the appropriate solution.

Over the long run we expect that the role of the state will expand to include supply-side policies in addition to (rather than in place of) Keynesian demand-side policies, though the shift to include supply-side policies will be long, controversial, and ambiguous in its effects. Just as there have been conservative and liberal versions of Keynesian policies, we can expect conflicting supply-side policies to develop. Conservative supply-side policies will emphasize old capitalist principles: market incentives over political allocations, inequality over equality, private prerogatives over public principles. Those policies can only lead to the elimination of costly though necessary federal controls on pollution and job conditions, continued profit subsidies in the name of increasing productivity, efforts to use public resources to subsidize private production and profit (as in subsidies for synthetic fuel plants), resistance to economic planning, energy policies that subordinate public goals to the power of large oil companies, regressive tax structures, inadequate social services, and outrageous defense budgets. In contrast, liberal supply-side policies will include efforts to increase competition and regulate corporate power, energy policies that diminish the role of existing corporations, efforts to use public resources for public purposes, more progressive taxes, public employment, and public investment; they will try to distribute the burden of macroeconomic policy more evenly, rather than letting the burdens fall on the poor. The development of new vocabularies and the new analytic apparatus of supply-side economics should not blind us to the continuing division: between those supporters of corporate capitalism seeking unrestricted license and public subsidies for private ends, and those who strive to control corporate power to achieve public goals. As long as these two sides are in contention, the promise that macroeconomic policy can resolve economic problems—a promise that assumes a reallocation of responsibility and resources from private to public units—will continue to be compromised by the power of private prerogatives.

Macroeconomic issues may seem arcane and unrelated to families and children. However, the outcomes of debates over macroeconomic policies will have the most fundamental impact on family life. The growth of the Keynesian state after the depression has meant that the material basis of the family has unavoidably become an issue of public policy. The well-being of families—their employment, earnings, the purchasing power of wages, what they are able to give their children—are no longer private decisions or dependent only on the health of the private economy, but depend in part on public and therefore political decisions about the economy. The success of efforts to develop post-Keynesian policies that will address supply-side problems will similarly affect the well-being of families and their children—especially low-income families—over the next generations. If we continue to deny that debates over macroeconomic policy are central to family life, then we will ensure that the well-being of families and children remain peripheral concerns.

The current search for a family policy reflects at least some of these concerns, and at its best recognizes just how important the state's macroeconomic decisions are to family life. In perhaps the strongest call for a national policy for families, Kenneth Keniston writes:

> Unemployment, low wages, and discriminatory barriers to employment that affect parents are directly translated into harmful effects on their children. . . . With children in the forefront of our minds, therefore, we believe that a family policy in the United States must provide *all* parents with the opportunity to choose employment at decent wages. . . . The goal of a jobs' component of a family policy must be to make employment available, fair, and humanly possible.[17]

Such an approach recognizes the public basis of family life; it addresses some of the causes of differences among children rather than trying to compensate for these differences after the fact, and it attacks problems that children's institutions cannot resolve. Yet the call for full employment in the interest of family well-being has a naive quality because it fails to confront the limitations on governmental policies as they have developed in the postwar era. Liberal family policy restates our historical aspirations for children and their families without recognizing why we have so often fallen short. The traditional liberal efforts to construct a comprehensive family policy that incorporates macroeconomic goals therefore must confront the constraints of the 1970s and 1980s: taxpayer revolts, conservative pressure to limit the state, and the structural limitations of Keynesian policies themselves.

The underlying issue is larger than the immediate balance of political power and will remain even after the political and ideological complexion of government shifts back from conservative to liberal. In constructing macroeconomic policy as part of family policy, the central dilemma of the American state emerges: how to implement public responsibility in an economy still considered private. At the same time as the state has become the guarantor of economic well-being and macroeconomic policy promises to minimize the worst economic conditions, the state has been restrained from "intrusions" into private enterprise and pressured into maintaining market mechanisms, private profits, and moderate unemployment. Even in liberal periods like the 1960s, macroeconomic policy has been inadequate to the task set for it. Until we remove these constraints, we stand no real chance of constructing an adequate family policy.

Politicizing Sex Roles

Since the mid-nineteenth century, the domestic ideal of the American family has been tied to specific roles of men and women. "Separate spheres," women at home and men at work, has defined the healthy family and by extension the best possible environment for children. Any transformation of those roles has been widely interpreted as threatening the family and destructive to children. The "family crisis" of the progressive era reflected in part the expansion of paid labor for women. The depression caused different worries about family life, as unemployment threatened to undermine the familial power of men. The debate over sex roles and their relationship to children has, not surprisingly, taken on a new intensity in the postwar period as women have dramatically increased their participation in paid employment, generating deep concern about the family's future and the health of children. Greater equality between men and women, rather than the functional differentiation of the domestic ideology, is the heart of the issue. As one opponent of the Equal Rights Amendment claimed, "We feel the family is under attack in America, and we feel the Equal Rights Amendment could be the turning point on whether family life as we know it will survive."[18] Battle lines have been drawn between those who assume that working mothers are "abandoning" their children and those who stress that maternal employment is good for children as well as mothers. From both a child-centered perspective and a concern for women, debates about sex roles have been more intense and politics more bitter than in any other area related to families and children.

Although women have always been in the labor market, the postwar changes constitute a qualitative shift. The proportion of all women working increased steadily from 18.2 percent in 1890 to 25.8 percent in 1940; after 1946, when the employment of women hit a postwar low of 30.8 percent, the participation of all women soared to 50.7 percent in 1979. The increase was not limited to working-class women, unmarried women, or married women without children, the traditional women workers. The greatest growth occurred among married women and mothers with children: the labor force participation of married women living with their husbands more than doubled, from 22 percent to 49.4 percent; mothers of school-aged children increased their participation from 26 percent to 61.6 percent, and mothers of children under six increased from 10.8 percent to 45.4 percent.[19] The narrowing of employment differentials between men and women, between married and unmarried women, and between mothers and other women has been one of the critical changes of the postwar period.

Conceptions of what working means to women have also changed. Economic necessity, the traditional reason for women working, has increasingly come to coexist with positive assertions of choice: work allows women to become independent, to develop a career, and to terminate unsatisfactory marriages, and it gives them greater power both outside the family and within it.[20] The pleasure many women find in employment, even when their jobs are menial and routine, testifies to the drudgery of being homebound. One factory worker described her work in these terms:

> I really love going to work. I guess it's because it gets me away from home. It's not that I don't love my home; I do. But you get awfully tired of just keeping house and doing those housewifely things. . . . You know, when I was home, I was getting in real trouble. I had that old housewife's syndrome, where you either crawl in bed after the kids go to school or sit and watch TV by the hour. I was just dying of boredom and the more bored I got, the less and less I did.

> On top of it I was getting fatter and fatter, too. I finally knew I had to do something about it, so I took this course in upholstery and got this job as an upholstery trimmer.[21]

The consequences of going to work extend beyond simply escaping from the home or even finding satisfaction in a particular job. Employed mothers tend to have more positive images of themselves than do unemployed mothers. Their feelings of competence are enhanced because they are valued by a larger circle of coworkers and by being productive at tasks that are more permanent than cleaning and cooking.[22] The benefits to women at work also extend to family relationships, especially in the power women gain within their families:

> I can't imagine not working. I like to get out of the house, and the money makes me feel more independent. Some men are funny. They think if you don't work, you ought to be home every day, like a drudge around the house, and that they can come home and just say, "Do this," and "Do that," and "Why is that dish in the sink?" When you work and make some money, it's different. It makes me feel more equal to him. He can't just tell me what to do.[23]

As long as employment for mothers could be considered temporary, expedient, and economically necessary, then it could be dismissed as inconsequential to their primary allegiances to family. But as working has come to have a new meaning for women, as it has become more central in their self-definition and status, it has become especially threatening to traditional conceptions of the family, to conventional relations between men and women, and to the domestic ideal of childrearing. Predictably enough, the response from the supporters of traditional domesticity has been to trumpet the dangers to children of maternal employment; they have complained about children denied their "birthright" to full-time mothering, damaged by the interruption of the maternal bond and by inadequate day care facilities, about the birth rate declining as women "abandon" childrearing for the self-centered pleasures of a career, and about the traditional family dissolving as the "basic unit of society."

Some of these claims, such as the fears for the death of the family, have been purely rhetorical; some, such as concern for the falling birth rate, have been irrelevant. Others have been proved false, as familial practices have changed in the postwar period, as more experience of working mothers has accumulated, and as fathers have begun to participate more in childrearing. While the necessity of strong, continuous, and affectionate bonds between parents and children still emerges as basic to healthy development, the necessity of a single maternal bond is no longer tenable.

In sharp contrast to earlier proclamations about the sanctity of the mother-child relationship, the empirical evidence indicates that two or more strong bonds are possible, that a strong role for fathers does not itself weaken the maternal bond, that a strong paternal relationship creates richer possibilities for a child, and that decent child care does not harm a child's normal development.[24] Rather than stunting the child's growth, maternal employment can benefit children by making their mothers more self-assured, less prone to depression and anxiety about the future, and less confined in their activities; and the higher income in families with working wives benefits children.[25] Most of the dire warnings of antifeminists, then, have proved to be simply untrue.

Yet working mothers and women contemplating both employment and children have discovered for themselves the truth of one warning: the satisfactions with work and the increased autonomy within families come at some cost because working women continue to bear the main responsibilities for childrearing and homemaking. Although they may reduce the time they spend in homemaking chores and rely more on child care, the traditional maternal responsibilities still rest with women even when they work: theirs are the responsibilities for making child care arrangements, and theirs the anxiety when those arrangements fall apart; they bear the responsibility for a clean home, and shoulder the blame if television-spotless standards are not maintained.[26] Even in those families where the husbands do take on additional household tasks, they tend to assume those which are relatively rewarding and more public—like the care of children—and leave the more repetitive and boring chores (cleaning and laundry) to their wives.[27]

The strain for women is partly one of time, but it is also a result of the conflict between the different responsibilities working women have. The ideological baggage surrounding maternal responsibilities—particularly the fear of working mothers that they are not providing their children the emotional support necessary for healthy development—adds a measure of guilt to the physical strain.[28] This is especially true among those least able to afford child care and other services to cushion the strains or, as with single mothers, those unable to call upon the support of a mate. The consequence is that women are pulled between two roles, finding satisfaction in both, but feeling uncertain about each:

> Working is hard for me. When I work, I feel like I want to be doing a real good job, and I want to be absolutely responsible. Then, if the little one gets a cold, I feel like I should be home with her. That causes complications because whatever you do isn't right. You're either at work feeling like you should be at home with your sick child, or you're at home feeling like you should be at work.[29]

Despite the tremendous changes in how women spend their time, the ideological and practical difficulties of combining employment and mothering remain powerful. Institutional and legal practices external to families are responsible for a great deal of the stress. Discrimination in employment means that women's wages and salaries are less than those for men; the most obvious and detrimental consequence for children is that they are likely to be in poverty—as 50.6 percent of them were in 1978—if they live in a female-headed household. For women, working conditions are worse and job satisfactions are less, creating strains that affect their family roles; and the structure of most employment—with inflexible hours and no provisions for family emergencies, suited to the conventional employment of men with full-time wives at home—has created yet other strains. The lack of social support for child care has made the care of children more difficult and more anxiety-ridden. The lack of enforcement of child-support obligations puts still other women in poverty, and sexual discrimination in education adds yet another disadvantage.

Many women have always recognized that public and political decisions shape sex roles and family functioning and have turned to the state and public policies to challenge their subordinate status. They have insisted that the "personal is political," not only because private negotiations (over responsibility for childrearing, for example) have public consequences but also because public decisions have consequences for private life. In the nineteenth century, women actively supported temperance legislation because alcoholism was a factor in poverty, desertion, and family violence. With few alternatives to marriage and the real fear of childbirth, feminists led the fight for state protection of birth control and abortion. In the progressive era, efforts to improve working conditions for women were justified by their benefits for family life. The suffrage movement took women directly into the political arena, with the hope that equality at the polls would bring equality within the family.[30]

In the last two decades, the range of issues debated, litigated, and legislated has been immense. Efforts to reduce discrimination in employment became institutionalized in the Equal Employment Opportunity Commission (EEOC) and the Office of Federal Contract Compliance (OFCC) that monitors discrimination among federal contractors. Discrimination in education, a factor in the crowding of women into "women's work," has been attacked through Title IX of the Civil Rights Act. The discriminatory treatment of women in various public and private programs—in Social Security, in health insurance, in access to credit—has become a public issue. Increasing demand for child care has stimulated efforts to expand public subsidies. The mistreatment of women in the courts—the cavalier attitudes toward rape and wife abuse, for example—has come under attack, and court-ordered procedures in the area of child custody have weakened the presumption that only mothers should care for young children. Other issues intimately connected to rights within the family—divorce laws and control over birth control, abortion, and sterilization—have similarly been opened to serious debate.

Because the underlying problems women face—employment and educational discrimination, equal treatment before the law, the availability of supports for childrearing—are social rather than private, the resort to the state has been necessary. Only by politicizing sex roles has it become possible for family relationships to be opened up, for women and men to acknowledge alternatives, for women to gain the personal and collective power to renegotiate long-established patterns, and for the political and public changes to be made that establish a social context for different kinds of sex roles. But the resort to the state has had ambiguous consequences; gains for women can be quickly reversed, as they have been in the Reagan administration, and the power of the state to promote greater equality has also been the power to maintain traditional domestic patterns.

The uncertain results of state action can be illustrated in three areas crucial to families—employment, child care, and reproductive rights.[31] Federal initiatives during the 1960s and 1970s to reduce pay and occupational differences between men and women were hampered by the strenuous resistance of employers and, in some cases, by the ineffective administrative structure of the Equal Employment Opportunity Commission, apparently designed to prevent quick and effective action. While an antidiscrimination policy was established, its influence has been small and employment discrimination continues almost unabated.[32] Even these minor advances are being reversed since President Reagan has further restricted the EEOC as part of reducing the "intrusion" of federal agencies into the workings of business. More women now work, and more can be found in managerial and professional positions, but on the whole women are in positions that are as sex-segregated as were occupational patterns in 1900, and they work for wages that continue to be approximately two-thirds of men's wages.[33] As a result the differences between the sexes have an economic basis that affects the family roles of women: the relatively higher wages of men mean that husbands still dominate familial decisions, that a husband's work seems more important than his wife's, and that it is "rational" for men to specialize in "market work" and women to specialize in "home production."[34]

The role of the state in child care has been similarly ambiguous. Government subsidies have expanded, but only grudgingly. The most effective motivation has been the desire to put welfare mothers to work and to provide compensatory education for lower-class children. Public funding for child care as a way of expanding roles for women has still not drawn widespread support; the child care tax credit, which as of 1978 funded 20 percent of child care costs through the income tax system, does not begin to offset the wage differences between men and women or the high cost of child care, and was still less than one-fourth of federal child care subsidies.[35] While there is more subsidized child care now than in the past, there is still relatively little, and it remains expensive relative to women's wages; child care still suffers from the stigma of deviance rather than being considered a normal consequence of maternal employment. As a result, some mothers are forced to make do with ramshackle arrangements of relatives, neighbors, and some paid care, while others arrange odd working schedules—nighttime and weekend work, for example—so that they need not use child care. The result is a strain for mothers and children alike.[36]

The sphere of reproductive rights has been the area most intimately connected to women's familial roles, and the most controversial. Access to contraception and abortion have been slow in arriving, despite being goals of feminists throughout this century. The major advances for women came not through legislation, but through litigation: *Griswold* v. *Connecticut* (1965) and *Eisenstadt* v. *Baird* (1968) prohibited government regulation of birth control; and *Roe* v. *Wade* (1973) seemed to put abortion beyond legislative control, with the Supreme Court arguing that state interference in a woman's right to obtain an abortion was unconstitutional. In the wake of *Roe* v. *Wade*, two developments occurred with major consequences for women: a tremendous increase in the numbers of women seeking abortion and an intense campaign to eliminate any public funding for abortion and to secure a constitutional amendment to override the Court's decision. The efforts against abortion have been directed at all women, but their most formidable consequences have been against the most vulnerable women—poor women for whom the "right" of safe abortion is empty without governmental subsidy. The elimination of federal funds for abortion, the refusal of all but a shrinking handful of states to continue subsidizing abortions with public money, and the growing effectiveness of political groups attacking politicians considered "soft" on abortion have testified to the power of the antifeminist position. The counterattack on the freedom to abort has drawn considerable strength from traditional conceptions of the family, especially the automatic assignment of women to childrearing.

In these areas, the potential gains for women—equality in employment,

253

more available child care, control over reproduction—are not necessarily gains for children. We can easily imagine conditions under which some children need full-time parenting or should not be in child care. Abortion is even more ambiguous: the unwanted child or its siblings might suffer if abortion did not take place, but the unborn child may have an interest in being born which conflicts with the mother's desire to abort. The potential ambiguity in these areas has been treated very differently by feminists and antifeminists, however. Those supporting expanded roles for women have sought to eliminate or minimize the conflict between mothers and children. They have pressed, for example, to assure that decent jobs with stimulating working conditions are available to women, rather than stressful and degrading work that might affect family life; they have sued against employment discrimination, so that working mothers would not have to face the strains of poverty. They have tried to expand part-time work and "flextime" so that work schedules and family responsibilities are congruent rather than antagonistic. In the area of child care, they have pressed for care of good quality, to allay the fears that child care might retard a child's development. In the difficult area of abortion, where even supporters admit to some qualms, feminists have tried to incorporate abortion into a broader program of reproductive issues addressed to both men and women, so that abortion does not become a substitute for contraception or an antidote for sexual irresponsibility but remains a last resort under extreme conditions.[37]

In contrast, antifeminists have made every effort to heighten the potential conflict between equality for women and the interests of children. Ironically, the policies they have espoused have by and large made matters worse for children (as well as women), even as they have claimed to speak for children. Rather than finding ways to facilitate the combination of employment and childrearing, antifeminists have insisted that part-time mothering is harmful to children, even though their insistence can do nothing to reduce the increasing numbers of mothers who work. They have attacked child care in every way possible, an approach that does nothing for those millions of children who are in child care regardless of antifeminist opposition. Rather than admitting the complexity of the issues involved in abortion, antifeminists have stridently publicized the most alarming aspects, publishing full-color photographs of fetuses and acting as if those women who choose abortion do so gleefully without the serious reservations that almost all of them feel. These have been extreme reactions, but they have drawn upon a widely accepted link between women and full-time mothering which remains powerful despite a century of feminist efforts and constantly increasing rates of maternal employment. Those supporting this link have pressured the state to recognize only traditional roles for women. As one critic of the Equal Rights Amendment put it, the amendment undermines the domestic rights of women who "wish to be full-time wives and mothers"; the intended effect of ERA to expand choices for women is ignored.[38] Only in welfare programs designed to force poor mothers into the work force has the tie between women and mothering been sundered by public policies—a measure of how little we are willing to pay publicly for women to stay home and care for their children, at the same time that many public policies assume that mothers ought to be caring for their children full-time.

The efforts to gain equality for women through state action have thus foundered on the most traditional assumptions about women's responsibilities. But they have also failed for another reason, one that is encountered over and over again in social policy: the continuing assumption that families and labor markets are private and should be as free from state intervention as possible. Despite the overwhelming evidence that neither families nor labor markets are private, state involvement in them is still viewed as corrupting. The casual treatment of wife abuse provides one example, reflecting the convention that husband-wife relationships are private; another instance is the consistent unwillingness of the state to enforce the fiscal responsibilities of men who abandon their wives and children, except when welfare costs can be reduced. The efforts to improve the economic conditions of women have similarly faltered on the political opposition to state interference with the prerogatives of private firms. The efforts to eliminate employment discrimination have been strenuously opposed by firms who benefit from the low wages they pay women and from the availability of women as a "reserve army" of potential workers who can readily be drawn into the labor market in periods of high demand and readily dismissed when demand slackens.[39] At the same time that growing employment for women has provided the economic basis for greater independence, the continued subordination of women to men in labor markets has retarded full equality between men and women. As long as those differences are seen to be rooted in "private" labor markets and in "private" family decisions, collective action on behalf of women by the state remains exceedingly difficult.

The resort to the state to develop more egalitarian sex roles has therefore been necessary but ambiguous in its results. Public policies have lagged behind the employment of women, with detrimental consequences for both children and mothers. Expanded employment has made it possible for women to remain single or to leave unhappy marriages that they were earlier condemned to endure; but continuing sex discrimination in employment means that female-headed families are much more likely to be poor. The failure to fund child care has not reversed the influx of mothers into the labor force, but has instead forced women who must work and who still suffer low wages to make do with haphazard arrangements. The unwillingness of employers to take measures that would facilitate combining employment and parenthood—"flextime," decent part-time work, maternity and paternity leaves—and the unwillingness of the state to promote such changes in employment conditions have placed women who choose not to forgo either employment or children under inordinate strain, and their children suffer the effects of that strain.

Many of the efforts to develop a coherent family policy have acknowledged the detrimental effects of unequal sex roles on women, family life, and children. They have then posed various policies—antidiscrimination measures, subsidized child care, the development of "flextime" and part-time work—to close the gap between men and women and to ease the strains of maintaining employment and family life simultaneously. If, like the call for full employment, these proposals sometimes seem naive, that is because they require more radical transformations than their authors envision. Eliminating sex discrimination requires public control over private institutions like the public control over firms, a direct attack against the dominance of nineteenth-century liberal tenets. It further requires breaking the ideological link between women and childrearing responsibilities, which means new thinking about sex roles as well as more social and paternal responsibility for children. Making employment and family life more compatible is similarly radical, since it requires recognizing the falsity of an ideological separation of home and work, and accommodating employment to the requirements of personal life rather than leaving family life to be shaped by capitalist labor markets.

The struggle by women to undo their subordinate status raises basic issues about the relation between personal life and work life. Reshaping sex roles requires reshaping the relations between work and family life so that employment is governed by concern for its effects on family life and parental responsibility. Such changes threaten the basic organization of capitalism as well as conventional relations between men and women; they cannot be accomplished without public and political action, involving the state and its potential power over the economy and the conditions of work. But efforts to use the state in such ways will remain frustrated unless the limits on the state's ability to accomplish fundamental changes in a capitalistic economy are transformed. Until they are, an appropriate family policy that promotes the well-being of children will remain elusive.

The Conflicts over Racial Discrimination

Of all children, minority children suffer the most. The simple fact of official poverty rates close to 30 percent, with perhaps 60 percent of black children and 40 percent of Hispanic children poor under other measures of poverty, is evidence enough. The special plight of black and Hispanic children has been recognized in the postwar efforts at childsaving—in the attempts to reform welfare, to establish compensatory education, in Great Society programs such as food stamps, housing subsidies, and Medicaid. In the efforts to improve the lives of minority children, in the real successes and the bitter setbacks of the last three decades, the dilemmas of the state's role with respect to children have been cast in their starkest form. For minority children the problems of poverty are the most hideous, the resistance to providing for other people's children the clearest. The fear of social disorder has above all been a fear of racial disorder, and impulse to control has been the strongest and most naked for minority children.

The issues surrounding black and Hispanic children have invariably been cast in terms of their families. The debate about the black family begun in the 1960s and the similar discussion, with less visibility, about Hispanic families constituted the most recent in a long series of efforts to examine the issue of race. Almost all of these efforts have emphasized the disorganization of minority families and their failure to raise their children adequately, implicitly blaming minorities themselves for their position in American society. Recent revisionist portrayals of minority families as strong and resilient have countered the dominant view, but they too have fallen into the pattern of examining family life itself rather than emphasizing the patterns of discrimination that have separated minorities from whites.[40] The conservative onslaught of the last few years has served to reinforce the emphasis on the "independent" minority family: without the weight of public programs to breed dependence, conservatives argue, resilient and determined minority families will be free to succeed.

Despite the fact that discussions about black and Hispanic families have tended to obscure the central issue of discrimination, the resolution to the problems which black and Hispanic families face has always been obvious. Even most commentators who have emphasized the degraded state of minority families and have blamed a "culture of poverty" have also acknowledged the necessity of antidiscrimination measures—in labor markets, in housing, in public institutions such as schools, in access to the legal system and to political power. For example, the Moynihan report on the black family, the symbol of white racism to the black community and the target of black rage since the mid-1960s, was itself subtitled "The Case for National Action" and proposed a policy "to bring the Negro American to full and equal sharing in the responsibilities and rewards of citizenship."[41] The attempts to implement such measures have yielded both major successes and limited gains. The Civil Rights Acts of 1957 and 1964 and the Voting Rights Act of 1965 consolidated the rights of minorities as citizens, rights that could be enforced by both private litigation and the Justice Department. Court decisions outlawed school desegregation. Equal access to educational facilities was enshrined in court decisions under the Constitution and Title VI of the Civil Rights Act of 1964, while various compensatory programs—Title I, bilingual programs, special admissions to higher education—provided other forms of equalization. Employment discrimination is now forbidden under the Equal Pay Act and Title VII of the Civil Rights Act; executive orders forbade discrimination by federal contractors, and some implementation of these laws by the Equal Employment Opportunity Commission occurred. The most important pieces of social legislation among the Great Society programs—welfare reforms, Medicaid, Medicare, food stamps, Head Start, the Community Action Program, federally sponsored legal aid—provided institutions for minority organizing and mechanisms to assure minority rights, giving minorities access to the state which they had never had before.

The postwar period has been important, therefore, in institutionalizing the struggles for racial equality. Yet in one area after another, the effects of these initiatives have been ambiguous, the promise of legislation and litigation to eliminate racial differences have been only partially realized and the attempts to remove the gains are still intense. In the critical area of earnings, there has been some improvement for blacks relative to whites, especially since 1963. For full-time male workers, the ratio of black to white earnings increased from 64 percent in 1947 to 77 percent in 1975, with similar increases for women; yet these improvements still leave blacks at a substantial disadvantage. Most of the improvement has come from the fact that the difference in schooling attainments of blacks and whites has narrowed dramatically, while the efforts of the federal government to eliminate employment discrimination have yielded no measurable results. There were some gains for Hispanics during the 1960s, though these gains may have been reversed during the 1970s, and a serious gap between Hispanic and white education levels remains.[42] Moreover, the relative economic gains of minorities have been concentrated among younger workers and may not persist as they grow older.[43] The improvement in the relative earnings of individuals has not yet affected the positions of minority families or their poverty rates: the median earnings of both black and Hispanic families relative to white families deteriorated slightly between 1970 and 1978. Relative rates of poverty also grew slightly worse for Hispanics and blacks during the 1970s; poverty rates for blacks remain three and a half times what they are for whites, and two and a half times as high as whites for Hispanics.[44] Progress in relative earnings among nonwhites has thus been small, erratic, and uncertain in its long-term effects. It has not yet yielded substantial gains for the overwhelming proportion of minority children.

In the area of education, the results are similarly mixed despite the narrowing of gaps in schooling attainments between blacks and whites. In 1930, black labor force entrants had an average of 5.9 years of schooling compared to 9.6 years for whites; by 1970 black attainments had risen to 11.4 years compared to 12.6 years among whites. Much of this improvement can be attributed to the end of *de jure* segregation in the South and the continued migration of blacks from the South to the North. In addition, the quality of black education has improved considerably.[45] Again, however, the gains are incomplete. The proportion of blacks with more than twelve years of schooling is still half of the proportion for whites, and this in a period when education beyond the high school level is increasingly necessary for decent jobs. Desegregation has not proceeded far outside the South, and internal mechanisms of segregation—principally tracking—keep minority pupils segregated in nominally integrated schools. Obvious differences in the quality of education between blacks and whites remain. The relative gains that blacks have made have not been extended to Hispanics, who often suffer the additional problems of language differences.

In still other areas of major impact on family life—in housing and health, for example—the gains have been mixed. Medicare and Medicaid programs have improved access to health care, but differences between whites and nonwhites in longevity, infant mortality rates, and other indicators of general health remain large. Public housing programs expanded during the 1960s, but housing discrimination continues unabated, and housing segregation is if anything becoming worse as minorities are trapped in central cities without adequate public resources. In fact, the problem of segregated housing reveals the racial division of this country in all its ignominy. Although many other problems stem from poor housing and the creation of racial ghettos—including segregated schools, crowding, health hazards, higher housing costs for those least able to afford it, and lack of access to jobs—the public efforts to reduce housing segregation have all failed. Antidiscrimination legislation has never been seriously enforced; efforts to "open up the suburbs" to minority housing have been strenuously resisted, as has public housing in white neighborhoods. Much as whites have resisted public funding for other people's children, they have been even more insistent that they be allowed to segregate themselves and their children from what they presume to be the evil influence of black and Hispanic families.

By the early 1980s, the era of improvements for minorities appears to have ended. The early initiatives of the Reagan administration confirmed the power of the backlash against previous gains. The strenuous resistance to desegregation, busing, and special admissions programs indicates the strength of white hostility to improvements in the educational standing of minorities. With the Department of Education barred by Congress from bringing school desegregation cases, the Department of Justice promising not to pursue desegregation, and the Reagan administration supporting public funds for private schools, the efforts of whites to resegregate the schools will go unrestrained. Underlying the taxpayer revolts at the state and federal level has been considerable racial animosity, with welfare—the symbol of fraud and abuse by minorities—generally leading the list of appropriate cuts. Spending cuts under President Reagan have been deepest for those social welfare programs on which minorities depend. As if that were not enough, the proposal to place most compensatory education programs in a block grant with a 25-percent reduction in funding and almost no federal oversight of how states spend the money promises to undermine significantly compensatory education. The early hearings on the reauthorization of the Voting Rights Act, due to expire in 1982, suggest that the procedural safeguards that have done so much to guarantee the right to vote to blacks and Hispanics might not endure. Under Ronald Reagan, the advances of Jimmy Carter in attacking employment discrimination have all been reversed: the Office of Federal Contract Compliance has indicated that it would reduce the number and scope of complaints, and the Equal Employment Opportunity Commission was reduced in its funding. The EEOC is headed by a black businessman who declared himself sympathetic to less government intrusion in business. With Reagan's principle advisor on minority affairs a black economist, Walter Williams, claiming that minorities in America do not suffer discrimination, blacks and Hispanics can look forward to still further efforts to weaken the fight against discrimination. These developments, disheartening by themselves, are still more discouraging because they indicate how fragile the gains of minorities always are. Even after more than a century of recognition that racial disparities are the most ignoble and threatening of all the divisions in American society, it proves impossible to sustain the public attack on these differences.

For nonwhites, as for women, the resort to the state has been necessary, but it has evidently not eliminated disparities due to discrimination. To some extent, the reasons for this are obvious. Hostility toward racial minorities is the most difficult aspect of discrimination to eliminate because the state has no real power over values and perceptions. But racial discrimination also has an economic basis: relegating racial minorities to the lowest positions in the occupational hierarchy has meant low incomes and unstable employment and has compounded racial discrimination with class distinctions. The economic basis of racial differences has been as difficult for the state to attack as ideological and cultural attitudes toward race: the efforts to eliminate employment discrimination, from the first feeble efforts during World War II, have inevitably required the state to intrude on the prerogatives of private firms, which have resisted all the more as it has become clear that complying with equal employment provisions is costly to both firms and to white workers. Above all, what was possible during the economic growth of the 1960s—when whites could gain in absolute terms while minorities were gaining relative to whites—is no longer possible in an era of slower growth and more limited opportunities.

Given racial inequalities and no real desire on the part of whites to eliminate them, the political tactics available to minorities have been relatively unconventional ones. The history of racial politics reveals how limited conventional access to the state by nonwhites has been: rather than acting through the traditional mechanisms of interest group politics, efforts to contest second-class citizenship have concentrated on protest and on legal challenges to existing practices.[46] Protest tactics, often uncertain in their effects, are the approach of last resort in American politics, an indication that the state is undemocratic and that traditional political mechanisms have been unavailable to nonwhites. Court challenges attempt to compel the state to enforce its own constitutional principles, and when they are used as a major instrument of social reform they indicate that the normal legislative process has been blocked. Both protest and litigation have yielded some success in the postwar period: court cases eliminated Jim Crow laws and *de jure* segregation, civil rights protests in the 1960s prompted the Civil Rights Act and the Voting Rights Act, and ghetto riots spurred welfare increases and other Great Society programs. But protest and litigation tactics are limited. Besides being difficult to sustain, protest is considered illegitimate and extremist, and it has so far proved difficult to convert protest movements into institutionalized pressure groups. Litigation is costly, time consuming, and—given changes in the Supreme Court—uncertain; more to the point, enforcement is usually reluctant and bitterly contested, as the desegregation efforts since *Brown v. Board of Education* indicate.

Given the limits of protest and litigation, the alternative strategy to improve the condition of minority families and the lives of minority children has been an appeal to justice. The evidence of how many blacks and Hispanics are poor, or have low schooling levels, or suffer poor health and bad housing, has been a demonstration of unfairness and discrimination as a justification for public action. But in an individualistic society such evidence has also been an admission of failure, an admission that opponents of racial equality have taken all too readily as a reason why public action is unwarranted and ineffective. (The opposite strategy—to counter the vision of minority families as failures by documenting their "strength and resilience"—has not fared much better, since this approach often works to deny the reality of discrimination and poverty.) The result of documenting the effects of racial discrimination on minority individuals has frequently led to inappropriate compromises: by ascribing failure to minorities themselves—the familiar logic of *parens patriae*—these approaches have led to public programs that attempt to change *individuals* through social services, compensatory education, and the vast array of programs for the educationally and culturally "deprived," rather than eliminating discrimination in all social institutions. Just as children's institutions have tried (and failed) to provide equal opportunity where inequality has seemed insuperable, so programs aimed at minority children have often been substitutes for more direct attempts to eliminate discrimination.

Minorities have been placed in a dilemma of the worst kind. For so long denied access to interest group politics, they have had to engage in protest and litigation, effective but self-limiting. Forced to prove the effects of discrimination, they have had to show how bad the material and psychological conditions of life are for them, or accept the efforts of white reformers to do the same. Invariably, findings that minority children are in trouble are ascribed to how minority families behave, ignoring the origins of racial discrimination. In the process, the limitations of *parens patriae* have come into play—denying the social and economic basis of family life, stigmatizing the clients of state intervention, and converting benevolent impulses into controlling institutions.

Because the issues of race are so stark, they make clear the essential challenge of family policy: the most appropriate approach to racial issues within family policy is to ignore issues of the family altogether and to concentrate instead on the most obvious and pernicious forms of discrimination—in employment, in education, in housing, and in access to political power. A family policy that focuses on minority families themselves will be inconsistent and incomplete, subject to cycles of public intervention and public withdrawal, depending upon how much families are blamed for their condition. Many of the recent calls for a comprehensive family policy acknowledge this, recognizing—as have child savers in every generation—that welfare programs, compensatory education, and other children's institutions will not eliminate racial discrimination. A family policy that concentrates on discrimination itself is therefore a progressive step, even though such an approach will, like all the postwar initiatives, be limited by racial hostility, adherence to old notions about private labor markets, economic competition from whites, and the use of public power for private ends.

The Absence of Class from the National Agenda

The problems of unemployment, poverty, sex discrimination, and racism have never been close to resolution in this country. Yet these issues are at least part of the national agenda, even during periods that are hostile to social reforms. Those debating family policy have been forced to acknowledge the magnitude of the state's role in guiding the economy, shaping income distribution, and modifying employment practices. They have recognized that public policy plays a role in defining sex roles and in the position of racial minorities, with profound implications for family life. In sharp contrast, issues of class have been absent from all national debates and from the efforts to generate a family policy.

The tendency to ignore class is especially appalling since it is impossible to understand the structural inequalities that so seriously affect children without understanding the nature of class. Divisions of income are also divisions of class, since much of the variation in income comes from earnings differences among occupations. Battles over unemployment represent, in veiled and indirect ways, forms of class conflict between those whose interests lie in expanded employment and those who benefit from the lower wages and more fluid labor markets associated with a modicum of unemployment. The inequalities of race and sex are in part explained by crowding women and minorities into low-status, low-paid occupations, giving discrimination economic and class dimensions in addition to its cultural and ideological origins. Beyond the fact that *all* the structural inequalities of a capitalist society are undergirded by class divisions, the variations of class have their own independent influences on children, through the values and attitudes parents pass on to their children and through the different levels of stress parents bring home from work. Class considerations in turn influence the state's relationship to children: through class-biased conceptions of children and of the socialization appropriate for children from different class backgrounds; through the fear of other people's children and the pressure to use public institutions for the advancement of one's own children; through the pressure toward the social control of unruly classes.

The failure of class issues to become part of the national agenda does not reflect a lack of efforts to politicize class. During the nineteenth-century transition to entrepreneurial capitalism, craft workers were conscious of their transformation into wage laborers and fought the domination of one class by another.[47] Throughout the century, the public vocabulary acknowledged the existence of class divisions, aided by the growth of class-conscious labor organizations such as the Knights of Labor and agrarian groups associated with Populism. The explosion of labor unrest around the turn of the century was widely discussed as class warfare, not (as is currently the fashion) in the depoliticized terms of battles over "income shares." A similar wave of interest in class-based politics took place during the 1930s as a result of the depression.

Yet these have been isolated episodes of class consciousness, and they have not culminated in a general recognition of class divisions. In each period of widespread class consciousness the reaction by the protectors of capitalism has been ferocious, with labor suppressed by overt violence exercised by both employers and the state. Business unionism under Samuel Gompers provided an institutional alternative to the classic dilemma of labor—whether to cooperate with capitalism or to oppose it—and its apparent success in raising wages and guaranteeing permanent employment provided an obvious and attractive alternative to the class-based politics of radical unions. Cultural institutions, especially schools, were used to teach "American" values: the sanctity of private property, the justice of class divisions, and the need to respect authority. After the progressive era, obvious class-based conflict sometimes developed—as happened during the efforts to unionize semiskilled workers into the Congress of Industrial Organizations during the depression—but such incidents were temporary and always followed by the cooling effects of business unionism. By the dawning of the postwar period—and partly because of its prosperity—class had disappeared from the vocabulary and the politics of most Americans, not for lack of efforts over the preceding century to bring class relations to the forefront but because of the strength of private and state resistance to raising issues in class terms.

The failure of class to be politicized or extensively analyzed in the United States, as compared with Europe—along with the associated failure to develop a strong brand of American socialism—has also occurred for other reasons. As de Tocqueville noted in the early nineteenth century, the ideologies of individualism and private property rights were always more powerful here than in Europe. The ideology of personal mobility and the "rags to riches" myth of the self-made man have tended to undermine the concept of class because they have fostered the notion that lower-class status is only temporary. Real levels of upward mobility have reinforced the ideology, although mobility has never been as great as the American dream assumed.[48] Business unionism hampered the discussion of class by preventing the development of a politically conscious union movement. The extraordinary ethnic and racial divisions within the working class have precluded a consciousness of class from emerging, especially as various forms of discrimination by sex and race (rather than by class) have been pervasive. The consequence of these historical forces has been to make class a dirty word in the United States: to suggest the existence of class divisions is to suggest that we are not an egalitarian society and that the limits of individualism and capitalism may be serious indeed.[49]

To some extent, the ideology surrounding family life has also been responsible for the absence of class consciousness. The American dream has often been expressed in terms of one's children: if a man did not experience upward mobility in his own life, he might at least expect his children to succeed. Even though the idea of living through one's children has expressed more hope than reality, it has been a critical force in demolishing a sense of class: if one's children could escape the class into which they were born, then class could not be a permanent condition. Struggles over class thus became individualized: the battle for parents has been to assure the mobility of their *own* children rather than to eliminate class conditions. To these ideological barriers have been added recent discussions of "pluralism" among American families. The efforts to recognize the legitimacy of different kinds of families based on ethnicity, race, religion or "life style" have hidden the class differences among families in favor of discovering the seemingly voluntary differences. The celebration of the "diversity" of American families, of all their "strengths and resiliance," is the ultimate evasion of class issues, since it suggests that class differences among families are not deep and that necessary reforms are relatively trivial.[50]

The result is that class is largely missing from public vocabulary and the national agenda. In those few instances where it appears, the concept of class is distorted and depoliticized, presented in a form that renders it meaningless and strips it of dangerous political content. Sociology, the academic discipline that has most consistently analyzed class-related issues, has converted class into "socioeconomic status," a combination of income and educational attainment. Inequalities of class are often portrayed as income or racial differences that appear to be amenable to the traditional measures of the welfare state—social services and income transfers. In the process, the origins of class differences in the organization of production and the use of class to describe fundamental power relationships have been abandoned.

Even where the effects of class differences are made obvious, their origins and the possibility of state action are left buried. For example, the 1973 report *Work in America* collected the available evidence about the destructive effects of working conditions on the physical and mental health, the satisfaction, and the sense of purpose of American workers; it clearly described the "blue-collar blues" and "white-color woes" of the early 1970s as the direct result of poor and unequal working conditions. But while the report was a powerful indictment of the effects of class-related conditions, its recommendations recapitulated those familiar from the liberal agenda: education, retraining, full employment, and perhaps federal funding of research and demonstration projects on job redesign.[51] The idea that the American state might do something about the origins of poor working conditions was never seriously raised.

Only in the area of health and safety conditions has there been a serious attempt to influence the conditions of work, and these experiences indicate the distortions of class in the public arena and the fragility of even minimal attempts to correct class-based inequalities. The Occupational Safety and Health Act of 1970 and the Occupational Safety and Health Administration (OSHA) that it created represented a real break from the tradition of minimal state interference in working conditions and minimal public concern for job safety and health.[52] Motivated by a growing consciousness of the economic cost of industrial accidents, the bill stressed the "lost production, wage loss, medical expenses, and disability compensation payments" caused by unsafe working conditions. The motive for reform was thus a simple cost-benefit calculation, rather than the effect of working conditions on workers' lives and the question of who should control job conditions. The battles over OSHA's implementation have, not surprisingly, divided along labor-management lines—or, as an earlier generation would have expressed the conflict, along class lines. Employers have consistently complained that OSHA inspections are intrusive and that health and safety-related modifications are costly; the labor position has been to eliminate as many unsafe working conditions as possible.

To some extent the battles over job conditions are conflicts over control of the workplace: greater power for OSHA means that decisions over the workplace are determined slightly more by political considerations than by the narrow economic calculations of individual firms, and the existence of OSHA has meant greater access to decision-making power for workers than would otherwise have been possible. However, the central principle has remained that of costs and benefits rather than the issue of control and class prerogatives. The conclusion that dangerous job conditions are uneconomic reflects the same instrumental logic and utilitarian thinking that has been so prominent in children's programs. Even here the economic costs of safety and health have become too high and the Reagan administration has begun to vitiate the limited controls of OSHA, perverting the basic cost-benefit rationale by emphasizing the costs to employers and ignoring the benefits to workers.[53] It is difficult to politicize class-related issues except in the most distorted ways: although the long-run effect of the Occupational Safety and Health Act may be to increase public control over the conditions of work, if it can survive conservative attacks, the acceptance of this idea has been possible only with justifications that ignore the origins of class and its ubiquitous influences. The consequences of class are sometimes addressed by the state, but in these cases the defining characteristics of class—the nature of job hierarchies and control over work—are left untouched.

The OSHA experience illustrates that resistance to state programs which might address class issues is in part an issue of costs. The goal of profit maximization has always driven firms to bear as few costs as possible and to push as many costs as possible onto society at large and onto workers. While the state has sometimes tried to reimpose hidden costs onto firms, firms have resisted because such efforts would infringe on profits. But the conflict is potentially much deeper than the issue of costs, because minimizing the adverse consequences of production on family life necessarily involves more than regulating the physical conditions of work. For example, because the most important determinants of job satisfaction include participation in decision making, it would be necessary to restructure decision making to increase satisfaction at work.[54] Because the strains of lower-class jobs come in part from the lack of power on the job and the nature of supervision, correcting the effects of class on family life requires a scrutiny of all elements of supervision and control. Because the values passed on to children result in part from the nature of an individual's control over work, this too would have to be considered. Once we begin to examine the effects of class on family life, the most fundamental elements of control over work and the structure of production must be open to public scrutiny. Indeed, calls for greater worker participation and economic democracy have drawn strength from the tie between satisfaction at work and familial satisfaction and from the obvious strains on family life created by class divisions.

Those who fail to address the origins of class divisions and their many consequences implicitly deny that class affects family life and childrearing. In so doing, they participate in the cover-up of class issues and guarantee that the structural inequalities that affect children will continue unmodified. One of the great failures of those modern liberals who have promoted a comprehensive family policy is that they have refused to consider the class structure of American society, even as they recognize how important the material conditions of family life are.[55] To most people concerned about the "crisis of family" and the plight of children, efforts to shape the conditions of work seem to have little to do with family policy, even though the conditions of work and family life have everything to do with one another.

Once we recognize that the family is no longer private, then the domain of family policy must extend beyond the conventional limits to all the economic and social conditions that influence families and children adversely, including the divisions of class. Once we recognize the variety of public influences on families, then it becomes illogical to delimit the concerns of the state. Once we have accepted the idea of a liberal democratic state—describing a state that responds to democratic pressures in order to enhance the freedoms and the capacities of all its citizens—then there is no justifiable reason to accept the political limits of capitalism in deciding what the scope of a state initiative should be. Inexorably, the very idea of a comprehensive family policy is a radical idea: under its banner we are forced to consider the origins and effects of class in a capitalist economy, and we must begin the politically difficult process of remedying the divisions of class through collective action.

10

Reconstructing the State

THE ATTEMPTS to improve children's lives have consistently driven Americans to elaborate public institutions for children. In turn, that strategy for child saving has proved inadequate; the effort to develop family policies, to improve the conditions of families as the best way to help children, has become more generally accepted. In analyzing the structural conditions of families, public issues that are normally beyond the scope of child advocates—macroeconomic policy, antidiscrimination efforts, the policies that support or undermine new roles for women, and the effects of class have emerged as central. In considering the problems of child caring and child welfare and how to resolve them through collective action, we have been led away from children and their immediate environments to much broader issues of social and economic policy.

Inexorably, our concern for children has led us to the most fundamental elements of the state's policy toward them: the most basic assumptions and practices that have limited both children's institutions and the larger policies that affect family life; the conditions under which the state normally intervenes in the lives of children; the role of professionals in public institutions; the different goals the state pursues and the contradictory effects of institutions for child welfare; the limits on direct intervention into the private economy; and the class and racial biases that pervade every institution and all attitudes toward children. The symptoms of collective failures are everywhere: in the cycles of reform and crisis in the sphere of families and children, repeated one more time in the "family crisis" of the 1970s and 1980s; in the condition of perpetual reform within most children's institutions, with little hope that the reforms proposed during the past decade will be adequate; in the contradictory nature of most children's institutions, providing "help that hurts"; in the greater polarization of political life, with increasingly fragmented groups battling furiously without any chance for rational and principled government to emerge.

We have summarized the problems within the American state as the dilemma of discharging public responsibility for children in a liberal society where private responsibility for childrearing and economic decisions dominates. The current manifestations of this dilemma are deeply rooted in the assumptions and practices of nineteenth-century America: the exaltation of the private family and the private economy, the dichotomy between public and private institutions, and the assumptions of *parens patriae* and of private responsibility for childrearing. Ironically, however, even as these were instituted, they were already inappropriate. At the moment when the ideology of the private family was codified in the antebellum period, the development of capitalism was replacing families as independent economic units with new units of firms, thereby undermining family privacy and self-sufficiency. The transition to an economy dominated by firms and then corporations has left only the family farm and the small family business, both of decreasing significance in the economy, as symbols of the self-sufficient families we would like to recreate but no longer can. Even as the state's involvement in the economic and social conditions that shape families has grown, we continue to insist that the family is private and that it should be interferred with only when it breaks down. Yet the ongoing concern for childhood poverty and the occurrence of family "crisis" during periods of economic change indicate how false the image of the private family has been. With families dependent on circumstances beyond their control—like the cycles of capitalist economies, inflation, unemployment, and discrimination—the old ideals of domestic privacy are no longer accurate.

The image of the private economy has been outdated for as long as has the image of the private family. The development of rudimentary monetary and transportation policies in the mid-nineteenth century, the growth of regulation in the progressive era, the early stages of macroeconomic management in the depression, and the expansion of state participation in the economy after World War II describe a history—slow, fitful, and uneven, to be sure—of increasing governmental responsibility to correct the worst faults of capitalism and to guarantee, insofar as possible, the economic health of the country. In an economy where 20 percent of the Gross National Product is generated in the public sector, where the federal government has become responsible for the health of the economy, and where regulatory activities are pervasive in guiding those activities not publicly funded, it has become ludicrous to speak of private enterprise as the foundation of the economy. The expansion of the state has sufficiently blurred the boundary between public and private decisions so that economic outcomes are almost always the result of both political and market forces.

By and large, the expansion of the state in economic and social policy has come about for good reason. It has occurred because serious economic and social problems could not be addressed through individualistic and private remedies, and so have required collective solutions. This was neither because of an ideological commitment to the state, which has been especially weak in the United States, nor because of the political power of the poor, which has been sporadic at best. As became clear in the Great Depression, capitalism operating by itself cannot reproduce the conditions of its prosperity. The need to stabilize the chaos of unregulated banking, to curb the gross abuses of large corporations, and to counter the vicious cycles that have regularly plagued capitalist economies have impelled the major expansions of state power. Since the demise of independent families in the nineteenth century, private families have been unable to fulfill the entire range of childrearing responsibilities (if indeed they ever could). To fill the gap, the state has expanded to eliminate the most hideous poverty, to assume public responsibility for education, to compensate for the unwillingness and inability of families to assume responsibility for delinquents, criminals, the mentally retarded, the aged, and others shunned by society. The growth of the state has been a mechanism for moderating the worst extremes of capitalism and smoothing the path of its development, rather than a direct challenge to capitalism. Similarly, children's institutions and the welfare state have developed to fulfill what were once familial responsibilities rather than to challenge private families directly. But because the expansion of public responsibility has always been accompanied by an ideological commitment to private responsibility for familial and economic decisions, Americans have never admitted the legitimacy of public responsibility. Nor have they eliminated the tendency to use public institutions for individual and private ends.

The duality of expanding state responsibility while maintaining the ideology of private responsibility has enabled most Americans to support the state. While modern liberals have consistently attempted to expand social and employment programs, contemporary conservatives who attack social welfare programs and "excessive" regulation are happy with high spending for defense, policing, and business subsidies. Even though fiscal conservatism and taxpayer revolts have become political rallying cries, and efforts to minimize governmental regulation have been given new impetus under Ronald Reagan, the activist state will still not wither away. Conservative supply-side economics requires an active program of tax subsidies to corporations and upper-income individuals, and the size of defense spending and tax cuts proposed by Ronald Reagan means that the federal deficit is certain to increase. Direct subsidies to corporations have always been popular among conservatives, and public funding for both the Export-Import Bank and synthetic fuel development were among the first Reagan budget cuts to be restored. The vague proposals to develop a program of "reindustrialization" will require other government initiatives, some of them specific to problem-ridden sectors like the steel and automobile industries. Sooner or later national policies for energy and raw materials will have to be developed. A conservative government in Washington does not foreshadow a return to a *laissez-faire* economy.[1] Only the modification of regulations that limit the powers of corporations and the direct attacks on social programs for the poor—both results of self-interested politics in a period of economic decline—have suggested a modification of public responsibility for economic and social problems. There remains a consensus among conservatives, moderates, and modern liberals—in action if not in ideology—on one essential principle: collective problems must be collectively addressed. What remains controversial is exactly how governmental solutions are to operate, in what interests, under whose control, and which problems are serious enough to merit public support.

Behind the currently fashionable rhetoric of removing the state from private matters is a very different reality. Over the long run the state will probably continue to expand, and the variety of its activities will become increasingly elaborate. The United States will in all likelihood follow the pattern of European states, where the public sector is much larger, the range of social programs more comprehensive, and the participation in the economy more elaborate (extending even to public ownership of corporations). The effects of that expansion are not at all certain, however. Contrary to the hopes of modern liberals, more government programs have not necessarily resolved underlying problems. Macroeconomic policy has not eliminated unemployment, inflation, or business cycles, though it has surely moderated all of them. Regulation has not eliminated the abuses of market mechanisms or eliminated the urgency of environmental safeguards. Although it has moderated poverty somewhat, the expansion of social services has not always benefited the poor. And public education does not guarantee that all will be literate or given an equal opportunity to succeed. More generally, as we have seen in children's institutions, humanitarian and principled impulses are often thwarted by self-interested politics or embedded in institutions of class and racial control.

While it is likely that the state will expand, the continued abuse of public policies is also possible—even probable, given the unequal distribution of political power and the constraints on the state originating in capitalist institutions. Even those programs that are generally considered "liberal" can be misused for illiberal ends. Public expenditures that stress extravagant defense equipment rather than a balance of sensible military expenditures and social programs are wasteful of public funds and harmful to the economy. A national energy policy can increase the profits of a few, highly monopolized corporations and increase the welfare of some areas of the country at the expense of other areas, rather than assuring that energy supplies will be equitably available to all. Public funds can be misused to shore up failing corporations without diverting profits from private hands or correcting the flaws of market allocations. Wage and price controls can just as easily be used to increase corporate profits or to favor high-income individuals as to moderate inflation and protect the most defenseless poor. Public employment programs can be and have been used to promote the employment of middle-class individuals rather than the poor and unemployed for whom they were originally intended. For families and children, the continued elaboration of public programs on the basis of old established principles—*parens patriae* and the assumptions of parental failure, cost-benefit justifications, class and racial divisions, and hostility toward other people's children—will guarantee that public programs remain inadequate and ambiguous in their effects on children.

The essential problem, then, is not simply the size of the state. Debates about the scope of the state—how much public responsibility ought to exist, what programs should be funded—are important, but they are insufficient. The policies that flow from them will be haphazard and unprincipled, unless public debates also involve the basic questions of who controls the state and in what interests it operates. The first of these questions involves the nature of democratic processes and political movements, and the second asks what principles and constraints shape the state's activities. Above all, the issues Americans will face over the next decades are whether it will be possible to move away from the fragmented, self-interested, unprincipled, and highly inegalitarian form of democracy they now have to a form more worthy of their democratic aspirations; whether the state continues to expand on the basis of the principles that have dominated public policies for more than a century or more progressive principles can emerge; and whether we can escape the endless cycles of crisis and inappropriate reform. To address those issues, we must first understand the most general principles that have shaped the American state. Only then will it be possible to transform the state in order to develop truly humane and just policies for children.

The Liberal Democratic State in a Capitalist Society

The United States is a society that is both liberal and democratic—liberal in the basic sense of devoted to the freedom of individuals and democratic in resorting to collective decision-making processes to resolve issues of collective importance.[2] However, the meanings of liberalism and democracy have changed over the past two centuries. What seemed necessary to enhance individual freedoms in the early nineteenth century, when small entrepreneurial firms were the most dynamic elements in an expanding economy, was very different from what is necessary in the late twentieth century, in an economy dominated by large corporations and an active state. Democracy has itself evolved, from the direct democracy of colonial communities to the representative democracy dominated by warring interest groups. To understand liberalism and democracy in America, we must understand their evolution and the ways capitalist development has transformed them.[3] Only then can we comprehend the state itself and the changes that will be necessary for the state to act on behalf of children.

In the eighteenth and early nineteenth centuries, the most freedom enhancing institutions were those of entrepreneurial capitalism. Capitalism freed individuals from the relics of feudal practices and from community restraints on trade, belief, and personal life. Above all, capitalism promised to free all individuals from the restraints of scarcity. Nineteenth-century liberalism therefore associated expanding freedoms with the institutions of entrepreneurial capitalism. Markets, market incentives, and market outcomes, were restricted as little as possible, as was private ownership of land and capital. Profit seeking was recognized as the basic incentive in production. Accumulation of profits in private hands (rather than in the hands of the public or the state) was approved, including the possibility for concentrating wealth in the hands of relatively few individuals. Individual initiative and economic freedom, including certain civil liberties necessary for the pursuit of private gain like freedom of association, freedom of speech, and the right to travel were also recognized. Although liberalism linked to capitalism stressed economic freedom, other rights—political freedom, artistic freedom, and religious liberty, for example—expanded as well. The links between capitalism and various individual freedoms became the institutional and the ideological basis of capitalism. They have with some justification allowed the defenders of capitalism to claim a historic commitment to freedom.

During the nineteenth century, the relation between the American state and the economy shifted, as the major tenets of economic liberalism—unconstrained markets and private gain—suffused both of them. In the colonial period and even in the early nineteenth century, state and local governments were active forces in economic development. Their concern was to promote the common good, to ensure both general prosperity and a harmonious social order. In phrases that reaffirmed colonial precedents, a Boston newspaper wrote in 1819 that it was "manifestly erroneous" to think that a commonwealth could survive and prosper by leaving industry alone and by assuming that individuals rather than government "are the judges of their interests." Although private ends were acknowledged, they were neither exalted above communal concerns nor thought of as legitimate substitutes for the common good.[4]

As the notion of the common good changed during the nineteenth century, the appropriate role of the state changed with it. As the American historian Roland Bertoff has written,

> The old commonwealth, in which private enterprise was expected to be regulated for the general welfare of society, dissolved into the nineteenth century liberal state which recognized no common social purpose greater than the sum of the many private purposes of individual farmers, merchants, railroad builders, and industrial entrepreneurs.[5]

Since the common good was now the sum of private interests, the state's role was to oversee the market place; the state might act where markets failed or were incomplete, but it was otherwise constrained from interfering in the operation of "free" markets. Through the legal system, banking regulations, powers of incorporation, and grants of land and money, the state tried to ensure that capitalist institutions (like markets) could operate stably. It promoted public investments like railroads and canals to facilitate private profit-making and communal goals simultaneously. These activities assumed that state involvement would be limited, and that where the state intervened it would seek to enhance private gain.

The changing nature of the state is epitomized in the relationship between the state and corporations. Between 1800 and 1850, a series of court decisions—the most famous being the *Dartmouth College* case (1819) and the *Charles River Bridge* case (1829)—severely limited the state's power over corporations. Once the state had created a corporation, it could not modify or eliminate it. The corporation, which had originally been conceived as a public agency performing public functions through the use of public and private capital, became primarily "a profit-making institution, a business vehicle serving the interests of investors" with little public control.[6] Of course, the nineteenth-century state could also act to ensure social peace, since social order was necessary for stable markets and private gain. Through newly established police forces and adult prisons and through public institutions like the schools and juvenile asylums, the state could incarcerate adults and socialize children so that class strife would be diminished.

Because liberalism in the nineteenth century was equated with capitalism, the liberal state has been essentially a capitalist state, supporting the different institutions of capitalism. The process has not been static. As the major institutions of capitalism have changed from small family businesses to large corporations, so too have the elements supported by the liberal state changed. Trying to maintain perfect competition is no longer a serious concern of the state, as corporations rather than small competitive firms have come to dominate capitalism in the twentieth century. In fact, the influence of corporate capitalism has made the state a prime sponsor of monopolistic practices: the regulatory mechanisms instituted in the progressive era favored large companies over small companies, and the failure to move vigorously against monopolies made the state a partner in the emergence of corporate capitalism.[7] As Theodore Roosevelt justified the waning of antitrust efforts:

> In the modern industrial world combinations are absolutely necessary. It is mischievous and unwholesome to keep upon the statute books unmodified, a law like the anti-trust law, which, while in practice only partially effective against vicious combinations, has nevertheless in theory been construed so as sweepingly to prohibit every combination for the transaction of modern business.[8]

Despite the demise of nineteenth-century competition, the nineteenth-century ideology has remained powerful: the renaissance of conservative thought in the 1970s and 1980s, with Milton Friedman the theoretician and Ronald Reagan the practitioner, confirms the power of old liberal convictions that the state should enhance freedom by promoting market mechanisms and private profits. Even as public responsibility for the economy has expanded, the legitimacy of the state's role has required a continuing deference to private gain.

The relationship between the family and the liberal state has also changed in similar ways. In the seventeenth and eighteenth centuries, the family and communal concerns were almost synonymous, and families had few privacy rights against communal supervision. During the eighteenth century, privacy rights for families expanded to protect a variety of political, religious, and economic freedoms that had themselves been forbidden in the earliest colonial communities. The private family—the family protected from intrusion by the state or community—was therefore a true liberal institution in the sense of one promoting freedoms. Because the family was a unit of production and of capital accumulation, its rights against state intervention were necessary to protect private capital accumulation and thus capitalist development in general. Nineteenth-century liberalism protected the private family as part of its general promotion of capitalism. At almost the same time, however, the link between families and capital accumulation was broken. In the nineteenth century the development of firms separate from families and then the domination of self-perpetuating corporations in the twentieth century slowly eliminated the family as a unit of production and capital accumulation. In the process, the private family as a central institution of economic liberalism became outdated.[9] This process has not always been acknowledged, as attested by generations of plans to resurrect the family farm and to restore the family as the "basic unit of society."

Even though the private family has become irrelevant to capitalism as a system of production, the family remains a potentially freedom-enhancing institution in a different sense. Since it remains the unit of income generation, wealth accumulation, and consumption, the family provides economic freedom—freedom from want, freedom to consume, a measure of independence from others—for those families with adequate incomes. But the private family thereby embodies the structural inequalities of income, class, and race that have been exacerbated by capitalist development. The defense of the private family as a liberal or freedom enhancing institution is in effect a defense of the inequalities generated by capitalism. The modern conservative position on the family has supported the private family, by stressing both the privacy rights of families against the intrusions of the state and the prerogatives of parents over teachers and other professionals. Pressing to reduce social programs that redistribute income from rich to poor families, that promote more equal access to schools, or that counter discimination, conservatives have also been the defenders of existing inequalities.

One strand of American liberalism has therefore embraced a nineteenth-century conception of economic and personal freedom as *freedom from constraints*, particularly governmental constraints, for both families and firms. This conception of liberalism has been supportive of capitalism, in allowing both capitalist firms to develop with a minimum of public restraint and inequalities among families to flourish with minimal correction. Almost from the very beginning, however, another conception of liberalism developed that challenged some aspects of capitalism. In contrast to those who emphasized the liberal elements of capitalism, others stressed that capitalism created such poverty and degradation that some individuals were not free, at least certainly not as free as others. Responding to the nineteenth-century appeal by the social theorist William Graham Sumner and others to stop interfering with the "natural laws of society as expressed in unreconstructed private enterprise and freedom of trade," the sociologist Lester Ward wrote that *laissez faire* means "mind your own business," a mandate that would be "nihilistic and suicidal." Workers regularly attacked the abuses of capitalist labor markets; progressive era reformers criticized monopolies for curbing rather than enhancing individual freedom.[10] From the time of the New Deal twentieth-century liberals have argued that whatever benefits capitalism brings, it must be limited in the interests of individual freedom. It must be limited by regulatory mechanisms, the transfer programs of the welfare state, the practice of macroeconomic policy, and more recently by environmental and consumer controls. Implicit in the criticism of capitalism has been the view that freedom from constraints as embodied in *laissez-faire* capitalism is not an appropriate conception of liberalism. This is so both because capitalism is often cruel and because it subjects all people to the constraints of markets. Instead, a conception of liberalism as the *freedom of individuals to develop their capacities* has motivated the efforts to curb the worst abuses of capitalism.[11]

In the realm of families, twentieth-century liberals have generally recognized that families are still bastions of freedom—even though we have a better appreciation of how families can work internally to deny freedoms to women, adolescents, and children. As a result most modern liberals want to protect families against unwarranted incursions by governments and corporations, such as intrusions of welfare workers and excessive data gathering, just as much as eighteenth-century liberals strove for the establishment of privacy rights. But since the link between families and capital accumulation has been broken, the private family can no longer be considered liberal in the sense of enhancing economic productivity, but only in the nineteenth-century sense of allowing inequalities to flourish. Even though the redistributive programs of the welfare state impose new constraints in the form of taxation, from the viewpoint of modern liberals these programs are freedom enhancing because they alleviate the poverty that otherwise makes the development of individual capacities (especially among children) almost impossible.

Much of the confusion and political debate over the liberal state arises from differences in what can be considered freedom enhancing. While the private family and capitalism appeared liberal in the nineteenth century, there is greater disagreement about the effects of capitalism in the twentieth century. In the twentieth century, the debates therefore have often involved battles between the defenders of capitalism—often considered conservatives—and those twentieth-century liberals who have been attempting to curb some of the worst abuses of capitalism. Yet modern conservatives have not always rejected state intervention. The expansion of the state has been accepted by capitalists anxious to constrain the instabilities and "destructive" competition of unfettered capitalism, and conservatives have rarely opposed public subsidies to business. On their side, modern liberals have tried to regulate capitalism, but they have never opposed capitalism itself. Even as they attacked monopolistic abuses and "vicious combinations," most progressive era reformers hailed the productive power of corporations. New Deal liberals hoped that the state might eventually wither away, even as they were implementing the programs of the welfare state and early Keynesian policies. The programs of the Great Society were hardly the radical departures that their critics have portrayed them to be. By and large the War on Poverty was conducted through conventional education and training programs and the transfer programs of the welfare state, all designed to change the income distribution without interfering with capitalist production itself. While they have fought its excesses, then, modern liberals have accepted many elements of capitalism, especially private ownership of capital and profits, market incentives and utilitarian logic, the prerogatives of private firms, and the extension of old liberal conceptions of the family in parental determinism, *parens patriae,* and the defense of the private family. Above all, the welfare of the population is dependent on the health of the economy, especially for poor people. Conservatives and liberals alike have therefore accepted the need for the state to promote a strong economy, which has in turn required that the state support rather than undermine capitalist prerogatives.[12]

The willingness of modern conservatives to use the state in their own interests and that of modern liberals to accept the essential elements of capitalism has given us the modern liberal state, with its preference for private over public solutions. The state intrudes into the economy and families only where markets or families are thought to have failed.[13] Government is generally prevented from engaging in activities that displace profit making or deny families the "right" to make private decisions. Profits and earnings are considered private, and the government derives its revenues by taxing private incomes rather than by engaging in public enterprise and public profit making. The state uses its public power to enhance private profit making in a variety of ways, and it does what is necessary to maintain social peace and prevent class warfare. Because of the dominance of these principles, accepted by both modern conservatives and modern liberals, the American state retains much nineteenth-century liberalism, presuming to promote individual freedoms by supporting capitalism.

The consequences of this presumption for children have been ubiquitous. As Americans have elaborated children's institutions, they have simultaneously constrained them by their allegiance to capitalism. They have done so by the subordination of public schooling to labor markets. They have required that welfare programs and public employment programs not dilute labor market incentives. They have restrained the state from taxing away "private" incomes, most obviously by taxpayer revolts. They have used the schools and the juvenile justice system to implement a class-biased conception of socialization to control lower-class children in the interests of social peace. These institutions have also been constrained by the respect for the concept of the private family and private responsibility for childrearing except under conditions of parental failure and by the class biases that manifest themselves in hostility to other people's children. Despite reform efforts that might alter inequalities, the state replicates the inequalities generated by capitalism, principally through the schools and constraints on welfare programs. Even the efforts to eliminate sexual and racial discrimination, both of which run counter to market-based meritocratic principles, have been strenuously resisted. As long as the dominant concept of liberalism remains that of freedom from constraints—especially the freedom to accumulate wealth privately, at the expense of others—these illiberal consequences will remain.

While the American state is liberal in ways consistent with capitalism, it is also democratic. Democratic mechanisms have always had the potential to modify the abuses of capitalism and even capitalism itself. Democratic decision making can replace market decisions and utilitarian logic with political decisions and humanitarian principles, as it does in regulating pollution, workplace safety, food and drugs. Too, it can limit the operation of markets, through wage and price controls, the regulation of oil prices, the operation of price stabilization programs for commodities, and the regulation of export markets for weapons and high-technology goods. The state can restrict private profits, as it does in regulating natural monopolies like utilities. It could even eliminate profit seeking as the way to allocate resources. It can reduce the inequalities that markets generate through tax and transfer programs, changing market incentives through tax policies. By regulating wages and working conditions and by creating public employment, the state can limit labor markets. And as it has in the national forests, public utilities, Conrail, and Amtrak, the state can replace private property with public ownership.

All of these modifications of capitalist practices have occurred to some extent, many of them through the programs of the welfare state. Democratic mechanisms—the ability of aggrieved groups to gain access to the state through voting and interest group politics, as well as through protest and litigation—have accounted for many of these constraints on capitalism. Certainly those who have successfully agitated for voting rights—women earlier in this century, blacks during the 1950s and 1960s—have recognized the potential of democracy to curb the worst inequalities of power. Yet democratic mechanisms have been unable to eliminate all the abuses of capitalism, as we have repeatedly seen in the case of children's issues. In part, support for capitalist institutions, even among liberals, has limited governmental constraints on capitalism. Liberals have pressed for tax and transfer programs to restrict poverty but have rarely challenged the hierarchical organization of production which breeds inequality. They have proposed public employment as a last resort but never as a fundamental replacement for private employment. They have fought for the necessity of some public ownership but have generally respected the institution of private property so that public enterprise is considerably more limited in this country than in Europe. Liberals have promoted Keynesian and other macroeconomic policies to limit business cycles and unemployment, but they have rarely promoted the national planning and more extensive direction of the economy that are common in other advanced capitalist countries. In every way, allegiance to capitalist institutions and the political power of corporations is much stronger in this country than in Europe.

One of the most serious reasons why democracy has not been more threatening to capitalism in this country is that democracy itself has taken a corrupted form. Just as capitalism has molded conceptions of liberalism, so too have democratic practices been shaped by capitalism. Most obviously, democracy has been degraded by the unequal distribution of political power. Despite the promise of formal equality in voting rights, the political impotence of the poor has always been an ignoble aspect of American democracy. Even as early American theorists of democracy like Thomas Jefferson acknowledged the legitimacy of hierarchy among people, they worried that inequalities could undermine the concept of citizenship. As Jefferson described the result of class divisions:

> Dependence begets subservience and venality, suffocates the germ of virtue, and prepares fit tools for the designs of ambition. . . . Generally speaking, the proportion which the aggregate of the other classes of citizens bears in any State to that of its husbandmen is the proportion of its unsound to its healthy parts, and is a good enough barometer whereby to measure the degree of its corruption.[14]

In some ways, class-based inequalities in political power have worsened. Although groups previously excluded from voting—blacks, native Americans, women—have gained access to the vote, the importance of voting has fallen relative to other forms of political activity, for example, lobbying by interest groups on specific issues. The development of increasingly expensive campaigns, with money rather than direct votes being the prime political resource, has also fostered political inequality. The result has been to defuse the dangerous potential of democracy to compromise capitalism, as democratic mechanisms themselves replicate the familiar patterns of structural inequalities.

The inequalities of power based on class have further prevented democratic decision making by limiting participation. In a class society, lower-class and working-class individuals experience relatively little power and participation in their work, and this sense of powerlessness spills over into other spheres of life including leisure time and politics.[15] With political representation becoming increasingly indirect—the United States has moved from direct democracy to representative democracy dominated first by parties and now by interest groups—the link between the individual voter and political outcomes has become increasingly tenuous. This has made it still more difficult for individual voters to see the point of participation.[16] As politics have come to be more spectacle and charade, the futility of participation has increased as well.[17] A consequence, then, is that participation has fallen to abysmally low levels. In the most widespread form of political behavior—voting—only 53 percent of eligible voters participated in the 1980 presidential election, and some national senators and representatives are elected with fewer than a quarter of the eligible voters at the polls.

Political participation has now become so low that many contemporary political theorists have turned the idea of democracy on its head. In contrast to some classic political theorists who stressed the importance of widespread participation, some current theorists have celebrated low participation as a contribution to the efficiency and stability of modern democracies. Samuel Huntington, a leading exponent of limited participation, has claimed: "The effective operation of a democratic political system . . . requires some measure of apathy and non-involvement on the part of some individuals and groups." By way of further defense Huntington adds, "In the past, every democracy has had a marginal population, of greater or lesser size, which has not participated in politics."[18] Such a view serves to justify what has already come to pass: a democracy where participation is limited, sporadic, skewed by class, and largely confined to the activity of voting. In this form of democracy, those who are most adversely affected by capitalism—the poor, lower-class individuals, and minorities—are the least likely to participate; those who benefit the most from the inequalities of capitalism are the most likely.

Finally, the very concept of democracy has been reformulated to be compatible with capitalist forms of liberalism. In the colonial period, political ideology assumed that a common good existed and considered political factions and "interests" illegitimate. In the words of John Adams, public virtue required "a positive Passion for the public good—established in the Minds of the People . . . Superior to all private Passions."[19] In the course of the nineteenth and early twentieth centuries, however, the colonial conception of public good dominating private interests was inverted. As de Tocqueville phrased the dilemma of democracy in America:

> For in a community in which the ties of family, of caste, of class, and craft fraternities no longer exist, people are far too disposed to think exclusively of their own interests, to become self-seekers practicing a narrow individualism and caring nothing for the public good.[20]

Rather than recognizing that self-interest is hostile to the common good, American political theorists since Joseph Schumpeter have described democracy as the clash of purely self-interested factions: the common good emerges from the competition among political groups, and no other conception of the common good exists. This construction of democracy has made political institutions analogous to the market. Competition among political groups for their own ends mimics the competition among firms for profit, and the assumption of pure self-interest as the basis of political activity parallels utilitarian assumptions about *homo economicus*.[21] Indeed, the analogy to the market goes further than many political theorists will recognize: just as consumers in the market place have unequal incomes and purchasing power, so groups in competition for political favors have unequal power and therefore achieve unequal political gains—not the equal political power that most Americans think of as democracy.

The competitive market model describes quite accurately the current stage of democratic practice, in which any conception of public responsibility—indeed, any form of principled politics—is torn to shreds under the pressure of self-centered interest groups and in which political power guides all public action. But as a normative guide, this conception of democracy confuses self-interest with collective interest and too often abandons any concern for the collective good. Its dominance means that Americans have essentially given up older conceptions of democracy in which individuals search for the collective good, in which they subordinate individual interest to the group's interest, and in which political participation is a way of forging a collective whole out of disconnected individuals.[22] The vocabularly once used to describe these conceptions—republican virtue, civic virtue, *civitas*, civic responsibility—has passed from public use. The very notion of public responsibility has become alien to a political system whose only function is to weigh which interest group has the most power.

The corruption of democracy reveals the disintegrating power of capitalism, its ability to take the old notion of democracy as a collective mechanism and to reduce it to the market-like interaction of individuals. In the process, capitalism has generated a form of democracy well suited to its maintenance, one in which the divisions of class and the inequalities of economic power have been replicated within the state itself. The result is that those who suffer the most under capitalism have the least ability to influence public decisions through democratic mechanisms. Those modern liberals who have tried to remedy some of the worst defects of capitalism have faced a political system that is a barrier to their goals.

By and large, then, the liberal democratic state in this country has tended to reproduce capitalism by accepting its essential elements—class divisions, the prerogatives of private ownership, the dominance of markets, the power of individualism, and the erosion of every conception of the collective. As a result, even as the state has enlarged its responsibilities in response to the most serious economic and social problems, the solutions have tended to replicate old patterns. This is the fundamental dilemma of public responsibility under capitalism. Capitalism generates a wide variety of problems which require collective resolution, yet capitalism also generates a set of barriers to their resolution, including a conception of liberalism as freedom from government interference and a distorted structure of democracy. These constraints are especially powerful for children, since the conception of childrearing as a private responsibility and the distrust of other people's children are so strong.

Yet to claim that the state merely replicates capitalism is quite wrong. The process of the state's expansion also transforms capitalism, and in this transformation we can find the openings for structural change in a democratic society.[23] Although capitalism has distorted the theory and practice of democracy, the expansion of the state still replaces economic decisions with political decisions that are theoretically democratic, or which *can be* democratic. This has consistently been the frustration of public institutions. While public institutions have tended to reproduce the inequities and irrationalities of capitalism, they have also presented new opportunities to correct these failures. The development of public education in the nineteenth century, for example, extended literacy and promised advancement to all children. The desperate efforts of blacks to gain access to schools for their children is testimony to that promise. The expansion of welfare programs, first in the progressive era, then during the 1930s, and again during the 1960s, has meant that one critical part of the income distribution—the low-income portion—is to some extent under public control, and that those in favor of changing the income distribution have another political mechanism at their disposal. Macroeconomic policy has similarly transformed the economic system by extending political influence over the economy and providing political access to groups, like organized labor, who in the past had never had any control whatsoever over the economy. In each case the potential inherent in democratic institutions has been limited, but that has not reduced the belief that public institutions should be responsive to the demands of all citizens.

There is, then, a solution to the central dilemma. Although the liberal democratic state has tended to reproduce capitalism, its actions have also transformed capitalism. As an activist state replaced a more *laissez-faire* state, private decisions were supplemented by public, political, and potentially democratic decisions. To some extent, then, the economy has come under public control, providing new opportunities for democratic participation. The process has been mirrored in the state's relationship to children: while state actions on behalf of children tend to reproduce structural inequalities, they simultaneously provide new opportunities for some and transform the conditions of childrearing for all, making decisions about children increasingly public and political. The challenge, now that the institutions of the activist state are well established, is to reassess the principles and structure of the liberal democratic state so that public responsibilities are not so quickly undermined by nineteenth century liberal assumptions. Since we assume that the state will continue to be powerful, we need to develop a set of normative principles to distinguish between progressive and regressive transformations of the state itself. Only then will it be possible to answer the questions of *to what ends* and *in whose interests* the state ought to work.

American Values and Progressive Principles

Although capitalist institutions and assumptions have corrupted the liberal democratic state, it is insufficient to call for socialism or the undoing of capitalism—as critics of capitalism have usually done—both because socialism is a nebulous concept and because capitalism is constantly being "undone" as corporate practices change and as the state itself changes.

Capitalism could give way to a form of socialism which is barbaric and illiberal. We can easily imagine forms of "democratic socialism" dominated by public enterprises which replicate the worst features of capitalism, in which private rights and private profit dominate communal concerns, inequalities and class divisions persist, and "democratic" practices have become overwhelmed by elite decision making and political apathy. Indeed, a variety of commentators think the United States is heading toward this form of state socialism, a "corporate socialism" or "lemon socialism" in which public ownership serves corporate interests on an ever-larger scale.[24] Without developing normative principles, therefore, we are likely to oscillate between expanding the state to moderate the abuses of capitalism and subordinating the state completely to the requirements of corporate capitalism—or to combine the two—without knowing why we are choosing one path rather than the other or where our choices will lead us.[25]

Generating normative principles to guide political action proves extremely difficult. Often grand principles sound like pieties adrift from concrete political realities, and there is inevitably an idiosyncratic element in choosing basic principles. Nonetheless, there is no serious alternative to establishing such principles and to creating a political structure that can implement these principles, once they have been debated and accepted. We assume that, in the absence of revolution, the principles guiding political action will emerge from existing American values, and that the transformations of American society over the next decades will proceed from existing institutions. The key question is whether American institutions and values can provide progressive principles upon which we can build or whether we must start the frightening task of breaking all historical continuity and generating principles *de novo*.

In fact, Americans have held several common ideals for some time. We can trace back to the colonial period a number of values, embodied in American institutions and consistently supported in public debate—individual freedom, democracy, the work ethic, family love, community, the value of education, the importance of children—which can form the basis for progressive principles.[26] The problem is that every one of these values has been corrupted by capitalism, so that what remain in practice are distorted and hollow vestiges of revered ideals. The distortions have too often left these ideals the property of conservatives. Lewis Mumford once noted the injustice "that patriotism should be monopolized by reaction-aries." Currently, assertions about the value of family (as in the "pro-family" movement), the sanctity of the work ethic, and the importance of literacy have become conservative euphemisms used to reimpose traditional sex roles, capitalist authority relationships, market incentives, and educational conformity. Modern liberals and radicals whose allegiance to family, work, and education is just as strong have been preempted. Unwilling to accept the specific political content of conservative appeals to basic values, they have been unable to use these values as guides for their own programs.[27] The challenge is to recognize how distorted these values have become and to disentangle those elements that remain valid and have appeal for the majority of Americans. Recognizing that normative principles will not eliminate conflict, we nonetheless propose to rescue some essential American values from their degradation under capitalism and to use them as the basis for judging future transformations produced by the state.[28]

The first and in many ways supreme American value is liberalism or the enhancement of individual freedom. Since the mid-eighteenth century, liberalism has been an essential basis of the American social contract, an ideology rarely in dispute. Its power has been apparent in the individual freedoms guaranteed by the Bill of Rights. A series of commentators beginning with de Tocqueville has testified to its special place in the United States compared to other Western liberal democracies. Though Americans differ as to what is required—emphasizing the freedom of the market place, religious or cultural liberty, or the limitations imposed by poverty, unemployment, and discrimination—Americans across the political spectrum have invariably phrased their arguments about the state in terms of individual freedom.[29] Yet, as we have seen, liberalism has been shaped by capitalist development. The conception that dominates state policies has most often stressed freedom from constraints (save those of the market place), especially the freedom from government interference with the "right" to accumulate. It has been, as de Tocqueville feared, a freedom in which people "become self-seekers practicing a narrow individualism and caring nothing for the public good," freedom for one's own children at the expense of other people's children. In this form, nineteenth-century liberals and modern conservatives have monopolized popular conceptions of freedom by claiming that capitalism—or "free enterprise"—is the only economic system that facilitates an individual's "freedom to choose." Evidently, not everyone has been admitted to the company of those who are free to choose; blacks and women have had to struggle hard for admittance, although their struggles have drawn moral force from the ideology of liberalism. The claims of the poor to exercise freedom of choice have never been taken seriously; what passes for economic "freedom" is based on inequality.[30] Other freedoms have been curtailed as everyone has been subject to the irrationalities and imperfections of markets—pollution, the social dislocation of economic development, the excess of business cycles, the banality of advertising, and other efforts to manipulate markets.

In liberalism, then, we confront a basic American value, the strength of which emerged early in American history but which has been shaped into a conservative and at times repressive social ideal. To resurrect liberalism in its original sense of enhancing individual freedom, we must shift to the alternative conception that stresses the equal right of all individuals to develop their capacities, a form of freedom which cannot be achieved when individuals are exceedingly unequal in economic and political power. Freedom from governmental constraints is not the issue; the constraints of markets can be every bit as harsh and repressive as governmental constraints. The new conception of liberalism requires action, including government action, to eliminate all barriers of discrimination which now prevent the equal freedoms of minorities and women, and—even more difficult—to eliminate or minimize the class divisions that are so pervasive. Since the development and protection of individual capacities require political action, this conception of liberalism also requires that political power be more equally distributed.

In the realm of children, the goal of developing human capacities has often been phrased as educating all children "to the limit of their abilities." This in turn suggests a series of reforms in educational institutions and training programs, in which warehousing and controlling functions recede in favor of the developmental functions that have so often been blocked. Accepting this interpretation of liberalism—essentially, the interpretation that modern liberals have often claimed—therefore generates an extensive roster of possible reforms, many of them beyond our capacity to imagine. The important point is that this principle can help disentangle those reforms that are truly freedom-enhancing from those that serve to replicate the inequalities and abuses of capitalism.

Along with liberalism, Americans have celebrated democracy, often in the most self-satisfied fashion. During the late eighteenth and early nineteenth centuries, Americans frequently voiced the view that democracy and its unique expression, the Declaration of Independence, were the new nation's most important contribution to the rest of the world. In their history textbooks. American youth have consistently learned of their country's democratic origins and of the triumphs of democratic processes.[31] The town meeting has been invoked as the quintessential American institution by such diverse citizens as the New England colonialists, Daniel Webster, and Jimmy Carter. Yet, like liberalism, democracy has changed over time. The obvious anachronism of the town meeting is one measure of the change. Another is the modification of a notion of democracy which underlay colonial practices and which has formed our most noble ideals of democracy. That concept of democracy required a society of relatively insignificant class divisions, in which all citizens enjoyed approximately equal status and independence because of their independence in production. It assumed that all citizens (free white males) would participate fully in democratic decision making. Citizenship was undifferentiated; there were citizens and noncitizens, not first-, second-, or third-class citizens.[32] This ideal of democracy assumed that the significant issue was who was to be a citizen; since nonwhites and women were not, the great battles over democracy in the nineteenth century involved their rights of citizenship. But these battles, significant as they were, often hid a more subtle transformation—the extent to which citizenship itself became unequal, as class and racial divisions shredded the one-class society of independent husbandmen. Over time, the expectation that citizens would actively participate in governing their communities and would subordinate individual interests to some conception of the community good was similarly transformed, eroded by the development of nonparticipatory democracy where self-interest rules, interest groups (rather than individual voters) hold the greatest power, and most individuals are politically alienated. Present conceptions of democracy as a marketlike mechanism have eliminated the conception of building an enduring and self-governing community.

The alternative to this debased conception of democracy is one that stresses widespread participation, among citizens relatively equal in political influence. Democratic decision making in this ideal would not be so thoroughly dominated by the goal of self-interest through the state, but would generate some principled conception of the common good to which citizens could defer. In Jefferson's words:

> Only lay down true principles, and adhere to them inflexibly. Do not be frightened into their surrender by the alarms of the timid, or the croakings of wealth against the ascendancy of the people. If experience be called for, appeal to that of our fifteen or twenty governments for forty years, and show me where the people have done half the mischief in these forty years, that a single despot would have done in a single year . . . the true foundation of republican government is the equal right of every citizen, in his person and property, and in their management.[33]

In Michael Walzer's more recent phrasing, the aim is a democracy in which "politics can be opened up, rates of participation significantly increased, decision making really shared, . . . a new politicizing of the state, a devolution of state power into the hands of ordinary citizens."[34] In this ideal, expertise and knowledge are used not to subvert participation but to enhance it. Like a revised conception of liberalism, a revision of democratic practices will require the narrowing of structural inequalities. It will also require fuller participation in all spheres of life, including economic democracy and workers' control, because political democracy will otherwise by undermined by the inequalities and passivity generated by capitalism.[35] A revitalization of older American ideals about democracy therefore stands as a basis for the radical transformation of the economy as well as the state.

Allegiance to work and the work ethic has been a third value central to American life. In this country, the work ethic has had its roots in the Puritan conception of work as a "calling," in which individuals gained a sense of purpose and meaning through serving God, family, and community as well as self. Indeed, work has seemed so integral to Americans' understanding of themselves that the decline of the work ethic has often been synonymous with the deterioration of the social fabric. Most concretely, unemployment has always been recognized as psychologically devastating as well as economically destructive, since unemployment denies an individual the purpose and the place in the social order that work provides.

The concept of work as intrinsically satisfying and as contributing to an individual's sense of efficacy and participation was initially tied to a conception of a broader moral order. As John Adams described this society, "an intelligent and honest" government could develop "virtues" and "habits" of industry. But it was hard to make work under capitalism moral, as jobs were stripped of self-direction and creativity, as layers of hierarchy reduced individual discretion and any sense of participation in a larger productive enterprise, and as earnings became the sole motivation. To ensure continued allegiance to work, workers had to be told exactly what to do. The directives in a reader for immigrants, distributed by the International Harvester Corporation just before World War I, and in the work rules of General Motors in 1971 are evidence of how closely work must be supervised:[36]

I hear the whistle. I must hurry.
I hear the five minute whistle.
It is time to go into the shop. . . .
I change my clothes and get ready to work.
The starting whistle blows.
I eat my lunch.
It is forbidden to eat until then.
The whistle blows at five minutes of starting time.
I get ready to work.
I work until the whistle blows to quit.

I leave my place nice and clean.
I put all my clothes in the locker.
I must go home.

EACH EMPLOYEE WILL BE INSTRUCTED ON THE FOLLOWING POINTS:

1. Be at their work assignment at the start of the shift.
2. Be at their work assignment at the conclusion of their lunch period.
3. All employe[e]s will be working effectively and efficiently until the bell of their scheduled lunch period and at the end of their scheduled shift.
4. Employe[e]s are to work uninterrupted to the end of the scheduled shift.

In these rules we have a sense of how much the conception of work has been desecrated, its primary purpose not intrinsic satisfaction but economic return. The work ethic has become an ethic of diligence, persistence, absolute obedience, and maximal effort in return for wages, rather than an ideal linked to the quality of jobs or satisfaction at work.[37] In this form, the work ethic has become a slogan for conservatives and employers seeking to exact greater effort from their lowliest laborers, in jobs that are often monotonous, dangerous, and poorly paid, rather than a conception of what work might be.

Corrupted as it has been, the ideal of work in America has nonetheless persisted. To resurrect it from its degradation as a tool to enhance profits and ensure social peace, however, requires emphasizing the importance of meaningful work for every individual. In turn, this requires not merely the kinds of job restructuring which became prominent in the 1970s—job enlargement, job rotation, work teams—but also the expansion of decision making by workers over their jobs, since expanded decision making is so critical to job satisfaction.[38] Because meaningful work is incompatible with the extensive class divisions of capitalism and with the process of continually degrading work, making work more satisfying will require breaking down class divisions and current patterns of control. As with revised conceptions of liberalism and democracy, then, we can use an ideal of work deeply rooted in American history to specify a number of progressive social and economic transformations.

Like the value of work, the value of love and intimacy is a widespread ideal, part of Freud's dictum that the psychologically mature adult should be able "to love and to work." In the United States, ideals of intimacy have usually been tied to family life, to love between husbands and wives and between parents and children. This itself narrows the potential of intimacy to individuals in family settings and attests to the monopoly of the "private" family as the setting for strong emotional attachments. The image of the family as a "haven in a heartless world" is one in which

291

relationships outside the family are usually competitive, cut-throat, antagonistic, uncaring—a statement of how capitalism has transformed relationships among people in the world of business and politics.[39] Given this transformation, it is no wonder that Americans have held so tenaciously to the ideal of "separate spheres" and the maintenance of a secure family life: the alternative has been to abandon any hope of intimacy.

But even within the family our conceptions of love have often been restricted. The domestic ideology made the family an emotional haven, but it did so by subordinating women to men and by denying children's rights to autonomy. As a consequence, attempts to introduce equality into familial relationships have almost always been perceived as attacks on the family itself. Even feminists have participated in this line of reasoning: some leaders of the women's movement in the 1960s proclaimed that women's liberation should eliminate the traditional family, a claim that most Americans interpreted as eliminating family life entirely. The prominence of hierarchical and authoritarian rather than egalitarian relationships has meant that the goals of "strengthening the family" and "upholding family values" have usually been the property of conservatives and antifeminists supporting traditional nineteenth-century conceptions of family life and personal relationships. Like individual freedom, democracy, and the work ethic, the family as a social value has been corrupted to accommodate inegalitarian social relationships.

The alternative, as most feminists have always contended and as many women and men came to understand during the 1970s, is to forge new conceptions of familial love based on equality between men and women rather than subordination of women to men, in which children are less the property of their parents and more individuals in their own right, childrearing is less authoritarian, men and women share childrearing responsibilities, and the boundaries of the private family are not so impregnable. These changes mean radical transformation in personal and social relationships, because the ideal of romantic love based on individual choice and intimacy cannot be fulfilled as long as sex roles are unequal. In turn, this means that all social practices that support sexual inequalities—including discrimination in employment and in education—must be eliminated. In addition, fulfilling the ideals of intimacy and love requires abolishing the economic barriers to family life—poverty, unemployment, and the economic precariousness of lower-class families—and eliminating the stresses of work life, all of which strain family relationships.[40] Achieving the ideals of intimacy and reconstructing the concept of the family implies subordinating production to family life—rather than subordinating family life to production, as is now the case—and thus the most fundamental transformation of capitalism.

Perhaps no value in American life has received stronger institutional expression than education; few societies have been willing to educate so many people for so long at public expense.[41] Like the value of work, education was initially tied to religion, and literacy and morality were inextricably linked. In the eighteenth century, the conception of a liberal education developed—the education of a free person in a republic, a literate, critical, and intellectually independent individual who could comprehend the threat of tyrants and could actively participate in a democratic political process to forge a community and a common purpose. Popular schooling existed "for the purpose of conveying literacy along with a certain common core of knowledge, morality, and patriotism."[42] But in the class-divided society that developed in the early nineteenth century, such an ideal was potentially revolutionary because independent thought and critical awareness might lead to class revolt—as slave-owners always knew. As the public schools expanded, they thus incorporated contradictory goals: societal control and individual emancipation, individual achievement and knowing one's place in the social order. The school was not simply the place where one learned the prerequisites of active citizenship but rather—as with democracy itself—where one learned the behavior appropriate for class-differentiated citizenship.[43]

During the twentieth century, the conversion of education into the primary mechanism for preparing individuals for labor markets has both extended the class divisions of schooling and further undermined the conception of liberal education. Schooling has become essential as a means of access to occupations, and learning itself is prized almost exclusively for its economic benefits. The prominence of schooling as a credential in the post–World War II period testifies both to the usefulness of schooling for individual advancement and to its intrinsic uselessness; the extraordinary commitment to education has simultaneously become a process of corrupting education. Older conceptions of liberal education have been eliminated at every level of schooling (including higher education) in favor of vocational conceptions. The alternative—to reestablish education as the elaboration of critical and creative processes—will require redefining education so that its primary concerns are no longer social control and individual economic gain. Such a redefinition in turn implies that we should cease to evaluate schooling by rates of return and reduce the exclusive emphasis on vocational goals. To fulfill the promise of education as a valued American ideal means reasserting literacy and critical thinking as the necessary attributes of any free individual, and reorienting all of schooling toward this goal.

The expectation that education would create free citizens has reflected still another value central to American life—a sense of community, the community to which citizens dedicate their energies. Since the first seventeenth-century settlements, Americans have defined their society as a "city on a hill," a special nation knit together by the promise of plenty, democracy, manifest destiny, and the heterogeneity of the melting pot. Obviously, the ideal was limited: not everyone enjoyed access to plenty, democratic power was not equally distributed, races and ethnic groups were coerced (where they resisted) into assimilation or were excluded. Yet the assertion of America as a community, a land where all could identify with one another, has remained a fundamental ideal. When social conditions suggested that the ideal was not being reached, individuals across the ideological spectrum have lamented that fact, conservatives bemoaning a community long past and liberals and radicals blaming the destruction of community on capitalism. Both laments have been right: colonial communities and small towns were often societies of mutual responsibility (in part because they made "strangers" so unwelcome) and so corresponded roughly to our notions, often romanticized, of community. But they were also societies in which elaborate social institutions dominated individual interest and enforced social responsibilities, and so were incompatible with the exalted privacy rights and individual freedoms of entrepreneurial capitalism.[44]

In place of mutual responsibility and dedication to the common good of older American ideals, corrupted conceptions of community have emerged which are more consistent with self-interest and individualism. One form of community is epitomized by the segregated upper-class suburb and the "community school." Both of them attempt to establish a community as a grouping of individuals (usually white) of similar class and homogeneous values, dedicated to privatism and investing as little as possible in public functions that support "others." The notion of community as the setting for people similar to one another has obviated the need to redistribute income to those who are poorer or to argue the appropriate conception of public responsibility. The difficulty of establishing public responsibilities—for children or any other group of individuals—has thus come partly from an inability to conceive of heterogeneous communities that encompass all individuals and within which public action considers the interests of all rather than the self-interest of a few selected individuals.

More progressive conceptions of community are difficult to find across the American landscape. The colonial communities that Americans take as ideals, a few utopian experiments like the Shakers, some other rigidly defined groupings like the Amish and the Hassidic communities, and more recent communal experiments that most Americans consider deviant are the only real models available. Nonetheless, the American ideal can be rather simply stated: it requires interpreting community as collectively formed by the participation of its members, in which the collective good supersedes the jousting for individual gain. According to this model, all individuals perceive themselves as better off for supporting the community, and constant critical evaluation and reformation replaces the mindless complacency of right-wing patriots and Chambers of Commerce. This alternative—the attempt to resurrect lost conceptions of civic responsibility—will not be easy to achieve. But as a goal it at least gives meaning to the historic search for community, and allows us to recognize when the call for community and common purpose supports selfish and exclusionary goals.

Finally, Americans have held a common set of values about children. They have persisted in viewing themselves as "child-centered," and have often acted on an ideal of disinterested behavior which suggests that Americans would like to provide as well as they can for the next generation. The sense of protectiveness of children and the motivation of child saving behind many reform movements have expressed truly humanitarian motives, consistent both with an ethic of social improvement through children and with a sense of community in extending to children all possible social benefits. Even the utilitarian expressions of child saving—the rhetoric of children as "our most precious natural resources"—indicate a concern for children which is potentially disinterested. The notion of allowing every child to develop "to the limits of his or her potential" expresses a concern for the well-being of children themselves, altruistic, benevolent and the most forceful expression of liberalism is the insistence that we should free all children to develop their essential capacities.

The ideals for children that Americans have consistently articulated have been relatively free of the corruptions that capitalism has inflicted on conceptions of liberalism, democracy, work, intimacy, and community. The problems have come in implementing these ideals: the real benevolence underlying reform movements and children's institutions has too quickly been converted to controlling impulses. Time and again efforts to "save the child" have been subverted by the conception of children as private responsibilities and the inherent limitations of *parens patriae*, class divisions, and hostility toward other people's children. The professional ethic of disinterested service, noble on its face, has been compromised by the drive for professional power and status. The private family, *parens patriae*, the discontinuity between public and private spheres, exaltation of capitalist labor markets and private profit, and class-based conceptions of children have corrupted our noblest aspirations for each suc-

295

ceeding generation. If we are to recapture our ideals for children and give them real content, the conditions that have so compromised those ideals must be changed.

The search for enduring American values need not stop here; there are others—religious values, ethical values, meritocratic ideals, perhaps aesthetic values—that we could explore as the normative basis for future transformations. However, those we have discussed so far—liberalism, democracy, the meaning of work, familial love, education, community, and the special position of children—are sufficient to establish the important point: they are specific values enunciated relatively early in American history, widely held by Americans, which can be used to reconstruct American society. Because these ideals have been corrupted in the course of capitalist development, using them to define progressive transformations requires returning to their original meanings.

Promoting these values, articulated in the seventeenth and eighteenth centuries, should not be understood as an exercise in nostalgia. There is no real alternative to taking our deepest principles from the past; principles become a part of our cultural heritage whose power we cannot escape, no matter how much economic and political practices have been at variance with those ideals.[45] The values we have emphasized were often far from realization even when they were first articulated. Jeffersonian democracy, for example, was hardly democratic when it supported slavery and denied citizenship to women. The colonial ideal of citizens acting in the common good often ran afoul of private interests and an emergent individualism. Yet we remain impressed with the vision of the colonialists and the political documents of the eighteenth century, enunciated in a time before capitalism was well formed, when ownership of capital was more equally distributed than it now is, when class divisions were not as pronounced, and when the individual interests of liberalism and collective interests were more in balance. If there is an element of nostalgia in reaching back to colonial times for basic American principles, it reflects a wish to re-create a society more egalitarian and less class-divided, a society that more nearly balances private interests and public responsibility, individual freedoms and collective decision making, liberalism and democracy.

This re-creation will be no easy task, since it is impossible—despite the nostalgic visions of some conservatives—to return to the small communities and the one-class agricultural economy that generated the earliest American values. The re-creation will be difficult for another reason, by now obvious. The principles we have offered embody at least two attributes: they require relatively egalitarian conditions, in contrast to older conceptions adapted to the class divisions of capitalism; they also require some modification of the intense individualism of nineteenth-century liberalism, particularly by establishing a sense of collective responsibility and an allegiance to community as well as to one's self. Progressive principles therefore require the transformation of capitalism, since capitalism in all of its many forms generates class divisions and inequality and constantly promotes individualism in place of collective responsibility.

Progressive Transformations for Families and Children

The task of reconstructing American institutions and revising the principles that govern political life is obviously immense, indeed never-ending. There are, however, small pieces of that task which can serve as interim goals and which begin to establish new conceptions of liberalism, new democratic forms, and institutions that allow our ideals for children to be fulfilled. The short-run political agenda has already been partly established, since much of the modern liberal program is progressive according to values we have outlined. Full employment, a decent welfare system, and the elimination of racial discrimination are necessary to set many families and children free from the constraints of poverty and economic uncertainty, and to allow the ideal of family life to flourish with its emotional ties free of economic strains. Efforts to eliminate sex discrimination remain necessary not only to minimize an important cause of poverty, but also to promote more egalitarian models of family life and to fulfill the ideal of liberalism in which all individuals (not just men) can fulfill their capacities and interests. As long as incomes remain highly unequal, a variety of publicly provided services—such as health care, child care, and family planning—are necessary for individuals to have real choices over the conditions of their lives. Changing the conditions of work to facilitate family life—through flexible schedules, parental leave, job sharing, and the like—would support family life, by minimizing the strains of employment which often subvert the ideals of familial intimacy. Current efforts to promote limited revisions of employment conditions—through OSHA, for example, and through experiments with job rotation and other mechanisms to make work less stultifying—promote conceptions of work as an intrinsically rewarding experience. The campaigns of child advocates represent efforts to implement public responsibilities for children, in such areas as health screening, health care, nutrition, the protection of children from advertisers and environmental hazards, the reformation of juvenile institutions, and the elimination of school biases. The efforts to develop new forms of parental participation in children's institutions—such as Title I parent councils and the public hearings once required for Title XX social services—may be limited, but they do allow greater participation in public institutions. These changes are necessary to moderate the worst effects of capitalism, and they promote greater equality and greater participation of all people in the institutions that shape their future.[46]

But the liberal agenda, for all its value, rarely goes far enough, and often proceeds in ways that enhance one social value to the detriment of another. For example, changing the income distribution through the tax and transfer system continues the division between private income and public taxes, which makes redistribution so difficult and so conflict-ridden. Redistributive programs also treat work as if it were valuable only for its monetary rewards, ignoring its potential role in providing meaning and a sense of participation. Liberal programs of public employment through CETA do little to alter conceptions of public employment as make-work or to change public perceptions of those in public employment as inadequate. Improved child care and health care for children will inevitably be frustrated as long as they are justified by familial inadequacy. Unless public programs incorporate new conceptions of professionalism, they will strengthen professional authority over families, providing still further ammunition for conservative complaints about government-run families. Much as they represent an advance over *laissez-faire* capitalism, the programs of the welfare state do little to advance economic democracy or political democracy, even though they expand the realm of political (and potentially democratic) decisions, because they do not enhance the participation of recipients.[47] To move toward the ideals outlined in the previous section, more thorough ideological and institutional transformations are necessary than the liberal agenda proposes.

In terms of children, it will first be necessary to replace *parens patriae* with other justifications for children's institutions. Implicit in modern liberal programs is the position that *all* children deserve adequate housing, health, and education. Yet almost invariably the public programs to achieve this ideal require that parents be considered inadequate, families pathological, and the children to be served "unlucky,"[48] with devastating consequences for the programs themselves. Alternatives to *parens patriae* are available, though they are not immediately obvious. One approach, for example, has been the effort of child care advocates to consider child care as a normal service for normal children, with subsidies varying by income (given a society of unequal incomes) but without interpreting subsidies as reflecting inadequacy. Services for crippled and handicapped children provide another partial alternative: in the best of circumstances they are offered without the stigma of parental failure, and the presumption of private responsibility more easily yields to an acceptance of public responsibilities. Finally, the influence of *parens patriae* can be weakened by acknowledging that the conception of the private family is an anachronism and that extensive federal subsidies to upper-income children contradict the image of public recipients as deficient.

One alternative to *parens patriae*, then, is to articulate a set of public responsibilities toward children—for education of a certain kind, for nutrition, for rehabilitative services for crippled children, for health care— with the corollary that public funds are to be allocated to those children most in need but without the current identification of need with parental failure. The process of developing such public responsibilities has already begun, at least implicitly, in the provision of public schooling, AFDC, Medicaid, and food stamps, but the process has been fitful, incomplete, and haphazard. It has invariably been contested as the transference of private income to other people's children. The abandonment of *parens patriae* will not eliminate conflict over public responsibility, especially where differences continue over what children need. But its abandonment can alter, in a self-conscious and explicit way, the stigma and miserliness that constrain public responsibilities for children.

Abandoning *parens patriae* also requires public action to revise professionalism. Professionals in children's institutions have always drawn power and self-definition from the presumption of familial inadequacy. Without this presumption, new conceptions of professionalism are possible—in which childrearing professionals acknowledge the uncertain nature of their expertise, in which they use their abilities and experience to work with "clients" and parents rather than to distance them, and in which professionals act according to their ideal of service rather than in the interest of greater power and status. Revisions along these lines are just barely underway in a few areas of medicine, law, teaching, and child care, and these innovations can provide some information on the prerequisites of "new professionals." Of course, such changes have consistently been challenged by conventional professionals. Particularly in a period of tight professional labor markets and escalating educational levels, there is every incentive to extend the conventional model rather than to revise it. Nonetheless, since most childrearing professionals are in public institutions officially open to political accountability, parents and citizens can assert public control to retain those elements of professionalism that are truly valuable while eliminating the objectional elements.

Beyond these general recommendations to revamp the assumptions underlying children's institutions, we can make more specific recommendations for particular institutions. In the area of schooling, much of the modern liberal agenda—particularly enhancing educational opportunities for minorities and lower-class children and eliminating sexual biases in the curriculum—are necessary if schools are ever to develop individuals to the limits of their capacities. But such reforms do nothing to correct the general degradation of education, which can be reversed only by reshaping education to promote liberal values, the values of free citizens. To do this, it will be necessary to limit the school's vocational purposes, first by eliminating the most obviously vocational parts of the curriculum: the vocational programs and other tracking mechanisms at the elementary and secondary levels, and the purely vocational curricula like business majors, prelaw, and premedicine at the college level. Once the notion of education as being primarily directed toward individual gain has been weakened, then it will be possible to reaffirm the historic purposes of education—literacy, critical citizenship, and possibly the creation of national cohesion and common purpose. Until then, the public roles of education will continue to be corrupted by the use of schools for private gain.

In the area of youth policy, the continued reliance on education and training programs alone is a mistake, given the general failure of such programs during the twentieth century. A more effective approach to the employment problems of young people—and therefore to some part of their unruly and even criminal behavior—is to address the structural causes of high rates of unemployment and underemployment. Revising the biases against young people, eliminating racial discrimination, reducing the demand for credentials which places teen-agers at a disadvantage, upgrading jobs so that the employment available to young people is not so abysmal, and expanding available employment are all more direct and appropriate measures than providing training and assuming that employment opportunities will develop accordingly. They are also more productive than enhancing employer profits through tax credits or through subminimum wages. Of course, these revisions are also more difficult than mounting training programs or offering profit incentives to employers. They require that the nature as well as the amount of employment be subject to public scrutiny; they indicate that the decentralized decisions and profit incentives of free labor markets need modification, for youth as for adults. In the long run, such modifications are part of the process of providing young people with valued roles. Without such provisions, there is no hope whatsoever that Americans can escape the youth problems they now regard as inevitable.

In the area of welfare programs, the limitations of purely redistributive programs (such as AFDC and the Earned Income Tax Credit) in correcting poverty among children have become obvious: not only are they always subject to conservative backlash, in a society where all taxpayers resent the use of their private income to support other people's children, but they also do nothing to encourage the participation of welfare recipients in the productive life of the community or to provide them with work as a source of meaning. The major alternatives—macroeconomic policies to reduce unemployment, public employment programs to create meaningful work directly, and efforts to eliminate race and sex discrimination—have been available for some time, but even under liberal governments their implementation has been uncertain. In the current conservative backlash, they are treated as desecrations of the natural laws of capitalism. It is therefore necessary to implement a more basic principle: since capitalist labor markets generate inequality, discrimination, poverty, and degrading and nonparticipatory work, they must no longer be regarded as sacred and beyond legitimate control by the state. Even with more thorough revisions of labor markets, it will still be necessary to retain purely redistributive programs for the severely disabled, the aged, and single parents with young children, for whom employment and antidiscrimination measures are largely irrelevant. The essential goal for those remaining redistributive programs is to integrate them into programs that are considered normal—for example, through negative income tax plans—so as to reduce the stigma of *parens patriae* and the intrusive power of the state.

In early childhood programs, both child care and parent education provide opportunities to create extraordinarily rich institutions that stimulate the development of children, relieve the stresses of family life and the uncertainties of parenting, reduce the isolation of the nuclear family, and form new communities around children. In the process of developing these possibilities, Americans will have to revise their justifications for children's institutions, the dominant conceptions of professionals, and sexual stereotypes about the appropriate roles of mothers and fathers, parents and professionals. These changes are already underway, even though they threaten at all times to disappear under the weight of conventional assumptions. It remains to create the conditions that encourage these changes in early childhood programs and to extend them to other children's institutions so that new models of child care and parent education are not buried by the practices of better-established and politically more powerful programs.

The proposals we offer to fulfill the promises Americans have consistently held out to children are sweeping, but they are still consistent with prevailing norms. The benevolence and humanitarianism implicit in *parens patriae*, the concern and expertise of professionals, the ideals of public education, the aspirations that youth should have fulfilling roles, the protection of the poorest children are all issues upon which the overwhelming majority of Americans have agreed. But to fulfill those promises requires looking beyond children's institutions and families to necessary transformations in the economic and political system—in macroeconomic policy, in the relationship between public and private ownership and employment, and in economic and political democracy. Ultimately, reforms to improve children's institutions or to strengthen families will lack much content without these larger transformations.

No matter who owns or controls large units of production, macroeconomic policy will remain critical to the welfare of the populace. Macroeconomic policy can, as is currently the case with conservative "supply-side" policies, strengthen the familiar mechanisms of capitalism, using public funds to subsidize profits and reducing public regulation of corporations. In the same fashion, macroeconomic policy can be used to formulate sector-specific policies—in the energy, steel, or automobile industries, for example—which rely on the decentralized and self-interested decisions of oligopolistic corporations, always searching for new forms of monopoly power, or it can develop mechanisms of national planning which simply replicate the power of existing corporations. However, this approach will only reproduce inegalitarian economic and social patterns. It is highly unlikely to reintroduce prosperity except in its most inegalitarian form. The conservative approach to macroeconomic policy—expanding the state to enhance rather than curb the power of corporations—will harm children indirectly, by maintaining unemployment and inequality; it will also undercut public support for children by labeling them as unproductive and wasteful, as the attacks on children's programs in Ronald Reagan's macroeconomic program illustrate.

The alternative is to use progressive principles to judge macroeconomic policy, making sure that it is relatively equitable in distributing the burdens of adjusting to new economic conditions rather than placing the burdens on the poor as has occurred in the Reagan administration. Rather than reproducing capitalist practices, a progressive macroeconomic policy would replace corporate and market-based decisions—inevitably undemocratic and socially costly, stifling widespread participation in economic decision making—with public and democratic decisions. Sector-specific policies and national planning must in similar ways develop a conception of the common good, rather than continuing to define the common good as the interests of those with the greatest political power. In macroeconomic policy, the fundamental issues of who controls the state and for what interests must be of dominant concern, or we will collectively continue to work toward prosperity in its capitalist version. For many children that is no prosperity at all, and for all children it means the continued degradation of their institutions and the American values embedded within them.

Urging a more activist and egalitarian macroeconomic policy in a capitalist society is itself filled with contradictions. The strategy of promoting public goals through the cooperation of self-interested corporations, particularly by enhancing private profits in the public interest—an idea that both conservatives and modern liberals have adopted—is not necessarily logically impossible, but its outcome has been uncertain; tax incentives are likely to be ineffective or abused, firms maximizing their own profits have been infinitely devious in getting around government regulation, and political pressure to undo government restraints has been the most logical and most profitable path for corporations. The alternatives, as European countries have already realized, has been to replace private ownership and private profit making with public ownership and public goal setting, particularly for crucial sectors of the economy like transportation, energy, and raw materials. Public ownership does not eliminate some central problems of the large corporation, of course—including the problems of efficiency and productivity, of forecasting demand and capital needs, of developing appropriate technologies. Public ownership also creates the danger of "corporate socialism," in which public ownership makes economic decisions and distributes social goods just as corporate capitalism does. But there are other problems whose solutions are enormously facilitated by public ownership: social evils such as pollution and dangerous job conditions (externalities, to economists) can be more easily minimized; attempts to create better working conditions can be more easily explored; worker participation is more readily introduced, without the fear that worker control will undermine the prerogatives of private capital. National planning, national investment decisions, and national security interests are all facilitated.

As in Europe, the opportunities for public ownership will arrive in different ways—through the near-failure of giant corporations, as has happened in this country with some railroads; through the demands of defense production suggesting nationalization of key industries; during particular crises affecting the American economy, as in the current energy crisis which has led to proposals to nationalize energy companies and to establish a public corporation to develop oil and gas on public lands. However, Americans have never taken full advantage of these opportunities, or they have twisted them into forms serving private interests. The takeover of the railroads reinforced the notion that public ownership should be burdened with the failures—the "lemons"—of private capital, giving the impression that the public sector is inefficient and creating "lemon socialism." Wartime crises and defense production have been used to enhance the profits of private companies even as they worked in the "public interest." The attempt to develop a coherent energy policy has resulted only in higher profits for existing corporations, benefiting from the high oil prices established by OPEC without increasing the supply of domestic energy. As in the case of macroeconomic policy, it will be necessary to develop conceptions of public ownership which serve the public interest rather than corporate goals. Many appropriate opportunities exist for public ownership, even if they are not ubiquitous and even if public ownership remains restricted in scope. The European experiences provide guides as to ways to make public corporations efficient and warnings to prevent their deterioration into corporate socialism. Only by taking advantage of these opportunities can we resurrect the principle of the common good, and eliminate the individualism and privatism that so consistently undermine our promises to children.

Just as public corporations can be used to allocate resources and produce goods according to public goals rather than private profits, public employment provides a way to allocate labor in ways free from the problems of capitalist labor markets. Public employment must not be considered, as has been assumed under CETA, as employment of last resort for the least desirable members of the labor force, nor as an indirect way for the federal government to subsidize local governments, nor as a disguised mechanism of "workfare." Rather, public employment must be thought of as a mechanism of allocating underutilized labor to the production of valued goods and services. Public employment can then furnish meaningful employment, provide a basis for developing new conceptions of job organization, and—perhaps the most important of all, at least in the short run—serve to eliminate poverty in ways that also promote work as a source of meaning and social participation. Public employment can also produce valued goods and services in short supply—housing for the poor, parks, social services for the young, old, and handicapped, the renovation of deteriorating public facilities including railroads and ports, and the reconstruction of central cities. But as long as it is subordinated to private labor markets none of these potential outcomes will materialize. Freed from these constraints, public employment can provide meaningful work to youth as well as adults, enhance participation, reduce poverty, and improve services to children.

Finally, it is necessary to reconstruct democracy, for without revising our understanding and practice of democracy, it is hard to imagine how our promises to give children a better life can be fulfilled. As we have argued, different forms of democracy are linked through social attitudes towards participation. The undemocratic employment practices of capitalism, where workers typically have no control whatsoever in the decisions that affect their employment, generate a citizenry for whom political participation is limited and easily manipulated by the media and other external influences. On a larger level, capitalism has fostered conceptions of democracy which celebrate low participation and which view democracy in marketlike ways. The forms of political democracy which are participatory and egalitarian therefore require economic democracy as well.[49] In place of the lack of participation and control typical of workers under capitalism, an economic system in which workers can participate in the decisions that affect their employment will at the very least promote job satisfaction, essential to family life. Workplace democracy will also enhance political participation and thus help reverse nonparticipatory forms of political democracy. In its most hopeful version, workplace democracy will reduce the divisions of class, by eliminating the stark contrast between manager and workers and by reversing the process of degrading work which strips jobs of their skills and meaning.[50] Beyond these instrumental justifications, workplace democracy is valuable in its own right, a necessary aspect of intrinsically satisfying conceptions of work and the liberal principle that free individuals must have some control over all aspects of their lives.

As in the case of public ownership, workplace democracy may emerge under different conditions. Plant closings have provided some opportunities for workers (and communities) to take ownership. Public aid to corporations can be used to require greater work control; admittedly a partial gesture, the *quid pro quo* worked out between the Chrysler Corporation and the United Auto Workers Union to place a union representative on the corporation's board as a precondition for government aid suggests a way to generate more democratic control of corporations. As in the case of public ownership, the European experiences with codetermination can provide some guide to the effectiveness of giving labor a place on corporate boards. Even though federal research and demonstration projects to guide job reorganization are relatively weak compared to the magnitude of the problem, they are an obvious place to begin.[51] OSHA provides a potentially valuable model for using state power to correct damaging job conditions, one that could be extended beyond the physical effects of work to the psychological effects, including damage to self-esteem, family relations, and sense of social participation. In other cases, we can use the principle of participation in decision making to see why some reforms are not especially progressive; for example, Peter Drucker's claim that we now have a form of "pension-fund socialism" because workers own a great deal of stock in American corporations is absurd because stock ownership promotes neither control nor participation.[52] Although the various proposals to establish worker control and revise class divisions remain largely undeveloped and untried, they make it clear that there is no dearth of mechanisms to begin revising class boundaries. The serious barrier remains the political problem of putting economic democracy and class differences on the national agenda. Until this is done, it will remain impossible to correct the inequalities that affect so many children's lives, to implement truly progressive conceptions of work, or to develop participatory forms of democracy.

In the long run, none of the economic and social transformations we propose will promote progressive ideals if we do not simultaneously reformulate political democracy. Democratic mechanisms are the only way of achieving progressive resolution of existing problems.[53] Yet the flaws in American democracy are now so serious as to undermine the potential for developing a truly liberal society. The limits on participation, the inequality of political power, the inadequacies of interest group representation (especially for children), and the conception of democracy in which self-interest dominates all principles have produced a form of democracy that retards progressive social and economic policies. The process of revising democratic mechanisms is to some extent underway. The efforts to increase the political visibility and power of women through the women's movement, the successful efforts to form consumer and environmental groups, and more powerful neighborhood organizations attest to the power of participatory democracy.[54] The examples of participatory democracy are heartening, particularly in the face of a long slide toward less representative forms of democracy; they illustrate once again that the opportunities for progressive reform are everywhere available.

The problem is that the various transformations we propose are all interrelated. Replacing *parens patriae* requires changing the conception of the private family, and that in turn requires a world where individuals can be sure that leaving the private family behind will not subject them to the cruelties of a "heartless world." For parents to abandon the use of public institutions for the private goals of their own children requires a conviction that public institutions will treat one's child decently, and requires the elimination of class boundaries and class hostility. Devising new conceptions of professionals requires the elimination of *parens patriae*, the development of public institutions which are truly benevolent rather than controlling, and the diminution of class divisions. The development of new economic institutions, designed to foster the intrinsic values of work and to reduce class divisions, depends on mounting a sustained political attack against those who would maintain capitalist institutions at all costs, which in turn requires a more active and participatory concept of democracy. The development of more participatory democratic mechanisms depends on more participatory forms of work and a more egalitarian class structure. Using the state to revise class barriers depends upon a conception of public power that can emerge fully only in a relatively egalitarian society in which individuals need not be constantly defending their private prerogatives against incursions by others. Because economic, political, social, and ideological institutions are so interdependent, it is difficult to know where to begin the process of conscious change.

At a time of conservatism and demoralization of liberals and radicals, our call for progressive transformations may seem wistful and naive. Nonetheless, we believe that in every area of economic and social policy there are more possibilities for progressive change than most Americans recognize. Every period of "crisis" is simultaneously a period of possibility, startling us out of old patterns, awakening us to problems which may not have been quite so obvious in more stable times, presenting new problems, and forcing us to develop new responses to old issues. Whether our responses are conscious, principled, and designed to resolve social problems without the ambiguities that have always marked the efforts of the state—whether it is possible to generate a "family policy" that is consistent and thorough, whether it is possible to reform children's institutions in ways that conform to our deepest ideals for children, and whether we can resurrect uncorrupted versions of the principles on which the United States was founded—remain the central issues. The outcomes will determine both the kind of society we live in as adults and our abilities to fulfill public promises to children.

POSTSCRIPT
Let Them Eat Ketchup:
The Plight of Children in the 1980s

THE 1980s have been rough on children. Poverty increased substantially, while government programs to protect children from destitution and to educate them have been cut. Educational reforms neglected many children, public support for early childhood programs dwindled, and the juvenile justice system became more punitive, less concerned with development and rehabilitation. A mounting federal deficit made it impossible to address any of the other pressing needs of children—the need for basic health care and nutrition, for better child protective services and foster care, for better education for the poor. As incomplete as programs for children were in the 1970s, they grew worse during the 1980s. The changes illustrate all too well the deeply-rooted limitations of what our government has done for children.

How the 1980s Have Harmed Children[1]

The most alarming development during the 1980s was the rise of poverty. The rate among children, as defined by the federal government, was halved during the 1960s, falling from 26.9 percent in 1959 to 13.8 percent in 1969. As the economy began to slip in the 1970s, poverty increased slightly to 16 percent in 1979. (During the same period poverty among the elderly fell from 25 percent to 15 percent because of expanding government programs, and the rate for other adults stayed roughly constant at around 9 percent.) Recession became more acute during the 1980s, as the Federal Reserve, with the blessing of the Reagan administration, deliberately engineered a slump to reduce inflation. The result was that poverty among children rose to a high of 21.8 percent in 1983, and about 3.5 million more children fell into poverty in just four years. When the recession eased, the rate dropped back to 19.8 percent in 1986, but the damage had been done: the rate in 1986 was worse than it had been in 1966. For some children, the figures are even more appalling: 42.7 percent of black children, 37.1 percent of Hispanic children, and 54.4 percent of children living only with their mothers were poor in 1986.

Dismal as they are, these trends have still been disputed, particularly since the definition of poverty has always been arbitrary. Fiscal conservatives have often complained that the official statistics are unnecessarily gloomy because they do not include some welfare benefits, like food stamps, Medicaid, and public housing. Martin Anderson, one of President Reagan's advisors on welfare, went so far as to claim that "the war on poverty has been won" because economic growth and income transfer programs have "virtually eliminated poverty."[2] But the official poverty standard also fails to subtract taxes—which, until the tax changes of 1986, were increasing more rapidly for the poor than for any group—and neglects changes in consumption patterns since the standard was established. It is also based on a food budget designed "for temporary or emergency use when funds are low"; only 10 percent of people whose food expenditures equal the cost of the plan can meet the Department of Agriculture's recommended daily allowances for basic nutrients.[3] Recalculating the poverty rate among children in 1982, when the official rate was 21.9 percent, yields a figure of 19.8 percent when various in-kind benefits are included and taxes are subtracted—depressingly far from a "virtual elimination" of childhood poverty. When more generous conceptions are used, a much higher figure of 27.7 percent is the result.[4] And no matter how poverty is defined, the trend is the same—up.

The causes of increasing need are not at all mysterious. The first of these is demographic: more children live with their mothers, rather than with both parents, because of increasing divorce, separation, and births out of marriage (including those to teenagers). In 1970, 10.8 percent of all children were living in female-headed families; by 1984 this proportion had nearly doubled to 20.4 percent. This group has the resources of only one parent rather than two, and mothers earn less than fathers—so these children are over four times as likely as others to be poor. The world of childhood is splitting into two: those with both parents usually stay out of poverty, while more than one half of the growing number of children living with their mothers are in need.

The second reason for the increasing problem among children is economic. Real earnings have decreased since the 1960s, pushing more families into poverty. The distribution of earnings has also become more unequal (particularly for males) since the late 1960s, so that relatively more earners have wages too low to protect their families.[5] These shifts are rooted in sweeping economic developments that are not yet clearly understood, but international competition, sectoral shifts, and the growth of part-time work are among the culprits. Increasing inequality also means that economic growth, the most popular antidote to poverty, doesn't benefit many of those in greatest need, especially mothers and their children. As the economy improved after 1983, commentators celebrated the strength of the recovery—but the poverty rate for children in families headed by women hardly budged at all, falling only 1 percentage point from 55.4 in 1983 to 54.2 percent in 1986. These economic changes, often left out of public discussions, have made the problem a moving target: in the absence of any welfare programs poverty would have increased about one third between 1973 and 1984.[6]

The final cause of the problem among children is the declining effectiveness of government programs. Ronald Reagan, taking office with a pledge to reduce the size of government, promised in his inaugural address that cuts in spending would be "equitable, with no one group singled out to pay a higher price." One month later he promised that "our spending cuts will not be at the expense of the truly needy", outlining the "social safety net" of programs exempt from any cuts: Social Security, Medicare, veterans' pensions, Supplemental Security Income (for the aged, blind, and disabled), school breakfasts and lunches for low-income children, nutrition services for the elderly, Head Start, and Summer Youth Employment. It was immediately clear that children were in trouble. Only 2 percent of the cost of the "safety net" programs were for children, and their three basic support programs—AFDC, Medicaid, and food stamps—were missing from the restricted list of programs immune from cuts. Even so, Reagan reneged on his promises. In its 1982 budget the administration proposed cuts of 50 percent in child nutrition programs, mostly from school breakfast and lunch, and eliminated separate authorization for Summer Youth Employment.

For 1982, Reagan proposed reducing AFDC by 17 percent, food stamps by 16 percent, and Medicaid by 11 percent. Planned cuts in categorical programs for children were even more drastic: 36 percent for WIC (Women, Infants, and Children, a nutrition program for pregnant women and small children), 50 percent for child nutrition, 27 percent for various child health programs, 38 percent for compensatory education, 35 percent for the education of handicapped children, 35 percent for bilingual education, and 45 percent for Job Corps and youth employment programs.[7] Congress, bamboozled into a frantic and complex legislative process that allowed no time for reflection, ratified most of these cuts.

Additional cuts were planned for 1983: another 18 percent in AFDC, 19 percent in food stamps, 11 percent in Medicaid, 33 percent in compensatory education, 32 percent in bilingual education, 33 percent in WIC, and an additional 10 percent in other child nutrition. But by the time these plans got to Capitol Hill, Congress had come back to life. Numerous discrepancies emerged in the administration's proposals. Reagan claimed his cuts in food stamps would not hurt the "truly needy," but the Congressional Budget Office said that 94 percent of the working poor would have their benefits terminated. Reports of children who were hungry, homeless, neglected, and abused began to pour in.

Cuts in food programs—particularly in WIC and school lunches—provoked the strongest outcry. When the Reagan administration proposed regulations to reduce the amount of food provided in school lunches, Nancy Amidei of the Food Research and Action Center brought three trays of food to congressional hearings. One held a pre-Reagan lunch: a two-ounce hamburger with a bun, two kinds of vegetables, and eight ounces of milk. The proposed reductions in serving size shrank the hamburger to 1 1/2 ounces on half of a bun; six french fries, nine grapes, and six ounces of milk completed the meal. The third tray showed the effects of new nutritional standards: it contained cake instead of bread, and four tablespoons of relish instead of vegetables or fruit. Administration officials branded her caricature of rule allowing ketchup to substitute for vegetables as exaggerated, which it was. The greater drawback was that the proposed rules allowed the new "mini-meals" to provide only 17 percent of a child's daily calorie needs, rather than 33 percent. But the proposed regulations, quickly withdrawn, became a vivid symbol for those who felt that the Reagan program for children offended both common decency and common sense.

Of the $9 billion in cuts proposed for 1983, Congress approved only $1 billion. Undaunted, the Reagan administration continued to press for cuts in children's programs for 1984—9 percent in AFDC, 7 percent in food stamps, another 9 percent in child nutrition—in what had become an annual ritual, recycling dozens of proposals rejected by Congress earlier. This pattern continued throughout the Reagan years. As late as 1988, after four years of having most spending cuts rejected by Congress, the administration proposed further cuts of 4.5 percent in AFDC, 2.3 percent in food stamps, 16.9 percent in child nutrition (a favorite target, despite the earlier promises about a "safety net"), 4.5 percent in Medicaid, and 31.1 percent in education.[8]

Although the torrent of Reagan budget reductions was stemmed by Congress, the 1981 and 1982 cuts were enough to cause substantial hardship. Slow increases in real spending since 1982 have been unable to restore the earlier cuts, and expenditures for the poor as of 1987 were 7.4 percent lower than in 1981—during a period when the number of poor children increased.[9] Children have borne the heaviest burden of reductions: while human resource programs overall were cut by 7 percent between 1982 and 1985, AFDC was cut by 13 percent, food stamps by 13 percent, children's nutrition programs by 28 percent, compensatory education by 17 percent, bilingual education by 30 percent, and other health services by 22 percent—all changes in programs that were already inadequate.[10]

The consequences of these reductions, during a period of increasing unemployment and poverty, were easy to predict. The General Accounting Office estimated that half a million families were eliminated from AFDC; they then lost access to Medicaid and other health programs. Many more had their food stamps cut or eliminated, and access to other nutrition and health programs became more difficult. For these children, life became precarious; a caseworker examining the effects of budget cuts described the "four to six month fallout syndrome" affecting mothers cut from AFDC:

> Victims of budget cuts hold their own for a few months, but a very fragile situation deteriorates over several months. First the children lose welfare and Medicaid benefits, the mother tries to continue working, but finds the money isn't enough. The family loses its phone, then the utility shutoff notices arrive. They start to borrow money. The parent takes a second job. Child care costs increase, and the mother is always tired. She never sees her kids anymore, and she still can't pay the bills. If one child gets even mildly ill, the whole situation may collapse. *These families are time bombs waiting for one small trigger to set off disaster.*[11]

Reductions in nutrition and health programs had some of the most obvious effects. In 1982, the trickle of reports about the reappearance of hunger swelled to a torrent. Food banks, soup kitchens, and food pantries—institutions best remembered from the Great Depression of the 1930s—appeared and expanded. Families began using these emergency sources, especially those whose unemployment benefits had run out or who found themselves without food stamps at the end of the month. Mayors in many cities reported inadequacies in their emergency food programs, finding new evidence of malnutrition and related health problems including low birth weight babies and infant mortality. Across the

country, improvements in infant mortality (long used as a summary indicator of maternal and child health) slowed. In some cities—including
Detroit, Pontiac, Flint (all hurt by the declining fortunes of the auto industry), Louisville, Milwaukee, Richmond, Indianapolis, and Los Angeles—infant mortality even began to rise, after several decades of steady
decline.[12] More instances of "failure to thrive" were reported by nurses
and pediatricians, and extreme cases of hunger surfaced in hospital emergency rooms and health clinics, including cases of "water intoxication"
caused by parents over-diluting baby formula to make it last longer. The
Citizen's Commission on Hunger in New England identified the problem:

> It is now 1984. Hunger has returned to America . . . Hunger returned as
> the result of governmental will and the weakening of programs that once
> worked so well . . . It returned under official watch as our leaders ignored
> the serious health threat it is to our nation.[13]

Other indicators of hardship were the reports of increasing child abuse.
The combination of higher poverty and dwindling public resources increased the stress within families, with sad consequences for children. In
Massachusetts, one social worker seeing more abused children articulated
the relationship between stress and abuse:

> The families closest to the edge feel the pressure first and worse . . . We
> see more abuse cases because some of our clients cannot afford a babysitter.
> The Work and Training Program has put a lot of pressure on mothers . . .
> More and more families are requesting foster care. Children are often scape-
> goated as a result of the outside pressure. Often families will ask for place-
> ment of just one child—the one who is acting out—and often a placement
> is not warranted.[14]

Many states reported more parents voluntarily giving up their children
to foster care, because they were no longer able to provide them with the
bare necessities. As one mother in California described her decision:

> I never thought that things would get this bad. I had to take my little girl
> to the welfare office and tell them that I couldn't take care of her, my own
> baby. But I was out of work and couldn't get welfare and there was no heat
> in the apartment because I didn't have the money to have the gas turned
> on and there was no food and I was worried that she would die from the
> cold and always be hungry. She started getting real slow and sleepy and I
> knew that I had to do something, and I didn't know what else to do. So I
> had to take her to that place and they arranged a foster home for her, but I
> don't know when I will get her back because I'm still just as broke and
> with no idea when things will be getting any better.[15]

Starting in 1985, in the midst of a much-celebrated economic recovery from the 1982–83 recession, the problem of homelessness garnered national attention. No longer were the homeless exclusively single men, derelicts, and junkies; increasingly those running shelters reported families with children on the streets, the victims of reductions in welfare programs as well as consistent cuts in federal funds for housing.

Each of these problems is disturbing not only because of the suffering of the children involved, but also because every extreme example is evidence of many more cases in which the problem has not become serious enough to provoke public attention. For every case of malnutrition that comes to an emergency room, there are more hungry children whose development may be retarded; for every baby who dies, many others are born underweight, or suffering from birth defects, respiratory ailments, and other health problems. For every case of child abuse that reaches the papers, there are many other parents and children living under undue stress, "time bombs waiting for one small trigger to set off disaster"; for every parent relinquishing a child to foster care, many others are just short of making this desperate move.

More "scientific" and less anecdotal evidence has confirmed the erosion of programs for poor children. The maximum AFDC benefit for a family of four, adjusted for inflation, fell 33 percent between 1970 and 1985.[16] The average cash transfer received by ready two-parent families fell 26 percent between 1973 and 1984, while the decrease was 37 percent for female-headed families, those with the fewest resources to start with.[17] With these and other cuts, the effectiveness of government programs in delivering children from poverty declined markedly. In 1973 cash transfers moved 24.7 percent of poor individuals in families with children out of poverty; by 1984 this had fallen by more than one third, to 18.7 percent. For children living with their mothers only—the group at greatest risk—the decline was even more drastic: The effectiveness of government programs fell by one half during this period—only 12 percent of poor individuals moved out of poverty, down from 24 percent.

The harsh treatment of children during the 1980s has been most obviously reflected in increasing poverty rates and declining welfare programs, but many other developments have reinforced the sense that children and youth are faring badly. Beginning in 1983, a movement for "excellence" in education energized the schools, quite rightly pointing out the deteriorating quality of American education and setting in motion a complex set of reforms. Some states increased academic requirements and developed new exit exams for graduation, and teachers reported increasing standards in the classroom. But many children were left out of these initial reforms, despite brave rhetoric promising to combine "excellence" with equity. The federal government had whacked away at the major programs for children with special needs—compensatory education, bilingual education, and education for the handicapped. The Reagan administration had also weakened the enforcement of laws governing equality of educational opportunity. The Office of Civil Rights of the Department of Education moved from enforcing civil rights laws to a voluntary compliance system. Because of its stress on voluntarism, it accepted large numbers of inadequate remedial plans, and refused to withhold federal funds from institutions that did not correct discriminatory practices. The Justice Department reinforced this neglect of equal opportunity statutes by opposing all desegregation orders, even those voluntarily adopted by school districts.[18] Minority children could count on little help from the federal government for their educational efforts.

In the few states that provided additional support for compensatory programs, tutorials, and other forms of educational aid, these efforts were often meager and failed to grapple with the basic deficiencies of the schools.[19] The state reforms came at a time of increasing dropout rates, and many feared that the changes would only worsen that problem. The modifications were necessary but too often lopsided: they provided sticks but no carrots, and neglected the special needs of those children who have been served badly by the schools.

For small children, who are increasingly in child care as more mothers have gone to work, the developments of the 1980s were no better. During the Reagan administration, any thought of federal support for child care was out of the question; funds for social services were cut by 29 percent between 1981 and 1987, and space for low-income children was reduced in almost every state.[20] A sense of crisis began to develop: the wages of child care workers, which average no more than the poverty line, are so low that serious shortages have developed and turnover has soared. Many communities under pressure formed commissions to study their options, and several states have enacted pilot preschool programs, but few of these efforts have generated real resources. Child care advocates pressed harder for support from corporations, but found only how chary big business is with its funds.[21] At the same time, a consciousness of the need for high-quality care has spread, and public debates now stress the positive consequences for low-income children of good early childhood programs. For child care providers, caught between dwindling resources and increased demands for quality, there was no way to respond to the conflicting demands. The sense of movement and development prevailing during the 1970s gave way to feelings of desperation.

The negative attitude toward young people during the 1980s became most obvious in the juvenile justice system, which grew increasingly punitive. Arrests of juveniles fell because the youth cohort was smaller; the rate at which young people were arrested also fell, while the rate of violent crime remained roughly constant. But the public seemed to believe that there was more juvenile crime rather than less; the system became more formal and restrictive, and oriented toward punishment rather than rehabilitation. The proportion of youth arrested who were referred to juvenile courts instead of being handled informally by law enforcement agencies increased; the proportion referred to adult courts increased. The average length of detention increased, leading to more juveniles in detention centers despite declining arrests; and admissions to training schools and lengths of stay there increased. The movement to decriminalize and deinstitutionalize status offenders, active in the 1960s and 1970s, lost steam, and many people called for status offenders to be brought back into the juvenile justice system. The abuses that had been identified earlier—the cruel treatment in many facilities and overcrowding in training schools, inappropriate placements in detention centers without facilities or programs for extended stays, and the lack of educational programs and constructive activities—continued more or less unabated.[22]

The Reagan administration signaled its position in the report of the National Advisory Committee for Juvenile Crime and Delinquency Prevention, *Serious Juvenile Crime: A Redirected Federal Effort*. The Committee recommended focusing on the "serious, violent, or chronic offender" and rejected basic aspects of the Juvenile Justice and Delinquency Prevention Act of 1974, especially grants to states for deinstitutionalization and for removing juveniles from adult jails. The Reagan administration repeatedly tried to eliminate the budget for the JJDPA, which has funded (if inadequately) many reforms and pilot programs. With the lack of federal direction, leadership in juvenile justice passed to the states. Some, like Utah and Massachusetts, developed model programs which carefully tried to distinguish serious offenders from others, to incarcerate the first group but provide treatment and education for the second. But many others— including California, which had earlier been the leader in juvenile justice reforms—became increasingly punitive.

Other changes affecting children were indirect. Efforts to reduce racial and gender-based discrimination in employment are important, because poverty is so much higher among black and Hispanic children and among those dependent on their mothers for support. But federal efforts to reduce discrimination, which had made real progress under President Carter, were consistently undermined during the Reagan administration. The staff of the Equal Employment Opportunity Commission was reduced, and the Commission began to pursue individual complaints (a time-consuming and ineffective approach) rather than charges of systematic discrimination. The Office of Federal Contract Compliance reduced its monitoring of all but the largest employers and diluted the punishment of those found guilty of discrimination. With a majority of new members appointed by Reagan, the U.S. Commission on Civil Rights, formerly an independent and powerful voice supporting civil rights, replaced many long-standing policies with those hostile to the legal rights of minorities, women, and other protected groups. Civil rights offices within federal departments, like education and agriculture, were similarly weakened.[23] The consistency of these actions was powerful: if children were victims of discrimination, direct or indirect, they could count on no help from the federal government.

Elsewhere children and youth were exposed to the full force of American consumerism, often with disastrous results. The decision of the Federal Trade Commission in 1983 to abandon its regulation of children's programming led to new and more creative ways of exploiting their gullibility. Starting with the Strawberry Shortcake programs, a series of shows developed featuring the exploits of heroes and heroines—many of them violent or perpetuating sexist stereotypes (Rambo, G. I. Joe, She-Ra and He-Man, Jem, the Thundercats, the Transformers, the Smurfs)—which were essentially extended commercials for toys. The constraints on advertising aimed at children, which had developed during the 1970s to limit the most misleading practices and the amount of advertising, fell apart. The sense that we as a nation ought to protect children and youth from the excesses of our culture vanished. Children had become consumers just like anyone else, easy prey for deceit, manipulation, and exploitation.

Rethinking Public Responsibility

If, as *Broken Promises* argues, the programs of the 1960s and 1970s were contradictory and inadequate, those of the 1980s have been much worse. Some reasons for this shift are obvious. Many changes, especially the decline in federal spending for children, reflected the old debate over "guns versus butter." The Reagan administration expanded defense spending enormously at the expense of social programs: in real terms programs for low-income families and children fell 78.4 percent between 1981 and 1987, while defense spending increased 36 percent to $1.6 billion. The size of the defense budget became so unfathomable, and the imbalance between defense spending and social spending so outlandish, that the Children's Defense Fund began counting in terms of missiles and tanks rather than dollars:

> For each [MX] missile we cancel, we could eliminate poverty for 101,000 female-headed families for one year. If we eliminated the whole program, we could eliminate poverty for all children *twice over* and have enough left to send all female heads of low-income families to college for a year.[24]

A double standard developed. Conservatives castigated welfare programs for fraud, waste, and ineffectiveness at precisely the time when good evidence about the benefits of welfare, nutrition programs, early childhood programs, and educational efforts had emerged. Meanwhile, they minimized information about the poor performance of defense systems and about the systematic fraud, waste, and abuse among defense contractors.[25] Other changes reflected the return of a laissez faire ideology, selectively applied, as when advertisers were released from FCC constraints as part of the general trend toward deregulation. The new harshness in the juvenile justice system represented yet another swing of the pendulum, away from the "permissiveness" of the 1960s toward more punitive norms.

But beyond these simple explanations, the developments of the 1980s illustrate the deeper dilemmas we examine in *Broken Promises*. The children's programs we have inherited, with their internal contradictions and innate limitations, will always be open to attack. Far from abberations, the changes of the 1980s have been the logical consequences of embedding certain assumptions in our programs. For the moment the pendulum may be swinging back, toward greater interest in children and more compassion for the plight of poor children. But unless we can rethink our perceptions and practices, the promising developments of the 1990s will themselves be incomplete and susceptible to being undone in decades still to come. The challenge to children's advocates is first to understand and then to reconceptualize the assumptions underlying our programs.

The first assumption to address is the limitation on public responsibility embedded in *parens patriae*, the doctrine that responsibility must be limited unless parents have failed their children. Too often the insistence on parental responsibility has been used to weaken *public* responsibility, including those programs that would help parents. The result has been to undermine support programs but without any success in encouraging parents to be more responsible, leaving children in the worst of all possible worlds. For example, the insistence on parental responsibility shows up in the limitation of welfare programs to the "truly needy"—a catchphrase indicating that children must be really badly off, and their parents complete failures, before the state will intervene. Otherwise parents must shoulder the responsibilities for children with no help from government despite high unemployment, rising poverty, and the continuation of employment discrimination against women and minorities.

The "rediscovery" of parental responsibility has dramatically affected debates about the causes of poverty and about welfare reform. During the 1980s, many individuals began to complain about the irresponsibility of poor parents; many of them blamed the welfare system itself (without good evidence) for creating "behavioral dependence."[26] This view is very old, of course, dating back at least to the nineteenth century fear that charity would "pauperize" the poor and make them forever dependent on the dole. The historic solution was to make charity as miserly as possible and to develop work obligations. The current solution, similar in every way, has been to make welfare less generous and to create new workfare programs, affirming the responsibility of welfare recipients to work and threatening loss of benefits if they refuse. To be sure, there are positive aspects to the current workfare programs, because many of them provide education, training, counseling, child care, and other forms of real support for workers. However, workfare has its dark side, especially where it asserts the responsibility of poor parents to work without making employment opportunities available. To insist on the obligations of parents during a decade of high unemployment, high rates of poverty, and declining benefits is at best a curious case of poor timing; it would be more appropriate to insist that parents should take the opportunities available to them during a period of economic boom and expanding benefits.

Other cases of the new insistence on parental responsibility abound. The opinion that parents should monitor television viewing helped to promote the Federal Communications Commission's decision not to regulate children's programming. The "squeal rule" to force teenagers to consult with their parents before obtaining birth control or abortions and the new interest in enforcing child support obligations of absent fathers provide other examples.

Of course, we should do everything possible to strengthen parental responsibility for children. But the emphasis on their roles rarely provides the kind of support that helps parents become more responsible. It has instead undermined the collective accountability for harm befalling children, and it has hurt them by denying access to those resources that could shield them from poverty and other woes. One way to reconceptualize programs for children, then, is to place their interests first and to stop using the issue of parental responsibility against them. Instead we should work to develop programs that provide support for children *and* for parents trying to act conscientiously—as the best of the current workfare and teenage prevention programs do—rather than behaving as if responsibility is a zero-sum game.

The developments of the 1980s also illustrate the powerful hostility toward the parents of poor children inherent in *parens patriae* (see chapter 2, pp. 50–51, and chapter 3, pp. 78–85). If parents must be failures before the state takes over, then our collective desire to provide for their children wars with our disgust at their failure. Indeed, one can read diatribes against the welfare system—such as Charles Murray's *Losing Ground* or George Gilder's *Wealth and Poverty,* with their assertions about the laziness and sexual irresponsibility of poor parents—and never find any mention of children whatsoever. Since critics of welfare are usually denouncing Aid to Families with Dependent Children, which was and is designed to provide for poor *children,* this omission is a serious oversight. Children have almost disappeared from current debates over welfare, which have focused instead on the behavior of parents: *we so despise poor parents that we are willing to let their children suffer.* Until this changes— until we are willing to accept collective responsibility for the support and education of poor children whatever the behavior of their parents, and to accept some public responsibility for their care as we improve their parents' ability to act responsibly—then it will be impossible to make good on the promise of protecting children from poverty.

The developments of the 1980s also indicate that we must confront the peculiar political weakness of the children's cause. The Reagan administration was hostile to almost all forms of social spending, but children's programs bore a disproportionate share of the cuts. The elderly still had political clout, so Social Security and Medicare were largely left intact, as were veterans' program; attempts to remove the disabled from Social Security and SSI were met with storms of protest; but children had no one to represent them. Their advocates were weakened by associations with the poor and with welfare, which had become dirty words. Child-oriented professionals, the groups most likely to espouse the cause of children, were out of favor, partly because of the right-wing description of them as "self-serving"—the facet of their professional character that has made their role as advocates for children so ambiguous (chapter 4, pp. 102–4). Teachers were under fire as incompetent, psychologists and child developmentalists were under suspicion, and social workers were discredited and demoralized.

Furthermore, poor children became the focus of diffuse hostility. Fiscal conservatives attacked "welfare" and the bloated budget for social spending; but resentment toward transfer programs—which include Social Security, Medicare, veteran's pensions, unemployment insurance, SSI for the aged, blind, and disabled, as well as programs for children—concentrated most intensely on AFDC, which accounts for less than 1 percent of the federal budget and only 2 percent of all social welfare spending. Politically this is understandable; other programs have stronger constituencies, and hostility toward poor parents made it easier to cut people from the AFDC rolls rather than from SSI or Social Security. But the result has been to force children to bear the burden of more general resentment toward transfer programs. If we are to change this, we need to consider fundamental changes to eliminate the inherent vulnerability of children in a political system based on self-interest.

Still another development of the 1980s, part of the Reagan antipathy for government spending, was the turn toward voluntarism and private charity as ways of fulfilling public purposes. Historically, the private precursors of public programs have played important roles in American social policy by identifying unmet needs and developing new ways of fulfilling them. But charitable resources have always been inadequate to their tasks, so reformers have been forced to turn to public funding as a way to meet more of the need for services. The Reagan administration attempted to reverse this process by exhorting private philanthropy to address the nation's problems, but it never developed a coherent approach to private efforts. Its cuts in social programs weakened nonprofit agencies, undermining rather than strengthening voluntarism as a response to social ills.[27] Most obviously, the amount of private giving was simply inadequate. During the recession of 1982–83, when unemployment and poverty rates were reaching new heights, private giving to nonprofit agencies increased by 5 percent; but this increase was only 40 percent of the cuts in government funding to these agencies. Reagan challenged the churches to provide for the poor, and they answered—quite rightly—that churches in this country are not adequate to the task. To help the increasing numbers of the hungry and homeless, charitable organizations expanded soup kitchens, food pantries, and emergency shelters, but they could not prevent hunger or homelessness from spreading; their staffs, hard-working and largely unrewarded, had never claimed that private charity was the best solution. Child care advocates pressured corporations for support to increase productivity, but received—except from a few of the largest, wealthiest, and most socially conscious firms—a pittance for their troubles (and much of that at the expense of the tax system).[28] Charitable efforts have been crucial during the 1980s in meeting the needs of families and children abandoned by public programs, but as sources of funding to meet massive needs they have been as insufficient in the 1980s as they were in the nineteenth century.

The 1980s have also been a period during which America's ambivalent but relatively benevolent feelings toward children changed, and controlling impulses came to dominate (see chapter 3, pp. 85–96). The punitive view of juvenile delinquents and the near-abandonment of rehabilitation efforts are the clearest illustrations. The initial reforms of the "excellence" movement, stressing new requirements and regulations rather than additional support for those trying to improve educational equity and quality, provide another.

Indeed, even the signs of hopefulness during the 1980s illustrate our dominant ways of thinking about children. Instrumental and utilitarian conceptions of children as "our most precious natural resource" have often corrupted what we can do for them (chapter 2, pp. 51–62). The greatest support for early childhood programs was generated by evaluations of the Perry Preschool Project, which claimed a benefit-cost ratio of seven to one. Head Start was insulated from cuts because of this simple economic argument. The WIC program of food supplements for pregnant women and their young children came to be widely supported, less because of humanitarian impulses than because evaluations indicated benefits in excess of costs. Workfare programs and child support enforcement were also praised after evidence about their net benefits came to light. Child advocates rushed to develop economic rationales for their programs, and the "bottom line" came to be the central element in any legislative presentation.

Instrumental conceptions of children and children's institutions also justified some of the most important reforms of the decade. A *Nation at Risk*, which many viewed as starting the "excellence" movement, promoted better education as the way to restore international competitiveness (without any evidence that poor education had contributed to the decline of the steel, automobile, or semiconductor industries). Those advocating programs for low-income and minority children argued that, in a country with increasing poverty rates and larger minority populations, these children should be better educated now because they would support the Baby Boomers in their old age; and some employers began to press for more attention to the education of poor and minority children because of looming shortages in the labor market, not because of any commitment to equity.

Such instrumental and utilitarian arguments do have merit, especially when they are based on fact rather than mythology. For children's advocates they are also unavoidable because of the political support they generate. But benefit-cost analysis is a technique for promoting efficiency; equity—the central concern for many children—has always held an uncomfortable position within benefit-cost analysis. The toughest questions arise when efficiency and equity point in different directions, as they often do in many welfare programs and school issues. In these cases utilitarian thinking is likely to impede the cause of poor children.

Above all, the claims on behalf of children have always been moral ones, and moral positions of all kinds—whether upholding the right of children to decent support, or the right of the populace to a clean environment and safe living conditions—have never had a place within benefit-cost analysis. The utilitarian approach may help children for the moment, but over the long run it will neglect those moral principles and noninstrumental goals that have always been at the center of claims for children.

What We Should Do for Children

The developments of the 1980s have been discouraging. But as the decade ends there are many signs of hope. Reagan's program of cuts in social programs was effectively slowed by Congress as far back as 1982. Many people have recognized how bad the increase in poverty among children since 1979 has been. A renewed concern with the well-being of families has shown up in recent writing on "family policy," in many ways similar to the search for a family policy of the late 1970s.[29] In 1986 Congress began a new debate over welfare, with Senator Moynihan offering the Family Security Act and Senators Evans and Durenberger promoting the Federalism Act of 1986 to provide greater federal financing for AFDC and Medicaid. The "excellence" movement has succeeded in turning public attention to children and youth. Many states have also begun to examine their options for early childhood programs. Some politicians have even suggested that the cause of children might dominate the 1988 elections.[30]

Given our analysis in *Broken Promises*, and the further decline in the status of children during the 1980s, what would a progressive agenda for children look like? Without a doubt, the first task will be to reconstruct the welfare state, to undo the damage of the Reagan years and to put into place some much-needed reforms. (With the benefit of hindsight, we now feel that we and others who attacked the limitations of the welfare state underestimated its importance.) One requirement will be to restore support levels, so that welfare programs lift all families with children out of poverty. Another will be to eliminate the intolerable variation among states that allows states like Texas and Mississippi to pay AFDC children so much less than California and Massachusetts do. A third will be to establish AFDC for two-parent families across the country, both to support children in these families and to eliminate the incentives for parents to remain apart. To accomplish these goals, it will be necessary to restore the federal role. While it is appropriate to allocate *administrative* responsibility to the states, the Reagan strategy of giving states *fiscal* responsibility for social programs is one that leads to low spending, wide interstate variation, and inadequate funding in states whose economies decline—precisely the places where the need for support is greatest.

In reforming welfare, three somewhat novel programs are now widely supported: workfare to urge welfare recipients into employment; child support enforcement plans, to prevent fathers from failing to support their children; and teenage pregnancy programs, to prevent the large numbers of births to teenage mothers that lead to the most intractable and long-lasting poverty. Each promises savings in current welfare programs; each also asserts a responsibility—of welfare recipients, of absent fathers, and of teenagers—that has made these changes attractive across the political spectrum. All three reforms should be supported, though they will not automatically benefit children. The best of the current workfare plans provide a variety of education, training, counseling, child care, and other supportive services to help mothers who are not on welfare; the worst of them are much more punitive, and expect recipients to find employment with little help. Current child support programs have tended to benefit state and federal treasuries more than children, since very little of the collections from fathers goes to their children; however, plans which can enhance the well-being of children have been devised and are now being tested.[31] Similarly, some approaches to teenage pregnancy, especially school-based clinics, are effective; but moralistic and punitive approaches should be avoided since they are ineffective in preventing teenage pregnancy.[32] In each case, then, the problem will be not simply to incorporate new features into the welfare system, but to make sure that they are

325

effective and are designed primarily to improve the well-being of poor children.

Many other children's programs of demonstrated effectiveness now serve only a small fraction of those who are eligible. Some have been seriously slashed in the past few years, and funding levels must be increased. In the area of nutrition, WIC still serves fewer than half of those who are eligible, despite its widespread appeal; school lunches and breakfasts, which have been proven worthwhile, should be restored. Compensatory education and bilingual programs were cut just as evidence of the conditions under which they are effective began to appear; these and other programs need to be rebuilt in order to make good on the promise of providing "excellence and equity too." Federal support for good quality child care should be increased, especially given evidence about the potential benefits of early childhood programs for low-income children. The declining federal support for model projects in the juvenile justice system must be reversed, and methods developed for dealing with the small amount of serious juvenile crime while enhancing chances for later success with less serious offenders. Correcting widespread abuse in state systems—overcrowding, harsh conditions, the continued use of inappropriate detention centers and adult jails, the lack of educational programs—may also require federal initiative and funding. The upsurge of homelessness, the increases in infant mortality and other signs of poor health among children, and the chaotic state of foster care all cry out for reform, for restoring programs cut during the 1980s and for correcting the flaws embedded in past practices.

Reconstructing the welfare state will require the attention and energy of reformers and advocates for years to come, particularly since there is nothing simple about designing and implementing effective programs. But there is a great deal of experience and evidence to guide this reconstruction. Welfare, education, health, and nutrition programs have been extensively studied; there is a great deal of evidence about what works and what doesn't that has accumulated over the past twenty years.[33] As long as the political will to provide for children exists, the technical means to do so can be developed.

At the same time, advocates should remember the inherent limitations of the welfare state, and work toward other solutions simultaneously. The most obvious flaw of the welfare state is that capitalism values self-sufficiency, and therefore views those who depend on the state as failures. The stigma attached to welfare recipients and the need to label the parents of poor children as "failures" are unavoidable, and they inevitably operate to limit public support and to create the cycles of generosity and stinginess that have characterized American social policy.

The system of transfers in the welfare state also has a structural flaw: during recessions, when welfare benefits are needed most, the tax revenues necessary to support welfare programs diminish, and support declines. This is a special problem of the current welfare system, under which states (which cannot run deficits) set eligibility conditions and benefit levels for many programs. Finally, as long as underlying economic conditions deteriorate the welfare system must expand merely to keep pace with increases in poverty, leading many to complain that the expansion of welfare has failed to "cure" poverty.

To avoid these limitations, it will be important to initiate reforms that go beyond the welfare state. Three approaches strike us as both necessary and fruitful. The first and most accessible is an attempt to shift away from the transfers that characterize the welfare state, in which some people are taxed to support others, and instead to reallocate earnings and property rights so that children benefit without having to rely on governments to force transfers. Child support enforcement programs can be viewed as one attempt to impose a different conception of property, by forcing fathers to recognize that their children have claims on their incomes regardless of their absence.

Another method of reallocation would be to eliminate employment discrimination against women and minorities—a redistribution of earnings that would benefit children enormously. The poverty rate among Anglo children living with two parents or with their fathers was about 9.8 percent in 1986, as compared to about 42 percent among other children; if we are able to eliminate the wage differentials associated with being female or a minority group member, we can eliminate up to 57 percent of poverty among children (as well as a good deal of it among adults). Eliminating discrimination against black men would be especially important, because their poor employment prospects have contributed not only to the poverty of black children but also to the break-up of their families.[34] Yet this proposal, simple in conception if complex in execution, is rarely mentioned in debates over welfare reform because it would involve a fundamental shift in labor markets, an approach quite different from that of existing welfare programs which take labor markets as given.

An additional area of reform has been the effort to establish parental leaves and flextime for working parents, in order to reduce the stress associated with working as well as parenting. We interpret these as attempts to establish the rights of children versus employers, and to require that employers recognize the primacy of childrearing over production. Such measures would benefit children in ways other than the provision of economic resources, but again they will be difficult to implement because they involve a restructuring of employment relations.

Still another mechanism of revising property rights to benefit children might be to create a children's allowance, common in European countries. The importance of such a provision would be to establish the prior claims of children on the country's resources, and to assert a collective responsibility for the costs of raising children. Political realists will recognize that a meaningful children's allowance is many years away; but for our purposes the important goal is to develop alternative conceptions of a policy which goes beyond the limitations of the welfare state.

A third area in which children's advocates must participate is that of economic policy. Of course, everyone's favorite antipoverty policy is economic growth; the trick is knowing how to achieve such growth. Appropriate macroeconomic policies are necessary, but in an increasingly international economic system they are no longer sufficient. The Reagan years, which emphasized laissez faire policies, clarified the bankruptcy of this approach: the country's trade deficit steadily worsened, and its international position deteriorated. The rise of trading partners with much more active economic policies, including Japan, confirms the inadequacies of the laissez faire approach. In the absence of economic leadership, a number of proposals have emerged for more active and interventionist perspectives on economic policy. Many of these fly under the banner of "industrial policies," and they have far greater potential to improve the economic standing of the United States.[35]

But economic growth per se may be insufficient, especially if such growth is lopsided. Two worrisome and interrelated trends became obvious during the 1980s: a deterioration of the equality in distribution of earnings (especially among men); and, contributing to that inequality, the relative growth of low-wage work and part-time work, much of it in services. The economic recovery after 1983 was very uneven. Some regions of the country (especially on the two coasts) benefited, but other areas stagnated. Unemployment fell from nearly 11 percent to 7 and then 6 percent (which many then claimed to be "full employment"). But poverty among black and Hispanic children and among children living with their mothers hardly moderated at all. These trends imply that it is possible to have economic and employment growth, but without jobs sufficient to lift families out of poverty. Even a full-time minimum wage job pays only $7,300 per year, well below the poverty-level income of $8,737 for a family of three; if work is sporadic then parents trying hard to support their

children may fall below even that level. Macroeconomic policy to stimulate growth may therefore be inadequate, and efforts to intervene more
directly—to change the distribution of jobs available—may be necessary.
Some of these, including public job creation programs, have been developed as aspects of proposed industrial policies; and public employment
also has the potential to create jobs of productive value which provide
more fulfilling work, at higher pay, than those available in the service
sector.[36]

A coherent economic policy, including one that improves the jobs at
the low end of the labor market, is important because many welfare programs can't work well unless the low-wage labor market is improved.
Workfare will not generate any savings, and will become increasingly
punitive, if unemployment is high and wages are too low to make employment (net of working expenses including child care) more lucrative
than welfare. Child support enforcement mechanisms will produce few
benefits, for either children or public treasuries, if fathers of AFDC children are low wage-earners. Above all, a continued deterioration in the
distribution of earnings and increasing rates of pretransfer poverty will
make the task of the welfare state more and more difficult. Then, no matter
how generous-spirited the reforms of the post-Reagan period are, we can
count on another backlash against poor children. Thus, reconstructing the
welfare state is inadequate without an appropriate economic policy, and
child advocates will need to participate in the development of both.

In *Broken Promises* we argue for the reconstruction of our political
system as well (chapter 10, pp. 305–7), and nothing over the past six years
has changed our minds. Indeed, the excesses of interest-group liberalism
have gone even further during the 1980s, as selfishness has dominated
all other political motives. Corporations and other groups with money
streamed to Washington and found ready access. The fiscal demands of
political campaigns increased enormously, politicians found themselves
raising money constantly, and even those who felt it a matter of principle
not to accept large donations—that is, from corporations and the wealthy—
found themselves unable to uphold these ideas.[37] A politics based on
appearance rather than substance flourished, as Ronald Reagan continued
to be enormously popular even as a majority of the population opposed
his policies. The separation of voter approval from voter opinions on issues
portends the end of representative democracy and the rise of a far more
demagogic politics, in which debates over policies and programs have
little bearing on elections. This will also be a future in which participation
in political issues continues to decrease as most citizens view themselves
as powerless, and in which the abysmal participation of the past elec-

tions—with only 53 percent of potential voters casting ballots in the 1984 Presidential election—grows even worse.

The development of this sort of political system, undemocratic and unprincipled, means that debates about the public interest, about moral goals, and about the rights of children cannot even begin. The ideas we promote in *Broken Promises* (chapter 10, pp. 299) about the need for a sense of collective responsibility for children, uncorrupted by *parens patriae* and class divisions, are simply impossible to develop, because any conception of public responsibility will be undermined by private interests. This is also a system in which the parents of poor children fail to vote in large numbers, so that the most direct representation of the worst-off children—including minority children—is weakened. Thus the most persuasive arguments are instrumental and utilitarian justifications in which we invest in children only if a program promises positive net benefits, only if it allows us to be better supported in our old age, only if children can be turned to our own advantage.

We need to work, then, toward a political system in which self-interest is muted, in which the influence of money is similarly muted, and in which participation is increased and made more active. This in turn means that child advocates need not only to improve their ability to work within the current political system, but also to change that system. Such efforts may seem far from the immediate needs of children, but they will be crucial to what we can accomplish on their behalf.

We envision, then, a series of nested initiatives. The reconstruction of the welfare state will be the first priority, undoing the ravages of the past few years. But over the longer run those concerned with children must also work for reform in three other areas—in creating new claims which benefit children, in developing new economic policies, and in reforming politics itself.

This approach offers some early improvement for children while keeping more fundamental changes, now completely out of reach, on the political agenda. It also promises some escape from the cycles of the past. After all, the swings of the last three decades—from the indifference to children and hostility toward youth of the 1950s, to the expansiveness of the 1960s, to the hostility of the 1980s—have appeared before in American history, and that provides some momentary comfort that things will not remain this bad. But these swings also suggest the potential impermanence of the current interest in children and of any benefits that might flow in the years to come.

Yet there is another pattern, an alternative to political cycles with their promise of contraction in another generation. The last half-century, since the Social Security Act of 1935, has been a period of remarkable progress for the elderly. In the past two decades the programs initiated during the 1930s have been expanded and extended, and the usual pattern—in which the elderly were always the poorest members of society—has been reversed. These gains have become largely irreversible, as the Reagan administration found when it tried to cut Social Security benefits. The political power of the elderly is partly responsible, of course, but a moral position is also involved: people should not have to fear poverty in their later years.

We should be proud of this progress. It proves that government can do good; it signifies that this country, otherwise so fragmented and individualistic, can accept a collective responsibility, even at great cost. It also shows that relatively permanent progress against a social problem is possible, in place of the cyclical pattern typical of social programs.

We should now devote the next several decades to such progress for children. Only in this way can we live up to rhetoric about "our most precious natural resources" and make good on our historic promises to children.

NOTES

Introduction

1. The emergence of the family as a political issue is an illuminating piece of social history in its own right. One of its first expressions was the debate triggered by Daniel Patrick Moynihan's memorandum on the black family in 1965; see Lee Rainwater and William Yancey, *The Moynihan Report and the Politics of Controversy* (Cambridge: M.I.T. Press, 1967). During the 1960s the women's movement developed a critique of the family as one source of women's oppression. Other early writings on family change and family crisis include a special issue of *Journal of Marriage and the Family* 29, February 1967; a volume by Abbott Ferris, *Indicators of Change in the American Family* (New York: Russell Sage Foundation, 1970); and the hearings of Mondale's Subcommittee on Children and Youth, *The American Family: Trends and Pressures, 1973* (Washington, D.C.: U.S. Government Printing Office, 1974). By the end of the decade, "family policy" had become an academic subspeciality. For reviews, see Janet Giele, "Social Policy and the Family," *American Review of Sociology* 5 (1979): 275–302; Gilbert Y. Steiner, *The Futility of Family Policy* (Washington, D.C.: The Brookings Institution, 1981).

2. See especially Mary Jo Bane, *Here to Stay: American Families in the Twentieth Century* (New York: Basic Books, 1976).

3. Quoted in Steiner, *Futility of Family Policy*, p. 22.

4. Quoted in Ibid., p. 16.

5. For a review of right-wing positions on the family, see Linda Gordon and Allen Hunger, "Sex, Family, and the New Right: Antifeminism as a Political Force," *Radical America* 11 (Nov. 1977/Feb. 1978): 9–25; see also the special issue on the "profamily" movement in *Conservative Digest* 6 (May/June 1980). The clearest expression of the liberal position is Kenneth Keniston and the Carnegie Council on Children, *All Our Children: The American Family Under Pressure* (New York: Harcourt Brace Jovanovich, 1977). For three other books similar in their recommendations, see Bane, *Here to Stay*; Advisory Committee on Child Development of the National Academy of Sciences, *Toward a National Policy for Children and Families* (Washington, D.C.: National Academy of Sciences, 1976); and Richard deLone, *Small Futures: Children, Inequality, and the Limits of Liberal Reform* (New York: Harcourt, Brace, Jovanovich, 1979).

6. Contrast Christopher Lasch, *Haven in a Heartless World: The Family Besieged* (New York: Basic Books, 1977), with the discussion of the "Bad Old Days" in Edward Shorter, *The Making of the Modern Family* (New York: Basic Books, 1975), and Lloyd deMause, ed., *The History of Childhood* (New York: Harper & Row, 1975).

7. The Carter speech on the family was delivered at the Mormon Family Unity Awards Ceremony on November 27, 1978.

1. Family Crises and Public Responsibility

1. Robert Bremner et al., eds., *Children and Youth in America: A Documentary History*, 3 vols. (Cambridge: Harvard University Press, 1970), 1:27–63; John Demos, *A Little Commonwealth: Family Life in the Plymouth Colony* (New York: Oxford University Press, 1970).

2. Nicholas Hobbs, *The Futures of Children: Categories, Labels, and Their Consequences* (San Francisco: Jossey-Bass, 1975), p. 261.

3. Sidney Ratner, James H. Soltow, and Richard Sylla, *The Evolution of the American*

Economy: Growth, Welfare, and Decision Making (New York: Basic Books, 1979), pp. 103–249; Clyde and Sally Griffen, *Natives and Newcomers: The Ordering of Opportunity in Mid-Nineteenth Century Poughkeepsie* (Cambridge: Harvard University Press, 1978); Peter Dobkin Hall, "Marital Selection and Business in Massachusetts Merchant Families, 1700–1900," in Michael Gordon, ed., *The American Family in Social-Historical Perspective* (New York: St. Martin's Press, 1978, 2nd ed.).

4. Alan Dawley, *Class and Community: The Industrial Revolution in Lynn* (Cambridge: Harvard University Press, 1976); Lawrence A. Cremin, *American Education: The National Experience, 1783–1876* (New York: Harper & Row, 1980), pp. 342–352.

5. On increasing inequality in the ante-bellum period, see Ratner, Soltow, and Sylla, *Evolution of the American Economy*, pp. 241–48; Peter Lindert, *Fertility and Scarcity in America* (Princeton: Princeton University Press, 1978), chap. 7; Edward Pessen, "The Egalitarian Myth and the American Social Reality: Wealth, Mobility and Equality in the Era of the Common Man," *American Historical Review* 4 (October 1971); Stuart Blumin, "Mobility and Change in Ante-Bellum Philadelphia," in Stephan Thernstrom and Richard Sennett, eds., *Nineteenth Century Cities* (New Haven: Yale University Press, 1969); Jackson Turner Main, *The Social Structure of Revolutionary America* (Princeton: Princeton University Press, 1965).

6. The literature on nineteenth-century institutions is a good source of information on alarm over the family. See, for example, Stanley Schultz, *The Culture Factory: Boston Public Schools 1789–1860* (New York: Oxford University Press, 1973); Carl Kaestle, *The Evolution of an Urban School System: New York City, 1750–1850* (Cambridge: Harvard University Press, 1973); David Rothman, *The Discovery of the Asylum: Social Order and Disorder in the New Republic* (Boston: Little, Brown 1971); Paul Boyer, *Urban Masses and Moral Order in America, 1820–1920* (Cambridge: Harvard University Press, 1978).

7. Schultz, *Culture Factory*, p. 58.

8. Richard Rapson, "The American Child as Seen by British Travelers," in Michael Gordon, ed., *The American Family in Social-Historical Perspective* (New York: St. Martin's Press, 1973), p. 195

9. Schultz, *Culture Factory*, p. 59; see also Rothman, *Discovery of the Asylum*, chap. 3.

10. Schultz, *Culture Factory*, p. 60.

11. Nancy F. Cott, *The Bonds of Womanhood: "Woman's Sphere" in New England, 1780–1835* (New Haven: Yale University Press, 1977); Ann Douglas, *The Feminization of American Culture* (New York: Knopf, 1977); Kathryn Kish Sklar, *Catharine Beecher: A Study in American Domesticity* (New Haven: Yale University Press, 1973); Ann Firor Scott, *The Southern Lady: From Pedestal to Politics, 1830–1930* (Chicago: University of Chicago Press, 1970), chap. 1; Kirk Jeffrey, "The Family as Utopian Retreat from the City: The Nineteenth Century Contribution," in Sallie Teselle, ed., *The Family, Communes and Utopian Societies* (New York: Harper & Row, 1971).

12. Jeffrey, "Family as Utopian Retreat."

13. David P. Handlin, *The American Home: Architecture and Society, 1815–1915* (Boston: Little, Brown, 1979), chap. 1.

14. Cott, *Bonds of Womanhood*, p. 74.

15. Carl Degler, *At Odds: Women and the Family in America from the Revolution to the Present* (New York: Oxford University Press, 1980), chap. 4.

16. Barbara Welter, "The Cult of True Womanhood, 1820–1860," in Gordon, *American Family*. See also Douglas, *Feminization of American Culture*, and Sklar, *Catherine Beecher*.

17. Cremin, *American Education*, p. 65.

18. Stephen Schlossman, "The Culture of Poverty in Ante-Bellum Thought," *Science and Society* 38 (Summer 1974): 150–66. For similar views, see also Schultz, *Culture Factory*, and Kaestle, *Evolution of an Urban School System*.

19. Herbert G. Gutman, *The Black Family in Slavery and Freedom, 1750–1925* (New York: Pantheon, 1976), p. xxi.

20. Rothman, *Discovery of the Asylum*, pp. 210, 212.

21. Schultz, *Culture Factory*, p. 67.

22. Kaestle, *Evolution of an Urban School System*, p. 117.

23. Schultz, *Culture Factory*, p. 67.

24. Henry Barnard, "Sixth Annual Report of the Superintendent of Common Schools to the General Assembly of Connecticut for 1851," in Michael Katz, ed., *School Reform: Past*

and Present (Boston: Little, Brown, 1971), p. 10.

25. Schultz, *Culture Factory*, p. 67.

26. Stephen Schlossman, *Love and the American Delinquent: The Theory and Practice of "Progressive" Juvenile Justice, 1825–1920* (Chicago: University of Chicago Press, 1977), p. 28. See also Rothman, *Discovery of the Asylum*.

27. Barbara Brenzel, "Domestication as Reform: A Study of the Socialization of Wayward Girls, 1856–1905," *Harvard Educational Review* 50 (May 1980): 196–213.

28. On the limited role of the federal government before 1900, see Morton Keller, *Affairs of State: Public Life in Late Nineteenth Century America* (Cambridge: Harvard University Press, 1977), chap. 8. On the shift toward more *laissez-faire* approaches to state government and away from colonial precedents, see Oscar Handlin and Mary Handlin, *Commonwealth: A Study of the Role of Government in the American Economy, Massachusetts, 1774–1861* (New York: New York University Press, 1947).

29. Ratner, Soltow, and Sylla, *Evolution of the American Economy*, pp. 253–359; Alfred D. Chandler, Jr., *The Visible Hand: The Managerial Revolution in American Business* (Cambridge: Harvard University Press, 1977); Gabriel Kolko, *The Triumph of Conservatism* (Chicago: Free Press of Glencoe, 1963).

30. Lindert, *Fertililty and Scarcity*, identifies 1916 as a year of peak inequality, though the data are sparse; Jeffrey Williamson, "The Sources of American Inequality 1896–1948," *Review of Economics and Statistics* 58 (November 1976): 387–97, documents increasing inequality up to World War I.

31. Robert Hunter, *Poverty* (New York: Harper & Row, 1955 ed.), pp. xxv–xxvi.

32. Daniel Rogers, *The Work Ethic in Industrial America, 1850–1920* (Chicago: University of Chicago Press, 1978).

33. Sheila Rothman, *Woman's Proper Place: A History of Changing Ideals and Practices, 1870 to the Present* (New York: Basic Books, 1978), pp. 42–60; Margaret Wilson, *The American Woman in Transition: The Urban Influence, 1870–1920* (Westport: Greenwood Press, 1979), chap. 6; Claudia Goldin, "Female Labor Force Participation Rates: The Origin of Black and White Differences, 1870 and 1880," *Journal of Economic History* 37 (March 1977): 87–108.

34. Marguerite Dixon, *Vocational Guidance for Girls* (New York: Rand McNally, 1919), p. 171.

35. Although not always accurate in its analysis, one of the best accounts of progressive era concerns with the family remains Arthur Calhoun, *A Social History of the American Family, From 1865 to 1919*, 3 vols. (New York: Barnes and Noble, 1960 ed.). This quote by Roger Swettland is from 3:134.

36. Ibid., p. 149.

37. S. Josephine Baker, *Fighting for Life* (1939); quoted in Bremner et al., *Children and Youth*, 2:16–17.

38. William O'Neill, *Divorce in the Progressive Era* (New Haven: Yale University Press, 1967), p. 62. See also Linda Gordon, *Woman's Body, Woman's Right* (New York: Grossman, 1976).

39. Calhoun, *Social History of the American Family*, 3:191.

40. Sheila Rothman, *Woman's Proper Place*, chap. 3; Barbara Ehrenreich and Deirdre English, *For Her Own Good: 150 Years of the Expert's Advice to Women* (Garden City: Anchor, 1978), chap. 5; Stephen Schlossman, "Before Home Start: Notes Toward a History of Parent Education in America, 1897–1929," *Harvard Educational Review* 46 (August 1976): 436–67; Handlin, *The American Home*, pp. 409–19.

41. Rothman, *Woman's Proper Place*, p. 103.

42. Mary Hill, *Charlotte Perkins Gilman: The Making of a Radical Feminist, 1860–1896* (Philadelphia: Temple University Press, 1980), p. 271.

43. O'Neill, *Divorce in the Progressive Era*, chap. 2.

44. Rochelle Beck, "White House Conferences on Children: An Historical Perspective," *Harvard Educational Review* 43 (1973): 653–68.

45. Mark Leff, "Consensus for Reform: The Mothers' Pension Movement in the Progressive Era," *Social Services Review* 47 (September 1973): 396–417; Schlossman, *Love and the American Delinquent*; Sheila Rothman, "Other People's Children: The Day Care Experience in America," *The Public Interest* 30 (Winter 1973).

46. Marvin Lazerson and W. Norton Grubb, *Vocationalism and American Education: A Documentary History, 1870–1970* (New York: Teachers College, 1974); David Tyack, *The*

One Best System (Cambridge: Harvard University Press, 1974); W. Norton Grubb and Marvin Lazerson, "Education and the Labor Market: Recycling the Youth Problem," in Harvey Kantor and David Tyack, eds., *Work, Youth and Schooling: Historical Perspectives on Vocational Education* (Palo Alto: Stanford University Press, 1982).

47. Bremner, et al., *Children and Youth*, 2:1420–22; David Tyack and Michael Berkowitz, "The Man Nobody Liked: Toward a Social History of the Truant Officer, 1840–1940," *American Quarterly* 29 (Spring 1977): 31–54.

48. David Rothman, "The State as Parent: Social Policy in the Progressive Era," in Willard Gaylin et al., *Doing Good: The Limits of Benevolence* (New York: Pantheon Books, 1978), p. 79. See also Schlossman, *Love and the American Delinquent*, chap. 4; David Rothman, *Conscience and Convenience: The Asylum and Its Alternatives in Progressive America* (Boston: Little, Brown, 1980).

49. Nancy Weiss, "Save the Children: A History of the Children's Bureau, 1903–1918" (Ph.D. diss., University of California, Los Angeles, 1974).

50. Grace Abbott, *The Child and the State*, vol. 2 (1938), in Bremner et al., *Children and Youth*, 2:751.

51. Ratner, Soltow, and Sylla, *Evolution of the American Economy;* Kolko, *Triumph of Conservatism;* James Weinstein, *The Corporate Ideal in the Liberal State, 1900–1918* (Boston: Beacon Press, 1968.)

52. Bremner et al., *Children and Youth*, 2:751.

53. The literature detailing the effects of the depression on family life includes E. Wright Bakke, *Citizens Without Work* (New Haven: Yale University Press, 1940); Mirra Komarovsky, *The Unemployed Man and His Family* (New York: Dryden Press, 1940); James Mickel Williams, *Human Aspects of Unemployment and Relief* (Chapel Hill: University of North Carolina Press, 1933); Glen Elder, Jr., *Children of the Great Depression* (Chicago: University of Chicago Press, 1974); Robert and Helen Lynd, *Middletown in Transition* (New York: Harcourt, Brace, 1937).

54. On the early welfare programs, see chapter 7.

55. The Family Protection Bill (S. 1808), introduced by Senator Paul Laxalt of Nevada, included a hodge-podge of measures like restrictions of federal regulations on religious issues, parental rights, child abuse, and spouse abuse, restrictions on Legal Services, and replacement of the Elementary and Secondary Education Act (the source of most compensatory education funds) with block grants. While generally antifeminist, homophobic, against civil liberties, and hostile to programs for the poor, the bill contains several liberal measures—repeal of discriminatory taxation of married couples and tax deductions for corporate child care support—to confuse the unwary reader looking for consistency.

56. Christopher Lasch, *Haven in a Heartless World: The Family Beseiged* (New York: Basic Books, 1977); Selma Fraiberg, *Every Child's Birthright: In Defense of Mothering* (New York: Basic Books, 1977); Peter Laslett, *Household and Family in Past Time* (Cambridge: Cambridge University Press, 1972).

57. Lee Rainwater and William Yancey, *The Moynihan Report and the Politics of Controversy* (Cambridge: MIT Press, 1967). For an excellent review of the literature on the black family see the appendix to Elmer Martin and Joanne Mitchell Martin, *The Black Extended Family* (Chicago: University of Chicago Press, 1978).

58. Octavio Romano-V, "The Anthropology and Sociology of the Mexican-American: The Distortion of Mexican-American History," *El Grito* 2 (Fall 1968): 13–26; Miguel Montiel, "The Social Science Myth of the Mexican-American Family," *El Grito* 3 (Summer 1970): 56–63; Nick Vaca, "The Mexican-American in the Social Sciences, 1912–1970, Part II, 1936–1970," *El Grito* 4 (Fall 1970): 17–51; Maxine Baca Zinn, "Political Familism: Toward Sex Role Equality in Chicano Families," *Aztlan* 6 (1975): 13–26.

59. Quoted in Robert Coles, *Children of Crisis: A Study of Courage and Fear* (Boston: Little, Brown, 1967), pp. 143–44.

60. On the historical literature, see Gutman, *Black Family in Slavery and Freedom;* Degler, *At Odds*, chap. 6. For comtemporary analyses, see Herbert Hyman and John Reed, "Black Matriarchy Reconsidered: Evidence from Secondary Analysis of Sample Surveys," *Public Opinion Quarterly* 33 (Fall 1969): 356–64; Delores Mack, "Where the Black Matriarchy Theorists Went Wrong," *Psychology Today* 4 (January 1971): 24, 86–87; Karl King, "A Comparison of the Negro and White Family Power Structure in Low Income Families," *Child and Family* 6 (Spring 1967): 65–74.

61. See Leo Grebler, Joan Moore, and Ralph Guzman *The Mexican-American* (New York: Free Press, 1970); Arthur Rubel, *Across the Tracks* (Austin: University of Texas Press, 1966), chap. 3. Other authors stress that the Chicano family has been changing rapidly in the direction of more egalitarian values; see, for example, the literature review in Zinn, "Political Familism," pp. 14–15.

62. Carol Stack, *All Our Kin* (New York: Harper & Row, 1974); Susan Keefe, Armado Padillo, and Manuel Carlos, "The Mexican American Extended Family as an Emotional Support System," in J. Manuel Casas and Susan Keefe, eds. *Family and Mental Health in the Mexican American Community* (Los Angeles: Spanish Speaking Mental Health Research Center, 1978).

63. See Martin and Martin, *Black Extended Family;* Andrew Bilingsley, *Black Families in White America* (Englewood Cliffs, Prentice-Hall, 1968); Robert Hill, The *Strengths of Black Families* (New York: Emerson Hall Publishers, 1971), Stack, *All Our Kin;* Robert Staples, "The Black American Family"; Montiel, "Social Science Myth"; Romano-V, "Anthropology and Sociology"; Vaca, "Mexican-American." The work of Robert Coles in his series *Children of Crisis* can be read as documenting the strengths of poor children, including black children in Vols. I and III and Chicano children in Vol. IV.

64. Quoted in Barbara Solomon and Helen Mendes, "Black Families: A Social Welfare Perspective," in Virginia Tufte and Barbara Myerhoff, eds., *Changing Images of the Family* (New Haven: Yale University Press, 1979), p. 271. For a criticism of the "strength-resiliency" perspective, see especially Martin and Martin, *Black Extended Family.*

65. Fraiberg, *Every Child's Birthright.* The quotations are from Rothman, *Woman's Proper Place,* p. 249.

66. Degler, *At Odds,* p. 392.

67. See, for example, Rothman, *Woman's Proper Place.*

68. These arguments are criticized in Milton Kotelchuck, "The Infant's Relationship to the Father," in Michael Lamb, ed., *The Role of the Father in Child Development* (New York: John Wiley and Sons, 1976); and James Levine, *Who Will Raise the Children? New Options for Fathers (and Mothers)* (New York: Lippincott, 1976).

69. This quote appeared in both the 1947 and the 1958 editions of *Baby and Child Care.*

70. See, for example Burton White, *The First Three Years of Life* (Englewood Cliffs: Prentice-Hall, 1975); and Fraiberg, *Every Child's Birthright.*

71. For reviews of the literature on the father's role, see Michael Lamb, *Role of the Father;* and Michael Rutter, *The Qualities of Mothering: Maternal Deprivation Reassessed* (New York: J. Aronson, 1974). For a careful review of the literature on childrearing, see Alison Clarke-Stewart, *Child Care in the Family* (New York: Academic Press, 1977). The best review of the effects of maternal employment is that of Lois Hoffman and F. Ivan Nye, *Working Mothers* (San Francisco: Jossey-Bass, 1974), especially chap. 6.

72. Urie Bronfenbrenner, "Beyond the Deficit Model in Child and Family Policy," *Teacher's College Record* 81 (Fall, 1979): 99.

73. Richard deLone, *Small Futures: Children, Inequality, and the Limits of Liberal Reform* (New York: Harcourt Brace Jovanovich, 1979), chap. 1.

74. For a similar argument—that the Supreme Court has been concerned with the instrumental role of the family in maintaining social order—see Robert Burt, "The Constitution of the Family," in Philip Kurland and Gerhard Casper, eds., *The Supreme Court Review: 1979* (Chicago: University of Chicago Press, 1980).

2. The Corruption of Public Responsibility for Children

1. As a legal doctrine, *parens patriae* is often treated as if it had a precise meaning and origin in the common law. However, the adoption of the phrase from English chancery law in the United States was a matter of convenience and justification after the fact rather than a careful reliance on English precedents. We use the concept of *parens patriae* as an approach to the state's treatment of children which extends to institutions other than the courts rather than as a specifically legal doctrine. On *parens patriae,* see Steven Schlossman, *Love and the American Deliquent: The Theory and Practice of "Progressive" Juvenile Justice, 1825-1929* (Chicago: University of Chicago Press, 1977), pp. 8–17; Douglas Rendle-

man, "Parens Patriae: From Chancery to the Juvenile Court," *South Carolina Law Review* 22 (1970): 147–81; Ellen Ryerson, *The Best-Laid Plans: America's Juvenile Court Experiment* (New York: Hill and Wang, 1978), pp. 63–72.

2. John Dewey, *The School and Society* (Chicago: University of Chicago Press, 1899), p. 3.

3. Sara Lawrence Lightfoot suggested the term "public love" to us.

4. David Rothman, *The Discovery of the Asylum: Social Order and Disorder in the New Republic* (Boston: Little, Brown, 1971), chap. 1; John Demos, *A Little Commonwealth* (New York: Oxford University Press, 1970); David Flaherty, *Privacy in Colonial New England* (Charlottesville: University of Virginia, 1972); Michael Zuckerman, "William Byrd's Family," *Perspectives in American History* 12 (1979).

5. Ryerson, *Best-Laid Plans*, pp. 67–77; and David Rothman, "The State as Parent: Social Policy in the Progressive Era," in Willard Gaylin, et al., *Doing Good: The Limits of Benevolence* (New York: Pantheon Books, 1978).

6. Edward Everett Hale, "The State's Care of Its Children" (1855), in Robert H. Bremner et al., eds., *Children and Youth in America: A Documentary History*, 3 vols., (Cambridge: Harvard University Press, 1970), 1:702–4.

7. This is drawn from an interview conducted in May 1977, which appears in Edward Zigler and Jeanette Valentine, eds., *Project Head Start: A Legacy of the War on Poverty* (New York: Free Press, 1979), pp. 57–58.

8. Martin Anderson, *Welfare: The Political Economy of Welfare Reform in the United States* (Palo Alto: Hoover Institution, 1978), p. 153. See also Peter Steinfels, *The Neo-Conservatives* (New York: Simon and Schuster, 1929), chap. 3 and chap. 9.

9. Gilbert Steiner, *The Children's Cause* (Washington, D.C.: The Brookings Institution, 1976), p. 255.

10. Kenneth Keniston and the Carnegie Council on Children, *All Our Children: The American Family Under Pressure* (New York: Harcourt Brace Jovanovich, 1977), p. 23.

11. For evidence on the effects of labeling in schools, see Robert Rosenthal and Lenore Jacobson, *Pygmalion in the Classroom* (New York: Holt, Rinehart and Winston, 1968); Ray Rist, "Student Social Class and Teacher Expectations: The Self-Fulfilling Prophecy in Ghetto Education," *Harvard Educational Review* 40 (August 1970): 411–51. For evidence on programs for juvenile delinquents, see Joan McCord, "A Thirty-Year Follow-up of Treatment Effects," *American Psychologist* 33 (March, 1978), 284–89.

12. On the "pathology" model, see especially Florence Ruderman, *Child Care and Working Mothers* (New York: Child Welfare League of America, 1968).

13. Sara Lawrence Lightfoot, *Worlds Apart: Relationships Between Families and Schools* (New York: Basic Books, 1978), p. 94; see generally chap. 3.

14. Letter of transmittal to Harvey Brenner, "Estimating the Social Costs of National Economic Policy: Implications for Mental and Physical Health, and Criminal Aggression," Joint Economic Committee, October 26, 1976, p. ix.

15. Report of the White House Conference on Child Health and Protection, section 3, "Education and Training" (Washington: U.S. Government Printing Office, 1931), pp. 211–12.

16. *Better Health Care for Our Children: A National Strategy*, quoted in *CDF Reports* 2 (January 1981), p. 4.

17. Lightfoot, *Worlds Apart*, p. 84.

18. For an early twentieth-century attempt to show the "money value" of schooling, see A. C. Ellis, *The Money Value of Education*, Bulletin no. 22 (Washington, D.C.: U.S. Bureau of Education, 1917). On the vocational role of schooling, see Marvin Lazerson and W. Norton Grubb, *American Education and Vocationalism: A Documentary History, 1879–1970* (New York: Teachers College Press, 1974); and W. Norton Grub and Marvin Lazerson, "Education and the Labor Market: Recycling the Youth Problem," in Harvey Kantor and David Tyack, eds., *Education and Work: Historical Perspectives on Vocational Education* (Palo Alto: Stanford University Press, 1982).

19. See especially Richard Freeman, *The Over-Educated American* (New York: Academic Press, 1976).

20. This is the result of a large literature that began with the Coleman report in 1966; for a typically pessimistic review of cognitive outcomes, see Harvey Averch, Stephen Carroll, Theodore Donaldson, Herbert Kiesling, and John Pincus, *How Effective is Schooling?* (Rand Report R-956-PCSF/RC, March 1972).

21. See Christopher Jencks's plea to reject the human capital model and replace it with a more "family-like" model that is less instrumental. Christopher Jencks et al., *Inequality: A Reassessment of the Effects of Family and Schooling in America* (New York: Basic Books, 1972).

22. On the politics of Head Start, see Steiner, *Children's Cause*, chap. 2. For the fruits of the efforts to find cognitive effects, see Irving Lazar et al., *The Persistence of Pre-School Effects*, Education Commission of the States, September 1977.

23. C. U. Weber, P. W. Foster, and D. W. Weikert, *An Economic Analysis of the Perry Preschool Project* (Ypsilanti, Mich.: High/Scope Educational Research Foundation, 1978).

24. On the dominance of cognitive criteria in publicly funded child care—and in the kindergarten before that—see W. Norton Grubb and Marvin Lazerson, "Child Care, Government Financing, and the Public Schools: Lessons from the California Children's Centers," *School Review* 86 (November 1977): 5–37.

25. This point has also been made in Lawrence A. Cremin, *Public Education* (New York: Basic Books, 1976); and Henry Aaron, *Politics and the Professors: The Great Society in Perspective* (Washington, D.C.: The Brookings Institution, 1978). For the only available evidence on the contention that changing one of several interacting influences may be insufficient, see Charles Benson et al., *Education and Nutrition: Performance and Policy*, University of California, Berkeley, April 1980.

26. A similar point is made by Aaron, *Politics and the Professors*, pp. 158–59.

27. For an excellent typology of different ways in which parents value children, see Lois Wladis Hoffman and Martin Hoffman, "The Value of Children to Parents," in J. T. Fawcett, ed., *Psychological Perspectives on Population* (New York: Basic Books, 1973). For empirical work based on this typology, see Lois Wladis Hoffman, Arland Thornton, and Jean Denby Manis, "The Value of Children to Parents in the United States," *Journal of Population* 1 (Summer 1978): 91–131.

28. Quoted in Arlene Skolnick, "The Myth of the Vulnerable Child," *Psychology Today* 12 (February 1978): 56–65.

29. Jerome Kagan, Richard B. Kearsley, and Philip R. Zelazo, *Infancy: Its Place in Human Development* (Cambridge: Harvard University Press, 1978), especially pp. 21–29. For a review article lamenting the domination of the "parent control" model, but providing little indication that any real alternative is being developed, see Barclay Martin, "Parent-Child Relations," in Frances Deyer Horowitz et al., *Review of Child Development Research*, vol. 4 (Chicago: University of Chicago Press, 1975). See, however, Richard Lerner and Graham Spanier, eds., *Child Influences on Marital and Family Interaction* (New York: Academic Press, 1978).

30. Studs Terkel, *Working* (New York: Pantheon Books, 1972), p. 32. A rich oral history describes the efforts to live through one's children, much of which focuses on working-class parents; see especially Richard Sennett and Jonathan Cobb, *The Hidden Injuries of Class* (New York: Knopf, 1972). For a scholarly discussion of this subject, see Arthur Kornhauser, *The Mental Health of the Industrial Worker* (New York: John Wiley and Sons, 1965); John Scanzoni, *Opportunity and the Family* (New York: The Free Press, 1970) chap. 7.

31. Lynnell Michaels, "Why We Don't Want Children," *Redbook Magazine*, January 1970, p. 10; reprinted in Ellen Peck and Judith Senderowitz, eds., *Pronatalism: The Myth of Mom and Apple Pie* (New York: Thomas Y. Crowell, 1974), p. 262.

32. Quoted in Paula Fass, *The Damned and the Beautiful: American Youth in the 1920s* (New York: Oxford University Press, 1977), p. 102.

33. Urie Bronfenbrenner, *The Ecology of Childhood* (Cambridge: Harvard University Press, 1978).

34. The concept of parents as managers is similar to the description of parents as "executives," in Keniston, *All Our Children*. However, Keniston appears to consider the managerial parent relatively powerless, an inaccurate assumption that makes the metaphor of the executive inappropriate. See also the concept of parents of handicapped children as managers who oversee and "orchestrate the services that professionals provide their children," in John Gliedman and William Roth, *The Unexpected Minority: Handicapped Children in America* (New York: Harcourt Brace Jovanovich, 1980), chap. 8.

35. The private use of public institutions is part of a more general tendency to interpret democracy in liberal terms, as marketlike institutions in which self-interested individuals or groups compete for favors from the state. See, for example, the discussion of modern

democratic theories in C. B. MacPherson, *The Life and Times of Liberal Democracy* (Oxford: Oxford University Press, 1977); and Carole Pateman, *Participation and Democratic Theory* (Cambridge: Cambridge University Press, 1970). We will return to this point in chapter 10.

36. "An Interview with Marion Wright Edelman," in *The Rights of Children* (Cambridge: Harvard Educational Review, 1974), pp. 71–72.

37. On tax expenditures for children and youth, see W. Norton Grubb and Patricia Griffin Heilbrun, *Far, Far to Go: Public Spending for Children and Youth in Texas* (Austin: Lyndon B. Johnson School of Public Affairs, 1982), especially Section I and Appendix C.

3. Public Responsibility in a Class Society

1. See Richard Bloom, Martin Whiteman, and Martin Deutsch, "Race and Social Class as Separate Factors Related to the Social Environment," *American Journal of Sociology* 70 (January 1965): 471–76; William Brinkhard and Louis Harris, *Negro Revolution in America* (New York: Simon and Schuster, 1964); Elliott A. Medrich, "The Serious Business of Growing Up: A Study of Children's Lives Outside of School," Childhood and Government Project, University of California, Berkeley, February 1977; J. Kenneth Moreland, "Kent Revisited," in *Blue Collar World* (Englewood Cliffs: Prentice-Hall, 1976), pp. 134–43; Richard Sennett and Jonathan Cobb, *The Hidden Injuries of Class* (New York: Knopf, 1972); Marc Fried, *The World of the Urban Working Class* (Cambridge: Harvard University, 1973).

2. Lawrence A. Cremin, *The Republic and the Schools: Horace Mann on the Education of Free Men* (New York: Teachers College Press, 1957) p. 87; Robert Bremner et al., *Children and Youth in America: A Documentary History, 1600–1865* (Cambridge: Harvard University Press, 1970), 1:460–61.

3. On *Plessy* v. *Ferguson*, the case establishing the constitutionality of "separate but equal" facilities, see J. R. Pole, *The Pursuit of Equality in American History* (Berkeley: University of California Press, 1978), pp. 195–200. On the conception of equal educational opportunity at the turn of the century, see Marvin Lazerson and W. Norton Grubb, *American Education and Vocationalism: A Documentary History, 1870–1970* (New York: Teachers College Press, 1974), pp. 136–40.

4. See especially Douglas Rendleman, "Parens Patriae: From Chancery to Juvenile Court," *South Carolina Law Review* 23 (1971): 205–59: Steven Schlossman, *Love and the American Delinquent: The Theory and Practice of "Progressive" Juvenile Justice, 1825–1929* (Chicago: University of Chicago Press, 1977), chap. 2.

5. Alexis de Tocqueville, *Democracy in America*, ed. Phillips Bradley, 2 vols. (New York: Vintage, 1955) 1:14.

6. T. B. Bottomore, *Classes in Modern Society* (New York: Random House, 1966), p. 105.

7. On the stability of the income distribution, see U.S. Bureau of the Census, *Money Income of Families and Persons in the United State: 1978*, Current Population Reports, series P-60, no. 123, June 1980, table 13. In fact, the distribution of income before transfers deteriorated—became more unequal—in the period of 1965 to 1974, but increasing welfare programs made the distribution of posttransfer incomes stable over this period. Sheldon Danziger and Robert Plotnick, "Demographic Change, Government Transfers, and Income Distribution," *Monthly Labor Review* 100 (April 1977): 7–11.

8. U. S. Bureau of the Census, *Characteristics of the Population Below the Poverty Level: 1978*, Current Population Reports, series P-60, no. 124, July 1980, table 1. The alternative poverty figures come from *The Measure of Poverty* (U.S. Department of Health, Education, and Welfare, April 1976), section 5, table 19; they are unavailable in such detail for years other than 1974.

9. Kenneth Keniston and the Carnegie Council of Children, *All Our Children: The American Family Under Pressure* (New York: Harcourt Brace Jovanovich, 1977), p. 26.

10. Survey Research Center, University of Michigan, *The Changing Economic Status of 5000 American Families*, May 1974, table 3. For another analysis of this data see Frank Levy, "How Big is the American Underclass?" *The Income Dynamics of the Poor Project Report*, University of California, Berkeley, January 31, 1977.

11. Lilian Rubin, *Worlds of Pain* (New York: Basic Books, 1976), p. 106. See also the first four volumes of Robert Coles, *Children of Crisis* (Boston: Little, Brown, 1967–77), which detail the precariousness of family life when poverty is a real threat.

12. Poverty thresholds for nonfarm families come from U.S. Bureau of the Census, *Characteristics of the Population Below the Poverty Level: 1978*, table A-3. Largely ignored in the postwar period, the special problems of the "working poor" have come to national attention only during the 1970s, and are now being addressed through a wage subsidy as part of the income tax and in proposed revisions of the welfare system. On the working poor, see Barry Bluestone, "The Tripartite Economy: Labor Markets and the Working Poor," *Poverty and Human Resources Abstracts* 5 (July/August 1970): 15–35.

13. Richard DuBoff, "Full Employment: The History of a Receding Target," *Politics and Society* 7 (January/March 1978); James Henry, "Lazy, Young, Female and Black: The New Conservative Theories of Unemployment," *Working Papers for a New Society*, 7 (March/April 1979): 71–79; and Glen Cain, "Labor Force Concepts and Definitions in View of Their Purposes," Special Report 20, Institute for Research on Poverty, March 1978.

14. Julius Shiskin, "Employment and Unemployment: The Doughnut or the Hole?" *Monthly Labor Review* 99 (February 1976): 3–10; Thomas Vietorisz, R. Miere, and J. Giblin, "Subemployment, Exclusion, and Inadequacy Indexes," *Monthly Labor Review* 98 (May 1975): 3–12.

15. Bureau of Labor Statistics, *Handbook of Labor Statistics*, 1978, table 67, p. 206. While this kind of data is unavailable for families, it seems reasonable that, because of multiple earners, spells of unemployment would have been relatively higher for families.

16. Rubin, *Worlds of Pain*, p. 35. See also Studs Terkel, *Working* (New York: Pantheon Books, 1972); Sennett and Cobb, *Hidden Injuries of Class*.

17. In 1978, 24.9 percent of families whose head was unemployed were in officially defined poverty, compared to 4.9 percent of families whose head was fully employed. In addition, 21.7 percent of families in which the head was not in the labor force were poor. Some of these represent "discouraged workers," those who have unsuccessfully looked for work for so long that they have given up the search and report themselves not in the labor force. U.S. Bureau of the Census, *Characteristics of the Population Below the Poverty Level: 1978*, table 25.

18. On the relation between unemployment and divorce, see Frank Furstenberg, "Work Experience and Family Life," in James O'Toole, ed., *Work and the Quality of Life* (Cambridge: MIT Press, 1974); and Heather Ross and Isabel Sawhill, *Time of Transition: The Growth of Families Headed by Women* (Washington, D.C.: The Urban Institute, 1975). For the relation between unemployment and seven indicators of stress—suicide, homocide, admission to state mental hospitals, mortality from cirrhosis of the liver, admission to state prisons, mortality from heart and kidney disease, overall mortality—see Harvey Brenner, *Estimating the Social Costs of National Economic Policy: Implication for Mental and Physical Health and Criminal Aggression*, Joint Economic Committee, Oct. 26, 1978. On the complex connection to child abuse, see Richard J. Light, "Abused and Neglected Children in America: A Study of Alternative Policies," *Harvard Education Review* 43 (November, 1975): 556–98.

19. See Rubin, *Worlds of Pain*, pp. 15–48.

20. Joseph Califano, "American Families: Trends, Pressures, and Recommendations," reprinted in "White House Conference on Families," Joint Hearings Before the Subcommittee on Child and Human Development, U.S. Senate and Subcommittee on Select Education, U.S. House of Representatives, Feb. 2 and 3, 1978, p. 285.

21. U.S. Bureau of Labor Statistics, *Workers of Spanish Origin*, Bulletin 1970, table C-22. However, the 1970 Census data indicate that in California, Chicano men earned 8 percent more than black men, and 4 percent more in Texas; Chicanas earned 8.6 percent more than black women in California, and 1 percent more in Texas. Vernon Briggs, Walter Fogel, and Fred Schmidt, *The Chicano Worker* (Austin: University of Texas Press, 1977), chap. 3. See also the 1959 data in Leo Grebler, Joan Moore, and Ralph Guzman, *The Mexican-American People* (New York: Free Press, 1970), chap. 8, indicating that Chicano men earned 11 percent more than black men in the Southwest.

22. Stanley Masters, *Black-White Income Differentials* (New York: Academic Press, 1975), chap 5. From one set of data, between 40 percent and 60 percent of the white-Chicano earnings difference is due to the differences in years of schooling, compared to

approximately 20 percent to 35 percent of the white-black difference. Calculated from Geoffrey Carliner, "Returns to Education for Blacks, Anglos, and Five Spanish Groups," *Journal of Human Resources* 11 (Spring 1976): 172–84. See also Dudley Poston, David Alvirez, and Marta Tienda, "Earnings Differences Between Anglo and Mexican American Male Workers in 1960 and 1970: Changes in the 'Cost' of Being Mexican American," *Social Science Quarterly* 57 (1976/77): 618–31, which indicates that 45 percent to 72 percent of Anglo-Chicano earnings differentials are due to differences in schooling levels (table 2).

23. For evidence on blacks, see Barbara Bergman, "The Effect on White Incomes of Discrimination in Employment," *Journal of Political Economy* 79 (March/April 1971): 294–313; for Chicanos see Grebler, Moore, and Guzman, *Mexican-American People*, chap. 4.

24. In March 1976, unemployment rates were 7.2 percent for white men, 10.5 percent for Chicanos, and 14.6 percent for black men. For women, Chicanas suffered higher unemployment rates than did black women, 14 percent versus 13.1 percent, both of these much higher than the 7.9 percent unemployment for white women. *Workers of Spanish Origin*, table C–14.

25. U.S. Bureau of the Census, *Characteristics of the Population Below the Poverty Level: 1978*, table 5; *Money Income of Families and Persons in the United States: 1978*, table 2.

26. Quoted in Barbara Bryant Solomon and Helen Mendes, "Black Families: A Social Welfare Perspective," in Virginia Tufte and Barbara Myerhoff, eds., *Changing Images of the Family* (New Haven: Yale University Press, 1979), p. 271.

27. For the best effort to clarify the complexities of class, see Erik Olin Wright, *Class, Crisis, and the State* (London: NLB, 1978), chap. 2. See also Bottomore, *Classes in Modern Society*, chaps. 1 and 2; Nicos Poulantzas, *Classes in Contemporary Capitalism* (London: NLB, 1978). The three groups we use correspond closely, though not perfectly, to independent primary sectors, dependent or routinized primary workers, and secondary workers. See, for example, Richard Edwards, *Contested Terrain: The Transformation of the Workplace in the Twentieth Century* (New York: Basic Books, 1979).

28. James O'Toole, et al., *Work in America* (Cambridge: The MIT Press, 1973), chap. 3; Arthur Kornhauser, *The Mental Health of the Industrial Worker* (New York: John Wiley and Sons, 1965), especially chap. 12.

29. Donald McKinley, *Social Class and Family Life* (New York: Free Press, 1964).

30. Terkel, *Working*, pp. 1–10.

31. Chaya S. Piotrkowski, *Work and the Family System: A Naturalist's Study of Working-Class and Lower Middle-Class Families* (New York: Free Press, 1979), p. 110.

32. John Scanzoni, *Opportunity and the Family* (New York: The Free Press, 1970); Robert Blood and Donald Wolfe, *Husbands and Wives: The Dynamics of Married Living* (New York: Free Press, 1960); Rubin, *Worlds of Pain*; McKinley, *Social Class and Family Life*.

33. Rosabeth Moss Kantor, *Work and Family in the United States: A Critical Review and Agenda for Research and Policy* (New York: Russell Sage Foundation, 1977); Rosabeth Moss Kantor, *Men and Women of the Corporation* (New York: Basic Books, 1977).

34. Kornhauser, *Mental Health of the Industrial Worker*, table 9–5, reported a positive correlation (.34) between job satisfaction and satisfaction with family and home. Another study found a correlation of .51 between job dissatisfaction and tension among family members; see O. A. Oeser and S. B. Hammond, *Social Structure and Personality in a City* (New York: MacMillan, 1954).

35. Robert and Helen Lynd, *Middletown* (New York: Harcourt Brace and World, 1929), p. 29.

36. Rubin, *Worlds of Pain*, p. 113

37. Terkel, *Working*, p. 10.

38. Rubin, *Worlds of Pain*, p. 207. On the importance of children surpassing their parents, see also the anecdotal material in Sennett and Cobb, *Hidden Injuries of Class;* Eli Chinoy, *Automobile Workers and the American Dream* (Garden City, N.Y.: Doubleday, 1975); Theodore Purcell, *Blue Collar Man* (Cambridge: Harvard University Press, 1960); and the more academic work of Scanzoni, *Opportunity and the Family*, chap. 7.

39. Rubin, *Worlds of Pain*, p. 207. On class differences in expectations (as distinct from aspirations), see also Fried, *World of the Urban Working Class*, p. 163.

40. Quoted in S. M. Millar and Ira Harrison, "Types of Dropouts: The 'Unemployables,' " in Arthur Shostak and William Gomberg, eds., *Blue Collar World: Studies of the American Worker* (Englewood Cliffs: Prentice-Hall, 1964), p. 479.

41. These tendencies hold when status and education are taken into account. See Melvin Kohn, *Class and Conformity* (Homewood, Ill.: Dorsey Press, 1969), especially chaps. 9 and 10; Sennet and Cobb, *Hidden Injuries of Class*.

42. Robert Hess and Virginia Shipman, "Early Experience and the Socialization of Cognitive Modes in Children," in Matthew Miles and W. W. Charrers, Jr., *Learning and Social Settings* (Boston: Allyn and Bacon, 1970) p. 178.

43. Ibid, p. 179.

44. Herbert Hyman, "The Value System of Different Classes: A Social Psychological Contribution to the Analysis of Stratification," in R. Bendix and S. M. Lipset, eds, *Class, Status, and Power: A Reader in Social Stratification* (Glencoe: Free Press, 1953), pp. 426–42; William Sewell and Vimal Shah, "Social Class, Parental Encouragement and Educational Aspiration," *American Journal of Sociology* 73 (March 1968): 559–72; Louis Schneider and Sverre Hysgaard, "The Deferred Gratification Pattern: A Preliminary Study," in Alan L. Grey, ed., *Class and Personality in Society* (New York: Atherton, 1969).

45. Rubin, *Worlds of Pain*, pp. 37–38.

46. Ibid.

47. The phrase "other people's children" comes from an insightful unpublished paper by Kenneth Keniston, "Notes on the Role of Children in American History," 1973. See also Sheila Rothman, "Other People's Children: The Day Care Experience in America," *The Public Interest* 30 (Winter 1973): 11–27.

48. On childrearing in the colonies see John Demos, *A Little Commonwealth: Family Life in Plymouth Colony* (New York: Oxford University Press, 1970); Philip Greven, *The Protestant Temperment: Patterns of Child-Rearing, Religious Experience and the Self in Early America* (New York: Knopf, 1977); Michael Zuckerman, "William Byrd's Family," *Perspectives in American History* 12 (1979): pp. 253–312.

49. See the documents in Philip Greven, ed., *Child-Rearing Concepts, 1628–1861* (Itasca, Illinois: F. E. Peacock, 1973).

50. Lilian Rubin, *Busing and Backlash* (Berkeley: University of California Press, 1972), p. 39.

51. Sennett and Cobb, *Hidden Injuries of Class*, pp. 135–36.

52. On wasteful defense spending see James Fallows, *National Defense* (New York: Random House, 1981). On health care costs, see Congressional Budget Office, *Tax Subsidies for Medical Care: Current Policies and Possible Alternatives*, January 1980. On tax expenditures, see W. Norton Grubb and Patricia Griffin Heilbrun, *Far, Far to Go: Public Spending on Children and Youth in Texas* (Austin: Lyndon B. Johnson School of Public Affairs, 1982), Section I and Appendix C; and Congressional Budget Office, *Tax Expenditures: Current Issues and Five-Year Budget Projections for Fiscal Years 1982–1986*, September 1981.

53. Martha Wolfenstein describes a "fun morality" of the 1950s in which all aspects of life—including childrearing—are supposed to be fun. While she criticizes this attitude as related to consumerism, it does represent—particularly in contrast to the childrearing literature of the 1970s—a much less anxious view of childrearing. Martha Wolfenstein, "Fun Morality: An Analysis of Recent American Child Training Literature," in Margaret Meade and Martha Wolfenstein, *Childhood in Contemporary Cultures* (Chicago: University of Chicago Press, 1955).

54. *Public Papers of the President of the United States: Lyndon Johnson, 1965* (Washington D.C.: U.S. Government Printing Office, 1966) 1:415.

55. Richard Freeman, *The Over-Educated American* (New York: Academic Press, 1976).

56. The cost of a "moderate budget" increased 79 percent. The 1976 figures come from Louis McGraw, "Family Budget Costs Continue to Climb in 1976," *Monthly Labor Review* 100 (July 1977): 35–39; the 1967 figures are from the U.S. Department of Labor, "Standards of Living for an Urban Family of Four," Bulletin 1560–5, April 1967. For a review of the literature on the costs of children, see Thomas Espenshade, "The Value and Cost of Children," *Population Bulletin* 32 (April) 1977: 3–47.

57. For evidence that the opportunity costs are substantial, see Espenshade, "Value and Cost of Children." On the "interruption effect," see Jacob Mincer and Solomon Polachek,

"Family Investments in Human Capital: Earnings of Women," in Theodore Schultz, ed., *Economics of the Family* (Chicago: University of Chicago Press, 1974).

58. These figures are taken from Charles Brecher and Raymond Horton, "Trends in Federal Expenditures for Youth," Conservation of Human Resources Project, Columbia University, May 9, 1980.

59. Quoted in Douglas Cater, "The Political Struggle for Equality of Educational Opportunity," in David S. Warner, ed., *Toward New Human Rights: The Social Policies of the Kennedy and Johnson Administration* (Austin: Lyndon B. Johnson School of Public Affairs, 1977), p. 339.

60. For reviews of the achievements of the Great Society and subsequent attacks, see Sar Levitan and Robbert Taggart, *The Promise of Greatness* (Cambridge: Harvard University Press, 1976); Henry Aaron, *Politics and the Professors* (Washington, D.C.: The Brookings Institution, 1978); and Peter Steinfels, *The Neo-Conservatives* (New York: Simon and Schuster, 1979), chap. 9.

61. The school financing reforms that came in the wake of the *Serrano* case uniformly included revenue limits. See W. Norton Grubb, "The First Round of Legislative Reforms in the Post-*Serrano* World," *Law and Contemporary Problems* 38 (Winter/Spring 1974): 459–92.

62. See, for example, "Public Opinion and Proposition 14," Education Commission of the States, February 1979, 61–69. Of the Californians polled, 61.6 percent responded that welfare services should be cut back. The next two favorite areas for cutbacks were day care (24 percent of the respondents) and parks and recreation programs (22.6 percent), both programs heavily used by children. On the early consequences, see Albert Lipson with Marvin Lavin, *Political and Legal Responses to Proposition 13 in California*, Rand Report R-2483-DOJ, January 1980.

63. Anthony Pascal et al., *Fiscal Containment of Local and State Government*, Rand Report R-2494-FF/RC, September 1979, p. 20–21.

64. On the "overload" thesis, see Steinfels, *Neo-Conservatives*, pp. 58–63; Michael Crozier, Samuel Huntington, and Joji Watanuki, *The Crisis of Democracy* (New York: The Trilateral Commission, 1975), pp. 65–74.

65. The data on children in poverty and the AFDC program are analyzed more completely in chapter 7.

66. Children's Defense Fund, "A Children's Defense Budget: A Response to President Reagan's Black Book," March 17, 1981.

67. Demos, *Little Commonwealth*, p. 134–35. See also Greven, *Protestant Temperament*; and Joseph Illick, "Child Rearing in Seventeenth Century England and America," in Lloyd DeMause, ed., *The History of Childhood* (New York: Harper & Row, 1974).

68. Quoted in Greven, *Child-Rearing Concepts*, pp. 140–43.

69. For the shift in conceptions of the child, see the discussions of childrearing literature in Ann Kuhn, *The Mother's Role in Childhood Education: New England Concepts, 1830–1860* (New Haven: Yale University Press, 1947). On the schools, see Barbara Finkelstein, "Pedagogy as Intrusion: Teaching Values in Popular Primary Schools in Nineteenth-Century America," *History of Childhood Quarterly* 2 (Winter, 1975): 349–78. On the importance of the work ethic to conceptions of children, see Keniston, "Notes on the Role of Children." On the persistence of work and play as images for pedagogy, see David K. Cohen and Marvin Lazerson, "Education and the Corporate Order," *Socialist Revolution* 2 (March/April, 1972): 47–72.

70. Lawrence A. Cremin, *The Transformation of the School* (New York: Knopf, 1962), pp. 207–15.

71. Jane Lazarre, *The Mother Knot* (New York: McGraw-Hill, 1976), p. 53.

72. Sennett and Cobb, *Hidden Injuries of Class*, p. 132.

73. Ibid, pp. 131–32.

74. For a good typology of writing on youth, see Vern Bengston, "The Generation Gap: A Review and Typology of Social-Psychological Perspectives," *Youth and Society* 2 (September 1970): 7–32.

75. In one survey only 3.3 percent of parents (though 11.5 percent of nonparents) mentioned a sense of immortality or carrying on the family line through their children as a valued aspect of parenthood. Lois Hoffmann, Arland Thornton, and Jean Denby Manis, "The Value of Children to Parents in the United States," *Journal of Population* 1 (Summer 1978): 91–131, table 2.

76. Boston Women's Health Collective, *Ourselves and Our Children* (New York: Random House, 1978), p. 19. This book can read as a summary of parenting values among young, white, middle-class, college-educated, feminist parents—a group with tremendous influence in defining childrearing norms.

77. James Gordon, "Demonic Children," *New York Times Book Review*, September 11, 1977.

78. On the mechanisms of splitting and displacement, see Keniston, "Notes on the Role of Children."

79. Winifred Cavanaugh, "My Child and Yours," *Better Homes and Gardens*, August 1950, p. 74.

80. George Gallup, "Eighth Annual Gallup Poll of the Public's Attitudes Toward the Public Schools," *Phi Delta Kappan* (October 1976).

81. William Chambliss, "The Saints and the Roughnecks," in Barry Krisberg and James Austin, eds., *The Children of Ishmael: Critical Perspectives on Juvenile Justice* (Palo Alto: Mayfield Publishing, 1978).

82. Quoted in Richard deLone, *Small Futures: Children, Inequality, and the Limits of Liberal Reform* (New York: Harcourt Brace Jovanovich, 1979), p. 89.

83. First Annual Report of the Superintendent of Common Schools, 1938; quoted in Bremner et al., *Children and Youth*, 1:453.

84. Quoted in Steinfels, *Neo-Conservatives*, p. 126; emphasis added.

85. See, for example, National Commission on the Reform of Secondary Education, *The Reform of Secondary Education* (New York: McGraw-Hill, 1973); President's Science Advisory Committee Panel on Youth, *Youth: Transition to Adulthood* (Chicago: University of Chicago Press, 1974); U.S Department of Health, *Work in America* (Cambridge: MIT Press, 1973). For criticisms of these developments, see W. Norton Grubb and Marvin Lazerson, "Ralley 'Round the Workplace: Continuities and Fallacies in Career Education," *Harvard Educational Review* 45 (November 1975): 451–74; Michael Timpane, Susan Abramowiz, Sue Berryman Bobrow, and Anthony Pascal, *Youth Policy in Transition*, Rand Report R-2006-HEW, June 1976; and the special issue "Symposium on Youth: Transition to Adulthood in Schools," *School Review* 83 (November 1974).

86. deLone, *Small Futures*, chap. 3.

87. Rubin, *Busing and Backlash*, p. 48.

88. For evaluations of child nutrition programs, see Congressional Budget Office, *Feeding Children: Federal Child Nutrition Policies in the 1980s*, May 1980, chap. 5.

4. Public Power and Children

1. For an excellent discussion of the politicizing of childhood, see Alan Wolfe, "The Child and the State: A Second Glance," *Contemporary Crises* 2 (1978); 407–35.

2. The expression "the children's cause" is taken from Gilbert Steiner, *The Children's Cause* (Washington, D.C.: The Brookings Institution, 1976).

3. Quoted in "200 Years of Child Health in America," in Edith Grotberg, ed., *200 Years of Children* (Washington, D.C.: HEW, n.d.), p. 122.

4. The literature on interest groups is vast. Much of it is directed to showing how the "broker state" within which interest groups function is compatible with democracy, and needs only to be made more equitable to be perfected. See, for example, David Truman, *The Governmental Process: Political Interest and Public Opinion*, 2nd. ed. (New York: Knopf, 1971). For critiques that stress the limits of interest group democracy in an inegalitarian society and the antidemocratic functions of interest groups, see Grant McConnell, *Private Power and American Democracy* (New York: Knopf, 1966); Theodore Lowi, *The End of Liberalism: Ideology, Policy, and the Crisis of Public Authority* (New York: W. W. Norton, 1969); Alan Wolfe, *The Limits of Legitimacy: Political Contradictions of Contemporary Capitalism* (New York: The Free Press, 1977), chaps. 4–5 and 8–10. The only volume that specifically addresses interest groups working on behalf of children is Steiner, *Children's Cause*, chap. 7.

5. Lorraine McDonnell, "Political Control and the Power of Organized Teacher," discussion draft, The Rand Corporation, March 1981.

6. Steiner, *Children's Cause*, pp. 73–74.

7. W. Norton Grubb and Marvin Lazerson, "Child Care, Government Financing, and the Public Schools: Lessons from the California Children's Centers," *School Review* 86 (November 1977): 5–37.

8. Steiner, *Children's Cause*, p. 243. On the issues of identification, see Angus Campbell, et al., *The American Voter* (New York: John Wiley, 1960), chap. 12. On self-interest as the basis of interest group cohesion, see especially Mancur Olson, *The Logic of Collective Action* (Cambridge: Harvard University Press, 1965). Others, especially Truman, have argued that some kind of psychological identification with the group is more important.

9. On the background of some nutrition programs, especially WIC, see Cheri Hayes, "Three Cases of Federal Policy Formation," and John Nelson, "The Special Supplemental Food Program for Women, Infants, and Children (WIC): A Case Study of Federal Policymaking," National Research Council, Panel for the Study of the Policy Formation Process, January 1979.

10. On Julia Lathrop, see Nancy Weiss, "Save the Children: A History of the Children's Bureau, 1903–1918" (Ph.D. diss., University of California, Los Angeles, 1974); on Mary Keyserling, see Steiner, *Children's Cause*, chap. 7.

11. See Campbell et al., *American Voter*, chap. 12; and McConnell, *Private Power*, chap. 5.

12. Steiner, *Children's Cause*, pp. 145–49.

13. "Towards an Inventory of Federal Programs with Direct Impact on Families," Family Impact Seminar, George Washington University, February 1978. See also the criticism in Gilbert Steiner, *The Futility of Family Policy* (Washington, D.C.: The Brookings Institution, 1981), chap. 2.

14. See Wolfe, *Limits of Legitimacy*, p. 154 *ff.*, for the argument that interest groups which go outside conventional limits are denied access to the state and to influence in decision making.

15. See especially Steiner, *Children's Cause*.

16. See especially Michael Zuckerman, *Peaceable Kingdoms: New England Towns in the Eighteenth Century* (New York: Knopf, 1970).

17. Bernard Bailyn, *The Ideological Origins of the American Revolution* (Cambridge: Harvard University Press, 1967).

18. Jeff Weintraub, "Virtue, Community, and the Sociology of Liberty: The Notion of Republican Virtue and Its Impact on Modern Western Social Thought" (Ph.D. diss., University of California, Berkeley, 1979).

19. C. B. MacPherson, *The Life and Times of Liberal Democracy* (New York: Oxford University Press, 1977), p. 47.

20. Jean Jacques Rousseau, *The Social Contract*, trans. Maurice Cranston (New York: Penguin, 1968).

21. Quoted in Jane Mansbridge, *Beyond Adversary Democracy* (New York: Basic Books, 1980), pp. 16–17.

22. Alexis de Tocqueville, *Democracy in America*, ed. Phillips Bradley, 2 vols. (New York: Vintage, 1955), vol 2.

23. Mansbridge, *Beyond Adversary Democracy*, chap. 2. See also MacPherson, *Liberal Democracy*, chap. 4, on "equilibrium democracy."

24. Truman, *Government Process*, p. 51.

25. George Gallup, *The Gallup Poll: Public Opinion, 1935–1971*, vol. 3: 1959–1971 (New York: Random House, 1972), p. 2192.

26. This point that interest groups prevent the achievement of principled politics is essentially the same as Lowi's contention that governments in interest group democracies cannot plan and cannot achieve justice. Lowi, *End of Liberalism*, Parts 1 and 2.

27. Hayes, "Three Cases of Federal Policy"; "Day Care and Child Development Reports," Jan. 29, 1979; *CCY Focus*, February 1979 and March 1979.

28. Center for Science in the Public Interest, "Nutrition Action," April 1981, pp. 10–13. See also the Children's Defense Fund, "A Children's Defense Budget: A Response to President Reagan's Black Book," March 17, 1981; and Jule Sugarman, ed., *Citizen's Guide to Changes in Human Services Programs* (Washington D.C.: Human Services Information Center, 1981).

29. John Mudd, "Services Coordination and Children," discussion draft, Children's Defense Fund, April 1, 1980.

30. *State Offices of Child Development*, Education Commission of the States, Report no. 55, September 1975.

346

31. Rochelle Beck, "White House Conferences on Children: An Historical Perspective," in *The Rights of Children* (Cambridge: Harvard Educational Review, 1974), pp. 653–68.

32. White House Conference on Families, *Listening to America's Families: Action for the 80s* (Washington, D.C.: White House Conference on Families, November, 1980).

33. Steiner, *Children's Cause*, p. 124.

34. This also seems to be Steiner's point, though in his assessment of the 1980 Conference he also blames the vagueness of "family policy." Steiner also places considerable blame on simple ineptness. Steiner, *Futility of Family Policy*, chap. 2.

35. This strategy is consistent with the contention that interest group politics is sound as long as all groups are adequately represented. See especially the summary and condemnation of pluralist theory in Lowi, *End of Liberalism*.

36. Marilyn Gittell et al., *Citizen Organizations: Citizen Participation in Education Decisionmaking*, Institute for Responsive Education, City University of New York, July 1979.

37. Polly Greenberg, *The Devil has Slippery Shoes: A Biased Biography of the Child Development Group of Mississippi* (New York: Macmillan, 1969).

38. For an analysis indicating the variability of liberal democracy and pointing out an emerging version in participatory democracy, see MacPherson, *Liberal Democracy*, chap. 5.

39. David Rothman, "The State as Parent: Social Policy in the Progressive Era," in Willard Gaylin, et al., *Doing Good: The Limits of Benevolence* (New York: Pantheon Books, 1978), p. 79.

40. Some commentators have interpreted *all* the turmoil of the 1960s as expressing hostility toward professionals in a variety of forms; see Rothman, "The State as Parent."

41. Christopher Lasch, *Haven in a Heartless World* (New York: Basic Books, 1977); Jacques Donzelot, *The Policing of Families* (New York: Pantheon Books, 1980).

42. The phrase "rearing children by the government" comes from an anonymous flyer circulated in opposition to the bill. See "Background Materials Concerning Child and Family Services Act, 1975, S. 626," Senate Subcommittee on Children and Youth, March 1976.

43. On the contradiction inherent in professionalized childrearing, see Carole Joffe, *Friendly Intruders: Childcare Professionals and Family Life* (Berkeley: University of California Press, 1977).

44. Sara Lawrence Lightfoot, *Worlds Apart: Relationships Between Families and Schools* (New York: Basic Books, 1977), p. 74.

45. Burton White, *The First Three Years of Life* (Englewood Cliffs: Prentice-Hall, 1975), p. 4. White's book has been heavily promoted with advertisements asking: "Will your child remember you for what you do *to* him or what you did *for* him?"

46. Lightfoot, *Worlds Apart*, p. 74.

47. For a recent statement of this position, used to criticize maternal employment and child care, see Selma Fraiberg, *Every Child's Birthright: In Defense of Mothering* (New York: Basic Books, 1977).

48. Lightfoot, *Worlds Apart*, pp. 113–14.

49. John Gliedman and William Roth, *The Unexpected Minority: Handicapped Children in America* (New York: Harcourt Brace Jovanovich, 1980), chap. 8.

50. Joffe, *Friendly Intruders*, p. 49.

51. Sheryl Ruzek, "Making Social Work Accountable," in Eliot Friedson, ed., *The Professions and Their Prospects* (Beverly Hills: Sage Publications, 1971), p. 229.

52. Nina Toren, "Semi-Professionalism and Social Work: A Theoretical Perspective," in Amitai Etzioni, *The Semi-Professions and Their Organization* (New York: The Free Press, 1969), p. 166.

53. Edward Lynch, "The White House Family Feud," *Policy Review* 13 (Summer 1980): 113. *Policy Review* is published by the conservative Heritage Foundation.

54. For an analysis of professionalization as a vehicle for market power, see Magali Sarfatti Larson, *The Rise of Professionalism: A Sociological Analysis* (Berkeley: University of California Press, 1977).

55. Joffe, *Friendly Intruders*, p. 53.

56. Ibid. p. 20

57. However, as doctors and lawyers have become publicly supported—through Medicaid, Medicare, and Legal Aid—there have been corresponding efforts to subject them to citizen and client control.

58. See especially Joffe, *Friendly Intruders*, pp. 133–35.

59. On semi-professionals, see Etzioni, *Semi-Professionals*.

60. The image of partners and antagonists is taken from Joseph Featherstone and Helen Featherstone, "Partners and Antagonists," *Working Papers for a New Society* 6 (May/June 1978): 8–10.

61. On these kinds of legitimate conflicts, see Lightfoot, *Worlds Apart*; and the third section of chapter 5.

62. See, for example, Ivan Illich, *Deschooling Society* (New York: Harper & Row, 1970); and Lasch, *Haven in a Heartless World*.

63. On the political battles over the Child Development Associate credential, see Steiner, *Futility of Family Policy*, chap. 4. On the hopes for the CDA, see Jenny Klein, "A New Professional for the Child Care Field—the Child Development Associate," *Child Care Quarterly* 2 (Spring 1973): 56–57; Offices of Child Development, *The CDA Program: the Child Development Associate, a Guide for Training*, DHEW publication No. (OCD) 73-1065, April 1973.

64. See, for example, "Activist Doctors Mixing Medicine, Radical Politics," *Los Angeles Times*, March 26, 1980, part 1, p.1.

65. On the importance of parents having some independent power to match the power of professionals, see Joffe, *Friendly Intruders*; Gliedman and Roth, *Unexpected Minority*.

66. For an excellent example of the tendency to both condemn professionals and urge them to do better, see Kenneth Keniston and the Carnegie Council on Children, *All Our Children: The American Family Under Pressure* (New York: Harcourt Brace Jovanovich, 1977); and Richard deLone, *Small Futures: Children, Inequality, and the Limits of Liberal Reform* (New York: Harcourt Brace Jovanovich, 1979).

5. Public Responsibilities and Private Gains: The Conflicts Within Schooling

1. Lawrence A. Cremin, *Traditions of American Education* (New York: Basic Books, 1977).

2. See, for example, Samuel Bowles and Herbert Gintis, *Schooling in Capitalist America* (New York: Basic Books, 1976); Marvin Lazerson, "Understanding American Catholic Educational History," *History of Education Quarterly* 17 (Fall 1977): 297–317; Richard Kluger, *Simple Justice: The History of Brown v. Board of Education and Black America's Struggle for Equality* (New York: Vintage, 1977); August Meier and Elliot Rudwick, *Across the Color Line: Explorations in the Black Experience* (Urbana: University of Illinois Press, 1976); George Counts, *School and Society in Chicago* (New York: Harcourt Brace, 1928).

3. Lawrence A. Cremin, *American Education: The National Experience, 1783–1876* (New York: Harper & Row, 1980); Carl Kaestle, *The Evolution of an Urban System: New York City, 1780–1850* (Cambridge: Harvard University Press, 1974); James Axtell, *The School Upon a Hill: Education and Family Life in Colonial New England* (New Haven: Yale Univerity Press, 1974).

4. Quoted in Stanley Schultz, *The Culture Factory: Boston Public Schools, 1789–1860* (New York: Oxford University Press, 1973), p. 67.

5. Steven Schlossman, "The Culture of Poverty in Ante-Bellum Social Thought," *Science and Society* 38 (1974): 150–66. See also Kaestle, *Evolution of an Urban School System*; Schultz, *Culture Factory*; Michael B. Katz, "The Origins of Public Education: a Reassessment," *History of Education Quarterly* 16 (1976): 381–407.

6. Quoted in Schultz, *Culture Factory*, pp. 252, 259.

7. Herbert Gutman, "Work, Culture, and Society in Industrializing America, 1815–1919," *American Historical Review* 78 (June 1973): 531–88; Alan Dawley and Peter Faler, "Working Class Culture and Politics in the Industrial Revolution: Sources of Loyalism and Rebellion," *Journal of Social History* 9 (Summer 1976): 466–80.

8. For discussions of the superiority of the school to family in training for adult life, see Robert Dreeben, *On What is Learned in School* (Reading, Mass.: Addison-Wesley, 1968); and Talcott Parsons, "The School Class as a Social System," *Harvard Educational Review* 29 (Fall 1959): 297–318. On the class basis of extended schooling at the turn of the century, see Joseph F. Kett, *Rites of Passage: Adolescence in America, 1790 to the Present* (New

York: Basic Books, 1977), chap. 6; and George S. Counts, *The Selective Character of American Secondary Education* (Chicago: University of Chicago Press, 1922).

9. For an excellent account of the corruption of liberal education, see Christopher Lasch, *The Culture of Narcissism: American Life in An Age of Diminishing Expectations* (New York: W. W. Norton, 1978), chap. 6; the quote from Jefferson is on p. 130.

10. Helen Lynd and Robert Lynd, *Middletown* (New York: Harcourt Brace and World, 1929), pp. 194–96. The vocationalization of schooling at the turn of the century is more fully analyzed in W. Norton Grubb and Marvin Lazerson, "Education and the Labor Market: Recycling the Youth Problem," in H. Kantor and D. Tyack, eds., *Work, Youth, and Schooling: Historical Perspectives in Vocational Education* (Stanford: Stanford University Press, 1982); Marvin Lazerson and W. Norton Grubb, *American Education and Vocationalism, A Documentary History, 1870–1970* (New York: Teachers College Press, 1974); and Jerry Nasaw, *Schooled to Order* (New York: Oxford University Press, 1979).

11. Charles Eliot, "Industrial Education as a Factor in Our National Prosperity" (1908) in Lazerson and Grubb, *American Education and Vocationalism*, p. 137; see also Edward Krug, *The Shaping of the American High School, 1880–1920* (Madison: University of Wisconsin Press, 1969), chap. 8.

12. Quoted in Sol Cohen, "The Industrial Education Movement, 1906–17," *American Quarterly* 20 (Spring 1968): 106. See also Marvin Lazerson, *Origins of the Urban School: Public Education in Massachusetts, 1870–1915* (Cambridge: Harvard University Press, 1971), chap. 6; David Cohen and Barbara Neufeld, "The Failure of High Schools and the Progress of Education," *Daedalus* 110 (Summer 1981): 69–90.

13. Quoted in Lazerson, *Origins of the Urban School*, p. 189.

14. See, for example, David Hogan, "Capitalism and Schooling: A History of the Political Economy of Education in Chicago, 1880–1930" (Ph.D. diss., University of Illinios, 1978).

15. Richard Freeman and S. Herbert Hollomon, "The Declining Value of College-Going," *Change* (September 1975): figure 1, p. 25.

16. Quoted in Paul Blumberg, *Inequality in an Age of Decline* (New York: New York University Press, 1980), p. 26.

17. The parallels between the expansion of the high school and the expansion of higher education have been developed by Martin Trow, "The Second Transformation of American Secondary Education," *International Journal of Comparative Sociology* 2 (1961): 144–65; and Jerome Karabel, "Community Colleges and Social Stratification," *Harvard Educational Review* 42 (November 1972): 521–62.

18. The demonstration that educational attainment of individuals in different jobs has risen faster than skill requirements is a common piece of evidence in the literature on schooling as a credential. See, for example, Ivar Berg, *Education and Jobs: The Great Training Robbery* (New York: Praeger Publishers, 1970), chap. 3; V. Lane Rawlins and Lloyd Ulman, "The Utilization of College-Trained Manpower in the United States," in Margaret Gorden, ed., *Higher Education and the Labor Market* (New York: McGraw-Hill, 1974).

19. National Center for Educational Statistics, *Digest of Educational Statistics, 1976 Edition* (Washington, D.C.: Government Printing Office, 1977), table 84, p. 86.

20. Karabel, "Community Colleges."

21. The classic study of cooling-out in the two-year community college is Burton R. Clark, *The Open Door College* (New York: McGraw-Hill, 1960).

22. For a full discussion of post–World War II challenges to segregation in education, including *Brown*, see Kluger, *Simple Justice*. On the treatment of Hispanics in schools, see George Brown et al., *The Condition of Education for Hispanic Americans* (Washington, D.C.: National Center for Education Statistics, 1980). Partly because of relative gains by blacks, Hispanics are now the group with the lowest educational attainments.

23. On ESEA, see Julie Roy Jeffrey, *Education for Children for the Poor: A Study of the Origins and Implementation of the Elementary and Secondary Education Act of 1965* (Columbus: Ohio State University Press, 1978). On Head Start see Edward Zigler and Jeanette Valentine, *Project Head Start: A Legacy of the War on Poverty* (New York: The Free Press, 1979).

24. *Serrano v. Priest*, 5 Cal. 3d 554, 487 P.2d 1241, 96 Cal. Rptr. 601 (1971); reprinted in *Harvard Educational Review* 41 (November 1971): 503–4, 531.

25. "Update on State-Wide School Finance Cases" (Washington D.C.: Lawyers Commit-

tee for Civil Rights Under Law, February 1978); W. Norton Grubb, "The First Round of Legislative Reforms in the Post-*Serrano* World," *Journal of Law and Contemporary Problems* 38 (Winter/Spring 1974): 459; Stephen Carroll, *The Search for Equity in School Finance: Summary and Conclusions*, Rand Report R-2420 NIE, March 1979.

26. James Smith and Finis Welch, *Race Differences in Earnings: A Survey and New Evidence*, Rand Report R-229F-NSF, March, 1978; Carroll, *Search for Equity*; Robert Brischetto, *Minorities, the Poor, and School Finance Reform*, vol. 9, "Summary and Conclusions," Intercultural Development Research Association, San Antonio, July 1979.

27. The most prominent academic research on the effects of integration has taken the form of examining the effects on school achievement; the Coleman Report of 1966 started this train of research, and work on educational production functions has continued it. For a review, see Harvey Averch et al., *How Effective Is Schooling?* Rand Report R-956-PCSF/RC, March 1972.

28. For evidence that the extent of local control is a function of state legislation rather than state funding, see Betsy Levin and Michael Cohen, "Levels of State Aid Related to State Restrictions on Local School District Decision-Making" (Washington D.C.: Urban Institute, n.d.). Historically, elementary and secondary schooling has become more homogeneous under the influence of national initiatives—testing programs, teacher unions, federal equalization policies—rather than state influences; see, for example, the impact of the College Entrance Examination Board in Michael S. Schudson, "Organizing the 'Meritocracy': A History of the College Entrance Examination Board," *Harvard Educational Review* 42 (February 1972): 34–69.

29. Jeffrey, *Education for Children of the Poor*, chaps. 5–7; and Averch et al., *How Effective Is Schooling?*, review the criticisms.

30. While the *Bakke* case stands as the most prominant symbol of the conflict, the Supreme Court's decision resolved nothing and in fact did more to frame the conflicts inherent in special admissions than resolve them: those against special admissions programs can find in the decisions some ammunition for their own cause, while special admissions programs in general were not ruled unconstitutional. The decision therefore paves the way for continuing legislative and legal battles, rather than disposing of this contentious issue definitively. See Joel Dreyfuss and Charles Lawrence, *The Bakke Case: The Politics of Inequality* (New York: Harcourt Brace Jovanovich, 1979).

31. Even with the considerable political support for Head Start, its supporters have still been forced into a frantic search for cognitive effects. See Irving Lazar et al., *The Persistance of Preschool Effects*, Summary Report to the Administration on Children, Youth, and Families, HEW, October 1977.

32. The formulation of "partners and antagonists" is drawn from Joseph and Helen Featherstone, "Partners and Antagonists," *Working Papers for a Democratic Society* (May/June, 1978): 8–10. This section has benefited enormously from one of the few works on the subject: Sara Lawrence Lightfoot, *Worlds Apart: Relationships Between Families and Schools* (New York: Basic Books, 1978). For a different analysis of inherent cooperation and conflict between schools and families, based on bureaucracy theory, see Eugene Litwak and Henry Meyer, "The School and the Family: Linking Organizations and External Primary Groups," in Paul Lazarsfeld, William Sewell, and Harold Wilenski, *The Uses of Sociology* (New York: Basic Books, 1967).

33. For analyses of the differention of family and school, see Dreeben, *On What Is Learned*; Parsons, "The School Class as a Social System"; Lightfoot, *Worlds Apart*.

34. Lightfoot, *Worlds Apart*, p. 74.

35. However, in this case our desire to maintain a pluralist society, in which communities like the Amish can survive, conflicts with the liberal principle of providing youth with "unlimited" choice over what they want to become. On this issue, *Yoder* decided for the rights of parents over children. The expectation of upward mobility has historically been challenged by parents wanting schools to maintain traditional group and familial values. See, for example, the desire of Slovak families for their own nationality and church-based schools, described in John Bodnar, "Materialism and Morality: Slavic-American Immigrants and Education, 1890–1940," *Journal of Ethnic Studies* 3 (Winter 1976).

36. "Censorship and the Teaching of English," *Arizona English Bulletin* 17 (February 1975); Paul Crosbie and Jacqueline Kasun, "The New Sex Education," *The Public Interest* 58 (Winter 1980): 120–37.

37. Quoted in Jonathan P. Sher, ed. *Education in Rural America: A Reassessment of Conventional Wisdom* (Boulder, Col: Westview Press, 1977), p. xiv.

38. On biases in the classroom, see Robert Rosenthal and Lenorea Jacobson, *Pygmalion in the Classroom* (New York: Holt, Rinehart, and Winston, 1968); Ray Rist, "Student Social Class and Teacher Expectations: The Self-Fulfilling Prophecy in Ghetto Education" *Harvard Educational Review* 40 (August 1970): 411–51.

39. Lightfoot, *Worlds Apart*, chap. 3.

40. See, for example, the evidence cited in Lightfoot, *Worlds Apart*, pp. 174–75, especially James Comer, "Improving the Quality and Continuity of Relationships in Two Inner-City Schools," *Journal of the American Academy of Child Psychiatry* 15 (Summer 1973). The evidence about parent-teacher collaboration in Head Start is similar; see Lazar, *Persistence of Preschool Effects.*

41. The irony of professionalism is that those teachers who are the least competent and sure of themselves—who lack *personal* authority—are the ones most in need of *positional* authority, an appeal to their professional status and presumed expertise. While all teachers rely on professional position to some extent, those who are incompetent are more likely to press their professional prerogatives. Lightfoot, *Worlds Apart*, p. 30. On the efforts of teachers to establish autonomy against parents, see Lightfoot, *Worlds Apart*, chap. 1.

42. On test bias, see Ronald Samuda, *Psychological Testing of American Minorities: Issues and Consequences* (New York: Harper & Row, 1975).

43. Richard Warren, "The Classroom as Sanctuary for Teachers: Discontinuities in Social Control," *American Anthropologist* 75 (February/June 1973): 280–91.

44. Ivan Illich, *Deschooling Society* (New York: Harper & Row, 1970).

45. For a similar argument in the context of an early childhood program, see Carole Joffe, *Friendly Intruders: Childcare Professionals and Family Life* (Berkeley: University of California Press, 1977). See also Lightfoot, *Worlds Apart*, for the argument that the power of parents must be brought into balance with that of professionals.

46. W. Norton Grubb, "The Phoenix of Vocationalism: Hope Deferred is Hope Denied," *New Directions for Education and Work* (Spring 1978): 71–89.

47. Marvin Lazerson, "Consensus and Conflict in American Education: Historical Perspectives," in James S. Coleman et. al., *Parents, Teachers, and Children* (San Francisco: Institute for Contemporary Studies, 1977). See also John E. Coons and Stephen P. Sugarman, *Education By Choice: The Case for Family Control* (Berkeley: University of California Press, 1978).

48. Delegating public responsibility to private institutions is characteristic of the "franchise state"; see Alan Wolfe, *The Limits of Legitimacy* (New York: The Free Press, 1977), chaps. 4–5.

49. The evidence on the growth of industry-based training is still limited, but see Harold Goldstein, *Training and Education by Industry* (Washington D.C.: National Manpower Institute, 1980); Seymour Lusterman, *Education in Industry,* (New York: The Conference Board, 1977).

50. For a review of the efforts at "diversion," designed to disperse high school students in workplaces and community settings, see Michael Timpane et al., *Youth Policy in Transition*, Rand Report R-2006-HEW, June 1976.

51. On the family as educator and the community as educator, see the special issues of *Teachers College Record* 75 (May 1974) and 79 (May 1978).

52. See Lightfoot, *Worlds Apart*, chap. 4; Kluger, *Simple Justice;* and the evidence on aspirations cited in chapter 3 herein.

6. Youth Policy: The Dilemmas of Development and Control

1. Carnegie Council on Policy Studies in Higher Education, *Giving Youth a Better Chance* (San Francisco: Jossey-Bass, 1979), p. 1.

2. The question of why the social conception of youth has coincided with the biological stage of adolescence has not been effectively answered. The mid-nineteenth century stage of youth came later than it does now, encompassing the late teens and the twenties. We also know that the age of onset of biological adolescence—as measured by the onset of menstru-

ation—has decreased from about age eighteen to about twelve during the last century or so. This suggests that the timing of biological changes and of the social conception of youth have coincided, though the nature of this relationship is unclear.

3. Phillip Greven, *Four Generations: Population, Land, and Family in Colonial Andover, Massachusetts* (Ithaca: Cornell University Press, 1970); and John Demos, *A Little Commonwealth: Family Life in Plymouth Colony* (New York: Oxford University Press, 1970).

4. Quoted in John Demos and Virginia Demos, "Adolescence in Historical Perspective," in Michael Gordon, ed., *The American Family in Social-Historical Perspective* (New York: St. Martin's Press, 1973). See also Joseph Kett, *Rites of Passage: Adolescence in America, 1750 to the Present* (New York: Basic Books, 1977).

5. Michael B. Katz, *People of Hamilton, Canada West: Family and Class in a Mid-Nineteenth Century City* (Cambridge: Harvard University Press, 1975); John Modell, Frank F. Furstenberg, Jr., and Theodore Hershberg, "Social Change and Transitions to Adulthood in Historical Perspective," Michael Gordon, ed., *The American Family in Social-Historical Perspective*, 2nd ed. (New York: St. Martins Press, 1978).

6. On the "problem of generations" caused by children becoming different from their parents, see Bruno Bettleheim, "The Problem of Generations," *Daedalus* 9 (Winter 1962): 68–96.

7. W. Norton Grubb and Marvin Lazerson, "Education and the Labor Market: Recycling the Youth Problem," in H. Kantor and D. Tyack, eds., *Work, Youth and Schooling: Historical Perspectives on Vocational Education* (Stanford: Stanford University Press, 1982).

8. Hall and Addams are quoted in Robert Bremner et al., *Children and Youth in America: A Documentary History*, 3 vols. (Cambridge: Harvard University Press, 1971) 2:81–85.

9. Note, for example, that the youth Kenneth Keniston wrote about in the 1960s were *The Uncommitted: Alienated Youth in American Society* (New York: Harcourt Brace and World, 1960) and *Young Radicals: Notes on Committed Youth* (New York: Harcourt Brace, 1968).

10. On the historical development of these distinctions, see Steven Schlossman and Stephanie Wallach, "The Crime of Precocious Sexuality: Female Juvenile Delinquency in the Progressive Era," *Harvard Educational Review* 48 (February 1978): 65–94.

11. For a review of the literature on the generation gap, emphasizing the difference between the "great gap" position and the "gap is an illusion" position, see Vern Bengtson, "The Generation Gap: A Review and Typology of Social-Psychological Perspectives," *Youth and Society* 2 (September 1970): 7–32.

12. *Wall Street Journal*, June 3, 1981, p. 18.

13. For a description of two delinquent gangs, one middle-class whose members grew up to be successes, and one lower-class whose members tended to accumulate police records and were later failures, see William Chambliss, "The Saints and the Roughnecks," in Barry Krisberg and James Austin, *The Children of Ishmael: Critical Perspectives on Juvenile Justice* (Palo Alto: Mayfield Publishing, 1978). On class and racial biases in the juvenile justice system, see the references in chapter 6, note 48 herein.

14. Paul Osterman, *Getting Started* (Cambridge: MIT. Press, 1980). For a different view of the consequences of unemployment, see Wayne Stevenson, "The Relationship between Youth Employment and Future Employability and Earnings," in *Supplementary Papers from the Conference on Youth Employment: Its Measurement and Meaning*, U.S. Department of Labor, October 1978.

15. Jane Gaskell and Marvin Lazerson, "Between School and Work: Perspectives of Working Class Youth," *Interchange* 11 (1980/81): 80–96.

16. Organization for Economic Cooperation and Development, *Youth Unemployment* (Paris: OECD, 1978), vol. I, p. 25.

17. Harvey Kantor and David Tyack, "Vocationalism in American Education: An Introduction," in Kantor and Tyack, *Work, Youth and Schooling*.

18. Marvin Lazerson and W. Norton Grubb, *Vocationalism and American Education, 1870–1970: A Documentary History* (New York: Teachers College Press, 1974).

19. Edward A. Krug, *The Shaping of the American High School, 1920–1940* (Madison: University of Wisconsin Press, 1972), pp. 319–27.

20. For a review of the effects of vocational education, see Beatrice Reubens, "Vocational

Education for *All* in High School?" in James O'Toole, ed., *Work and the Quality of Life* (Cambridge: MIT. Press, 1975); the most recent and sophisticated analysis is John Grasso and John Shea, *Vocational Education and Training Impact on Youth* (Berkeley: Carnegie Council on Policy Studies in Higher Education, 1979). See also W. Norton Grubb, "The Phoenix of Vocationalism: Hope Deferred is Hope Denied," *New Directions for Education and Work* 1 (Spring 1978): 71–89.

21. On manpower programs of the 1960s, see Jon Goldstein, "The Effectiveness of Manpower Training Programs: A Review of Research on the Impact on the Poor," Joint Economic Committee, November 20, 1972.

22. Vice President's Task Force on Youth Employment, *A Review of Youth Employment Problems, Programs, and Policies*, 3 vols. (Washington, D.C. 1980). See also Congressional Budget Office, *Policy Options for the Teenage Unemployment Problem*, Background Paper no. 13, especially table 1; and *Employment and Training Report of the President*, 1978, especially table A-19.

23. On unemployment rates for blacks and Hispanics, see *Employment and Training Report of the President*, 1978, table A-20, and *Workers of Spanish Origin: A Chartbook*, Bureau of Labor Statistics, Bulletin 1970, 178, table C-14. For evidence that racial differences reflect discrimination and cannot be explained by the educational and demographic differences between white and black youth, see Osterman, *Getting Started*, chap. 5.

24. James Smith and Finis Welch, *Race Differences in Earnings: A Survey and New Evidence*, Rand Report R-2295-NSF, March 1978.

25. Dale Mann, *Chasing the American Dream: Jobs, Schools, and Employment Training Programs in New York State* (New York: Community Service Society of New York, 1980), pp. 28–29.

26. See Paul Barton, "Youth Unemployment and Career Entry," in Seymour Wolfbein, ed., *Labor Market Information for Youth* (Philadelphia: Temple University Press, 1975); *Youth Unemployment and Minimum Wages*, Bureau of Labor Statistics Bulletin 1655, 1970; Daniel Diamond and Hrach Bedrosian, *Hiring Standards and Job Performance*, U.S. Department of Labor Manpower Research Monograph no. 18, 1970; Osterman, *Getting Started*.

27. For evidence that child labor laws seem to affect employment patterns for those under eighteen, see Daniel Mitchell and John Clapp, "The Effects of Child Labor Laws on Youth Employment," *Conference Report on Youth Unemployment*. However, employers are not generally able to indicate what child labor laws are actually violated, and so hiring older workers appears to be a way of avoiding the trouble of investigating the child labor laws completely and the risk of unwittingly violating them.

28. The uncertain evidence on the impact of minimum wage labor is discussed in CBO, *Policy Options for Teenage Unemployment*, pp. 33–39; Osterman, *Getting Started*. For conservative claims, see M. Stanton Evans, "A Youth Differential," *National Review*, August 1977, p. 888.

29. For evidence that educational attainments in occupations have been increasing faster than the cognitive requirements of jobs, see V. Lane Rawlins and Lloyd Ulman, "The Utilization of College-Trained Manpower in the United States," in Margaret Gordon, ed., *Higher Education and the Labor Market* (New York: McGraw-Hill, 1978). See also Mann, *Chasing the American Dream*, and Grubb and Lazerson, "Education and the Labor Market."

30. Carol Leon, "Young Adults: A Transitional Group with Changing Labor Force Patterns," *Monthly Review* 101 (May 1978): 3–9.

31. The evidence that better information leads to higher earnings and occupational status is inconclusive. For some evidence on variations in information, see *Career Thresholds*, U.S. Department of Labor Manpower Research Monograph no. 16, 1970, vol. 1, chap. 5.

32. Three influential reports appeared toward the end of the 1960s, each of them calling for a reorientation of schooling around work: the report of the President's Science Advisory Committee, *Youth: Transition to Adulthood* (Chicago: University of Chicago Press, 1974); the report of the National Panel on High Schools and Adolescent Education; and that of the National Commission on the Reform of Secondary Education. These reports have been summarized and criticized in Michael Timpane et al., *Youth Policy in Transition*, Rand Report R-2006-HEW, June 1976.

33. We have previously examined and criticized career education in W. Norton Grubb

and Marvin Lazerson, "Rally 'Round the Workplace: Continuities and Fallacies in Career Education," *Harvard Educational Review* 45 (November 1975): 451–74. On the resurrection of vocational education, see Grubb, "Phoenix of Vocationalism."

34. Eleanor Farrar et al., *The Walls Within: Work, Experience and School Reform* (Cambridge: Huron Institute, 1980).

35. Good summaries of the programs include *CETA: An Analysis of the Issues*, National Commission for Manpower Policy, Special Report no. 23, May 1978; *Employment and Training Report of the President, 1978*; OECD, *Youth Unemployment*, vol. II.

36. For YEDPA enrollments, see *Employment and Training Report of the President 1979*, pp. 41–45.

37. For information on the fast-moving and uncertain developments during the first six months of the Reagan administration, see the "Employment and Training Reporter" (Washington, D.C.: Bureau of National Affairs), various issues in March–September 1981.

38. For a review of the evidence, see Bradley Schiller, "Program Outcomes," in *CETA: An Analysis of the Issues*. The initial evaluations of CETA, using the Continuous Longitudinal Manpower Survey data, have been unable to disentangle the effects of CETA on participants from the effects of improving economic conditions. Westat Inc., *CLMS Follow-up Report No. 3*, Office of Program Evaluation, Employment and Training Administration, Department of Labor, January 1981.

39. Charles Killingsworth and Mark Killingsworth, "Direct Effects of Employment and Training Programs on Employment and Unemployment: New Estimates and Implications for Employment Policy," in *Conference Report on Youth Unemployment*.

40. See the discussion in the fourth section of chapter 9, herein. Even the study by HEW which documented the effects of poor job conditions could only offer the most pallid recommendations for government initiatives, largely in the form of funding demonstration programs, and even these have not been established. HEW, *Work in America* (Cambridge: MIT. Press, 1973), chap. 6.

41. For data on trends in juvenile crime, see U.S. Department of Justice, *Crime in the United States, 1975*, table 30, and *Crime in the United States, 1978*, table 26. The Office of Youth Development, *Juvenile Court Statistics*, reports that between 1950 and 1972, the ratio of arrests to the population between eleven and eighteen rose from 1.6 percent to 3.4 percent.

42. On the history of the juvenile justice system, see Steven Schlossman, *Love and the American Delinquent: The Theory and Practice of "Progressive" Juvenile Justice, 1825–1926* (Chicago: University of Chicago Press, 1977); Anthony Platt, *The Child-Savers: The Invention of Delinquency* (Chicago: University of Chicago Press, 1969); Ellen Ryerson, *the Best-Laid Plans: America's Juvenile Court Experiment* (New York: Hill and Wang, 1978); David Rothman, *The Discovery of the Asylum: Social Order and Disorder in The New Republic* (Boston: Little, Brown, 1971); David Rothman, *Conscience and Convenience: The Asylum and Its Alternatives in Progressive America* (Boston: Little, Brown, 1980); Douglas Rendleman, "Parens Patriae: From Chancery to Juvenile Court," *South Carolina Law Review* 23 (1971): 205–59.

43. Quoted in Bremner, *Children and Youth*, 2: 504–6.

44. President's Commission on Law Enforcement and the Administration of Justice, *Report of the Task Force on Delinquency* (1967), p. 7.

45. *1974 Report of the Law Enforcement Assistance Administration*, U.S. Department of Justice; see also *Children in Custody*, Report on Juvenile Detention and Correctional Facility Census of 1971 (LEAA, 1971). One study reported that in 1971 85,000 children were in custodial juvenile facilities, a rise of 15,000 over the previous year. But a far greater number—about 500,000—were processed through juvenile detention facilities during the year (though on any given day the detention population numbered about 10,000), and an equal number were processed through *adult* jails, as part of the trend to try older juveniles in adult courts and place them in adult prisons. See Rosemary Sarri, *Under Lock and Key, A Report of the National Assessment of Juvenile Corrections* (Ann Arbor: University of Michigan Press, 1974).

46. See N. Morris, *An Honest Politician's Guide to Crime Control* (Berkeley: University of California Press, 1970).

47. J. Williams and M. Gold, "From Delinquent Behavior to Official Delinquency," *Social Problems* 20 (Fall 1972): 209–29.

48. Marvin Wolfgang, M. Figlio, and T. Sellin, *Delinquency in a Birth Cohort* (Chicago: University of Chicago Press, 1972). Variables other than race and class associated with a court penalty include the seriousness of the offense and having previously committed some offense, as one might expect; the point is that class and race—especially race—remain important even when the nature of the offense has been controlled. Other evidence on the differential rates of referral into the juvenile justice system comes from Yeheskel Hasenfeld, "Youth in the Juvenile Court: Input and Output Patterns," in *Brought to Justice? Juveniles, the Courts, and the Law* (Ann Arbor: National Assessment of Juvenile Corrections, 1976), which reports that referral rates are three times as high for nonwhites as for whites.

49. Mimi Goldman, "Women's Crime in a Male Society," *Juvenile Court Judges Journal* 23 (Summer 1971): 33–35. See also N. Greene and T. C. Esselstyne, "The Beyond Control Girl," *Juvenile Court Judges Journal,* 23 (Summer 1971); Kristine O. Rogers, "For Her Own Protection . . . : Conditions of Incarceration for Female Juvenile Offenders in the State of Connecticut," *Law and Society Review* 7 (Winter 1972): 223–46; "Note: Ungovernability: The Unjustifiable Jurisdiction," *Yale Law Journal* 83 (June 1974): 1383–1409. On the history of the separate treatment of girls, see Schlossman and Wallach, "Crime of Precocious Sexuality."

50. For descriptions of different programs, see Krisberg and Austin, *Children of Ishmael*, chaps. 7 and 8.

51. Krisberg and Austin cite unpublished work by Wolfgang, Figlio, and Thornberry indicating the dominance of psychiatric or psychological approaches to the causes of crime; Ibid., p. 118. For one example of a work-based therapeutic program, see Delbert Elliot and Brian Knowles, "Social Development and Employment: An Evaluation of the Oakland Youth Work Experience Program," in *Conference Report on Youth Unemployment.*

52. For program evaluations, see Marc Riedel and Torence Thornberg, "The Effectiveness of Correctional Programs: An Assessment of the Field"; and William Davidson II and Edward Seidman, "Studies of Behavior Modification and Juvenile Perspective," both in Krisberg and Austin, *Children of Ishmael.* As in the case of vocational education, the generally negative findings of these studies probably represent an agglomeration of completely worthless (and even harmful) programs with some that are effective. For a review of effective programs, see Paul Gendreau and Bob Ross, "Effective Correctional Treatment: Bibliotherapy for Cynics," *Crime and Delinquency* 25 (October 1979): 463–89.

53. Joan McCord, "A Thirty-Year Follow-up of Treatment Effects," *American Psychologist* 33 (March 1978): 284–89.

54. On the relationship between school failure and juvenile offenses, see the review in Daniel Glaser, *Crime in Our Changing Society* (New York: Holt, Rinehart, and Winston, 1978); Daniel Glaser, "Economic and Socio-cultural Variables Affecting Rates of Youth Unemployment, Delinquency and Crime," in *Conference Report on Youth Unemployment.*

55. On the relationship between juvenile crime and employment opportunities, see Llad Phillips, Harold Votey, and Darold Maxwell, "Crime, Youth, and the Labor Market," *Journal of Political Economy* 80 (May/June 1972): 491–504; Glaser, "Economic and Socio-cultural Variables."

56. See R. Sarri and R. Vinrer, "Justice for Whom: Varieties of Juvenile Correctional Approaches," in M. Klein, ed., *The Juvenile Justice System* (Beverly Hills: Sage Publications, 1976); Y. Hasenfeld, "The Juvenile Court and Its Environment," in *Brought to Justice? Juveniles, Courts, and the Law* (National Association of Juvenile Courts, 1976). On diversion, see D. R. Cressy and R. A. McDermott, *Diversion from the Juvenile Justice System* (Washington, D.C.: U.S. Government Printing Office, 1973); F. Allen, *Borderlands of Criminal Justice* (Berkeley: University of California Press, 1964); N. Morris, *The Future of Imprisonment* (Berkeley: University of California Press, 1974); Paul Lerman, *Community Treatment and Social Control: A Critical Analysis* (Chicago: University of Chicago Press, 1975); Paul Nejelsk, "Diversion: Unleashing the Hounds of Heaven?" in Margaret Rosenheim, ed., *Pursuing Justice for the Child* (Chicago: University of Chicago Press, 1976).

57. On decriminalization, see W. Sheridan, "Juveniles Who Commit Noncriminal Acts: Why Treat in a Correctional System?" *Federal Probation* 31 (March, 1967): 26–30; Adrian Gough, "The Beyond-Control Child and the Right to Treatment: An Exercise in the Synthesis of a Paradox," *St. Louis University Law Journal* 182 (1971):182–200; Judge David

Bazelon, "Beyond the Control of the Juvenile Court," *Juvenile Court Judges Journal* 21 (Summer 1970): 42–45; E. Lemert, "The Juvenile Court—Quest and Realities," in *Juvenile Delinquency and Youth Crime,* Report to National Commission on Law Enforcement and the Administration of Justice (1967).

58. In the most extreme case of deinstitutionalization, Massachusetts has experimented with closing its state correctional facilities altogether. But this nationally noted experiment has not necessarily reduced the number of juveniles confined to facilities, since a great deal of the caseload has been transferred to therapeutic facilities. See Andrew Rutherford, "Youth Corrections in Massachusetts," in Sheldon Messinger, ed., *The Aldine Crime and Justice Annual* (Chicago: Aldine-Atherton, 1976). On deinstitutionalization efforts and subsequent enlargement of the juvenile justice system in the progressive era, see Rothman, *Conscience and Convenience.*

59. *Kent* v. *United States* 383 U.S. 541 (1966), at 556.

60. *In re Gault,* 375 U.S. 1 (1967). *In re Winship,* 397 U.S. 358 (1970) extended juvenile rights further, extending adult standards of proof to juveniles.

61. Paul Goodman, *Growing up Absurd* (New York: Random House, 1960), pp. 33–34.

7. Welfare Policy and the Needs of Other People's Children: The Limits of Redistribution

1. U.S. Bureau of the Census, *Characteristics of the Population Below the Poverty Level: 1978,* Current Population Reports, series P-60, no. 124, July 1980, table 1.

2. Robert H. Bremner, *From the Depths: The Discovery of Poverty in the United States* (New York: New York University Press, 1956); Stephan Thernstrom, "Poverty in Historical Perspective," in Daniel P. Moynihan, ed., *On Understanding Poverty: Perspectives from the Social Sciences* (New York: Basic Books, 1969).

3. Quoted in Richard deLone, *Small Futures: Children, Inequality, and the Limits of Liberal Reform* (New York: Harcourt Brace Jovanovich, 1979), p. 20.

4. For survey evidence indicating that children are generally not blamed for their poverty, especially compared to adults, see Fay Lomax Cook, *Who Should Be Helped? Public Support For Social Services* (Beverly Hills: Sage Publications, 1979), chap. 4.

5. Mollie Orshansky, "Counting Up the Poor," *Social Security Bulletin* 28 (January 1965): 6.

6. The figures on the incidence of poverty under alternative definitions are taken from *The Measure of Poverty* (U.S. Department of Health, Education, and Welfare, April 1976), table 19. These alternative figures are available for 1974 only. The figures are not broken down by both age and race: the poverty rates of 40 percent and 60 percent for Hispanic children and black children are rough estimates devised by applying racial differentials to official statistics. For a more extensive discussion of the unrealistic nature of official poverty standards, see Kenneth Keniston, *All Our Children: The American Family Under Pressure* (New York: Harcourt Brace Jovanovich, 1977), pp. 26–31.

7. There has been some improvement; however, since in 1965 only 14.5 percent of poor families with children were moved out of poverty. Almost all of the increased effectiveness comes from the improvements in programs to children in *male*-headed families. See Robert Plotnick and Felicity Skidmore, *Progress Against Poverty: A Review of the 1964–1974 Decade* (New York: Academic Press, 1975), table 6.4. The contrast in the effectiveness of transfer programs in alleviating poverty among aged families and non-aged families (those most likely to have children) has if anything become worse over time: in 1976 transfer programs moved 93 percent of aged poor families over the official poverty line, while transfer programs moved only 42 percent of families with a head under sixty-five over the poverty threshold. See *Poverty Status of Families Under Alternative Definitions of Income,* Congressional Budget Office, Background Paper no. 17, January 13, 1977, table 6.

8. See, for example, "Poll Discloses Property Taxes Cuts Are Widely Backed Around Nation," *New York Times,* June 28, 1978.

9. Despite publicity surrounding welfare "queens" who intentionally defraud the AFDC system, the evidence from the negative income tax experiments (cited in chapter 7, note 38) suggests that disincentives are relatively low. See also Leonard Goodwin, *Do the Poor Want to Work?* (Washington, D.C.: The Brookings Institution, 1972).

10. Mildred Calvert, "Welfare Rights and the Welfare System," in Milwaukee County Welfare Rights Organization, *Welfare Mothers Speak Out* (New York: W. W. Norton, 1972), pp. 29-30.

11. On mothers' pensions, see Mark Leff, "Consensus for Reform: The Mothers' Pension Movement in the Progressive Era," *Social Service Review* 47 (September 1973): 397-417; on "scientific philanthropy," see James Lane, "Jacob Riis and Scientific Philanthropy During the Progressive Era," *Social Service Review* 47 (March 1973): 32-48.

12. Francis Fox Piven and Richard Cloward, *Regulating the Poor: The Functions of Public Welfare* (New York: Random House, 1971); and Lester Salamon, *Welfare: The Elusive Consensus* (New York: Praeger Publishers, 1978), especially chap. 3.

13. See in general "Work Tests," *Materials on Welfare Law*, (New York: Center on Social Welfare Policy and Law, 1972), chap. 5.

14. Barbara Boland, "Participation in the AFDC Program," in *Studies in Public Welfare*, Paper no. 12 (part 1), Joint Economic Committee, Subcommittee on Fiscal Policy, 1973; see also Cynthia Rence and Michael Wiseman, "The California Welfare Reform Act and Participation in AFCD," Working Paper no. 81, Institute of Business and Economic Research, University of California, Berkeley, July 1976. Two-thirds of growth in the welfare rolls was due to increased participation, with one-third due to increases in the eligible population; Salamon, *Welfare*, chap. 2, table 2.5.

15. Most data on social security programs are from the *Social Security Bulletin*, published monthly by the Social Security Administration of HEW. The food stamp figure is for the fiscal year, from "Medicaid Statistics, Fiscal Year 1975," National Center for Social Statistics, March 1976.

16. In New York, for example, the average family on AFDC received an additional $501 a year through food stamps and $1,606 worth of health services through Medicaid. David W. Lyon et al., *Multiple Welfare Benefits in New York City*, Rand Report R-2002-HEW, August 1976, table S-1. These subsidies represented 8.2 percent and 26.4 percent of the total income available to AFDC recipients, but these figures might be low relative to other AFDC recipients across the country since New York City is one of the most generous jurisdictions.

17. For a review of WIN, see Leonard Goodwin, *The Work Incentive (WIN) Program and Related Experiences*, R and D Monograph 49, U.S. Department of Labor, 1977. The most sophisticated evaluation found that WIN participation did not significantly decrease welfare payments or increase the rate of leaving AFDC, even though WIN increased earnings slightly. See *The Impact of WIN II: A Longitudinal Evaluation of the Work Incentive Program (WIN)*, Report MEL 76-06, Office of Policy, Evaluation, and Research, Employment and Training Administration, U.S. Department of Labor, September 1976.

18. These regulations and HEW's Quality Control System have been briefly described by Frances Fox Piven, "Welfare Reform and the Redistribution of Income," *Public Welfare* 34 (Spring 1976): 14-18. For extensive commentary, see "Comments on Proposed Regulations Relating to Methods of Determining Eligibility, Fair Hearings, and Recoupment of Overpayment, Submitted on Behalf of National Welfare Rights Organization," National Center on Social Welfare Policy and Law, May 1973. On the various attempts to curtail welfare costs in the 1970s, see Christopher Leman, *The Collapse of Welfare Reform: Political Institutions, Policy, and the Poor in Canada and the United States* (Cambridge: MIT Press, 1980).

19. On the complexity and ambiguity in welfare standards, see "Issues in Welfare Administration—An Administrative Nightmare," *Studies in Public Welfare*, Paper no. 5 (part 1), Joint Economic Committee, Subcommittee on Fiscal Policy, Dec. 31, 1972. Errors are as much the fault of caseworkers as clients: the Center on Social Welfare Policy and Law cited New York statistics that 45 percent of errors were made by the welfare agency alone, and additional 10.8 percent of errors were made jointly by the agency and the recipient but could have been prevented by the agency itself (in the report mentioned in chapter 7, note 18 herein).

20. In the 1973 survey of AFDC recipients, 49.7 percent of families were female-headed because of divorce or separation, and an additional 44.6 percent were female-headed because of illegitimacy. See *Findings of the 1973 AFDC Survey*, part 1, table 22, p. 44. On the growth of female-headed families, see Heather Ross and Isabel Sawhill, *Time of Transition: The Growth of Families Headed by Women* (Washington, D.C.: The Urban Institute, 1975). For documentation of movements on and off welfare, see David Lyon, *The*

Dynamics of Welfare Dependency: A Survey, Welfare Policy Project, Institute of Policy Sciences and Public Affairs, Duke University, Spring 1977.

21. On the harms of the child support system, see Judith Cassety, *Child Support and Public Policy*, (Lexington, Mass.: D.C. Heath, 1978); Colin Blaydon and Carol Stack, "Income Support Policies and the Family," *Daedalus* 106 (Spring 1977): 147–61. Legislation provides exceptions from the Child Support Enforcement Program where it would be in the "best interests of the child," but HEW has written regulations that allow exception only in cases of rape and incest.

22. Quoted in Leman, *Collapse of Welfare Reform*, p. 215.

23. See the evidence on WIN cited in chapter 7, note 17 herein. While he was governor of California, Ronald Reagan introduced a "workfare" plan that was a total failure; see State of California, Employment Development Department, "Third Year and Final Report on the Community Work Experience Program," April 1976.

24. On the replacement of "discretionary paternalism" with administrative and managerial techniques, see Mark Aaronson, "Legal Advocacy and Welfare Reform: Continuity and Change in Public Relief" (Ph.D. diss., University of California, Berkeley, 1971).

25. On the relative ineffectiveness of administrative practices, see Lyon, *Dynamics of Welfare Dependency*, pp. 33–40.

26. Further negative effects can be seen in declining rates of application approval (from 88.1 percent in early 1970 to 76.5 percent in 1975); rates of discontinuing welfare cases increased 136.4 percent between 1970 and 1975, while AFDC cases rose only 39.3 percent. All data is from *AFDC Rates of Approval* published by the Social and Rehabilitation Service for three-month intervals.

27. Data on average monthly payments per recipient comes from table M-32 of the *Social Security Bulletin* for various years.

28. Quoted in Andrew Hacker, "Up for Grabs," *New York Review of Books*, April 30, 1981.

29. On the changes in AFDC, see the revised regulations in the *Federal Register*, vol. 46, no. 182, September 21, 1981, pp. 46750-773.

30. "Reagan Reaffirms Determination to Cut Federal Aid Even Further," *New York Times*, 22, November 1981, p. 1.

31. The fullest discussion of this argument is Piven and Cloward, *Regulating the Poor*, and their subsequent volume, *Poor People's Movements: Why They Succeed, How They Fail* (New York: Random House, 1977).

32. To some, reducing work disincentives is the prime issue; see, for example, Henry Aaron, *Why Is Welfare So Hard to Reform?* (Washington, D.C.: The Brookings Institution, 1973). The concern over work disincentives stimulated the greatest amount of welfare-related research during the 1970s, in the form of the various negative income tax experiments. The dominance of economists in this work and their concerns over the effectiveness of labor market incentives and the disincentives of transfer programs has strengthened this focus.

33. See, for example, David Gold, Clarence Lo, and Erik Wright, "Recent Developments in Marxist Theories of the State," *Monthly Review* 20 (October/November 1975); James O'Connor, *The Fiscal Crisis of the State*, (New York: St. Martin's Press, 1973); and Jurgen Habermas, *Legitimation Crisis* (Boston: Beacon Press, 1975).

34. Social and Rehabilitation Service, *Public Assistance Annual Statistical Data, 1975*.

35. Incentives for splitting up families are universally acknowledged to exist in the present welfare system, but there is no consensus on the effects of these incentives on actual behavior. One review of the literature does indicate some effect, but its magnitude is probably smaller than has been assumed and causal interpretations are uncertain. See "The Effects of Welfare Reform on the Family," Institute for Research on Poverty, University of Wisconsin, March 11, 1977, section 7.

36. A Harris survey of July 1979 showed that a majority felt that welfare spending could be cut by one-third without serious consequences, while two-thirds favored protecting Social Security and a majority opposed cuts for publicly-subsidized jobs. Natalie Jaffe, "Attitudes Towards Public Welfare Programs and Recipients in the United States," in Salamon, *Welfare*.

37. Comparability among programs is difficult because of different ways of treating dependents and differences in family composition. Data are taken from the *Social Security Bulletin* 44 (March 1981), various tables.

38. This evidence has been generated by the various negative income tax experiments. For a summary, see Albert Rees and Harold Watts, "An Overview of the Labor Supply Results," in Joseph Pechman and Michael Timpane, eds., *Work Incentives and Income Guarantees in the New Jersey Negative Income Tax Experiment* (Washington, D.C.: The Brookings Institution, 1975).

39. For two clear statements of the "equity" argument, see *Income Security for All Americans*, Studies in Public Welfare, Paper no. 20; and Michael Barth, Joseph Carcagno, and John Palmer, *Toward an Effective Income Support System: Problems, Prospects, and Choices* (Madison: Institute for Research on Poverty, 1974).

40. For justification of the incremental approach, see Richard Nathan, "The Case for Incrementalism," *City Almanac* 11 (December 1977); and Frederick Doolittle, Frank Levy, and Michael Wiseman, "The Mirage of Welfare Reform," *The Public Interest* 47 (Spring 1977): 62–87.

41. The best developed of the comprehensive programs is the Griffiths plan, described in *Income Security for All Americans*. Other plans similar in structure include Nixon's Family Assistance Plan, the revision of FAP known as H.R.1, Weinberger's Income Supplement Program, and, with the most complete integration into the income tax system, McGovern's demogrant proposal and the credit income tax proposal of the National Urban League.

42. Prior to Carter's proposed reforms, three-track systems were proposed by Russell Long, described in Robert Haveman, "Earnings Supplementation as an Income Maintenance Strategy: Issues of Program Structure and Integration," in Irene Lurie, ed., *Integrating Income Maintenance Programs* (New York: Academic Press, 1975); by Arnold Packer, "Categorical Public Employment Guarantees: A Proposed Solution to the Poverty Problem," *Studies in Public Welfare*, Paper no. 9 (part 1), August 20, 1973; and in the JOIN plan, described in Robert Lerman, "JOIN: A Jobs and Income Program for American Families," *Studies in Public Welfare*, Paper no. 19,. Dec. 30, 1974.

43. For a similar conclusion based on the New Deal experience with public employment, see Richard Hegner, "The WPA: Public Employment Experience in the New Deal," *Studies in Public Welfare*, Paper no. 19, Dec. 30, 1974.

44. Ross and Sawhill, *Time of Transition*, are especially emphatic about antidiscrimination policies as an alternative to current welfare reform proposals.

8. The Frontiers of Public Responsibility: Child Care and Parent Education

1. Carole Joffe describes this program in *Friendly Intruders: Child Care Professionals and Family Life* (Berkeley: University of California Press, 1977).

2. For the history of child care, see Virginia Kerr, "One Step Forward, Two Steps Back: Child Care's Long American History," in Pam Roby, *Child Care—Who Cares?* (New York: Basic Books, 1973); Margaret O'Brien Steinfels, *Who's Minding the Children? The History and Politics of Day Care in America* (New York: Simon and Schuster, 1973); and Sheila Rothman, "Other People's Children: The Day Care Experience in America," *The Public Interest* 30 (Winter 1973): 11–27.

3. Quoted in Rothman, "Other People's Children," p. 16.

4. For a summary of developments in the 1920s, see National Society for the Study of Education, *Preschool and Parent Education*, Twenty-Eighth Annual Yearbook (Bloomington, Ill.: Public School Publishing, 1929).

5. On the power of the public school model to legitimize public funding, in the earlier example of the kindergartens, see Marvin Lazerson, *Origins of the Urban School: Public Education in Massachusetts, 1870–1915.* (Cambridge: Harvard University Press, 1971), chap. 2.

6. Howard Dratch, "The Politics of Child Care in the 1940s," *Science and Society* 38 (Summer 1974): 167–204; Ruby Takanishi, "Federal Involvement in Early Childhood Education (1933–1973): The Need for Historical Perspectives," in Lilian G. Katz, ed., 3 vols., *Current Topics in Early Childhood Education*, vol. 1 (Norwood, N.J.: Ablex, 1977).

7. For a review of programs as of 1973, see Stevanne Auerbach, "Federally Sponsored Child Care," in Roby, *Child Care—Who Cares?*

8. *Summaries and Characteristics of States' Title XX Social Services Plan for Fiscal*

Year 1977 (HEW, March 1, 1977), especially Technical Note no. 2, "Eligibility Standards for Services."

9. Congressional Budget Office, "Childcare and Preschool: Options for Federal Support," September 1978, table 9.

10. For an exposition and criticism of the "pathology" model, see especially Florence Ruderman, *Child Care and Working Mothers* (New York: Child Welfare League of America, 1968).

11. The educational requirements of the 1968 Federal Interagency Day Care Requirements have never had much content, but some Title XX programs have still prided themselves on the "educational" components. This is true, for example, of the school-based programs reviewed in W. Norton Grubb and Marvin Lazerson, "Child Care, Government Financing, and the Public Schools: Lessons from the California Children's Centers," *School Review 86 (November 1977):* 5–37.

12. This phrase comes from an anonymous flyer that circulated around the country in opposition to the Child and Family Services Act of 1975; see *Background Materials Concerning the Child and Family Services Act, 1975,* Subcommittee on Children and Youth, U.S. Senate, March 1976. Particularly since much of this attack was inaccurate and scurrilous, it has been easy for child care advocates to dismiss it as coming from a crazed rightwing fringe. In our view this reaction fails to appreciate the intensity and spontaneity of the opposition to professional and state-dominated childrearing which has been voiced across a wide ideological spectrum.

13. For the position of the American Federation of Teachers, see *Putting Early Childhood and Day Care Services into the Public Schools* (AFT Task Force on Educational Issues, Winter 1976). For a critical and historical perspective, see Grubb and Lazerson, "Child Care, Government Financing, and the Public Schools."

14. On the contradictions of "professionalized childrearing," see Joffe, *Friendly Intruders.*

15. Two examples must suffice. One involves the literature on utilization: see, for example, Suzanne Woolsey, "Pied Piper Politics and the Child-Care Debate," *Daedalus* 106 (Spring 1977): 127–45; Meredith Larson, *Federal Policy for Pre-School Services: Assumptions and Evidence,* Stanford Research Institute, May 1975. These papers (and others based on them) find that most parents use home-based care; they then conclude that since federal subsidies have been confined to center care there should be no increased federal subsidies, a *non sequitur* that fails to consider the possibility of more flexible federal programs. Another example is the widely cited "conclusion" that federal subsidies are neither efficient nor equitable, based on Mordecai Kurz, Philip Robins, and Robert Spiegleman, *A Study of the Demand for Child Care by Working Mothers,* Stanford Research Institute, Research Memorandum 27, August 1975 (restated, for example, in the Congressional Budget Office report cited in chapter 8, note 9 herein, p. 50.) However, the underlying paper provides no examination of efficiency issues whatsoever, and the conclusion of inequity is based on the unnecessary and unlikely assumption of equal subsidies for all income groups.

16. Selma Fraiberg, *Every Child's Birthright: In Defense of Mothering* (New York: Basic Books, 1977).

17. See, for example, Alison Clarke-Stewart, *Child Care in the Family* (New York: Academic Press, 1977); Greta Fein and Alison Clarke-Stewart, *Day Care in Context* (New York: John Wiley, 1973), chap. 4; Jerome Kagan *Infancy* (Cambridge: Harvard University Press, 1978); Arthur Emlen and Joseph Perry, "Child Care Arrangements," in Lois Hoffman and F. Ivan Nye, *Working Mothers* (San Francisco: Jossey-Bass, 1974).

18. One exception to this pattern was the Child Care Act of 1979, which explicitly encompassed both employment-related and developmental goals. For an analysis of this act in terms of the three basic issues presented here, see W. Norton Grubb, "Testimony on the Child Care Act of 1979," Senate Subcommittee on Child and Human Development, Feb. 6, 1979.

19. Ellen Galinsky and William Hooks, *The New Extended Family: Day Care That Works* (Boston: Houghton Mifflin, 1977).

20. Polly Greenberg, *The Devil Has Slippery Shoes* (New York: Macmillan, 1969).

21. Alice Collins and Eunice Watson, *Family Day Care* (Boston: Beacon Press, 1976), describes this method for organizing networks for family day care homes.

22. On some experiences in work-site child care that have failed, largely because of lack

of interest of employers who saw them only as cost-reducing mechanisms, see Cookie Avrin and Georgia Sassen, *Corporations and Child Care* (Cambridge: Women's Research Action Project, 1974).

23. For a discussion of "utopian" child care, see Steinfels, *Who's Minding the Children?* Self-styled "radical" child care to socialize children in new ways is described in the newsletter "People About Childcare," published by the Child Care Organizing Committee in New Haven.

24. Laura Lein, "Parental Evaluation of Child Care Alternatives," *Urban and Social Change Review* 12 (Winter 1979): 13.

25. Mary Jo Bane et al., "Child Care in the United States," Family Policy Note no. 11, Joint Center for Urban Studies of MIT and Harvard University, February 1979.

26. One powerful example is the demands black parents make on child care and Head Start to teach their children reading. See, for example, Joffe *Friendly Intruders*, chap. 5.

27. On various "models," including parent-based conceptions, see Gwen Morgan, "The Trouble with Title XX," Day Care and Child Development Council of America, 1977.

28. "The Child Development Associate Consortium's Credential Award System," The Child Development Associate Consortium, Washington, D.C., December 1970.

29. On the necessity for parents having some countervailing power against professionals, see Joffe, *Friendly Intruders*. On the importance of parent involvement, see the "Hearings Before the Subcommittee on Child and Human Development: An Examination of How Best to Shape Future Federal Legislation Involving Child Care and Human Development" (Washington, D.C.: U.S. Government Printing Office, 1978), and the summary statement by Senator Alan Cranston, "The Shape of New Child Care Legislation," *Congressional Record* vol. 124, August 24, 1978, pp. 1–5.

30. For the argument about the kindergarten, see Grubb and Lazerson, "Child Care, Government Financing, and the Public Schools." For the prediction that child care can expand only under public school control, see Gilbert Steiner, *The Children's Cause* (Washington, D.C.: The Brookings Institution, 1976), chap. 10.

31. Grubb and Lazerson, "Child Care, Government Financing, and the Public Schools."

32. Our discussion of parent education borrows heavily from Steven Schlossman, "Before Home Start: Notes Toward a History of Parent Education in America, 1897–1929," *Harvard Education Review* 46 (August 1976): 436–62; and "The Parent Education Game: The Politics of Child Psychology in the 1970s," *Teachers College Record* 79 (May 1978): 788–808.

33. For a discussion of social and political activism by Women's Clubs during the progressive era, see David Thelen, *The New Citizenship: Origins of Progressivism in Wisconsin, 1885–1900* (Columbia: University of Missouri Press, 1972). See the discussion of "educated motherhood" in Sheila Rothman, *Woman's Proper Place* (New York: Basic Books, 1978), chap. 3.

34. Steiner, *Children's Cause*, pp. 1–9; Nancy Weiss, "Save the Children: A History of the Children's Bureau, 1903–1918" (Ph.D. diss., University of California, Los Angeles, 1974).

35. Doubt about compensatory programs are summarized in Julie Roy Jeffrey, *Education for Children of the Poor: A Study of the Origins and Implementation of the Elementary and Secondary Education Act of 1965* (Columbus: Ohio State University Press, 1978). On the Westinghouse Report, see Steiner, *Children's Cause*, chap. 2.

36. See, for example Alison Clarke-Stewart, "Parameters of Parent Education in the United States Today," unpublished; David Weikart, "Parental Involvement Through Home Teaching," in *High/Scope Report of 1974–75* (Ypsilanti, Michigan: High/Scope Educational Research Foundation, 1975); Earl Schaefer, "Parents as Educators: Evidence from Cross Sectional, Longitudinal and Intervention Research," *Young Children* 4 (April 1972): 227–39; Urie Bronfenbrenner, "Is Early Education Effective?" *Teachers College Record* 76 (December 1974): 279–302.

37. On the bureaucratic and political needs of OCD, see Steiner, *Children's Cause*, chaps. 3 and 4.

38. On the PCDCs, see Mary Robinson, "Parent Child Development Centers: An Experiment in Infant-Parent Interventions and Systematic Testing of Social Innovations," R and D Planning Memorandum, Office of Research Plans and Evaluation, Office of Economic Opportunity, 1972; Office of Child Development, "Parent Description and Status Report,"

U.S. Department of Health, Education, and Welfare, April 1976; and Dale Johnson, *Houston Parent Child Development Center* (Washington, D.C.: Office of Child Development, Final Report, Grant No. DHEW-90=C-379, 1976).

39. OCD, "Parent-Child Development Centers," p. 2.

40. The Houston program is reputed to cost over $5,000 per year per child—in a state where the maximum welfare grant in 1978 for a family of four was $1,680, with another $2,124 available through food stamps, and where Title XX day care cost perhaps $1,500 per year.

41. On Home Start, see the Office of Child Development, *A Guide for Planning and Operating Home-Based Child Development Programs* (Washington, D.C.: U.S. Department of Health, Education, and Welfare, 1974); Steiner, *Children's Cause*, chap. 4; OCD, *The Home Start Demonstration Program: An Overview* (Washington, D.C.: U.S. Department of Health, Education, and Welfare, 1973); OCD, *Report of a Joint Conference: Home Start/Child and Family Resource Program* (Washington: U.S. Department of Health, Education, and Welfare, 1975). The quote about the "happy home environment" is from *A Guide for Planning*, p. 34.

42. Ann O'Keefe, *Head Start Home-Based Programs: A Preliminary Report* (Washington: U.S. Department of Health, Education, and Welfare, 1976).

43. On EFP see Elizabeth Ogg, *Preparing Tomorrow's Parents* (New York: Public Affairs Committee, Inc., 1975); Duane J. Mattheis, "Education for Parenthood and the Schools," *PTA Today* 1 (May 1975): 3; Priscilla S. Jones, "Parenthood Education in a City High School," *Children Today* 4 (March/April 1975): 7–11; Education Development Center, *Exploring Childhood: Program Overview and Catalog of Materials* (Newton, Mass.: EDC School and Society Programs, 1976); Education Development Center, *Exploring Childhood: Summary of Evaluation Findings* (Cambridge: EDC Social Studies Program, 1975); Education Development Center, *Exploring Childhood: Summary of Evaluation Findings* (EDC School and Society Programs, 1976); and Behavior Associates, *Evaluation of Education for Parenthood Programs: An Overview* (Tucson: Behavior Associates, 1976).

44. Clarke-Stewart, "Parameters of Parent Education."

45. For a description of one parent education program which engaged the attention of parents as long as they were actively participating but which bored them whenever an expert lectured, see Joffe, *Friendly Intruders*, pp. 84–87.

46. One example that symbolized the potential of child care and parent education as a political focus—the Head Start program in Mississippi—also illustrates the pressure within the pluralist state to eliminate challenges. The successes of the Mississippi groups for a time threatened to cause the abolition of the entire Head Start program as conservative senators like John Stennis attempted to eliminate funding. Greenberg, *The Devil Has Slippery Shoes*.

9. The Search for a Family Policy

1. For a general critique of the "family policy" area, see Gilbert Steiner, *The Futility of Family Policy* (Washington, D.C.: The Brookings Institution, 1981). On the general nature of "family policy," see Sheila Kamerman and Alfred Kahn, "Explorations in Family Policy," *Social Work* 21 (May 1976): 181–86; Sheila Kamerman and Alfred Kahn, eds., *Family Policy: Government and Families in Fourteen Countries* (New York: Columbia University Press, 1976); Alvin Schorr, "Family Policy in the United States," in *Explorations in Social Policy* (New York: Basic Books, 1968); Janet Giele, "Social Policy and the Family," *American Review of Sociology* 5 (1979): 275–302.

2. Alva Myrdal, *Nation and Family* (1941; reprint ed., Cambridge: MIT. Press, 1968); the quote is from Moynihan's foreword, pp. vi–vii, x.

3. See Peter Berger and John Neuhaus, *To Empower People: The Role of Mediating Structures in Public Policy* (Washington, D.C.: American Enterprise Institute, 1977). Another conservative document is the Family Protection Act of 1979 (S. 1808).

4. See especially John Mudd, "Services Coordination and Children," Children's Defense Fund, May 1, 1980.

5. A Sidney Johnson, "Preface," in Ruth Hubbell, *Foster Care and Families: Conflicting Values and Policies* (Philadelphia: Temple University Press, 1981), p. xi. On family impact analysis, see also Steiner, *Futility of Family Policy*, pp. 28–32.

6. See especially Richard deLone, *Small Futures: Children, Inequality, and the Limits of Liberal Reform* (New York: Harcourt Brace Jovanovich, 1979); Kenneth Keniston and the Carnegie Council on Children, *All Our Children: The American Family Under Pressure* (New York: Harcourt Brace Jovanovich, 1977); Mary Jo Bane, *Here to Stay: The American Family in the Twentieth Century* (New York: Basic Books, 1976); Advisory Committee on Child Development, *Toward a National Policy for Children and Families* (Washington, D.C.: National Academy of Science, 1976).

7. Herbert Stein, *The Fiscal Revolution in American* (Chicago: University of Chicago Press, 1969); David A. Gold, "The Rise and Decline of the Keynesian Coalition," *Kapitalistate* 6 (Fall 1977): 129–62. For a full account of the Employment Act, see Stephen K. Bailey, *Congress Makes a Law: The Story Behind the Employment Act of 1946* (New York: Columbia University Press, 1950).

8. For a theory of the business cycle as a form of class struggle, see Rafford Boddy and James Crotty, "Class Conflict, Keynesian Policies, and the Business Cycle," *Monthly Review* 97 (October 1974): 1–17. The economic policies of the late 1970s provide a fine illustration of this process. As unemployment abated throughout 1977 and 1978 and inflation rates began to climb, pressure from the business community mounted to replace unemployment as the prime target of macroeconomic policy with inflation. Carter's 1979–80 anti-inflation policy was the concrete result, with labor and advocates of the poor resisting this shift in policy.

9. Lester Thurow, "How to Wreck the Economy," *New York Review of Books*, May 28, 1981.

10. The trade-off between unemployment and inflation is not universally accepted, but the evidence against it is more theoretical than empirical, and the conception of a trade-off still dominates macroeconomic policy. For a review of the literature on inflation and employment, see Anthony Santomero and John Seater, "The Inflation-Unemployment Trade-Off: A Critique of the Literature," *Journal of Economic Literature* 16 (June 1978): 499–544.

11. The index of spendable average weekly earnings fell almost 20 percent between 1967 and 1981. U.S. Bureau of Labor Statistics, "Real Earnings in April, 1981," table 1. See also H. M. Douty, "The Slowdown in Real Wages: A Post-War Perspective," *Monthly Labor Review* 100 (August 1977): 7–12.

12. For evidence that the poor lose both absolutely and relatively from inflation, see Edward Budd and David Seiders, "The Impact of Inflation on the Distribution of Income and Wealth," *American Economic Review* 61 (May 1971):128–38; John Palmer and Michael Barth, "The Distributional Effects of Inflation and Higher Unemployment," in Marilyn Moon and Eugene Smolensky, eds., *Improving Measures of Economic Well-Being* (New York: Academic Press, 1977). The finding that inflation is *favorable* to the poor rests on the fact that inflation erodes the wealth of upper-income groups; see, for example, John Palmer, *Inflation, Unemployment, and Poverty* (Lexington, Mass: Lexington Books, 1973); Joseph Minerik, "Who Wins, Who Loses from Inflation?", *Brookings Bulletin* 15 (Summer 1978): 6–10.

13. The poor are somewhat better off with a choice of low unemployment. Palmer and Barth, "Distributional Effects of Inflation"; Edward Gramlich, "The Distributional Effects of Higher Employment," *Brookings Papers on Economic Activity*, 1974, 293–336.

14. The basic argument can be simply expressed: the price level (or the rate of inflation) and the quantity of output (roughly, employment) are a function of both aggregate demand and aggregate supply. Keynesian policies have manipulated aggregate demand through tax, expenditure, and monetary policies, but the real culprit in stagflation has been upward shifts in the aggregate supply curve. Reducing inflation by reducing aggregate demand increases unemployment, but policies to shift the aggregate supply curve downward reduce the inflation and increase employment (or output)—though at the costs of intrusions into the private economy, the further replacement of market mechanisms with political decisions. The implication is that Keynesian policies are not wrong, but are incomplete in ignoring aggregate supply. See "Plugging in the Supply Side," Joint Economic Committee, Senate Report 96–618, March 4, 1980. For a rudimentary textbook attempt to integrate the supply side, see Rudiger Dornbusch and Stanley Fischer, *Macroeconomics* (New York: McGraw-Hill, 1978), part 3.

15. Robert Heilbroner, "The Supply-Side Fad," *New York Review of Books*, June 11, 1981.

16. On the ineffectiveness of balancing the federal budget, see Jesse Burkhead, "Balance the Federal Budget?" *Public Affairs Comment*, Lyndon Baines Johnson School of Public Affairs, May 1979; Ansel Sharp and Phyllis Smith Fleuniken, "Budget Deficits: A Major Cause of Inflation?" *Public Finance Quarterly* 6 (January 1978): 115–27; William Niskanen, "A Friendly Case Against the Balanced Budget Amendment," *Taxing and Spending* 3 (Spring 1980): 41–47.

17. Keniston, *All Our Children*, pp. 84–85.

18. Quoted in Sheila Rothman, *Woman's Proper Place: A History of Changing Ideals and Practices, 1870 to the Present* (New York: Basic Books, 1978), p. 250.

19. *Historical Statistics of the United States*, Series D-36. Figures for 1948 come from *Historical Statistics*, Series D-59, D-61, D-71, and D-72; 1979 figures have been taken from *Marital and Family Characteristics of Workers, March 1979*, Bureau of Labor Statistics, Special Labor Force Report 237, tables 1 and 4. On the history of working women, see W. Elliott Brownlee and Mary M. Brownlee, *Women in the American Economy: A Documentary History, 1675–1929* (New Haven: Yale University Press, 1976); Rosalyn Baxandall, Linda Gordon, and Susan Reverby, eds., *America's Working Women: A Documentary History, 1600 to the Present* (New York: Vintage Books, 1976); Elisabeth Pleck, "Two Worlds in One: Work and Family," *Journal of Social History* 10 (Winter 1976): 178–95.

20. On the effect of employment on familial power, see Stephen Bahr, "Effects on Power and Division of Labor in the Family," in Lois Hoffman and F. Ivan Nye, *Working Mothers* (San Francisco: Jossey-Bass, 1974).

21. Lillian Rubin, *Worlds of Pain* (New York: Basic Books, 1976), p. 170. See also Louise Kapp Howe, *Pink Collar Workers* (New York: Avon Books, 1977).

22. Nye and Hoffman, *Working Mothers*, chap. 9; Rubin, *Worlds of Pain*, chap. 9.

23. Rubin, *Worlds of Pain*, p. 175. The theory which has dominated the empirical literature suggests that the power of individuals in a family is related to the resources they bring to the marriage, including financial, emotional, and affective resources and skills involved in running a household. The familial resource theory was first developed in R. O. Blood and and D. M. Wolfe, *Husbands and Wives* (New York: The Free Press, 1960). For a recent review, see Stephen Bahr, "Effects on Power and Division of Labor Within the Family," in Hoffman and Nye, *Working Mothers*, chap. 7. The evidence on the effects of increasing employment among women suggests that American marriages have become more egalitarian. But not, of course, completely egalitarian; for some caveats, see Dain Gillespie, "Who Has the Power? The Marital Struggle," *Journal of Marriage and the Family* 33 (August 1971): 445–58.

24. Michael Lamb, ed., *The Role of the Father in Child Development* (New York: John Wiley and Sons, 1976); Michael Rutter, *The Qualities of Mothering: Maternal Deprivation Reassessed* (New York: J. Aronson, 1974); Alison Clarke-Stewart, *Child Care in the Family* (New York: Academic Press, 1977).

25. Hoffman and Nye, *Working Mothers*, chap. 6; Lois Hoffman, "Maternal Employment 1979," *American Psychologist* 34 (October 1979): 844–50.

26. On changes in the allocation of time to housework, see Nye and Hoffman, *Working Mothers*, chap. 2; Laura Lein has stressed that even when husbands increase the amount of time they spend in housework, the *responsibility* still rests with wives. Laura Lein, "Work and Family Life," Preliminary Report, Working Family Project, 1974.

27. Lein, "Work and Family Life"; Milton Kotelchuck, "The Infant's Relationship to the Father," in Lamb, *Role of the Father*.

28. Nye and Hoffman, *Working Mothers*, chap. 6.

29. Rubin, *Worlds of Pain*, p. 172.

30. Linda Gordon, "The Struggle for Reproductive Freedom: Three Stages of Feminism," in Zillah Eisenstein, ed., *Capitalist Patriarchy and the Case for Socialist Feminism* (New York: Monthly Review Press, 1979); Ellen DuBois, "The Nineteenth Century Women Suffrage Movement and the Analysis of Women's Oppression," in Eisenstein, *Capitalist Patriarchy*; Barbara Easton, "Feminism and the Contemporary Family," *Socialist Review* 8 (May/June 1978): 11–36.

31. For one perspective on these issues, see Rothman, *Woman's Proper Place*, chap. 7.

32. Andrea Beller, "The Impact of Equal Employment Opportunity Laws on the Male/Female Earnings Differential," in Cynthia Lloyd, Emily Andrews, and Curtis Gilroy, eds., *Women in the Labor Market* (New York: Columbia University Press, 1979). Although Beller interprets her results as showing that federal efforts have had some impact on earn-

ings differentials, her regression coefficients are statistically insignificant and therefore indicate the uncertainty of federal impact.

33. Edward Gross, "Plus Ca Change . . . ? The Sexual Structure of Occupations Over Time," *Social Problems* 16 (1968/69): 198–298; *Economic Report of the President, 1973* (Washington, D.C.: Government Printing Office, 1973), 155. See also Valerie Kincaid Oppenheimer, "The Sex-Labeling of Jobs," *Industrial Relations* 7 (May 1968): 219–34. On wage differences see Beller, "Impact of Equal Opportunity Laws."

34. This is the approach of the Chicago school of economics to the economics of the family. See, for example, Theodore Schultz, ed., *Economics of the Family: Marriage, Children, and Human Capital* (Chicago: University of Chicago Press, 1973); Gary Becker, *A Treatise on the Family* (Cambridge: Harvard University Press, 1981).

35. Congressional Budget Office, *Child Care and Preschool: Options for Federal Support* (September 1978), table 9.

36. Laura Lein, "Parental Evaluation of Child Care Alternatives," *Urban and Social Change Review* 12 (Winter 1979); Mary Jo Bane et al., "Child Care in the United States," Family Policy Note no. 11, Joint Center for Urban Studies of MIT and Harvard University, February 1979.

37. Carole Joffe, "The Abortion Struggle," *Dissent* (Summer 1981).

38. Quoted in Rothman, *Woman's Proper Place*, p. 260.

39. For a review of various aspects of female unemployment, see Marianne Faber and Helen Lowry, "Women: The New Reserve Army of the Unemployed," in Martha Blaxall and Barbara Reagan, eds., *Women and the Workplace: the Implications of Occupational Segregation* (Chicago: University of Chicago Press, 1973).

40. See the references cited in notes 57–64 of chapter 1.

41. Lee Rainwater and William Yancey, *The Moynihan Report and the Politics of Controversy* (Cambridge: MIT Press, 1967), p. 94.

42. See especially James Smith and Finis Welch, *Race Differences in Earnings: A Survey and New Evidence*, Rand Report R-2295-NSF, March 1978; Sar Levitan, William Johnston, and Robert Taggert, *Minorities in the United States: Problems, Progress and Prospects* (Washington, D.C.: Public Affairs Press, 1975).

43. Edward Lazear, "The Narrowing of Black-White Income Differentials is Illusory," *American Economic Review* 69 (September 1979): 553–64.

44. For evidence on the small deterioration of black and Hispanic family incomes during the 1970s, see *Money, Income and Poverty Status of Families and Persons in the United States: 1978* (Advance Report), Current Population Reports series P-60, no. 120, November 1979, table 3. For data on poverty rates and trends, see tables 18, 20, and 21.

45. Smith and Welch, *Race Differences in Earnings*.

46. On the dominance of these tactics, see Dorothy Newman et al., *Protest, Politics and Prosperity: Black Americans and White Institutions, 1940–75* (New York: Pantheon Books, 1978), especially chap. 1. See also Richard Kluger, *Simple Justice* (New York: Knopf, 1976); and Francis Fox Piven and Richard Cloward, *Poor People's Movements: Why They Succeed, How They Fail* (New York: Random House, 1977).

47. See, for example, Alan Dawley, *Class and Community: The Industrial Revolution in Lynn* (Cambridge: Harvard University Press, 1976).

48. Stephan Thernstrom, *The Other Bostonians* (Cambridge: Harvard University Press, 1973).

49. The failure to develop a consciousness of class as an important consequence of capitalism is linked to—though not the same as—the lack of a strong socialist movement in the United States. On the latter issue see Jerome Karabel, "The Failure of American Socialism Reconsidered," *New York Review of Books*, February 8, 1979; T. B. Bottomore, *Classes in Modern Society* (New York: Random House, 1966); Robert Bellah, *The Broken Covenant: American Civil Religion in a Time of Trial* (New York: Seabury Press, 1975), chap. 5; John Laslett and Seymour Martin Lipset, *Failure of a Dream? Essays in the History of American Socialism* (Garden City: Doubleday, 1974).

50. Stephen Steinberg, *The Ethnic Myth: Race, Ethnicity, and Class in America* (New York: Atheneum, 1981).

51. James O'Toole et al., *Work in America* (Cambridge: MIT. Press, 1973); see chap. 6 for the weak recommendations. Nonetheless, the report generated tremendous controversy and was charged with being a socialist document.

52. For the political and legislative background to the Act, see *The Job Safety and*

Health Act of 1970 (Washington, D.C.: Bureau of National Affairs, 1971). On its implementation, see John Mendleoff, *Regulating Safety: An Economic and Political Analysis of Occupational Safety and Health Policy* (Cambridge: MIT. Press, 1979).

53. "Budget Boys Cripple OSHA," *In These Times*, April 8–14, 1981, p. 6.

54. Victor Vroom, "Industrial Social Psychology," in Gardner Lindsey and Eliot Aronson, eds., *The Handbook of Social Psychology*, vol. 5 (Reading, Mass: Addison Wesley, 1968); Victor Vroom, *Work and Motivation* (New York: Wiley, 1964), chap. 5.

55. For example, deLone, *Small Futures*, goes further than any other writer in identifying the effects of class on children but fails to incorporate any discussion of class into his recommendations.

10. Reconstructing the State

1. For a similar argument, see Robert Heilbroner "The Supply-Side Fad," *New York Review of Books*, June 11, 1981.

2. Our debts to several political theorists are enormous. See especially C. B. MacPherson, *The Life and Times of Liberal Democracy* (London: Oxford University Press, 1977); C. B. MacPherson, *The Political Theory of Possessive Individualism: Hobbes to Locke*, (London: Oxford University Press, 1962); Michael Walzer, *Radical Principles: Reflections of a Unreconstructed Democrat* (New York: Basic Books, 1980); Alan Wolfe, *The Limits of Legitimacy: Political Contradictions of Contemporary Capitalism* (New York: The Free Press, 1977). In addition, we have often used the vocabulary of Charles Lindblom, *Politics and Markets* (New York: Basic Books, 1977). The most coherent efforts to develop theories of the state which are both empirically powerful and normatively progressive are those of neo-Marxists; In addition to Wolfe, see especially James O'Connor, *The Fiscal Crisis of the State* (New York: St. Martin's Press, 1973); Jurgen Habermas, *Legitimation Crisis* (Boston: Beacon Press, 1975); Ernest Mandel, *Late Capitalism* (London: NLB, 1975), chap. 15; David Gold, Clarence Lo, and Erik Wright, "Recent Developments in Marxist Theories of the Capitalist State," *Monthly Review* 27 (Oct./Nov. 1975).

3. On changes in the definitions of liberalism and democracy, see MacPherson, *Political Theory of Possessive Individualism;* and John Dunn *Western Political Theory in the Face of the Future* (Cambridge: Cambridge University Press, 1979). The question of whether capitalism was necessary for liberal thought to flourish has been much debated and remains unresolved. MacPherson argues that liberalism was a direct expression of capitalism. Dunn, in contrast, suggests that there was no necessary connection. That liberalism and capitalism paralleled each other and became linked is, however, beyond dispute.

4. Oscar Handlin and Mary Handlin, *Commonwealth: A Study of the Role of Government in the American Economy—Massachusetts, 1774-1861* (Cambridge: Harvard University Press, rev.ed. 1969), pp. 52–53 and passim.

5. Rowland Bertoff, *An Unsettled People* (New York: Harper & Row, 1971), pp. 170–72.

6. Handlin and Handlin, *Commonwealth*, chap. 6; Morton J. Horwitz, *The Transformation of American Law, 1780-1860* (Cambridge: Harvard University Press, 1977).

7. On the progressive era as a turning point for the liberal state under corporate capitalism, see James Weinstein, *The Corporate Idea in the Liberal State: 1900-1918* (Boston: Beacon Press, 1968); and Gabriel Kolko, *The Triumph of Conservatism* (New York: The Free Press, 1963).

8. Quoted in Kolko, *Triumph of Conservatism*, p. 128.

9. See, for example, Peter Dobkin Hall, "Marital Selection and Business in Massachusetts Merchant Families, 1700-1900," in Michael Gordon, ed., *The American Family in Social-Historical Perspective*, 2nd ed. (New York: St. Martin's Press, 1978).

10. Henry Steele Commager, ed., *Lester Ward and the Welfare State* (Indianapolis: Bobbs-Merrill, 1967), pp. 63–68; David Montgomery, *Workers' Control in America* (New York: Cambridge University Press, 1979).

11. The distinction between freedom from constraints and freedom to develop has been made many times, but rarely as clearly as by MacPherson, *Life and Times of Liberal Democracy.*

12. This point has been particularly stressed by Lindblom, *Politics and Markets.*

13. The dominant theory within mainstream economics of what the state should provide, the theory of public goods, is a catalogue of different forms of market failure as justifications for public regulation or provisions of goods and services. The dominant theory of social policy, we have argued, is essentially the same.

14. From *Notes on Virginia* (1791), quoted in MacPherson, *Life and Times of Liberal Democracy,* p. 18. On citizenship more generally, including examination of who was not granted the rights of citizenship, see Edmund Morgan, *American Slavery, American Freedom: The Ordeal of Colonial Virginia* (New York: W. W. Norton, 1975); and James H. Kettner, *The Development of American Citizenship, 1608-1870* (Chapel Hill: University of North Carolina Press, 1978).

15. Carole Pateman, *Participation and Democratic Theory* (Cambridge: Cambridge University Press, 1970).

16. On the extent of political participation in the mid-nineteenth century, see de Tocqueville, *Democracy in America,* ed. Phillips Bradley, 2 vols., (New York: Vintage, 1955), vol. 2. The roots of declining participation at the end of the century are discussed in Walter Burnham, "The Shape of the American Political Universe," *American Political Science Review* 59 (March 1965): 7-28. On participation generally, see J. Roland Pennock and John Chapman, eds., *Participation in Politics: Nomos XVI* (New York: Lieber-Atherton, 1975).

17. Christopher Lasch, *The Culture of Narcissism* (New York: W. W. Norton, 1978), chap. 4.

18. Quoted in Walzer, *Radical Principles,* p. 96.

19. Quoted in Jeff Weintraub, "Virtue, Community, and the Sociology of Liberty: The Nation of Republican Virtue and Its Impact on Modern Western Social Thought" (Ph.D. diss., University of California, Berkeley, 1979), p. 41. On the hostility to "interests" and the subsequent changes in political theory in the decades surrounding the American Revolution, see Bernard Bailyn, *The Origins of American Politics* (New York: Random House, 1968).

20. Quoted in Weintraub, "Virtue, Community, and the Sociology of Liberty," p. 153; but see also pp. 142-93.

21. Pateman, *Participation and Democratic Theory,* chap. 1.

22. On alternative conceptions, see Pateman's discussion of participatory democracy; the discussion of "developmental democracy" in MacPherson, *Life and Times of Liberal Democracy,* chap. 3; the discussion of republican virtue in Weintraub, "Virtue, Community, and the Sociology of Liberty"; and Walzer, *Radical Principles.*

23. Our major quarrel with the neo-Marxist theory of the state is its functionalism: neo-Marxist theory stresses the reproduction of capitalism by the state, particularly by aiding the accumulation of profit in private hands and by legitimizing capitalism, but tends to ignore that the state by its very actions also transforms capitalism.

24. See for example, Bertram Gross, *Friendly Facism: The New Face of Power in America* (New York: M. Evans, 1980); Sidney Lens, "Socialism for the Rich," *The Progressive* 39 (September 1975): 13-19.

25. For other pleas to construct coherent normative principles, see Walzer, *Radical Principles*; Boris Frankel, "On the State of the State: Marxist Theories of the State after Leninism," *Theory and Society* 7 (Jan.–March 1979): 199-242.

26. Our assumption that we should build on American values is similar to the assertion of Robert Bellah that the failure of socialism in America has in part been a failure to erect socialism on specifically American values. Bellah does not make clear what those values have been, but the proposal to begin with established principles remains admirable. Robert Bellah, *The Broken Covenant: American Civil Religion in a Time of Trial* (New York: Seabury Press, 1975), especially chap. 6.

27. For a parallel argument, see the discussion of individual freedom in Walzer, *Radical Principles,* pp. 3-19.

28. This is of course a huge enterprise, one which can only be outlined in this section. Its completion requires tracing the emergence and successive corruption of core values in American history. This enterprise has been suggested by Christopher Lasch; see "Politics and Social Theory: A Reply to the Critics," *Salmagundi* 46 (Fall 1979): 194-202.

29. The power of the liberal ideology is discussed in Richard deLone, *Small Futures: Children, Inequality, and the Limits of Liberal Reform* (New York: Harcourt Brace Jovanovitch, 1979).

30. See Walzer, *Radical Principles*, especially pp. 273–90.

31. See Ruth Miller Elson, *Guardians of Tradition: American Schoolbooks of the Nineteenth Century* (Lincoln: University of Nebraska Press, 1964), and Frances Fitzgerald, *America Revised: History Schoolbooks in the Twentieth Century* (Boston: Little, Brown 1979).

32. Kettner, *Development of American Citizenship*, chaps. 8–10; Lawrence A. Cremin, *American Education: The National Experience, 1783–1876* (New York: Harper and Row, 1980).

33. Walzer, *Radical Principles*, p. 70. The Jefferson quote is from a letter to S. Kerchoral in 1816, cited in Saul Padover, ed., *Democracy by Thomas Jefferson* (New York: Greenwood Press, 1939), p. 53.

34. Walzer, *Radical Principles*, p. 70.

35. For the argument that political democracy requires economic democracy, see Walzer, *Radical Principles*, especially pp. 273–91; and Pateman, *Participation and Democratic Theory*.

36. Herbert Gutman, *Work, Culture, and Society in Industrializing America* (New York: Vintage, 1976), pp. 5–7.

37. On changes in the work ethic, see Daniel Rogers, *The Work Ethic in Industrial America, 1850–1920* (Chicago: University of Chicago Press, 1978). On the degradation of work, see Harry Braverman, *Labor and Monopoly Capital* (New York: Monthly Review Press, 1974); and Richard Edwards, *Contested Terrain* (New York: Basic Books, 1979).

38. On the persistence of the value of work, along with experiments to revise working, see James O'Toole, *Work in America* (Cambridge: MIT Press, 1973), especially chap. 1 and the appendix. On the relationship between decision-making power, job satisfaction, and the sense of participation, see Victor Vroom, *Work and Motivation* (New York: Wiley, 1964); and the literature review in Pateman, *Participation and Democratic Theory*.

39. Christopher Lasch, *Haven in a Heartless World: The Family Besieged* (New York: Basic Books, 1977).

40. On conceptions of romantic love, see Ann Swidler, "Love in Adulthood in American Culture," in Neil Smelser and Erik Erikson, ed., *Themes of Love and Work in Adulthood* (Cambridge: Harvard University Press, 1980).

41. See, for example, Lawrence Cremin's argument that the "genius" of American education has been the demand that schooling be made universal. Lawrence A. Cremin, *The Genius of American Education* (New York: Random House, 1965).

42. Cremin, *American Education*, p. 104.

43. On the degradation of liberal education, see especially Lasch, *The Culture of Narcissism*, chap. 6.

44. Richard Bushman, *From Puritan to Yankee* (Cambridge: Harvard University Press, 1967). On the decline of community responsibility, see David Rothman, *The Discovery of the Asylum: Social Order and Disorder in the New Republic* (Boston: Little, Brown, 1971), chap. 1.

45. See Walzer, *Radical Principles*, p. 10.

46. Excellent examples of the liberal agenda directed at children and families are the reports of the Carnegie Council on Children, especially Kenneth Keniston and the Carnegie Council on Children, *All Our Children: The American Family Under Pressure* (Harcourt Brace Jovanovich, 1977); deLone, *Small Futures*; John Gliedman and William Roth, *The Unexpected Minority: Handicapped Children in America* (New York: Harcourt Brace Jovanovich, 1980).

47. This succinct statement of the limits of the welfare state comes from Walzer, *Radical Principles*, p. 9.

48. The term "unlucky children" is from Gilbert Y. Steiner, *The Children's Cause* (Washington, D.C.: The Brookings Institution, 1976).

49. See especially Pateman, *Participation and Democratic Theory*; Walzer, *Radical Principles*, especially chap. 17.

50. On working control and economic democracy, see Gerry Hunnius, David Garson, and John Case, *Workers' Control: A Reader on Labor and Social Change* (New York: Vintage, 1973); Martin Carnoy and Derek Shearer, *Economic Democracy: The Challenge of the 1980s* (Armonk, N.,Y.: M. E. Sharpe, 1980).

51. See appendix to O'Toole, *Work in America*.

52. Peter Drucker, *The Unseen Revolution: How Pension Fund Socialism Came to America* (New York: Harper & Row, 1976).

53. For a similar argument based on populist and socialist movements in the Southwest at the turn of this century, see Lawrence Goodwyn, "The Cooperative Commonwealth and Other Abstractions: In Search of a Democratic Premise," *Marxist Perspectives* 3 (Summer 1980): 8–42.

54. On a variety of organizing efforts, see the special issue on organizing neighborhoods of *Social Policy* 10 (September/October 1979).

Postcript: The Plight of Children in the 1980s

1. Much of this section was orginally written with Julia Brody, and was previously published as W. Norton Grubb and Julia Green Brody, "Ketchup and Other Vegetables: The Plight of Children under Ronald Reagan," in J. Boulet, A. M. DeBritto, and S. A. Ray, *Understanding the Economic Crisis: The Impact of Poverty and Unemployment on Children and Families*, Bush Program in Child Development and Social Policy, University of Michigan, 1985.

2. Martin Anderson, *Welfare: The Political Economy of Welfare Reform in the United States* (Palo Alto: Hoover Institution Press, 1978), p. 15.

3. "Food and Nutrition Issues in the Food Stamp Program," Food Research and Action Center, 1981.

4. Congressional Budget Office, *Reducing Poverty Among Children*, May 1985, table A–2.

5. Peter Henle and Paul Ryscavage, "The Distribution of Earned Income Among Men and Women, 1958–77," *Monthly Labor Review* 103 (April 1980); Martin Dooley and Peter Gottschalk, "Earnings Inequality Among Males in the United States: Trends and the Effects of Growth," *Journal of Political Economy* 92 (February 1984); Sheldon Danziger and Peter Gottschalk, "Do Rising Tides Lift All Boats? The Impact of Secular and Cyclical Change on Poverty," *American Economic Review* 76 (May 1986); W. Norton Grubb and Robert Wilson, "The Distribution of Wages and Salaries, 1960–1980: The Contributions of Gender, Race, Sectoral Shifts, and Regional Shifts," Working Paper no. 39, LBJ School of Public Affairs, 1987.

6. Among those individuals living in families with children, 14.9 percent would have been poor in 1973 without any government transfers; the comparable figure in 1984 was 20.4 percent. Calculated from Danziger and Gottschalk, "How Have Families with Children Been Faring?" Joint Economic Committee, Nov. 1985, tables 7 and 14.

7. *A Children's Defense Budget: An Analysis of the President's Budget and Children* (Washington, D.C.: Children's Defense Fund, 1982). Some corrections based on OMB figures have been provided by Robert Greenstein of the Center on Budget and Policy Priorities.

8. Center on Budget and Policy Priorities, "One Third of President's Proposed Spending Cuts to Come from Programs for the Poor," table 1; Children's Defense Fund, *A Children's Defense Budget, FY1988*, Appendix A (Washington, D.C.: Children's Defense Fund, 1987).

9. *A Children's Defense Budget, FY1988*, p. 241.

10. Congressional Budget Office, "Major Legislative Changes in Human Resources Programs Since January 1981", August 1983. These figures describe average cuts over the period between 1982 and 1985 as a result of the legislative changes of 1982–83, as compared to what spending would have been under Carter policies.

11. *For Want of a Nail: The Impact of Federal Budget Cuts on Children in Massachusetts* (Boston: Massachusetts Advocacy Center, 1983).

12. *The Widening Gap: The Incidence and Distribution of Infant Mortality and Low Birth Weight in the United States, 1978–82*, Food Research and Action Center, January 5, 1984.

13. Citizen's Commission on Hunger in New England, *American Hunger Crisis: Poverty and Health in New England* (Boston: Harvard University School of Public

Health, 1984). For the most comprehensive evidence about hunger, see *Hunger in the Eighties: A Primer*, Food Research and Action Center, 1984.

14. *For Want of a Nail*, pp. 63–64. For information on child abuse soon after the early round of Reagan cuts, as of January 1983, see National Committee for Prevention of Child Abuse, "Incidence of Child Abuse Climbing," Working Paper no. 008.

15. *A Children's Defense Budget: An Analysis of the President's FY1985 Budget and Children* (Washington, D.C.: Children's Defense Fund, 1984), p. 15. For other reports on parents giving up their children to foster care, see *For Want of a Nail*. See also Nancy Amidei, "Poor Children and Social Responsibility," in *The Impact of Poverty and Unemployment on Children and Families*, Bush Program in Child Development and Social Policy, University of Michigan, 1985.

16. *Reducing Poverty Among Children*, Congressional Budget Office, May 1985, table III–4.

17. Danziger and Gottschalk, "How Have Families with Children Been Faring?" table 10.

18. *An Oath Betrayed: The Reagan Administration's Civil Rights Enforcement Record*, Civil Rights Leadership Conference Fund, October 1983.

19. On the reforms, see *Barriers to Excellence: Our Children at Risk*, National Coalition of Advocates for Students, January 1985; W. Norton Grubb, "Educational Reform and the New Orthodoxy: The Federal Role in Revitalizing the U.S. Labor Force," Joint Economic Committee, December 1986; and Marvin Lazerson et al., *An Education of Value* (New York: Cambridge University Press, 1985).

20. *A Children's Defense Budget, FY1988*, pp. 210–11. These are cuts in real rather than nominal terms.

21. On developments in child care, see W. Norton Grubb, "Young Children Face the States: Issues and Options in Early Childhood Programs," Center for Policy Research in Education, Rutgers University, May 1987.

22. On developments during the 1980s, see Barry Krisberg et al., "The Watershed of Juvenile Justice Reform," *Crime and Delinquency* 32 (January 1986), and other articles in this special issue. See also the special issues of *Crime and Delinquency* on "Youth Policy and Juvenile Justice Reform," July 1984, and on "Rethinking Juvenile Justice," July 1983; and *A Children's Defense Budget, FY 1988*, Chap. 13.

23. Janet Schroyer-Portillo, "Civil Rights in Crisis: The Reagan Administration's Reforms," National Council of La Raza, July 20, 1984.

24. *A Children's Defense Budget: An Analysis of the President's FY 1984 Budget and Children* (Washington, D.C.: Children's Defense Fund, 1983), p. 21.

25. A large literature has developed on the ineffectiveness of the military and the astounding cost of its failures. For a judicious summary of the evidence, indicating modest increases in military capability despite enormous increases in the defense budget, see "Defense Spending: What Has Been Accomplished," Congressional Budget Office, April 1985.

26. For refutations of the view that welfare has caused poverty, see Robert Greenstein, "Losing Faith in *Losing Ground*," *The New Republic*, March 25, 1985; "*Losing Ground*: A Critique," Institute for Research on Poverty, Special Report no. 38, August 1985; and David Ellwood and Lawrence Summers, "Poverty in America: Is Welfare the Answer or the Problem?" in Sheldon Danziger and Daniel Weinberg, eds., *Fighting Poverty: What Works and What Doesn't* (Cambridge: Harvard University Press, 1986). The phrase "behavioral dependency" comes from Michael Novak, *The New Consensus on Family and Welfare* (Washington, D.C.: American Enterprise Institute, 1986). Despite some distortions, especially about the poverty statistics themselves, this book is correct in reporting that a "new consensus" has developed around the need to assert parental responsibility, especially through workfare and child support enforcement; but it is utterly fantastic to claim that the perception of "behavioral dependency" is new.

27. Lester Salamon, "Nonprofit Organizations: The Lost Opportunity," in John Palmer and Isabel Sawhill, *The Reagan Record* (Cambridge: Ballinger Publishing Co., 1984).

28. On effort to gain support from employers, see Alfred Kahn and Sheila Kamerman, *Child Care: Facing the Hard Choices* (Dover, Mass.: Auburn House, 1987), chap. 6.

29. On family policy, see Daniel Patrick Moynihan, *Family and Nation* (New York: Harcourt Brace Jovanovich, 1986); Marion Wright Edelman, *Families in Peril: An Agenda*

for Social Change (Cambridge: Harvard University Press, 1987); and Ruth Sidel, *Women and Children Last* (New York: Penguin Books, 1986).

30. "Children Emerge as Issue for Democrats," *New York Times*, September 27, 1987, p. 14.

31. See, for example, Irwin Garfinkel and Sara McLanahan, *Single Mothers and Their Children: A New American Dilemma* (Washington, D.C.: The Urban Institute, 1986), chap. 5.

32. Edelman, *Families in Peril*, chap. 3.

33. For example, see Sheldon Danziger and Daniel Weinberg, eds., *Fighting Poverty: What Works and What Doesn't;* and *What Works: Research About Teaching and Learning*, U.S. Department of Education, 1986.

34. Irwin Garfinkel and Sara McLanahan, *Single Mothers and Their Children.*

35. See, for example, Lester Thurow, *The Zero-Sum Solution* (New York: Simon and Schuster, 1985); Ira Magaziner and Robert Reich, *Minding America's Business* (New York: Harcourt Brace Jovanovich, 1982); Samuel Bowles, David Gordon, and Thomas Weisskopf, *Beyond the Waste Land: A Democratic Alternative to Economic Decline* (Garden City, N.J.: Anchor Books, 1984); Gar Alperowitz and Jeff Faux, *Rebuilding America* (New York: Pantheon Books, 1984).

36. *Job Creation Through Public Service Employment*, National Commission for Manpower Policy, Report no. 6, March 1978; J. Ball, D.M. Gerould, and P. Burstein, *The Quality of Work in the Youth Entitlement Demonstration* (New York: Manpower Development Research Corporation, 1986).

37. For vivid descriptions of the corruptive influence of money, we especially like Elizabeth Drew, *Money and Politics: The New Road to Corruption* (New York: MacMillan, 1983).

NAME INDEX

Aaron, Henry, 315n25, n26, 320n60, 334n32
Aaronson, Mark, 334n24
Abbott, Grace, 26, 27, 97–98, 312n50
Abramowitz, Susan, 321n85
Adams, John, 283, 290
Addams, Jane, 159, 328n8
Allen, F., 331n56
Alvirez, David, 318n22
Anderson, Martin, 48, 314n8
Andrews, Emily, 340n32
Aronson, Eliot, 342n54
Auerbach, Stevanne, 335n7
Austin, James, 321n81, 328n13, 331n50–52
Averch, Harvey, 314n20, 326n27
Avrin, Cookie, 337n22
Axtell, James, 324n3

Bahr, Stephen, 340n20, 340n23
Bailey, Stephen K., 339n7
Bailyn, Bernard, 322n17, 343n19
Baker, Josephine, 21–22, 68, 311n37
Bakke, E. Wright, 312n53
Bane, Mary Jo, 309n2,n5, 337n25, 339n6, 341n36
Barnard, Henry, 310n24
Barth, Michael, 335n39, 339n12, n13
Barton, Paul, 329n26
Baxandall, Rosalyn, 340n19
Bazelon, David, 90–91, 331n57
Beck, Rochelle, 311n44, 323n31
Becker, Gary, 341n34
Bedrosian, Hrach, 329n26
Bellah, Robert, 341n49, 343n26
Beller, Andrea, 340n32

Bendix, R., 319n44
Bengston, Vern, 320n74, 328n11
Benson, Charles, 315n25
Berg, Ivar, 325n18
Berger, Peter, 338n3
Bergman, Barbara, 318n23
Berkowitz, Michael, 312n47
Bertoff, Roland, 275, 342n5
Bettleheim, Bruno, 328n6
Blaxall, Martha, 341n39
Blaydon, Colin, 334n21
Blood, Robert, 318n32, 340n23
Bloom, Richard, 316n1
Bluestone, Barry, 317n12
Blumberg, Paul, 325n16
Blumin, Stuart, 310n5
Bobrow, Sue Berryman, 321n85
Boddy, Rafford, 339n8
Bodnar, John, 326n35
Boland, Barbara, 333n14
Bottomore, T. B., 316n6, 318n27, 341n49
Bowles, Samuel, 324n2
Boyer, Paul, 310n6
Brademas, John, 217
Braverman, Harry, 344n37
Brecher, Charles, 320n58
Bremner, Robert H., 309n1, 311n37, 312n47, n50, n52, 314n6, 316n2, 321n83, 328n8, 330n43, 332n2
Brenner, Harvey, 314n14, 317n18
Brenzel, Barbara, 311n27
Briggs, Vernon, 317n21
Brinkhard, William, 316n1
Brischetto, Robert, 326n26
Bronfenbrenner, Urie, 36, 313n72, 315n33, 337n36
Brown, George, 325n22
Brownlee, Elliott, 340n19
Brownlee, Mary M., 340n19
Budd, Edward, 339n12

Burkhead, Jesse, 340n16
Burnham, Walter, 343n16
Burt, Robert, 313n74
Bushman, Richard, 344n44
Bushnell, Horace, 86
Byrd, William, 79

Cain, Glen, 317n13
Calhoun, Arthur, 21, 311n35, n39
Califano, Joseph, 72, 317n20
Calvert, Mildred, 333n10
Campbell, Angus, 322n8, n11
Carcagno, Joseph, 335n39
Carliner, Geoffrey, 318n22
Carlos, Manuel, 313n62
Carnoy, Martin, 344n50
Carroll, Stephen, 314n20, 326n25, n26
Carter, Jimmy, 4, 9, 72, 103, 109, 111, 112, 194, 196, 203–5, 235, 260, 288, 309n7, 335n42, 339n8
Casas, J. Manuel, 313n62
Case, John, 344n50
Casper, Gerhard, 313n74
Cassety, Judith, 334n21
Cater, Douglas, 320n59
Cavanaugh, Winifred, 321n79
Chambliss, William, 90, 321n81, 328n13
Chandler, Alfred D., Jr., 311n29
Chapman, John, 343n16
Chapp, John, 329n27
Charrers, W. W., Jr., 319n42
Chinoy, Eli, 318n38
Clark, Burton R., 325n21
Clarke-Stewart, Alison, 313n71, 336n36, 338n44, 340n24

SUBJECT INDEX

Abortion rights, 253

Adolescence, *see* Youth

Adolescence, Its Psychology, Anthropology, Sex, Crime, Religion, and Education (Hall), 158

Adversarial democracy, 107–10, 113

AFDC, *see* Aid to Families with Dependent Children

AFL-CIO, 105, 204

Agriculture, U.S. Department of, 109, 187

Aid to Families with Dependent Children (AFDC), 8, 39, 66, 67, 81, 82, 93, 188, 199–202, 206, 238, 239, 299, 332n9, 333n16, n20, 334n26, n29; AFDC-U program, 188, 199, 202; hostility to funding of, 51, 84; limitations of, 301; maternal employment vs., 209, 213; progressive era precursors of, 24; reduction of social spending and, 100; structure of, 189–97

Altruism, public, 58

American Association of University Women, 223

American Dilemma, An (Myrdal), 31

American Federation of Teachers, 98, 101–3, 105, 215–16, 336n13

American Home Economics Association, 223

American Psychological Association, 101

American revolution, 107

Amish, 294, 326n35

Aspirations, class differences in, 75–76

Bakke v. Board of Regents of the University of California, 141, 143, 326n30

Behaviorism, 61

Bill of Rights, 287

Bitter Cry of the Children, The (Spargo), 186

Black Child Development Association, 112

Blacks, 31–33; labor market discrimination against, 72; poverty among, 187; in public schools, 134–36, 139, 141; under slavery, 16–17; unemployment among, 167–68; *See also* Minorities; Racial discrimination

Boston, public education in, 135

Boston School Committee, 132

Boston Women's Health Collective, 321n76

Boy Scouts, 157, 159

Brown v. Board of Education (1954), 139, 141, 262, 325n22

California: public education in, 140; tax limitation movement in, 84, 151; "workfare" program in, 334n23

Capitalism: entrepreneurial, rise of, 13–14; laissez-faire, 97; liberal democratic state under, 274–85

Carnegie Council on Children, 49, 70, 155, 309n5, 314n10, 316n9, 324n66, 339n6, 344n46

Carnegie Council on Policy Studies in Higher Education, 327n1

Catholics, 133, 145

Census Bureau, U.S., 316n7, n8, 317n12, n17, 318n25, 332n1

Center for Science in the Public Interest, 322n28

Center on Social Welfare Policy and Law, 333n19

Chambers of Commerce, 105, 295

Charles River Bridge case (1829), 275

Chicanos, *see* Hispanics; Minorities; Racial discrimination

Child care, 208–22; alternative futures for, 216–22; continuities in, 210–16; future of public responsibility for, 230–32; in progressive era, 24; reform of, 301; role of state in, 252–53

Child Care Act (1979), 107, 214, 217, 336n18

Child Development Associate, 103, 124–25, 220, 324n63

Child and Family Services Act (1975), 115, 215, 336n12

Children's Bureau, U.S., *see* Federal Children's Bureau

Children's Cause, The (Steiner), 48

Children's Defense Fund, 65, 101, 104, 320n66, 322n28

Child Study Association of America, 223

Child Support Enforcement Program, 194, 199, 201, 334n21

Child Welfare League of America, 104, 105

Christian Scientists, 124

Chrysler Corporation, 305

City University of New York, 138